A practical guide to the teaching of Spanish

A practical guide to the teaching of
SPANISH

WILGA M. RIVERS

MILTON M. AZEVEDO

WILLIAM H. HEFLIN, Jr.

RUTH HYMAN-OPLER

New York
OXFORD UNIVERSITY PRESS
1976

Permission to reprint copyright material is hereby gratefully acknowledged:

To Doubleday and Company, Inc. for permission to quote from the English translation of J. M. Gironella's *Un Millón de Muertos,* entitled *One Million Dead.*

To Editorial Contenido, S.A., for material from Federico Gallardo Cortés, "Los
melenudos envidian a la mujer."

To José Maria Gironella and Editorial Planeta for permission to quote from *Un
Millón de Muertos.*

To Harcourt Brace Jovanovich, for material from *A-LM Spanish,* Level One, Second
Edition. Copyright © 1969 by Harcourt Brace Jovanovich, Inc. and reprinted with their
permission.

To Holt, Rinehart and Winston, for material from Jimenez, "El Viaje Definitivo"
and Becquer, "Rimas" in *Lecturas Hispanicas,* Book One, eds. del Rio and Hespelt
(1946).

To the Heirs of Juan Ramón Jiménez for the poem by Jiménez, "El Viaje Definitivo,"
in *Canción* (Madrid: Aguilar, S.A. de Ediciones, 1961).

To Oxford University Press, for "Prohibido Fumar en el Tranvía" in J. K. Leslie,
Cuentos y Risas, A First Reader in Spanish (1952).

To Prentice-Hall, for material by A. Díaz-Cañabate in *La España Moderna,* eds.
Thomas R. Hart and Carlos Rojas (1966).

To Charles Scribner's Sons, for A. M. Matute, "La Conciencia" in *Maestros del
Cuento Español Moderno,* ed. Cano-Ballesta (1974); and "El Gato que Nunca
Murió" in P. G. Evans, *An Elementary Spanish Reader* (1960).

To Colley F. Sparkman, for "La Gitanilla" in *De Todo un Poco,* Book 1, eds.
Carlos Castillo and Colley F. Sparkman (D. C. Heath and Co., 1936).

To University of California Press, for material from "Letrilla Satirica" in *A Critical
Anthology of Spanish Verse,* ed. E. Allison Peers (1949).

To University of Miami Press, for material from Tomas Navarro Tomas, *Studies in
Spanish Phonology* (1968).

Preface

Foreign-language teaching is an interesting and exciting occupation. Since the nature of language and its complex operations is still a matter of controversy and since the psychologists have still much to learn about how language is acquired—the native language as well as a second or third language—foreign-language teachers have an open field. They are free to experiment and innovate. They can appropriate what has proved successful in other times and other places. They can repeat and refine what they have found to be effective in their own circumstances with their own students. They can share successes and explore failures with their colleagues, learning much from each other.

Learning to use a language freely and fully is a lengthy and effortful process. Teachers cannot learn the language for their students. They can set their students on the road, helping them to develop confidence in their own learning powers. Then they must wait on the sidelines, ready to encourage and assist, while each student struggles and perseveres with autonomous activity. Some students learn the language well, even while the teacher observes. For those who find the task more difficult, we should at least make every effort to ensure that their language learning is an enjoyable and educational experience.

As foreign-language teachers we must remain optimistic. Rarely will we see the fully developed product: the autonomous, confident language-user, although we will often be stimulated by the enthusiasm of those we have started along that path. Let us not be discouraged by the jeremiads of those who tell us our task is an impossible one in the time at our disposal. Our colleagues in mathematics and physics do not produce batches of Einsteins after three or four years of study and Stravinskys are rare in the music room. Students interested in language and uninhibited in using the little they have assimilated will have a foundation on which to build when the opportunity presents itself. Surely all true education is beginnings. It is the hope of the author that this book and its companion volumes will play some part in stimulating imaginative and resourceful teaching which will arouse and sustain effective self-motivated learning.

In these books we do not provide final answers. What we have written is intended to provoke lively discussion. This is clearly an age when flexibility is a prime attribute for the young teacher. As prospective and practicing teachers consider the many techniques we have described and understand the rationale behind them, recognizing their strengths and weaknesses, they will be establishing a solid basis for choice when they are faced in a local situation with a wide variety of students of different ages and personal objectives. Ultimately, their selection should accord with their educational ideals, their own personality potential, and the needs and learning preferences of their students. The one all-sufficient answer for the classroom teacher is an alluring panacea but as illusory and unattainable as the philosopher's stone.

Method books for the preparation of foreign-language teachers abound. Some students using this book may have a background in general methodology such as is provided in *Teaching Foreign-Language Skills** and books of a similar nature. The range of material in that book, however, is not considered in detail in this one. Rather, many ideas implicit and explicit in the earlier book have been developed in practical detail in the light of more recent emphases in the various branches of linguistics and the psychology of language. (Teachers are provided with much information without the confusions of overly technical language.) Stress is laid throughout on using language from the earliest stages for the normal purposes of language. Attention is also paid to contemporary developments in the study of the French language.

For all of the volumes in the series, the basic theoretical discussion and the elaboration of techniques remain parallel but for every exercise or activity, and for the types of study materials discussed, examples are supplied in the language the student will be teaching. The books are, therefore, appropriate for simultaneous use in a multiple-language methods class as well as for language-specific courses in foreign-language departments, whether for future high school teachers or for those preparing for a future in undergraduate instruction. The material will also be useful for inservice

* Wilga M. Rivers, 1968. Chicago: The University of Chicago Press.

training courses and institutes, enabling teachers of different languages to consider general problems together while penetrating to the heart of the matter through the language with which each is most familiar. The books will also provide a treasury from which practicing teachers can draw many ideas for individualized learning packets and for small-group activity, as well as for stimulating learning in a more conventional classroom.

A few additional explanations may facilitate the use of the book. Although there is some detailed discussion of points of Spanish syntax and phonology, these are subordinate to the discussion of the preparation of teaching and testing materials and the elaboration of techniques; no attempt has been made to treat them systematically or exhaustively. Other books are available to meet this need. On the other hand, material used in the examples has been selected with a view to opening up discussion of areas of language about which the non-native speaker of Spanish may not be quite clear, particular emphasis being laid, in a number of places, on the differences between spoken and written language. Examples, as given, are not intended to be complete but illustrative of technique. The suggested exercises, indicated by an asterisk *, then draw the application into other areas of possible confusion or difficulty. One cannot teach what one does not fully understand oneself. Teachers in training will thus have a further opportunity to clarify matters which have worried them in the past.

It should be noted, at this point, that it is the intention of the authors that the asterisked activities be assigned, so that students actively participate in creation of new materials and in the adaptation and refinement of those provided in current textbooks. The close examination and judicious adaptation of text, test, and taped materials should be part of every trainee teacher's experience, along with the trying out in actual teaching situations of what has been developed (whether in micro-lessons or in practice teaching with a class). Students should be encouraged, during their training period, to begin a permanent indexed file of personally culled teaching materials, together with ideas for activities and projects. They should keep on file reading passages, cultural information, poems, scenes from plays, songs, and games appropriate for various ages and levels, informal visual aids, interesting and amusing variations of techniques, practical activities in which their students can use the language informally and spontaneously, and sources of information and supplementary assistance. If students share what they gather during this important period of preparation, they will not approach their first year of full-time teaching empty-handed.

The artificiality of dealing with various aspects of language use in separate chapters is apparent (e.g., the separation of listening and acceptable production of sounds from communicative interaction and both of these from knowledge of the rules of grammar). Students will need to hold certain questions in abeyance until they can see the whole picture.

For those who wish to consider questions in a different order from that supplied, numerous cross-references are included in the text, in addition to the comprehensive information in the detailed list of contents and the index. To facilitate the finding of examples dealing with various aspects of language use, initial letter classifications have been used throughout different sections, viz., C: Communicating, both speaking and listening; G: Grammar; S: Sounds; R: Reading; and W: Writing.

Examples go beyond the elementary course. Although it is difficult to establish a level of difficulty in the abstract, E has been used to indicate the elementary level (first or second year of high school, first or second semester of beginning college study), I for intermediate level (second or third year of high school, second or third semester of college), and A for advanced level (fourth or fifth year of high school, fourth semester or above in college). This classification is non-scientific and indicative only. It will be for the instructor, the student, or the practicing teacher to adjust the interpretation of levels of difficulty to particular situations.

In conclusion, the authors wish to thank most warmly the numerous persons, scholars and teachers in the field, who have contributed to the development of their thinking through discussion, demonstration, or published work. Special thanks must, however, go to the editors at Oxford University Press, John Wright and Ann Lindsay, for their constant encouragement and meticulous assistance in production; to Arlene Vander-Werff, for her invaluable work in coordinating our manuscripts, for her meticulous care in advising us on discrepancies and omissions and for her many suggestions for improvements to the final text; to José M. Rodríguez, Jorge M. Guitart, Rafael Castillo, Manuel Puerta, and Montserrat Dejuán-Espinet who provided helpful assistance in verification of numerous points of Spanish usage; to David Nasjleti for his valuable suggestions which were incorporated in the final version of Chapter 5 and for the many improvements which were made on his advice after he had kindly read the entire text for inconsistencies or inadvertent errors; to Janet Feigenbaum, Harriett Weatherford, and Tobie Kranitz for their help in the preparation of the manuscript, and to René Coppieters for his assistance with the index. We also wish to express our appreciation of the material help in the realization of the task which was accorded by the Research Board and Center for Advanced Study of the University of Illinois at Urbana-Champaign.

Cambridge, Massachusetts   W. M. R.
Urbana-Champaign, Illinois   M. M. A.
Knoxville, Tennessee   W. H. H., JR.
Buffalo, New York   R. H.-O.

October 1975

Contents

A practical guide to the teaching of Spanish

I
COMMUNICATING

Communication acts

In Part I, speaking and listening are discussed in separate chapters, although in a communication act one clearly complements the other. The reader will bear in mind that being able to speak a language without understanding what is being said by native speakers is of limited use, while being able to understand a language but not speak it can have specialized utility (for the enjoyment of foreign-language films, broadcasts, plays, and songs, or for professional monitoring purposes) but is very frustrating in normal communication situations. Being able to speak comprehensibly does not necessarily ensure ability to comprehend normal native speech; on the other hand, many people develop a very high level of aural comprehension without being able to express themselves freely. Both areas require serious attention.

In a well-rounded program, success in each will be recognized as a separate achievement and given equal importance in the eyes of the students. Nevertheless, practice of each should normally be in relation to the other if communicating is the ultimate goal.

Developing skill and confidence in communication

When selecting learning activities, we must always remember that our goal is for the students to be able to interact freely with others: to understand what others wish to communicate in the broadest sense, and to be able to convey to others what they themselves wish to share (whether as a reaction to a communication or as an original contribution to the exchange). To do this effectively, however, the students must understand how the Spanish language works and be able to make the interrelated changes for which the system of the language provides mechanisms.

The following schema will help us to see the essential processes involved in learning to communicate.

C1 Processes involved in learning to communicate

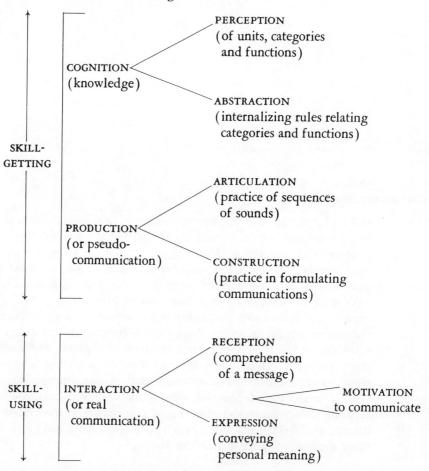

SKILL-GETTING

COGNITION (knowledge)
→ PERCEPTION (of units, categories and functions)
→ ABSTRACTION (internalizing rules relating categories and functions)

PRODUCTION (or pseudo-communication)
→ ARTICULATION (practice of sequences of sounds)
→ CONSTRUCTION (practice in formulating communications)

SKILL-USING

INTERACTION (or real communication)
→ RECEPTION (comprehension of a message)
→ EXPRESSION (conveying personal meaning)
← MOTIVATION to communicate

Note: 1. This is not a sequential but a parallel schema, in the sense that skill-getting and skill-using[1] are continually proceeding hand in hand. There is genuine *interaction from the beginning,* with students exploring the full scope of what is being learned.

2. *Bridging the gap* between skill-getting and skill-using is not automatic. Skill-getting activities must be so designed as to be already *pseudo-communication,* thus leading naturally into spontaneous communication activities.

3. The terminology of this schema will be used in discussing appropriate activities for skill-getting and skill-using.

Knowledge and intensive practice (skill-getting) are not enough to ensure confident interaction. The latter requires practice in actual, purposeful conversational exchange with others. In Chapter 1 we shall discuss linguistic aspects of the spoken language with which the students need to be familiar if their communication is not to be stilted and various types of bridging activities (e.g., the many uses of dialogues, Cummings devices, and action chains); in Chapter 2 we shall turn our attention to ways of involving students in real interaction.[2] In Chapter 3, the problems of understanding the spoken language are considered in depth. Chapters 4 and 5 give the rationale for techniques and activities for perception, abstraction, articulation, and construction.

1
Structured interaction

Opposing views on the development of speaking skill

According to the *progressive development* view, ability to speak the language derives from the systematic study of grammar, phonology, and lexicon. This is the approach of grammar-translation texts, where it is assumed that accuracy in expressing oneself orally is dependent on prior study of language forms through reading and written exercises; of audio-lingual or aural-oral texts where oral imitation, memorization, and drilling techniques precede attempts to speak spontaneously (although in this case the latter is attempted much sooner than in traditional grammar-translation texts); and of texts which begin with narrative and conversational reading passages.

The *immediate communication* view holds that speaking skill is developed from the first contact with the language. The student may be encouraged to express himself in simple ways under the guidance of the teacher (*¿Qué es esto? Es un libro; ¿Dónde está el libro? El libro está en la mesa*). Alternatively, in a simulation of the total immersion experience of the foreigner in another culture, he may be expected to use for the expression of his own message anything he has acquired of the language from hearing it, supplemented by gestures, pantomime, or the showing of objects, with the teacher suggesting words and expressions only when the student falters.

This chapter takes a *middle position* between these two approaches, advocating that students be encouraged to express themselves freely in the

6

language from the beginning, through carefully presented experiences and games which provide them with a framework for spontaneous communicative creation while presupposing they will use what they have been learning through an orderly progression of study and practice. The Type B exercises described in Chapter 4 prepare students to use the language for expressing their own meanings[1] and are paralleled from the beginning with extensive opportunities for autonomous interaction of the type discussed in Chapter 2. If students are to develop as uninhibited communicators who seize opportunities to use the language with native speakers, they must early overcome their timidity and the fear of being embarrassed when they express themselves simplistically or awkwardly, as they will often do when their knowledge of the language is at an elementary stage.

Differences between spoken and written Spanish

Much of any foreign language learned at school is acquired from books. Even where conversations and dialogues appear, they are often unrepresentative of authentic speech. Tapes and records attempt to bring the oral language into the classroom, but some of these are no more than stilted oral recitations of written forms of the language. If students are to learn to use authentic speech, their teachers must be aware of the features which differentiate the spoken language from the conventional written forms, and particularly from the literary usages to which they have become accustomed in their own advanced studies.

For conciseness and precision of meaning, Spanish speakers usually employ in written material more complicated structures and a wider vocabulary than in speech. This is one reason why learning to write Spanish well is an advanced art. In one sense, written Spanish is *less redundant* than the spoken form of the language (that is, it contains fewer signals of the same aspect of meaning) in that repetitions and duplications are avoided and the additional clues provided by such things as rising and falling intonation and tone of voice are absent. In another sense it is more redundant, in that it contains many signals to meaning which are completely lost when the written form is presented orally. Phenomena involving contiguous vowels provide several instances of this. For example, in a sentence such as *me he equivocado* there are three occurrences of /e/ in succession; in careful speech, these vowels can all be pronounced in linked fashion: /meeekibokádo/. In rapid speech, however, they can coalesce into only two or even one occurrence of /e/: /mekibokádo/. In other words, one or two /e/'s are eliminated and an untrained hearer becomes confused because he does not recognize where one word ends and another begins.

C2 Analysis of some sentences from a modern literary work highlights a number of differences between the written and spoken codes in Spanish.

Algunos días más tarde, iba a la escuela por la playa, al pie de las casitas cuyas terrazas llegan hasta la orilla. Como no tenía prisa, me senté a descansar, contemplando el mar y el muelle, que estaba a la izquierda. Volví la cara al oír algunas palabras en la terraza que tenía a mi espalda, y ví a una niña muy pálida, muy delgada, sentada, mirando el mar. Era Miss Orquídea, en un gran sillón, envuelta en una manta verde.

ABRAHAM VALDELOMAR, "El vuelo de los condores."[2]

If recounted orally, this incident might have been expressed as follows:

Algunos días más tarde—no más de dos o tres días—iba a la escuela por la playa. Tú sabes, por allá donde están las casitas con terrazas que llegan hasta la orilla. Pues, no tenía prisa, y así me senté a descansar un rato y a contemplar el mar y el muelle. Este estaba a la izquierda, ¿sabes? Luego oí hablar a alguien en la terraza detrás de mí—a mi espalda. Volví la cara y ví allá a una niña muy pálida, sin color alguno y muy delgada... Era Miss Orquídea, en un gran sillón y envuelta en una manta verde. Ella—la señorita—miraba el mar.

Commentary

1. Not only would the second version when spoken contain more clues to meaning (that is, be more redundant) because of the prosodic features of intonation and pitch, and the expressive features of tone of voice, gesture, and facial expression with which it would be accompanied, but it is expressed in simple declarative sentences, with considerable repetition of semantic detail (*algunos días más tarde—no más de dos o tres días; por la playa—por allá donde* . . . ; *detrás de mí—a mi espalda; muy pálida—sin color alguno*); with grammatical substitutions with the same referent (*ella—la señorita*); and with expletives and conversational tags and cliches like *tú sabes, ¿sabes?, luego, pues,* which add little to the message, but give the speaker time to organize the succeeding segment for production.

2. *Sinalefa:* The speaker would pronounce *iba a la escuela* as /ibalaeskuéla/, where the two equal unaccented vowels ib*a a* coalesce in the single syllable /ba/ and where the two different unaccented open vowels in l*a e*scuela are also reduced to a single syllable /lae/. In substandard and even in rapid colloquial speech, final /e/, /a/, and /o/ are often dropped before a following unequal vowel (/leskuéla/). While this is a practice the student should avoid in learning to pronounce, he should be aware of its occurrence and be able to recognize the linked forms.

3. *Loss or alteration of phonemes.*

a. In rapid informal speech the [d] within the participial ending -*ado* tends to be very much weakened, often to the point of disappearing entirely, as in [delgáᵈa], [sentáᵈa]. (Weakening of this phoneme also occurs frequently in word final position when the final syllable carries the stress, e.g., [libertáᵈ], [ciuᵈáᵈ] (Lat. Am.), [ustéᵈ].)

b. Alveolar /n/ is characterized by its tendency to assimilate to the point of articulation of an immediately following phoneme. Thus, *sin color* [siŋkolór].

✱ Be sure that you know and understand the rules for *sinalefa*. A useful reference is T. Navarro Tomás, *Pronunciación española,* 16th ed. (Madrid: Raycar, S.A., 1971), pp. 147–60.

Effects of the position of stress

The term *stress* is used to refer to the relative prominence given either to syllables of a single word (*word stress*) or to one or more syllables of a sequence of words (*sentence stress*). Word stress plays an essential role in Spanish, since it serves to differentiate between otherwise similar words, as exemplified by the pairs *hablo* vs. *habló, tome* vs. *tomé,* and so on. There are two degrees of word stress in Spanish, namely *primary* or *strong* and *weak.* (Some linguists posit an intermediary degree, called *secondary,* but this need not concern us here.)

If pronounced in isolation, every Spanish word has a primary stress (which may or may not be indicated by an *acento agudo* in ordinary orthography). In the stream of speech, however, words are usually strung together, as it were, and some classes of words—usually the so-called "bound forms" such as unstressed pronouns, prepositions, definite articles, and so on—always occur with weak stress. Typically, a Spanish *grupo fónico* (that is, a phonemic phrase or breath group) consists of one or more stressed syllables, each preceded and followed by one or more unstressed syllables. For example, a sentence such as *La casa de la muchacha que vimos ayer* contains a sequence of strong (′) and weak (˘) stresses which, in a phonemic transcription, may be represented thus: /lăkásădělămŭčáčăkěbímŏsăyér/.

Sentence stress occurs as the most prominent primary stress in a given phonemic phrase and usually fulfills the function of signalling the "information focus" of a sentence. For example, the sentence *¡Ya se fue tu taxi!* may be uttered with sentence stress on either *fue* or *taxi.* In the former case, it would be equivalent to "Your taxi has already *left*," whereas in the latter it would mean something like "Your *taxi* has already left."

✻ Consider the possible ways of pronouncing a sentence such as *My math teacher is coming tomorrow* as a reply to each of the following questions:

1. When is your math teacher coming? My math teacher is coming tomorrow.
2. Will your math teacher stay home tomorrow? No, my math teacher is coming tomorrow.
3. Who is coming tomorrow? My math teacher is coming tomorrow.
4. Is it your music teacher who is coming tomorrow? No, my math teacher is coming tomorrow.
5. Is it your sister's math teacher who is coming tomorrow? No, it's my math teacher who is coming tomorrow.

As the above examples illustrate, English makes wide use of placement of sentence stress to indicate variations in the focus of information. In Spanish, however, this recourse is not nearly so important as variations in word order, which may or may not be used with special lexical and syntactical devices. As a consequence of this, sentence stress is inextricably bound to the position of major parts in the Spanish sentence. As a general rule, if a word is to receive sentence stress, it is brought to the end of the *grupo fónico*.

For example, in *Bebe mucha agua cuando hace calor,* sentence stress would fall on the word *calor;* in *Cuando hace calor, bebe mucha agua,* two *grupos fónicos* have been created by the change in word order, and now both *calor* and *agua* receive sentence stress. In the first sentence, there is only one focus of information; in the second, there are two.

C3 Notice the different speech effects of the following pairs.
— Algunos creen que la guerra es inevitable.
— La guerra, creen algunos, es inevitable.

— Avíseme cuando llegue él.
— Cuando llegue él, avíseme.

✻ Practice taking simple statements or questions and reordering them to emphasize different elements in the utterance, e.g.:

¿Tu hermano ya se fue?
¿Ya se fue tu hermano?
¿Ya se fue el hermano tuyo?

Another device which brings particular words into the position of stress is the construction *ser . . . quien/ . . . el que/ . . . cuando/ . . . donde.*

C4 Compare:

Mi hermano ganó el *premio.*
Fue mi *hermano* quien ganó el *premio.*

Mañana vamos al *centro.*
Es mañana cuando vamos al *centro.*

* Make the changes necessary to replicate the emphasis of the following in Spanish:

I sold my house.
I sold my *house* (not my car).
I sold *my* house (not my father's).
I *sold* my house (I did not rent it).
I sold my house (not the realtor).

Notice that these common patterns of speech make the spoken utterance more redundant than a simple written declarative sentence would be. This fact is significant for the aural comprehension of fleeting combinations of sounds. The teacher must be aware of these basic patterns and encourage students to use them when expressing themselves orally in Spanish.

* For a more comprehensive account of stress in English and Spanish, read J. B. Dalbor, *Spanish Pronunciation: Theory and Practice* (New York: Holt, Rinehart and Winston, 1969), Chapter 34.

Style of language (register or level of discourse)

We use different styles of language in diverse situations—when we are speaking to a person in an official position, to an acquaintance, to a close friend, or within the family circle. Students should be made conscious of this fact and learn to recognize, and eventually use, Spanish in these different styles. They should be able to distinguish *lenguaje culto* from *lenguaje coloquial* or *corriente.* They should be able to understand rather than use *lenguaje popular.* (These distinctions also help them to recognize the author's intent in conversational material in written Spanish.) Werner Beinhauer's *El Español Coloquial* (Madrid: Editorial Gredos, 1963), although outdated in parts, contains information on the colloquial language which can be of use to teachers and advanced students alike. The *Gramática del Español Contemporáneo,* by Martin Alonso (Madrid: Ediciones Guadarrama, 1968), has a chapter entitled *Laboratorio de la Palabra Hablada,* in which the reader will find an interesting analysis of the characteristics of different levels of language use. Articles on the subject also appear regularly in *Hispania,* the official journal of the American Association of Teachers of Spanish and Portuguese.

Joos distinguishes for English five styles: intimate, casual, consultative, formal, and frozen. Applying the criteria set out by Joos in *The Five Clocks* we may develop the following sequence in Spanish for a similar situation treated at the five levels.[3]

C5 In an *intimate* situation, a parent may say to a child who is embarrassingly present and has shown some reluctance to leave: *¡Vete de aquí!* (According to Joos, in intimate style the utterance contains no information that is known to the participants.) This is *lenguaje familiar.*

In a *casual* style the parent may say: *Déjanos solos, ¿quieres?* (Once again complete information is not supplied, and this style involves the use of well-known formulas.) This is *lenguaje coloquial* and, like the preceding style, also employs the *tuteo.*

Consultative style, the style of standard exchange between strangers, would require rather something like: *Salga Ud. de la sala por un momento, por favor.* (Since consultative style is used for persons outside the intimate circle, the *tú* form would not be used. Consultative style supplies all necessary background information.) In such a situation one would use *lenguaje cuidado.*

A *formal* situation, on the other hand, may require: *Tenga Ud. la bondad de ausentarse por algunos minutos.* (In formal style, the speaker often does not refer to himself and he does not anticipate any immediate participation on the part of the person addressed.) Here *lenguaje formal* is used.

Frozen or printed style may be observed on a notice outside a door: *Se ruega no interrumpir la reunión.* This is usually *lenguaje administrativo.*

Compare the following series:

¿Y la sal? ¿Me alcanzas la sal? Alcánceme la sal, por favor. Ud. que es tan amable, ¿quiere tener la bondad de alcanzarme la sal? Se ruega no monopolizar la sal.

* Try constructing a similar series on the themes: "Please do not talk" and "Write to me about it."

C6 In the light of the above discussion on styles of language, examine the following passage from the play *El Carrusell* by Victor Ruiz Iriarte.[4]

MÓNICA   ¡Chis! ¡Chis! (*Tomy se vuelve hacia ella. Sonríe. Durante unos segundos se miran los dos largamente, intensamente. Y, de pronto, como respondiendo al mismo impulso, corren el uno hacia el otro y se abrazan, se estrechan, se besan apasionadamente.*) ¡Oh! Tomy, Tomy. ¡Te quiero tanto!

TOMY   Nena . . . (*Se vuelven a besar. Un silencio. Y, de pronto, se oye la voz de Ramonín que grita estentóreamente.*)

RAMONÍN   (*Dentro.*) ¡Cru, cru, cru! (*Mónica y Tomy se separan, aterrados.*)

MÓNICA   ¡Ayyy!

TOMY   ¡¡Porras!!

MÓNICA   ¡Oh! Un día nos sorprenderán . . . (*Mónica escapa corriendo, sofocadísima, y entra en la habitación de la izquierda. Tomy, casi de un salto se zambulle en el sofá. Y por la puerta de la derecha aparece Ramonín, recitando como siempre para su inexistente auditorio.*)

RAMONÍN   ¡Cru, cru, cru! ¡Mírela! ¡Ahí está! ¡Oh, Madame Fix, la vieja prostituta! Jajajá. ¡Kikirikí! Canta el gallo. ¡Oh, no! Es el agente de bolsa de madame Fix. ¡Guardias! ¡Protejan a la bondadosa, a la hermosa, a la poderosa madame Fix! (*Transición.*) Bueno. Se acabó el ensayo . . .

TOMY   ¡Ah! Pero ¿estabas ensayando?

RAMONÍN   ¡Naturalmente! ¿Es que no se nota? Pues para que te enteres: dentro de ocho días debutaré como actor en un teatro de cámara . . .

TOMY   (*Estupefacto*). ¿Quién? ¿Tú?

RAMONÍN   ¡Yo! ¿Que te parece?

TOMY   ¡Ramonín! Me has dejado de una pieza. (*Ramonín se sienta en el sofá, junto a Tomy.*)

RAMONÍN   Un suceso, ya verás. Me presento con una obra extranjera, como un profesional. Una comedia revolucionaria, muy de izquierdas, ¿sabes? Algo extraordinario. Figúrate tú que se levanta el telón y los personajes hablan y hablan y siguen hablando, y hasta el final nadie sabe de qué se trata. Pero, cuando llega ese final . . .

TOMY   (*Interesadísimo.*) ¿Qué? ¿Se casan?

RAMONÍN   Un cuerno, chalao.

✱ Discuss in the above passage: indications of rapid speech; structures commonly used in *lenguaje familiar;* words which are particularly indicative of *lenguaje familiar and lenguaje popular;* allusions which may reflect Spanish customs; the contrast between the language used by the characters and that in the stage directions.

The style of language in dialogues of the sort found in textbooks may not always be used consistently.

C7 La señora Martínez y una amiga se encuentran en el centro de Madrid:

SRA. MARTÍNEZ   Buenos días, señora González. ¿Cómo está Ud.?
SRA. GONZÁLEZ   Muy bien, gracias.
SRA. MARTÍNEZ   ¿Y su hijo?
SRA. GONZÁLEZ   No está mal.

Commentary

1. If Sra. González were really *una amiga* of Sra. Martínez, the latter would normally say something like, *¿Qué tal, Ana?* She might also (but not necessarily so) use the *tú form.* By the tone of her address, Sra. González is more probably a *conocida* or a *vecina.*

2. In response to Sra. Martínez's very polite greeting, Sra. González should add to her reply a repetition of the formula *buenos días* or *¿qué tal?* as well as an inquiry such as, *¿y usted?*

3. Sra. González's *no está mal* after Sra. Martínez's polite inquiry is very brusque and out of keeping with the general tone of the exchange. If the son has not been well, something like *Está bastante bien, gracias* would have been more polite.

* Examine dialogues in current textbooks to see if they use different levels of discourse appropriately and consistently.

Bridging activities

All that we can teach students in a foreign language is how to construct the appropriate framework, in all its detail, for the expression of meaning. We cannot teach students to express their own meaning; we can provide opportunities which stimulate motivation for this personal activity to take place and we can help the student to improve the framework so that it can really carry the message intended. We can develop activities where the student constructs various types of frameworks and help him try them out to see if they will carry effectively the meanings he intends. Searle calls language "rule-governed intentional behavior."[5] We can help the student internalize the rules; we cannot supply the intention, although we can stimulate it by contriving situations and encounters. One way in which we help students try out frameworks of varying degrees of complexity and subtlety (that is, to perform "speech acts"[6]) is by providing practice in *pseudo-communication.* This is communication in which the content is structured by the learning situation, rather than springing autonomously from the mind and emotions of the student. *We bridge the gap to true communication by encouraging the student to use these structured practices for autonomous purposes from the early stages.* In this way, the average student acquires confidence in his ability to function on his own. (Linguistically gifted students will always develop confidence in their own way, with or without special guidance.)

The concept of *individualization of instruction* has to be very carefully analyzed in relation to the development of communication skills: it can mean small-group practice and interaction, but not independent study, because communication by definition involves someone other than the communicator. Students also learn a great deal from listening to the way other people formulate their communications. At the other extreme, communication cannot be efficiently practiced in large groups. For a discussion of suitable groupings of students for communication practice, see Wilga M. Rivers et al., "Techniques for the Development of Proficiency in the Spoken Language" in H. B. Altman and R. L. Politzer, eds., *Individualizing Foreign Language Instruction* (Rowley, Mass.: Newbury House, 1971), pp. 165–74.

RULE-GOVERNED BEHAVIOR

In language use, we fit our meaning into a framework which conforms to many types of rules, or recurring regularities: not only syntactic, morphological, and phonological, but also semantic and cultural. Once we have an intention to express, not only do we have to select the "right words" for our purpose, but these choices entail other lexical selections within the sentence which we must respect, but which function according to rules at present only vaguely understood. Semantics also dictates our choices in syntax,[7] and syntactic selection forces certain morphological adjustments. We cannot operate effectively in speech or writing until we have understood the possibilities the rules afford and are able to put into operation the sheer mechanics of the language at the level of verb endings for person and tense, required agreements, conventional word order and so on.[8] Cultural expectations come into play as well, that is, rules of relationships and obligations in interpersonal communication within a society, expressed in part through registers or levels of discourse, but also through expected and implied questions and reactions, social taboos, and the mutually understood references of words used in certain associations.

C8 El no me dejó hacer lo que yo quería.
    El impidió la realización de mis planes.

The decision to express this intention at a more formal level in the second sentence motivated the choice of *impedir* instead of *dejar,* and this lexical choice entailed other lexical choices and a different syntactic framework from that in the first sentence.

Siento no poder acompañarle pero hoy es el día del santo de mi madrina y vamos a celebrarlo juntos.

Comprehension of this sentence is dependent on comprehension not merely of the individual words but of certain extended family relationships and obligations of Spanish society.

Supplying the student with a basic corpus

The first problem we face in teaching students to speak a foreign language is how to plunge them into using natural language when they know little or nothing of the new tongue. Proponents of the grammar-translation approach have usually maintained that conversing in the language should not be attempted until students control the essentials of the syntactic and morphological systems intellectually and in graphic form and have acquired through reading and memorization an extensive vocabulary, at which stage they can learn to express themselves orally quite rapidly by drawing on what they have learned. But with the modern emphasis on the importance of oral communication and the present generation's greater familiarity with aural-oral rather than graphic presentations of information, this approach can be discouraging for many students.

A number of approaches have been proposed at different times for plunging the student into active language use. All have proved effective in the early stages when intelligently and imaginatively implemented. We need some way of supplying the student with a basic corpus with which to work.

We can identify four main approaches to this problem: the object centered, the melody and rhythm centered, the verb centered, and the situation centered.

OBJECT CENTERED

In this approach, students begin by discussing objects in the classroom in imitation of the teacher. The grammatical structures introduced are demonstrable in relation to these objects, so that students hear and practice them in a realistic setting.

C9 He aquí el libro. Allá está la ventana . . . ¿Qué es esto? Es el libro. Es la ventana . . . ¿Dónde está el libro? El libro está en la mesa . . . El libro es verde . . . Es el libro de Pedro . . .

The class then goes on to discuss persons in the classroom in much the same terms:

Pedro es un alumno. Es grande.
María es una alumna. Es pequeña.
Es la hermana de Pedro.

Variant: Teachers sometimes use the contents of a handbag or shopping basket instead of classroom objects. Later, pictures of houses, gardens, airports, farms are used to expand the environment for purposes of description and discussion. Sometimes these pictures are in the textbook. Otherwise, use is made of commercially available wall-pictures, full- or double-page scenes cut from magazines, or projected slides. Students often construct posters, with items labeled in Spanish, to illustrate these environments, and these are posted on the bulletin board so that students can assimilate the vocabulary casually through frequent contact. (Unless the teacher is watchful, however, an overemphasis on acquiring names for a multiplicity of objects may develop.)

This approach sometimes limits students to accurate production of very trite sentences which they would not conceivably wish to use in spontaneous conversation: *Esto es un libro. Es verde. Está en el escritorio del profesor. Este es el libro del profesor.* Modern students find this approach boring and trivial. It is well to remember that in real conversation we rarely comment on things which are visible unless the situation is exceptional: *¡La silla está en el escritorio del profesor! ¿Por qué?* A little whimsy will help to enliven the exchanges and keep the students alert.

MELODY AND RHYTHM CENTERED

In a very different approach, only one noun is used for quite a long time: *una regleta* (a rod). Called "the silent way"[9] by Gattegno, its originator, this method concentrates at the beginning on developing sensitivity to the melody and flow of the language. Students listen to tapes of a number of languages trying to recognize which of the speeches they hear is in the language they have been studying.[10] Gattegno considers that

since babies learn to talk their mother tongue first by yielding to its "music," we can . . . trace the first elements of the spirit of a language to the unconscious surrender of our sensitivity to what is conveyed by the background of noise in each language. This background obviously includes the silences, the pauses, the flow, the linkage of words, the duration of each breath required to utter connected chunks of the language, the overtones and undertones, the stresses as well as the special vowels or consonants belonging to that language.[11]

The teacher works with only about thirty words in the initial lessons, mainly the feminine articles *la* and *una* for use with *regleta,* pronouns in the direct and indirect object forms (*la, las, me, se, le*), some color adjectives in the feminine form, possessives (*mí, su*), a few numerals, some forms of *tener, poner* and *estar* (*tengo, tiene, tienen; ponga; está, están*), the command forms of *dar* and *tomar,* the preposition *a,* the conjunction *y; sí, no,* and a few adverbs like *también, allí, aquí.* Using a box of colored rods, the teacher induces the student to utter fluent sentences with native-like facility, while talking as little as possible himself. There is a minimum of imitation of the teacher and a maximum of concentration by the student on constructing sentences with the help of the rods. The teacher does not explain grammatical features but encourages the students to think about what they hear and to try to construct utterances which conform to the rules they have discovered for themselves.

C10 Types of sentences practiced with the rods:

Tome una regleta azul (roja, verde).
Démela a mí.
Tome una regleta amarilla y désela a Roberto.
Tome dos regletas verdes y démelas a mí.

The rods continue to be used for learning such things as comparatives, temporal relationships, and tenses.

Later, through the technique of *visual dictation,*[12] students are given practice in recognizing the printed equivalents of the words they have been using orally as they created situations with the rods, and also in the fluent constructions of sentences using these words. Here the teacher points silently and rapidly, but only once, to a succession of words on a chart of scrambled words with phonic color coding, and in a short time students are able to produce with acceptable diction long sentences like *Tome una regleta azul y una regleta verde; déle la regleta azul a Roberto y déme la regleta verde,* as well as to demonstrate through action that they have understood what they are saying.

Gattegno claims to be "rejecting the learning of vocabularies and grammar . . . and replacing it with as thorough a penetration of the spirit of a language as possible."[13]

VERB CENTERED

One of the best-known devices under this head is the *Gouin series*.[14] Gouin had observed the way his child commented on his own actions and he developed from this the idea of an *action series* or *action chain*. He divided common events into five general series: the home, man in society, life in nature, science, and occupations. These were subdivided and resubdivided into shorter series centering around the verb, which, according to Gouin, is "the generating element of the sentence."[15] The language was then taught through a series of commonly performed actions, first orally, then in writing. A different verb was used in each statement, and students were expected to acquire the situational vocabulary along with the verb through performing or miming the actions while they described what they were doing. The teacher first demonstrated the series in the native language and then, when the students had understood it clearly, in the foreign language. The students next repeated the actions under the guidance of the teacher or of other students, describing what they were doing in the foreign language as they were doing it. (Gouin advocated peer teaching, saying that "in Nature, one child can and does teach another child to talk."[16]) While the students were trying to reproduce the series the teacher would make encouraging remarks in the language. After this aural-oral phase, the series would be read and then written out by the students.

The example Gouin himself gives[17] is the following (the verb is emphasized orally in the initial demonstration):

C11 YO) ABRO LA PUERTA

voy	Voy hacia la puerta.
me aproximo	me aproximo a la puerta.
llego	llego a la puerta.
me paro	me paro cerca de la puerta.
alargo	alargo el brazo.
tomo	tomo la empuñadura.
volteo	volteo la empuñadura.
halo	halo la puerta.
cede	la puerta cede.
gira	la puerta gira sobre sus goznes.
suelto	suelto la empuñadura.

We may be surprised at the amount of specialized vocabulary this method entailed. Gouin considered that general terms were infrequently used in comparison with specific vocabulary. His emphasis was, of course, on the verb, but the verb in complete sentences.

This approach can be extended to provide practice in all persons and different tenses.

C12   STUDENT A   ¿Qué hago?
        STUDENT B   Tu abres la puerta.

        STUDENTS A & B   Escribimos en la pizarra.
        TEACHER   ¿Qué hacen ellos?
        STUDENT C   Escriben en la pizarra.

        STUDENTS A & B   ¿Qué hacemos?
        STUDENT C   Uds. escriben en la pizarra.

        TEACHER   ¿Qué hicieron?
        STUDENT C   Escribieron en la pizarra.

        STUDENT A   Vea lo que haré la semana que viene. (Miming action)
        STUDENT B   Tú harás tus maletas.
        STUDENT C   Ella hará sus maletas.

Through mime the variety of the actions can be expanded considerably and the activity becomes a competitive game, with students describing each movement and then guessing what is being mimed. In an individualized or group work program this may be a completely student-to-student activity.

C13 (I) In another variation, the student is given an order or a series of orders (of increasing complexity) by the teacher or another student:

Vaya[18] a la puerta; abra la puerta; ponga el libro en la gaveta del escritorio; abra el libro en la página veinte y lea la primera frase en voz alta.

The student obeys the order saying what he is doing or, if he is learning the *pretérito,* what he has done. If he makes a mistake another student can describe what he actually did and what he should have done. (*Puso el libro en el escritorio. Debió haber puesto el libro en la gaveta del escritorio.*) This provides a useful situational context for learning the expression *deber +infinitive* or the useful *en vez de + infinitive.*

Recent revivals of this type of activity learning have been the *strategy of the total physical response*[19] (in which students respond physically to commands in the foreign language of increasing morphological and syntactical complexity) and *Situational Reinforcement*[20] (which uses the techniques of C12).

The Gouin approach can be developed in considerable detail beyond these simple examples and can be the basis of factual learning about the geography of Spain, the monuments of Madrid, activities at festivals, matters of etiquette, and so on.

C14 (I) A map of Spain is drawn, as a cooperative project, on the floor of the classroom, and students are asked to undertake journeys. (A posted map and pointer may be substituted, but this reduces the physical response to a symbolic one.)

TEACHER OR ANOTHER STUDENT: Saliendo de Madrid, pase por el río Tajo. Vaya hacia Aranjuez. No entre en la ciudad, sino siga camino hacia Toledo.

The student addressed then describes his journey in the *pretérito* with personal embellishments.

STUDENT: Salí de Madrid, donde hacía mucho calor. Pasé por el río Tajo a las nueve de la mañana. Llegué a Aranjuez pero no entré en la ciudad porque ya estaba lloviendo. Seguí camino hasta Toledo, donde almorcé.

Recognizing its debt to Gouin and to the subsequent work of Emile de Sauzé of Cleveland, whose influence can still be perceived in many a modern textbook, is the *verbal-active approach,* which has also been called "a rationalist direct method."[21] Yvone Lenard says, "The sentence arranges itself around the verb" and "it is, therefore, imperative that the student learn to listen for the verb in the sentence, recognize its form, and answer immediately with the appropriate form."[22] In essence, this echoes Gouin, although Lenard's method adds a question-answer sequence to the action series. Since this is a direct method, unlike the Gouin approach it excludes the native language from the classroom and the textbook.

In this approach, grammar is learned inductively and through action rather than through deductive grammar rules. Diller says, "Knowing a rule and being able to act on it is quite independent of being able to formulate the rule adequately. The rule can be psychologically real without any formulation of it. . . . Rules for action are best learned in conjunction with demonstration and practice of the action."[23] Both Diller and Lenard emphasize the necessity for the learning stage to develop into opportunities for innovative sentence creation on the part of the student. Quoting de Sauzé's viewpoint, Lenard says, " 'Language is invention.' It has no existence apart from the speaker or the writer who recreates, reinvents the language for his own needs each time he uses it."[24] She lays great stress on the daily oral composition as "the most important exercise of the verbal-active method in building the elements of which fluency is composed."[25] In these oral compositions, prepared in advance in writing but delivered orally in front of their fellows, students try to use only what everyone else is learning, thus cultivating "originality, free invention, and personal expression within a strictly controlled structural framework."[26] (Note that the verbal-active method moves from listening and speaking to writing before reading, another deviation from Gouin which is traceable to de Sauzé.)

C15 *Verbal-active action series*

Declaración y pregunta	*Respuesta*
Por la mañana *me despierto* temprano. ¿A qué hora *se despierta* Ud.?	*Me despierto* a las siete.
Me levanto en seguida. ¿*Se levanta* Ud. en seguida?	No, no *me levanto* en seguida. No *me gusta levantarme* en seguida.
Luego *me visto: me lavo la cara* (con agua y jabón), *me lavo los dientes* (con el cepillo de dientes) y *me cepillo el pelo* (con el cepillo para la cabeza). Y luego *me peino.* ¿Ud. *se peina?*	Sí, *me peino.*
Un hombre *se afeita* por la mañana (probablemente con una máquina de afeitar eléctrica). ¿Ud. *se afeita,* señor?[27]	Sí, *me afeito,* pero *me dejo* las patillas y el bigote.

SITUATION CENTERED

For many centuries, situationally based dialogues have been in and out of fashion for providing students with a corpus of foreign-language words and expressions with which to work.[28] They are very frequently found in present-day textbooks. The situations chosen may be experiences common to both the native and the foreign culture, or may introduce the student to typically Spanish ways of interacting and reacting. Sometimes they are printed with a parallel idiomatic translation; at other times students are expected to comprehend the meaning through action or through simple Spanish explanations.

Dialogue construction can be indicative of diverse philosophies. Some dialogues are designed to *demonstrate grammatical rules* and examples of rules in use and the variations of paradigms are introduced systematically in the exchanges.

C16   PABLO   ¿Adónde vas esta noche?
       MADELENA   Voy al centro con mi familia. Vamos al cine.
       PABLO   ¿Qué van a ver Uds.?
       MADELENA   *El Bolero,* con Cantinflas. Mis primos van a ver la misma película mañana.

The aim of grammar-demonstration dialogues is to lead students to inductive recognition of the rule or the paradigm. These dialogues need not be memorized: they can be studied and discussed in Spanish, dramatized, and used as a basis for recombinations. They lead naturally to grammatical explanations and intensive practice exercises through which the operation of the rule, or paradigm, becomes clear to the student, enters his active repertoire, and is then used by him in a genuinely communicative interchange.

Other dialogues, which we shall call *conversation-facilitation dialogues,* are intended primarily to provide students with a stock of useful expressions (clichés of conversation, frequently used expressions, conventional greetings, expletives, and rejoinders) with which to practice conversing, while the teaching of the grammar proceeds as a parallel but distinct activity.

C17   FERNANDO   Hola, Jorge. ¿Cómo estás?
       JORGE   Bastante bien. ¿Y tú?
       FERNANDO   Bien, gracias. ¿Vienes conmigo?
       JORGE   Con gusto. ¿Ahora mismo?

Students memorize the segments, which have been selected because of their potential usefulness, and then practice using them in recombinations to form new dialogues involving different personalities.

Many dialogues combine both of these functions: grammar-demonstration and conversation-facilitation. It is important to recognize the type of dialogue with which you are dealing so that it may be used for the purpose for which it was constructed.

A third type of dialogue we may call *recreational.* This is the familiar skit. This activity has always been popular with students and teachers in an orally oriented approach. It is a true bridging activity which provides for spontaneous creation within the limits of what is being learned. It is discussed under *Dialogue Exploitation,* p. 36.

Dialogue construction and adaptation

You should be able to recognize the good and bad features of dialogues for several reasons:

—so that you can select well-written materials for use in classroom teaching or in individualized learning packets;

—so that you can rewrite poorly constructed dialogues when you are forced to use materials selected by others;

—so that you can write dialogues yourself, if you wish to supplement available materials (e.g., you may decide to prepare a dialogue based on a story which has been read).

GRAMMAR-DEMONSTRATION DIALOGUES

C18

1. MARÍA   ¿Adónde irá Ud. mañana?
2. LUISA   Iré a visitar a mi amiga Josefina, que reside en una pequeña aldea.
3. MARÍA   ¿Qué harán Uds. allá?
4. LUISA   Visitaremos la antigua abadía y pasearemos por el parque.
5. MARÍA   ¿Qué se puede ver en una aldea pequeña?
6. LUISA   Muchas cosas—casas viejas, jardines, animales y una escuela.
7. MARÍA   ¿Se quedará Ud. unos días?
8. LUISA   Por supuesto. No volveré hasta la semana que viene.
9. MARÍA   ¿Prefiere Ud. una aldea pequeña o una gran ciudad?
10. LUISA   Prefiero la pequeña aldea.
11. MARÍA   A mí me gusta más la gran ciudad.

Commentary

1. As a sustained exchange between two friends, this dialogue is very artificial and stilted. It has been laboriously constructed to include various persons of the future tense of regular -*ar* verbs and of certain common irregular verbs.

2. *Contemporary usage.* Certain features of authentic modern speech have been completely ignored.

a. Two friends of school age would use the *tú* form. There is some controversy about the usefulness of the *tú* form for foreign students. Some say that foreigners rarely reach a stage of intimacy where the use of *tú* is acceptable and may offend by using it too freely. It is, of course, commonly used among students. Offense can be caused by the person who is insensitive to the right moment for using *tú* as well as by the person who uses it inappropriately. Furthermore, students who have not experienced through use the different relationships which *tú* and *Ud.* imply in various situations will miss many nuances in their later reading. It is the teacher's role to train students in correct use of the two forms.

b. *Tenses.* In sentence 1, the *present tense* would certainly be used in conversation for a project so close at hand, instead of the future tense which pushes the action into a more remote, less certain domain: *¿Adónde va Ud. mañana?* (Contrast: *¿Qué hará el año que viene?*)

This choice of present tense in the question would attract a response in the *immediate future* form in 2: *Voy a visitar a mi amiga.* The immediate future would also be used in 3: *¿Qué van a hacer...*, in 4: *Vamos a visitar... vamos a pasear...*, and in 7: *¿Vas a quedarte?*

In 8: *No volveré hasta la semana que viene,* the future tense would be retained because it demonstrates the use of this tense to refer to an event still to take place and which has no relation to a present situation or action.

c. In 7, another possibility is *¿Tú vas a quedarte?* with rising inflection. (Practice in the latter form which is in very frequent use in conversation is often neglected in the classroom.)

d. *Reside* in sentence 2 is a rather formal word in this sense; *vive* would be used in contemporary Spanish.

3. *Weaknesses in the construction of the dialogue*

a. In sentence 4, unnecessarily stilted vocabulary is used in *antigua abadía.* The simpler familiar words *vieja iglesia* are perfectly good substitutes in this context. The same is true of *una aldea pequeña* in sentences 2, 5, 9, and 10. The more colloquial *un pueblecito* is preferable.

b. Sentence 6 is extremely artificial for a conversation of this type. (The variation in position of *aldea* in adjoining sentences could also be confusing to a student at this level.) *Una escuela* is hardly a novelty to the city visitor. *La primera escuela rural de la región* would make for a more natural text.

c. Certain questions which seem clearly to have been introduced into the dialogue because of their usefulness for an unimaginative question-answer period in class add to the artificiality of the dialogue: *¿Prefiere Ud. una aldea pequeña o una gran ciudad? Me gusta más... ¿Prefiere Ud. la vida en el campo o en la ciudad grande? ¿Prefiere Ud. las vacaciones en el campo o en la playa?* (Similarly: *¿Qué se puede ver...?*)

C19 *Rewritten,* with sentences shortened and language and usage modernized, this dialogue might read as follows:

MARÍA   ¿Adónde vas mañana?

LUISA   Voy a visitar a mi amiga Josefina. Ella vive en un pueblecito no muy lejos de aquí.
MARÍA   ¿Qué piensas hacer allá?
LUISA   Vamos a ver la vieja iglesia y quizás a pasear por el parque.
MARÍA   ¿Te quedarás unos días?
LUISA   Claro. No volveré hasta la semana que viene.

Commentary

This shorter dialogue demonstrates the use of the immediate future and the future tense in the matrix of a possible conversation which could be exploited in various ways apart from its grammatical purpose. Clearly the complete morphology of the future tense cannot be appropriately taught through a dialogue, but this short version which includes three persons of the immediate future and two forms of the future tense, provides a basis for discussion of the contemporary uses of these forms. In C18 three irregular and four regular forms of the future tense appear in a very unrealistic dialogue, with no use of the immediate future. Not only is there no clear demonstration of appropriate use, but the student is given a very false view of conversational possibilities.

* Find some grammar-demonstration dialogues in textbooks in current use, comment on their good and bad features, and practice rewriting the least effective of them.

CONVERSATION-FACILITATION DIALOGUES

Many textbooks include dialogues purely for the purpose of providing students in the early stages with *useful utterances and exclamations* which, with variations of vocabulary, can be recombined in all kinds of personal ways to make possible active classroom conversation and creative skits. Well-written and presented, such dialogues can provide the student with a fund of very authentic expressions for use at a stage when his overall knowledge of the language is still quite minimal. This ability to put together something meaningful encourages him with a sense of progress.

C20
1. JUAN PABLO   Buenos días, Pedro.
2. PEDRO   Buenos días, Juan Pablo. ¿Adónde vas? ¿Al cine?
3. JUAN PABLO   No. Tengo hambre. Me voy a almorzar.
4. PEDRO   ¿De veras? Yo también tengo hambre.
5. JUAN PABLO   Ven conmigo, si quieres.

6.   PEDRO   Seguro. ¿Adónde vamos?
7. JUAN PABLO   Hay un buen restorancito cerca de la estación.
8.   PEDRO   Pues bien. Mira, ahí viene María Teresa. No quiero
                  verla.
9. JUAN PABLO   Ni yo tampoco. Vámonos ahorita.

Commentary

1. With this type of dialogue, students are expected to memorize the sentences (through active role-playing) so that they can produce them quickly in new situations. This provides practice in the rhythm of the phrase and in specific intonation patterns.

2. The dialogue would be learned and practiced in sections (1-3, 1-7, 1-9). In other words, the dialogue is open-ended.

3. Utterances are short or are easily divided into short, meaningful segments (*tengo hambre, cerca de la estación, vámonos*). The aim of the memorizing is for the students to be able to use these segments freely in new combinations, and to learn to vary segments semantically, not to know the sixteen utterances by heart so that they can produce them parrot-fashion in the original sequence.

4. Students will learn short utterances like these easily by acting out the dialogue in small groups. The memorization and recall process are aided by visuals: flashcards, stick figures, flannel board, puppets, vanishing techniques (where the dialogue is written on the chalkboard with major elements of the phrase being obliterated one by one until students know the complete utterance thoroughly).

5. Small groups will perform their version of the dialogue for the others. Meaningful deviations from the original wording and paraphrases will be welcomed as indications that the students have indeed assimilated the material in a more than superficial way. The students will be encouraged to develop new situations, including as often as possible material learned in other dialogues or in other classwork. (See *Dialogue Exploitation*, below.)

6. Conversation-facilitation dialogues do not follow a question-answer, question-answer sequence. This is not the natural mode of ordinary conversation. C20 consists of greeting, greeting returned, question, question, answer, explanation, statement, exclamation, statement, suggestion, acceptance, question, oblique answer, exclamation, statement, statement, suggestion.

7. Items are not exploited grammatically or paradigmatically as they

would tend to be in a grammar-demonstration dialogue. Here students are familiarized, in a meaningful context, with constructions which they may not study systematically for some time (e.g., *no quiero verla*) but which are immediately useable in their present form and in semantic variants (*no quiero quebrarla, no quiero leerlo*).

8. Many modern textbook writers would consider C20 too long for an early dialogue. The material in it can easily be rewritten as a spiral series.

SPIRAL SERIES OF DIALOGUES

Short dialogues are usually more useful than longer dialogues. The interrelated content of two response pairs is more easily remembered than the development of thought in six response pairs. One response pair (A to B) allows little scope for an interesting mini-situation, although it is used as the basic unit in the Cummings device illustrated in C29.

Sometimes several short dialogues develop a continuing theme, each in succession using some of the linguistic material from the one preceding. Such a succession of dialogues is called a spiral series. As students exploit each section, they are consolidating material already learned and the now-familiar material makes the learning of the new material more meaningful. Dialogue C19 could be developed spirally as follows:

C21 1. MARÍA TERESA ¿Adónde vas mañana, Ana?
          ANA Voy a ver a mi amiga Josefina.
     MARÍA TERESA ¿Dónde vive ella?
          ANA Vive en un pueblecito no muy lejos de aquí.

     2. MARÍA TERESA ¿A quién vas a ver mañana?
          ANA A mi amiga Josefina que vive en un pueblecito.
     MARÍA TERESA ¿Está lejos de aquí?
          ANA No, es ese pueblecito de la vieja iglesia.

     3. MARÍA TERESA ¿Cuándo vas a ver a tu amiga Josefina?
          ANA Mañana. Vamos a visitar una vieja iglesia del pueble-
               cito.
     MARÍA TERESA ¿Ese es el pueblecito cerca de la Alhambra, ¿no es
               verdad?
          ANA Sí, ése. Y quizás pasearemos por los jardines durante
               mi visita.

     4. MARÍA TERESA ¿Vas a pasear por los jardines con tu amiga Josefina?
          ANA Claro. Me quedaré unos días en su casa.
     MARÍA TERESA ¿Vas a visitar también la vieja iglesia de la Santa Cruz?

ANA Sí, tendré tiempo. No volveré hasta la semana que viene.

Commentary

Practice with expanding dialogues gives students the confidence for making up their own recombinations and original skits and provides a useful link with writing. The spiral sequence above gives experience with immediate future and future tenses, different types of questions, and the varied possibilities of use of simple adverbial phrases.

✱ Rewrite C20 as a spiral series.

INTRODUCING CULTURAL CONTRASTS INTO DIALOGUES

Many textbook writers are criticized for writing dialogues which are culturally neutral, that is, which deal with situations like the one in C20 which could take place in any culture.

Some critics would argue that C20 would convey a feeling for Spanish everyday culture if its content were more like the following:

C22 JUAN PABLO Buenos días, Pedro.

PEDRO Buenos días, Juan Pablo. ¿Adónde vas?

JUAN PABLO Tengo una carta que echar al correo pero me faltan estampillas.

PEDRO Hay un estanco calle arriba. ¿Quieres que te lo enseñe?

This dialogue conveys the useful piece of information for a visitor to Spain that he should look for a tobacconist's shop if he wants to buy stamps for his postcards, whereas in most other countries he would expect to buy them in a post office. This kind of superficial difference in social organization has no deep significance and, if such snippets of information are over-emphasized by repetition and exploitation in dialogues, students may well develop the attitude that the Spanish persist in doing things in odd ways for no apparent reason. This type of factual information can also become outdated overnight as a result of a shift in social organization or habit. (Note, for instance, the influence of the increasing number of refrigerators and supermarkets on the Spanish housewife's traditional routine.)

True cultural understanding means an appreciation of basically different attitudes and values which are reflected in the things people do, but are not necessarily explicitly stated. It is difficult to work such concepts into

short situational exchanges without oversimplifying and stereotyping social
behavior.

The following dialogue,[29] obviously for students with some experience in
reading, does convey a basic Spanish value which is reflected in many
aspects of individual and social life.

C23 PEDRO   Benito, ¡qué sorpresa encontrarte hoy en Madrid!

BENITO Pedro, ¿hace mucho que estás aquí?

PEDRO   Hace cuatro días y todavía no doy pie con bola en esta gran
ciudad.

BENITO Bueno, es que Madrid no es nuestra capital de provincia. Es la
capital de España. Aquí se siente la fiebre del progreso que do-
mina a España.

PEDRO   Sí, mucho progreso pero hasta ahora no encuentro trabajo.

BENITO Pues, si no tienes enchufe no hay forma de colocarte.

PEDRO   ¿Enchufe? ¡Pero esas son cosas del pasado!

BENITO Mira, Pedro, no te olvides que a pesar del progreso, ésta es
España y aquí el que tiene padrino se bautiza y el que no, ¡mala
suerte!

PEDRO   Así que la tradición del padrino no cambia, ¿eh?

BENITO Muchas cosas están cambiando pero "la recomendación" sigue
siendo parte de nuestra idiosincracia.

PEDRO   En ese caso mañana regreso a León porque yo no conozco a nadie
en Madrid.

BENITO Hombre, parece mentira, me conoces a mí y para algo somos
amigos. Mira, aquí está mi teléfono. Me llamas esta noche y nos
ponemos de acuerdo para presentarte a mi jefe que está buscando
un nuevo empleado.

* Examine some textbook dialogues which purport to convey some understanding of Hispanic culture. Analyze the cultural content in the following
terms: Is the cultural content of a superficial nature, reflecting interesting
but insignificant aspects of behavior or social organization, or are the
features portrayed surface indicators of deeper attitudes and values?

CHECKLIST FOR ORIGINAL OR REWRITTEN DIALOGUES

1. Do I intend this to be a grammar-demonstration, a conversation-
facilitation, or a recreational dialogue?

2. Is the conversation interesting and natural? Do the participants say
something worthwhile? Have I avoided the question-answer-question-
answer format?

3. What points of grammar (or conversational items) do I wish students to assimilate?

4. Is my list so ambitious that it has made the dialogue stilted and unnatural? (What can I omit while still achieving my purpose? See C18.)

5. Can I increase the redundancy to make the conversation more natural? (See C2.)

6. Can I include more expletives and rejoinders to make it sound more spontaneous? (See Chapter 4: G44.)

7. Are the levels of language I have used appropriate and consistent? (See C5.)

8. Is the dialogue of a reasonable length for classroom use and exploitation? (Is it open-ended? Should I rewrite it as a spiral series?)

9. Are individual utterances short enough to be assimilated or, alternatively, do they break naturally into useful segments?

10. Have I reentered lexical items, idioms, and grammatical structures from previous dialogues to refresh the students' memory?

11. In how many ways can this dialogue be exploited? (See below.)

12. Does the situation lend itself naturally to interesting or amusing recombinations? Is it likely to stimulate students to produce their own recreational dialogues or skits?

Dialogue exploitation

The dialogue as a teaching technique has come in for much criticism because it has been used unimaginatively and its full potential ignored. There is more than one way to use a dialogue. In fact, the possibilities are so extensive that one could actually exploit each dialogue differently for a whole semester, if one wished.

DIALOGUE MEMORIZATION

The most criticized way of teaching through dialogues has required of each student that he memorize every dialogue completely and thoroughly (and this often for dialogues of fifteen or twenty sentences) and that he be able to recite the whole sequence on demand. This type of activity is time-consuming and tedious and gives indefensible importance to a particular sequence of utterances. As a result, students are at a loss when they do not hear the precise cue they are expecting. They become discouraged and exasperated by the mistakes they make in recalling memorized materials—mistakes which have nothing to do with their comprehension and assimilation of the material.

As has been noted earlier, there is no need for memorization of *grammar-demonstration dialogues*. A certain amount of repetition to ensure correct, fluent production is sufficient. Thorough exploitation with variety, in the ways suggested below, paralleled by as much grammatical explanation as the students need, will ensure understanding of the principles behind the structures used, while judicious practice in their meaningful use in all kinds of variations of their original setting will prepare students to use them perceptively in utterances of their own creation. Similarly, vocabulary will be retained more thoroughly if used frequently in various contexts.

Conversation-facilitation dialogues, which are short and full of expressions of wide applicability, may be memorized to the point where the useful segments, rather than the original sequence, are immediately available for use. Meaningful variations of the sequence will be welcomed as signs of real assimilation of the material. Recall may be aided by the use of a series of pictures on film, flashcards, or transparencies for overhead projection. Some teachers in the early stages like to have an English translation readily available when the student momentarily forgets the sequence of the dialogue; others reject this aid, preferring to concentrate on direct association of utterance and action.

WAYS OF PRESENTING AND LEARNING FROM THE DIALOGUE

With imagination the teacher can vary ways of presenting the dialogue. There are *five aspects* of the dialogue activity which need to be provided for if the energy expended is to yield any fruit in terms of the students' growing ability to function freely in the language.

1. Some *setting of the scene* to arouse student interest in the content of the dialogue and facilitate comprehension of the language used.

For example: acting out the conversation first of all in English or in mime with appropriate props; discussion of the content of the dialogue with the help of pictures, slides, flashcards, projected diagrams, maps, plans; discussion of some aspect of life or some social situation for which the dialogue will supply a cultural contrast; some classroom language activity of the direct method or Gouin type (C11-13) which relates to the content of the dialogue; some preparing of the semantic area through discussion or through a competition or game; the recounting in the foreign language of an incident or anecdote of related interest, or the showing and discussion in English of a cartoon or a series of stick figures related to the theme. For a *grammar-demonstration* dialogue: raising some questions about the grammatical problem to arouse interest in its manifestations in the script and as a stimulus to the students to find out for themselves from the dialogue how the rule works.

2. Some technique for *focusing student attention* on the meaning of the interchange.

For example: students may be asked to listen to the whole dialogue on tape several times as a listening comprehension exercise with opportunity between each hearing for group piecing together of the meaning; students may listen to the dialogue as they watch a series of slides, or look at a series of sketches illustrating the content of the interchange; students may be supplied ahead of time with a set of questions for which they should find answers as they listen to the dialogue; sometimes, for variety, students may be given the written script of the dialogue to peruse and ask questions about before listening to it without the script.

3. Some *familiarization* of students with the actual utterances in the dialogue through an activity which makes cognitive demands on them.[30]

For example: as students in the initial stage repeat the lines of the dialogue to develop fluency in their production, they take roles, group speaking to group or class to teacher, until they can handle the material with reasonable efficiency; after hearing an utterance two or three times, students try to reconstruct it as a group endeavor; the teacher writes the material on the board and gradually erases sections to see if students are repeating meaningfully and can supply the erased portions (erasures increase in length). For a *conversation-facilitation* dialogue: some students mime the dialogue while the class supplies the words; students go off in pairs and practice taking roles, testing each other on knowledge of the material; students act out the roles on an individual basis or as group presentations.

4. Some *formal manipulation* of the material in the dialogue, exploiting the useful expressions in a *conversation-facilitation* dialogue or the morphological and syntactic items in a *grammar-demonstration* dialogue.

For example: directed dialogue or guided conversation (see C24); group recombinations for similar but slightly different situations; chain dialogue (see C25). For *grammar-demonstration* dialogues: analysis of rules demonstrated in the material, leading into intensive practice through the various kinds of oral exercises described in Chapter 4. For *conversation-facilitation* dialogues: items of the dialogue may be used as personal questions to students who either answer for themselves or pretend through their answers to be someone else (the teacher or other students guess who they are); the teacher, or a student, establishes a situation by a remark and another student responds with a suitable expletive or rejoinder:

A No puedo almorzar contigo.
   No tengo dinero.
B ¡Que lástima!

for a given expletive, the student creates an utterance:

A *¡Oye!* ...   B ¡Oye, ahí viene tu prima!
A *Perdón* ...   B Perdón, ¿dónde está la Puerta del Sol?

5. Some ways in which the dialogue material can be used in the *creation of new utterances and new dialogues* expressing the students' own whims, feelings, and imaginings. The suggestions below encourage students to draw on anything they know from previous dialogues, from group conversation or from reading, in preparing their versions. (They should, however, be discouraged from seeking extra vocabulary in dictionaries at this stage.)

For example: the creation of a similar situation in another setting (the irate shopper demanding money back for a faulty appliance becomes the irate air traveler demanding a refund for a ticket, or a householder trying to get rid of a door-to-door salesman becomes a television viewer trying to cut off a telephone advertiser); group preparation using a series of pictures of a different setting and a climactic utterance (*¡Pero está quebrada!*) as a basis for a dialogue with a similar denouement to the one already studied. See also suggestions for *Recreational Dialogues,* below.

DIRECTED DIALOGUE OR GUIDED CONVERSATION

The teacher prompts pairs of students to reproduce sections of the dialogue. Directed dialogue may be conducted in several ways.

C24 (Working from C20)

a. TEACHER TO STUDENT A
   Ask B where he's going.

   STUDENT A   ¿Adónde vas, Miguel?
   TEACHER TO STUDENT B
   Tell him you're going to lunch.
   STUDENT B   Voy a almorzar.

b. TEACHER TO STUDENTS A & B
   You meet each other in the corridor and one of you asks the other where he's going. The other replies he's going to lunch.

   STUDENT A   ¿Adónde vas, Miguel?
   STUDENT B   Voy a almorzar.

c. TEACHER TO STUDENT A
   Pregúntale (pregúntele)[18] a Miguel adónde va.
   STUDENT A   ¿Adónde vas, Miguel?
   TEACHER TO STUDENT B

Contéstale (contéstele) a Pedro que tú vas (Ud. va) a almorzar.

STUDENT B   Voy a almorzar.

Commentary

Directed dialogue is more difficult than most teachers realize because it involves a transformation of the teacher's cue for which students must be well prepared. Any potential usefulness is often negated by the amount of time devoted to the pure mechanics of the performance. It is sometimes helpful to perform the operation several times in English to accustom the students to the procedure before using any of the approaches suggested.

d. TEACHER TO STUDENTS A & B

Uds. se encuentran en el pasillo y uno de Uds. le pregunta al otro adónde va él, y éste contesta que va a almorzar.

STUDENT A   ¿Adónde vas, Miguel?

STUDENT B   Voy a almorzar.

Commentary

Here the language of the directions is more complex than the language, possibly memorized, of the response. This can make the exercise confusing and difficult for an elementary-level student.

CHAIN DIALOGUE

This is a challenging and amusing way for students to practice retrieval of many expressions and structures they have learned. It can begin with very recent material (for instance, a response pair from C20) but should soon develop into a competition to think up questions and answers of all kinds.

C25 TEACHER TO A   ¿Adónde vas, Miguel?

A   Voy a almorzar.

A TO B   Ven conmigo, si quieres.

B   Seguro.

B TO C   ¿Adónde vamos?

C   Al cine.

C TO D   ¿Te gustan las películas?

D   No, me gusta más la televisión.

D TO E   ¿Cuántos años tienes?
    E   Tengo catorce años.
E TO F   ¿Y tú?

Rubbishing the dialogue

As a variation of the chain dialogue, but with a similar aim of developing flexibility by drawing on all kinds of expressions which the students have acquired, one team of students (Juan) undertakes to keep to the utterances in the dialogue recently studied, the other team (Pedro) thinks up possible responses other than those learned. (Later the teams exchange roles.) Students try to remain within the bounds of what they have learned but may ask the teacher occasionally for a few new expressions, thus adding to their repertoire things they would like to say. (Since this is a satirical approach there is no need for the resulting sequence to be semantically probable.)

C26 (Based on C20.)

JUAN   Buenos días, Pedro.
PEDRO   Buenos días, señor. ¿Le conozco a Ud.? (*or* no entiendo, señor; *or* Perdón, ¿(es que) me habla Ud.?)
JUAN   ¿Adónde vas? ¿Al cine?
PEDRO   No, me quedo aquí. (*or* No, voy a acostarme; *or* No le importa a Ud.; *or* ¿qué es un cine?)
JUAN   Ven conmigo, si quieres.
PEDRO   ¡Qué idea! (¡Vaya una idea! *or* No, no quiero ir; *or* De acuerdo, si tú pagas el billete.)

THE DIALOGUE AS A CULMINATING ACTIVITY

It has become customary to think of the dialogue as an introductory teaching technique, but it can also come at the end of a unit of study, whether dialogues are or are not used as a technique in the body of the lesson. In this case, it demonstrates in operation in a realistic situation what has been studied analytically. It is then enjoyed as an opportunity to express oneself in language and structures which are now familiar. This is the place for the *recreational dialogue* or skit.

As a bridging activity, the *recreational dialogue* should have as its starting point a situation for which the student has some vocabulary and expressions available to him. "Situation" here is used in its broadest sense: a person alone in a house who hears a strange noise outside the window experiences a similar nervous reaction to a person watching a spider weave its web from the ceiling to a shelf of his bookcase and may very well exclaim in the same fashion: "¡Dios mío! ¡Qué voy a hacer!"

Most students need the stimulus of seminal ideas such as the following, which take them from the shelter of the cove further and further into the open sea.

1. Skits may be based on an adaptation of the type of situation in a dialogue they have just been studying: two people discussing their meal in a restaurant become the seven dwarfs grumbling about the meal Snow-White has prepared; two people meeting in a supermarket become a boy meeting a girl at the school dance.

2. Students are given one side of a conversation which is not explicit and are asked to create a dialogue. Different groups act out their versions.

C27 A Perdón, ¿qué tiene Ud. ahí?

B ....

A Pues, ¡jamás he visto nada semejante!

B ....

A Con todo, ¿a Ud. le gusta él (ella)?

B ....

A Dispense. Desafortunadamente, tengo trabajo que hacer.

3. Students are given a response pair beginning: A: *¿Quién te dijo eso? ¿Tu hermana?* B: *Claro que no. Ella no estaba en casa.* They extemporize a response-pair completion (or prepare a longer completion). Students should not strive each time for wit, which requires fairly sophisticated manipulation of language, but rather for a sensible conclusion.

C28 ANDRÉS ¿Quién te dijo eso? ¿Tu hermana?

BERNARDO Claro que no. Ella no estaba en casa.

ANDRÉS Pero la ví en el balcón.

BERNARDO No, ésa era mi madre. Ellas se parecen.

4. Students are given a punch line and different groups work out short skits leading up to it. (*¡Pero ya se fue!* or *¡No, no, no, yo no, yo no!*)

5. Skits are based on a list of words providing basic elements (*tren, una vieja, dos estudiantes de vacaciones, frontera, aduana, pequeña envoltura blanca, el día siguiente*).

6. Students prepare puppet plays using the particular settings of recent dialogues (*restaurante; banco; en casa de la abuela*). Timid or reticent students will often express themselves in the voice of a puppet.

7. Students create original dialogue arising from an ambiguous picture, or a cartoon without caption. The pictures chosen should show an obviously emotional situation or a predicament involving two or more people, or some incongruity.

8. Students invent dialogues based on problems caused by differences in

everyday living in Spain; e.g., a foreign visitor to a Spanish home finds himself looking at a plate of *menudos;* problems of two tourists trying to find a Spanish acquaintance in an apartment building (*timbre de llamada, conserje, ascensor, primer piso*).

The Cummings device[31]

One attempt to link structural practice and lexical exploration to communication is Stevick's Cummings device, based on the two-utterance communication. Stevick says, "The shorter a dialog, the less unexplained, confusing clutter it contains."[32] As a technique for moving from manipulation of structures to communication at each learning step, the Cummings device merits a place in this section on bridging activities.

Cummings device is Stevick's preferred term for what he earlier called his "microwave cycle." He describes the device as follows:

The . . . format itself, in what we may a little wryly call its "classical form," contained a basic utterance (usually but not always a question) and from four to eight potential answers or other appropriate rejoinders. If the basic utterance and the rejoinders are well chosen, they can lead to almost immediate real or realistic . . . conversation in class, and are also likely to find use in real life outside of class. At the same time, new structures and new vocabulary can be kept to a minimum.

A . . . "cycle" was divided into an M-phase and a C-phase. *M* stood for *m*imicry, *m*anipulation, *m*echanics and *m*emorization, and *C* for *c*ommunication, *c*onversation, and *c*ontinuity. Within the M-phase, the first section usually introduced the answers or rejoinders, often in the form of a substitution drill with a separate column for cue words. The second section contained the question(s) or other basic utterance(s). The C-phase combined the elements of the M-phase with each other and, ideally, with material from earlier lessons, to form a short sample conversation.[33]

The C series is so designed that lexical items are easily substitutable (substitutable items being placed in parentheses as a guide). As Stevick explains,

it is only through this kind of "delexicalization" that one can get away from content words chosen either at the whim of the textbook writer, or for their high frequency in the language as a whole, and that one can insure the use of the content words that are of high frequency in the student's immediate surroundings. In this way, through localization and personalization of vocabulary, we improve the likelihood that language *study* will be replaced by language *use*, and that language *use* will become a part of the group life of the students.[34]

The usefulness of this technique is that the teacher who has mastered the principle can derive Cummings devices, as need and interest suggest, from any materials—lessons in books, newspaper articles, material heard on tape, radio, or film track, or ongoing communicative activities. As with any device, it is intended, not as the whole of the course, but as one among the many possible activities which provide variety for student learning.

C29 *The Cummings device*

M-1   Juan trabaja en la ciudad.

Nosotros   Nosotros trabajamos en la ciudad.

Ana y Pedro   Ana y Pedro trabajan en la ciudad.

todos los días   Ana y Pedro trabajan todos los días.

ocho horas por día   Ana y Pedro trabajan ocho horas por día.

Ud.   Ud. trabaja ocho horas por día.

Josefina   Josefina trabaja ocho horas por día.

en una oficina   Josefina trabaja en una oficina.

hoy   Josefina trabaja hoy.

Nosotros   Nosotros trabajamos hoy.

M-2 ¿Trabaja Ud. todos los días?
No, no trabajo todos los días.

M-3 ¿Dónde trabaja Ud.?
¿Cuándo trabaja Ud.?
¿Cuánto tiempo trabaja Ud.?

C-1 A ¿Trabaja Ud. en (una oficina)?
B No, no trabajo en una oficina.

A ¿Trabaja Rosa en (una oficina)?
B No, ella trabaja en (una tienda).

A ¿Trabaja Ud. (hoy)?
B Sí, trabajo (todos los días) . . .

C-2 A ¿Dónde (trabaja) Ud.?
B Trabajo (en la ciudad).

A ¿Trabaja Ud. (en Chicago)?
B Sí, trabajo (allá).

A ¿Cuándo (trabaja) Ud.?
B Trabajo (todos los días).

A ¿Cuántas (horas) por (día) (trabaja) Roberto?
B Trabaja (ocho) (horas) por (día).

A   ¿Cuántos (días) por (semana) (trabaja) Ud.?
B   (Cinco) (días) por (semana).

C-3 A   ¿(Ud.) trabaja en Chicago?
     B   Sí, (yo) trabajo allá.

     A   ¿(Se) trabaja (ocho) (horas) por (día) aquí?
     B   No, (nosotros) trabajamos (siete) (horas) por (día).

Note that in the C (Communication) phases the questions will be
personalized: names and activities used will be those of members of the
class.

Stevick warns his readers that the device "is not a theory, nor a method,
but only a format,"[35] that there are a number of pitfalls to be avoided in
writing individual cycles (these are discussed in Chapter 6 of Stevick,
1971), and that no course should consist of just one format. "Procedures
and systems and approaches," he says, "supplement one another more than
they supersede one another."[36]

THE CUMMINGS DEVICE AND CULTURAL INFORMATION

In C29, questions and answers refer to general activities of daily life in
any society. The device can also be used to interest students in differences
between daily activities in their own country and in Spain or another
Spanish speaking country. The following types of information could be
incorporated in a Cummings device based on question forms.

C30 En México se pueden comprar pajaritos por las calles.
     ¿En España se compran envolturas en la farmacia?
     ¿Dónde se compran latas de pintura? (En la botica.)

✱ Try to construct a Cummings device incorporating the type of information
in C30.

Oral reports

Up to this point most of the bridging activities discussed have involved
questions and answers, short statements and comments, requests, and exclamations. Another important facet of communicating includes describing,
narrating, and explaining, all of which involve more sustained speech. Very
early in the language course, students should have opportunities to practice
these skills, taking as topics whatever suggests itself in the course of their
reading or classroom activities. Reading passages, dialogues, sets of pic-

tures, films, magazines, or class discussions of aspects of the country, its achievements, and the people who live in it provide basic vocabulary and ideas from which the students fan out in a creative way.

1. Reports at first are *short* (four or five sentences), later expanding as the students gain in confidence and experience. Students are always encouraged to ask the presenter questions about details of the report.

2. Initial efforts may be combined ones. Students in small groups construct their reports orally, with one student writing the group production on a chalkboard while the others criticize and improve on it until all are satisfied. When the class is next reassembled, a spokesman for the group gives the description or narration orally, without referring to a script, and students from other groups ask questions. (The role of presenter is taken by different members of the group on successive occasions.)

3. In Lenard's verbal-active method, oral compositions play an important role.[37] She reiterates to her students the slogan: "An excellent composition is original, imaginative, correct. Dictionary? No, no, absolutely no."[38] After the composition has been thoroughly discussed and worked over orally in class, it is written out and corrected by the teacher. "There is no point," Lenard says, ". . . in permanently recording . . . anything that has not reached its best possible form."[39]

We may add that, at least by the intermediate level, teachers need to give students help in the effective use of the dictionary and some oral reports can then be devised as demonstrations of successful dictionary search. (See Chapter 9: *Exploring the Dictionary.*) In these cases, presenters explain in simple Spanish paraphrases any specialized vocabulary they have used, thus developing another useful skill.

4. Early reports may be guided in a number of ways.

a. A sequential series of questions is provided on what has been read, viewed, or discussed, or on a similar, but personalized, situation.

C31 (Based on R38.)

Ud. está en Madrid. ¿Adónde quiere ir? ¿Por qué? ¿Cuál modo de transporte escoge Ud.? Descríbalo. Un hombre vestido de uniforme le habla. ¿Quién es? ¿Qué le pregunta a Ud.? ¿Dónde se baja Ud.? ¿Qué ve Ud.?

With an undefined series such as this, the students' answers become very diverse: they may be drawn directly from the text or may deviate considerably from it; e.g., instead of going to the Puerta del Sol by bus, the student may decide to go to Burgos by train to see the cathedral, or to the Prado by *taxi*.

b. The student is given a series of pictures with no questions attached, the interpretation being left entirely to his imagination or invention.

c. A framework of key words forms a skeleton outline.

C32 Ud. va a salir por avión.

Preparativos — coche — estacionamiento — equipaje — billete — andén — sala de espera — diario — dos amantes jóvenes — un niño desagradable — dos marineros — aviso — embarco — salida.

d. Persons, places, or things in the students' own environment lead to mystery descriptions for which the other students guess the referent.

5. A simple form of oral report is a regular *Show and Tell* session, where students of their own volition share with their classmates things they have discovered about Spain, Mexico, Puerto Rico, Cuba, or South America, and show objects imported from these countries, stamps, postcards, maps, menus, objets d'art, and bric-a-brac brought back by touring relatives.

6. Oral reports are an essential part of learning about the great figures and artistic, scientific, and social achievements of the people as well as their pleasures and aspirations in daily living; students prepare individual and group presentations as a culmination to their research on specific topics.

7. At more advanced stages, many opportunities arise for students to explain and discuss what they have been reading, hearing, or seeing in films, or to discuss topics of general interest arising from these or from current events in the news.

Situation tapes

Cartier[40] reports experimentation with situational conversations on tape for individual practice. The student hears the voices of two or more persons who are ostensibly conversing with him: spaces are left for him to record his parts of the interchange. The conversations are so designed that the student is led to make replies consistent with their drift, although what he actually says and how he says it are his own choice. The interlocutors call each other by their names and soon the student feels that he knows them and that they are actually speaking to him. After he has recorded his responses, he listens to the completed conversation and then re-records it as often as he wishes until he is satisfied with his part. (After all, we always think of that clever response after the crucial moment has passed.) The context can also be filled in with visuals. No monitoring or correction is supplied, the student being perfectly free to express himself to the best of his ability. In this way, the less confident student is able to practice real communication without the embarrassment of expressing himself inadequately in front of others.

C33   Pedro y Joaquín se encuentran con Ud. delante del cine.

The student is shown a picture of the cinema, with the name of the film being shown and a notice stating the times at which it will be shown. Italicized speeches are on the tape. A blip* indicates when the student is expected to reply.

PEDRO	*Hola, chico. ¿Tú también vienes a ver esta película?* *
ESTUDIANTE	Sí, dicen que es una buena película.
or	Sí, no tengo otra cosa que hacer.
or	No, solamente pasaba por aquí.
JOAQUÍN	*Mi hermana me dijo que es una película estupenda.*
PEDRO	*Pues yo, personalmente, no sé. ¿Y tú?* *
ESTUDIANTE	Tengo unos amigos que la han visto.
or	Yo tampoco sé nada.
or	Yo nunca he oído decir nada de esa película.
PEDRO	*¿Qué vas a hacer ahora, Joaquín?*
JOAQUÍN	*Nada. Pasear un rato quizás.*
PEDRO	*Te acompañamos si quieres. ¿Es que esperas a alguien?* *
ESTUDIANTE	Sí, espero a una amiga (un compañero).
or	No, estoy solo.
PEDRO	*Tenemos un poco de tiempo. ¿Quieres tomar algo, Joaquín? Hay un café aquí a la vuelta.*
JOAQUÍN	*¡Buena idea! ¿A qué hora empieza la película?* *
ESTUDIANTE	Dentro de diez minutos, creo.
or	A las ocho, me parece.
or	Empieza pronto.

* Imagine that you are at a party in Mexico or another Spanish-speaking country. Try to make up a series of taped utterances for a situation tape. Then see whether different kinds of responses can be inserted without destroying the coherence of the sequence.

2
Autonomous interaction

Returning to the schema C1, we observe the gap between skill-getting and skill-using. Some indications have been given of ways in which production or pseudo-communication activities can become bridging activities, facilitating and stimulating autonomous interaction. (See also Chapter 4: *Oral Practice,* Type B exercises, p. 129.)

The crossing from bridge to shore, however, will not necessarily take place without encouragement. Many students will remain on the bridge, rather than face the unprotected autonomy of real communication, unless they are given opportunities very early to develop confidence and self-reliance through frequent, pleasant incursions into autonomous territory. In other words, the student will prefer the safety of the structured exercise and develop a nervous attitude toward the unstructured which will be hard to change. He must learn early to express his personal intentions through all kinds of familiar and unfamiliar recombinations of the language elements at his disposal. "The more daring he is in . . . linguistic innovation, the more rapidly he progresses."[1] This means that priority must be given to the development of an adventurous spirit in trying to convey one's meaning to others in the foreign language.

How can we develop this necessary confidence and self-reliance? We must create, and allow to develop naturally, opportunities for our students to use the foreign language for the normal purposes of language in relations with others—as Birkmaier puts it, "to use language in a natural, useful way, in a significant social setting."[2] Such activities link listening and speaking, since, without ability to comprehend the speech of others, "communication" becomes an uninteresting and frustrating one-way street. In some approaches, activities such as those described in this section are the chief preoccupation. Even where this is not so, they must be given time and place if students are to communicate in uninhibited freedom.

Categories of language use

The student needs situations where he is on his own (that is, not supported by teacher or structured exercise), trying to use the foreign language to exchange with others messages of real interest to him. Yet we cannot send students off in groups or pairs and tell them to interact. *Motivation to communicate* must be aroused in some way. We must propose, or encourage students to develop, activities which have an intrinsic interest for them—activities in such natural interactional contexts as the following: (1) establishing and maintaining social relations, (2) expressing one's reactions, (3) hiding one's intentions, (4) talking one's way out of trouble, (5) seeking and giving information, (6) learning or teaching others to do or make something, (7) conversing over the telephone, (8) solving problems, (9) discussing ideas, (10) playing with language, (11) acting out social roles, (12) entertaining others, (13) displaying one's achievements, (14) sharing leisure activities.

These types of interactional activity lend themselves to various patterns of individualization, with students naturally seeking out partners with whom they feel at ease. Maslow[3] has shown that each individual has a hierarchy of needs to be satisfied, rising from physiological needs through the needs for feelings of security, belongingness, esteem (of others and for oneself), and self-realization. These are reflected in complex interrelationships within any group. Since genuine interaction springs from the depths of the individual personality, all of these needs affect student reactions in a truly autonomous situation. For these reasons, only the student himself knows whether he feels more at ease with a fluent speaker who can help him along, a less fluent speaker whose lesser ability encourages him in his own efforts, or a good listener who inspires him with confidence. Some students, by their nature, interact very fully with few words. Students thus form their own small, natural-affinity interactional groups which select or generate activities as the group becomes a compatible unit.

An imaginative teacher and involved students will think of many absorbing and exciting interactional activities. Listed below are some expansions, by no means exhaustive, of the possibilities for language use within each category and some sample activities which would lead to the use of language in the terms of the category. Naturally, once an activity becomes truly autonomous, the student automatically draws on elements from other categories, e.g., while making something (category 6), he overturns a container of paint and apologizes (category 1), then solves a problem by suggesting how such a situation could be avoided by a different arrangement of working space (category 8).

All of the activities suggested will obviously not be possible for all students from the earliest stage of learning. The teacher will *select and graduate activities to propose* from these categories, so that the attitude of seeking to communicate is developed early in an activity which is within the student's growing capacity. An impossible task, which bewilders and discourages the student too early in his language learning, is just as inhibiting of ultimate fluency as lack of opportunity to try what he can do with what he knows. The sample activities within each category are broadly labeled E (Elementary), I (Intermediate), and A (Advanced). This is obviously not a hard-and-fast guide since the maturity, capabilities, and goals of groups are so diverse.

1. ESTABLISHING AND MAINTAINING SOCIAL RELATIONS

(E) Greetings between persons of the same and different age and status, introductions, wishes for special occasions, polite enquiries (with attention to the permissible and the expected questions in the culture), making arrangements, giving directions, apologies, refusals; (I) excuses, mild rebukes, conventional expressions of agreement and polite disagreement, encouraging, discouraging, and persuading others; (A) expressing impatience, surprise, dismay, making promises, hedging (the gentle art of non-communication), teasing.

Conversation capsules or *mini-incidents* can be developed by interaction groups to demonstrate how to handle various situations. These need not be lengthy. Students learn appropriate gestures as they enact the situations.

(E) Answering the door and politely getting rid of an unwanted caller; calling on the phone with birthday greetings, congratulations on a successful achievement, an enquiry about the health of a friend, or to make some arrangements; enacting urgent situations (fire, drowning, street attack) which require quick vocal responses with set phrases; (I) welcoming visitors at home, customers in a shop, or clients in an office.

(A) These uses become inextricably interwoven within other activities. Reality is achieved when students are able to greet, escort, and entertain a Spanish-speaking visitor to the school or the town, interact in Spanish with an exchange student, or participate in a visit abroad or an informal activity of category 14.

2. EXPRESSING ONE'S REACTIONS

The student can be put in real or simulated situations where he has to react verbally throughout a television show, at an exhibition of pictures or photographs, during a friendly sharing of slides, or at a student fashion show. (In these cases the clever or amusing remark, instead of being frowned upon as presumptuous, is welcomed, as long as it is in Spanish.)

3. HIDING ONE'S INTENTIONS

(I) Each student may be given a mission which he must not reveal under any provocation, but which he tries to carry out within a given period of time. This activity carries purposeful use of the language beyond course hours as students try to discover each other's missions. (E) Selekman[4] has developed for this category a game called *Super Spy* (*Super Espía*). One group forms a team of spies who decide on a mission. Each spy goes to a different group, the members of which try to find out his mission through astute questioning. The group which is successful first then explains how their spy's mission was discovered. This activity also involves (5), (8), and (13).

4. TALKING ONE'S WAY OUT OF TROUBLE

Simulated or real situations of increasing verbal difficulty should be set up where the student must use his wits to extract himself from his dilemma; e.g., giving non-answers to an inquisitive neighbor anxious to know the origin of a loud noise he heard in the middle of the night; redirecting the course of an awkward or embarrassing conversation; answering the complaint: *"Te llamé por teléfono anoche, como convinimos, pero nadie contestó"* without revealing where one was or what one was doing.

5. SEEKING AND GIVING INFORMATION

a. *Seeking information* on subjects for which students have some basic vocabulary. (A) Finding out specialized vocabulary for a special interest can be part of this type of interaction, particularly in connection with (6). (I) Students may be sent to find out specific information from a monolingual Spanish speaker or an informant who pretends to be monolingual, or the students seek the information from other Spanish speakers outside of the course or the school. The information may be useful for activities in categories (1), (6), (8), or (12).

b. *Giving information* (E and I) about oneself, one's family background, the area where one lives, one's career aspirations, vacation preferences, pet peeves; (I and A) about some subject in which one is proficient (the student may be giving information to other students learning to do or make something, perhaps explaining what he is doing while he is doing it).

Combining (a) and (b). (E and I) All kinds of classroom opportunities arise for students to wonder why and ask the teacher or each other. Students should be encouraged to ask questions in Spanish about what they are to do and to seek information about Hispanic customs and institutions. If a new student has joined the class, if there is a new baby in the family, if some student has returned from a vacation or a summer job, or if someone saw an accident on the way to school, other activities should be suspended while students ask about it in Spanish. *Simulated settings* like bank or airline counters, customs desks, workshops, or restaurants may be used to expand the school setting. Advertisements from magazines can give an initial fillip to the interaction, with students enquiring about advertised services. Students may use Spanish air schedules, customs forms, menus, or maps (often brought home by traveling relatives or the teacher) as a basis for asking and answering questions or giving directions. The *interview technique* also combines these two aspects of information-sharing. (A) The interview may be based on social roles adopted by the participants, thus linking (5) with (11). The results of the interview may be written up for a wall newspaper, as a link with writing practice.

6. LEARNING OR TEACHING HOW TO DO OR MAKE SOMETHING

Here, language is associated with action. The possibilities for increasing the interest and motivation of students of all kinds of abilities and interests are limitless. It is the basic technique of foreign-language camps and should be incorporated automatically into the programs of foreign-language clubs. On a smaller scale it can become part of a regular course. The pressure of intensive courses is certainly relieved by sessions in the foreign language where students actually work with real-life materials and activities (sports, hobbies, crafts, physical exercise, dances).

7. CONVERSING OVER THE TELEPHONE

This is always difficult in a foreign language because of the distortions of sound, interference, and lack of situational, facial, and body language clues to meaning. It should, therefore, be practiced early. The students should learn to use a phone book from the country where the language is spoken, and, where this is possible, make actual calls enquiring about goods, services, or timetables for transport.

The help of monolingual, or presumed monolingual, contacts outside the course should be enlisted. Some incapacitated persons, older persons living alone, and retired teachers would enjoy participating in this type of activity. They should be instructed to act strictly as monolinguals[5] and should be informed of the specific nature of the student's assignment. Where none of these are available, teachers will act as informants for A students from their colleagues' classes, and A students will act as informants for E and I students.

The telephone practice is usually associated with (6) or (8).

8. PROBLEM SOLVING

The problem should require verbal activity for its solution. It may involve (5) or (6), even (3), (4), (9), or (10).

a. (E) Such well-known games as *Veintiuna Preguntas, Identificación, Animal-Vegetal-Mineral,* and their derivatives are popular. One student thinks of something (or someone, or a historical incident . . .), the others try to guess what it is with the fewest possible yes-no questions. (See G43.) (I and A) These games can become very sophisticated as versions of television panel series like *Aquí no hay secretos, ¿Quién dice la verdad?* (where three people pretend to be the person who performed some particular acts and the students try to decide which one is telling the truth), and *¿Cuál es mi profesión?* (where the questioners try to decide the occupation of the one being questioned).

b. (E and I) Selekman has experimented with a game called *Guilty Party*[6] (*El Culpado*), where one student is accused by the group of an unspecified crime which he must discover through a series of questions (When did I do this? Where did I do it? Why did I do it? Did anyone help me? . . .). After he has discovered his crime, the accused must attempt to defend himself to seek an acquittal. (A) This game can follow a study of the Spanish legal system and incorporate relevant features of Spanish justice.

c. (E and I) Lipson,[7] in an attempt to focus the students' attention on the *content* of the sentences they are producing, has worked out materials which take up the principle of the well-known type of puzzle:

A, B, and C live on X, Y, and Z streets.
A works in an office.
B is a lawyer.
C stays home while his wife goes to work.
The people on X street all work in factories.
The people on Y street are all single.
The people on Z street all own their own businesses downtown.

—On which streets do A, B, and C live?

Lipson's materials are about hooligans who steal in factories, conduct themselves badly in parks, like to smoke on trolley buses, and are often uncultured people (uncultured people never wash). Later we find out that hooligans are of two types: those who conduct themselves badly in parks never wash, while those who steal in factories like to smoke on trolley buses. The plot thickens when we find out that there are two gangs of hooligans, Borodin's and Gladkov's: Borodin steals at Gladkov's factory and Gladkov at Borodin's. This complicated background leads to questions such as the following:

Which hooligans often wash?	Hooligans who steal at factories
	OR
	hooligans who don't conduct themselves badly in parks . . .
When does Borodin steal at his own factory?	He never steals at his own factory.
Why not?	Borodin steals at Gladkov's factory.
What does Gladkov do when Borodin is not stealing?	As far as I know, Gladkov steals at Borodin's factory.

Both Selekman[8] and Lipson[9] report that students become so involved in these problem-solving activities that their verbal participation becomes really creative and personally meaningful. As Lipson puts it: "What often happens is that members of the class start arguing with each other, and the teacher steps aside and lets the argument run."

d. (A) Problem-solving activities may be associated with some project for another course. Students may want to find answers to such questions as the following:

i. Why does Panama want to renegotiate the present treaty with the United States concerning the Panama Canal? What changes does Panama seek in the new treaty?

ii. Why does my *paella* not taste the same as that I had in Spain last summer?

The answer to (i) may be sought through library research, listening to speeches, interviews with Panamanian visitors, reading of newspapers and magazines, and finally classroom discussion of what each student has gleaned, thus interweaving (5), (8), (9), and (13). Question (ii) may require some of the same procedures, along with experimentation in the kitchen (6).

9. DISCUSSING IDEAS

(E and I) Factual details of things read, seen, or heard provide a basis for discussion. Mystery stories are useful. Cultural differences are most likely to provoke lively discussion. Since students at the E and I stages are at a disadvantage in such discussions because of the teacher's wider command of the language, the teacher must refrain from taking over and doing all the talking. At these levels, topics for discussion are normally kept to areas for which the students know some vocabulary and expressions. Otherwise, they come after a project of research into the area; or, students are provided with some written or recorded material from which they can acquire the necessary Spanish terms for use in the discussion.

(A) Students decide on controversial subjects they wish to discuss, prepare their points for discussion, but make their remarks without a written script; two groups prepare the same topic and discuss it with each other while students from other groups ask questions; one student takes a viewpoint and tries to convince other students that this viewpoint is tenable.

Stevick's *microtexts*[10] are useful as starters. A short text in Spanish on any subject may be selected by teacher or students. This text is distributed, shown on the overhead projector, or written on the chalkboard; students then discuss and elaborate on the details of the text and any implications of it. The text should not be more than fifty words in length, or, if delivered orally, should not take longer than thirty seconds to relate. With experience, teachers and students can draw an astonishing amount of interesting discussion from almost any text. Possible microtexts are: (E) a menu, a concert program, an airline timetable, selections from letters from Spanish correspondents, or a paragraph from a newspaper about the official activities of a leading political figure; (I) newspaper accounts of the dog that saved its master during a fire, a bank robbery, two children lost in the mountains, a recent Spanish Nobel Prize winner, a swing in fashions for dress or hair styles, or selected letters from the *Consultorio Sentimental*. (A) accounts of recent decisions on Spanish domestic or foreign policy (editorial comments from two different Spanish-language newspapers or from a Spanish- and an English-language newspaper may be compared), new developments in the Spanish educational system, the latest approaches to the drug problem in Latin America, letters to the editor raising interesting questions.

10. PLAYING WITH LANGUAGE

Newspapers and magazines have for years published regularly all kinds of word games (crossword puzzles, acrostics and double-acrostics, vocabulary expansion quizzes). Books on language enjoy a perennial popularity, and magic and esoteric words continue to mesmerize devotees. From early childhood people are fascinated by language. This natural love of language can be exploited in the foreign-language class.

(E, I, A) *Scrabble* games geared to the letter frequencies of different languages are obtainable.

(E) Nonsense and counting rhymes may be learned by heart and recited for fun. Songs with repetitive refrains are popular. Students like to learn onomatopoeic expressions (animal cries, rain dripping, doors banging) and these can be used in games and classroom drama.

(I) Oral construction in groups of crossword and other language puzzles can stimulate much discussion in the language, particularly when the construction becomes complicated in the final stages. *Charades* provide amusing themes for classroom dramatization. Students take a two-syllable word (*soldar*) and for each syllable they improvise a short episode which brings in the word it represents (*sol/dar*). They then act out an episode which brings in the complete word (*soldar*) and students guess which word it is. (Other possibilities are: *banca/rota/bancarrota; para/sol/parasol;* or two segments: *mano/tener/mantener,* or three syllables: *es/pan/tos/espantos*).

(A) Students may seek out and discuss word origins, word histories, and borrowings. They may examine Spanish-language popular magazines like *Vanidades Continental* to see the extent of contemporary Spanish borrowings from English. At this level too, students may begin to take an interest in regional differences in the Spanish language (e.g., the accent and common expressions of peninsular Spanish as contrasted with Latin American Spanish).

11. ACTING OUT SOCIAL ROLES

Psychologists point out that we are constantly taking on different roles and the style of language which goes with them.

Dramatic improvisation is an excellent technique for eliciting autonomous interaction. Situations and participating characters are suggested in a very sketchy fashion. Students are allowed a short time to plan what they will do before they enact the scene, improvising the dialogue as they proceed. Several groups or pairs may improvise the same situation with very different results. Even inhibited students feel free to express themselves when they are being someone else in a recreational activity.

(E) Students act out roles in which they can use expressions learned in (1).

(I and A) Situations are proposed which represent various social settings with characters of different occupations, relationships, and levels of authority:

a. The job interview with a timid (or overconfident) applicant.

b. The overbearing bureaucrat and the applicant for a visa extension.

c. The *conserje* trying to find out all about the reticent new *inquilino* on the fourth floor.

d. The hippie son asking his very proper father for money.

e. The cocktail party at the *Embajada de España:* the vapid female talking about nothing at great length or echoing what other people say (*Es la primera*

vez que me invitan a la Embajada. / *¿Verdad? ¿Ud. está aquí por primera vez?*);
the boastful type (*¡Yo soy el autor de veinte novelas que han tenido un éxito
fenomenal! Seguramente Ud. ha leído Y manaña, el mundo.*); the parallel monologue (A: *Mi hija acaba de casarse hoy mismo.* B: *¿Verdad? Yo tengo hijos
(varones) solamente.* A: *Ella se casó con un profesor de la Universidad Nacional.*
B: *¿Ah sí? Mi hijomenor es estudiante en la Facultad de Medicina*); the igno-
ramus talking to the Nobel Prize winner (*¿Es difícil ganar ese premio? ¿Qué
se tiene que hacer para ganarlo?*) . . . .

    f. Situations based on proverbs.

    g. Well-known political figures or characters in films or television programs
may be mimicked in familiar situations.

12. ENTERTAINING OTHERS

The student should be given the opportunity to use his natural talents for
singing, making music, or acting as host for a radio call-in program or a
TV talk show. Groups of students may prepare and present radio or TV
commercials. (These may involve more or less talking interspersed with
mime, and are, therefore, very suitable for the early stages of a course.)
A complete radio or TV program with news, situation comedy, commercials, weather report, interview, give-away show, sports, song and dance
routine, and the national anthem of a Spanish-speaking country may be
prepared for presentation to another class, for a *Día de la Raza* celebration,
for an Open Day, or for a school assembly.

13. DISPLAYING ONE'S ACHIEVEMENTS

(E, I, and A) Students may tell the group about what they did in (3),
(4), (5), (6), or (8), or present and explain special projects, which will
often be interdisciplinary (e.g., the study of an aspect of Spanish art, music,
architecture, or history). (A) As a climax to (9), groups may present their
different viewpoints in a full-scale debate.

    Some kind of public presentation can become a regular culminating
activity to draw together many individualized interaction projects.

14. SHARING LEISURE ACTIVITIES

Students should have the opportunity to learn, and become proficient in,
the games and diversions of the Hispanic people. They should be able to
participate in verbal competitions. Where there are special activities traditionally associated with festivals or national holidays, students should be
able to engage in them at the appropriate time (*la Nochebuena, la
Navidad, el Año Nuevo, el Día de los Reyes Magos, el Día de los Difuntos,
el Día de la Raza, el Día del Santo* . . .).

Much autonomous interaction takes place at Spanish clubs, Spanish tables, class picnics, or at Spanish language camps. Visits are arranged to see exhibitions of Spanish paintings, eat at Spanish restaurants, see Spanish films, or attend performances by visiting theatrical companies. Groups within a class may take turns preparing a Spanish meal and inviting the others. Schools should investigate possibilities for inviting Spanish-speaking exchange students and assistants. Spanish-speaking residents of the district or visitors passing through should be invited to talk with Spanish classes on a formal or informal basis. Students should undertake to show their town or their school to Spanish-speaking visitors or tourists on a regular basis.

At the advanced level, students often opt for *purely oral courses* to perfect their ability to communicate. For these courses, activities such as those described above which plunge students into normal uses of language are essential.

* Take three of the categories listed and for each try to think of three more activities which would lead to these particular normal uses of language. If you are studying this book in a class group, have a brain-storming session to see what you can add to the suggestions given.

Perfeccionamiento, *not perfection*
CORRECTION OF ERRORS IN AUTONOMOUS INTERACTION

It is during intensive practice exercises, or construction practice, that immediate corrections may be made. Even then, we should not jump in before our students have had time to think and often to correct themselves. Our task is to make our students conscious of possible errors and to familiarize them to such a degree with acceptable, rule-governed sequences that they are able to monitor their own production and work toward its improvement in spontaneous interaction. In interaction practice we are trying to develop an attitude of innovation and experimentation with the new language. Nothing dampens enthusiasm and effort more than constant correction when the student is trying to express his ideas within the limitations of his newly acquired knowledge of the language. Teachers who are non-native speakers of the language know that they are very often fully conscious of a mistake they have just made, even mortified by it, but unable to take it back. We should be happy when our students have reached the same level of awareness of acceptable usage, since it means they are becoming autonomous learners as well as autonomous speakers.

The best approach during interaction activities is for the instructor silently to note consistent, systematic errors (not slips of the tongue and occasional lapses in areas where the student usually acquits himself well).

These errors will then be discussed with the student at a time when the instructor is helping him evaluate his success in interaction, with particular attention to the types of errors which hinder communication. The instructor will then use his knowledge of the areas of weakness of a number of students as a basis for his emphases in instruction and in review. In this way, we help students focus on what are problem areas for them as they learn from their mistakes. Steady improvement will come only from individual motivation and purpose—that personal desire to perfect one's communicative effectiveness which is stimulated by genuine interest in what one is doing.

WHAT LEVEL OF CORRECT SPEECH CAN WE EXPECT FROM OUR STUDENTS?

The first question we must ask ourselves is: How does a native speaker frame his utterances when he is thinking only of expressing his meaning?

C34 Es muy difícil, ¿verdad?, llegar a dominar un idioma extranjero, con todas . . . su pronunciación correcta, tanto que fuese capaz una persona de engañar; esto cuando se trata del estudio, por ejemplo, entre, vamos a decir, un idioma que no sea muy similar al castellano, vamos a suponer, una persona que hable e-e-el inglés, o el francés o el italiano, y al hablar el castellano, pues, es lógico pensar que . . . no se va a tomar un ciento por ciento la pronunciación siempre, por más que haya el . . . exista el . . . el empeño de la pronunciación, pues será reconocido de que es un extranjero el que está hablando el castellano. Y . . . en mi concepto, de repente se encuentran, pues, gentes con una . . . vamos, con . . . con una facilidad de asimilación, de . . . de . . . de pronunciación tan, tan grande que es bastante difícil, bastante difícil poderlos reconocer.[11]

This passage, transcribed from a taped conversation, shows clearly how we feel our way toward the most effective framework for expressing our meaning, leaning heavily on hesitation and transition expressions (*¿verdad?, pues, vamos . . .*) and repetitions (*con . . . con una facilidad, bastante difícil, bastante difícil, tan . . . tan grande . . .*), changing our minds in midstream about choice of words (*haya el, exista el . . . el empeño . . .*) and about the type of sentence which will best express our meaning (*vamos a decir, y . . . en mi concepto . . .*). Note that we do not make basic errors in morphology or syntax. (In "*con todas su*," the word *todas* acts as a transition expression while the speaker chooses the precise noun he needs to express his meaning—*toda su pronunciación*—and indicates hesitancy in formulating the sentence.) The repetitions also help the listener to process each segment at the speed of utterance by providing redundancy to reinforce the meaning he is extracting.

It is clear that we cannot expect our students to speak Spanish always in well-formed sentences in the heat of personal expression, when they do not do so in their native language. We must also expect students to hesitate, restructure sentences, and make sudden changes of lexical choice which may temporarily affect agreements of person and gender in the immediate vicinity. These imperfections are important only if they affect comprehensibility.

THE SI LINE

Stevick draws to our attention an interesting fact about simultaneous interpreters. "These remarkable individuals," he observes, "perceive both lexical meaning and grammatical form, and come out with their own reformulations in the other language after only a few seconds delay. Even as they speak, they are taking in new data for interpretation. . . . But if they are to continue, there is a line that they dare not cross: they must not become personally involved in what they are saying. Once the content of the message begins to make a difference to them, they lose the power of speaking and listening at the same time."[12] Stevick calls this boundary the SI (simultaneous interpretation) line: "Above it," he says, "lie grammatical form and dictionary meaning; below it lies everything that matters to speaker and listener."[13]

In view of this psychological phenomenon we have no reason to be surprised that students engaging in genuine interaction make many slips which we know they would not make in structured activities. Correcting them immediately and frequently will force students, for self-protection, to keep their attention above the SI line and will result in speech which is more carefully correct but which never goes beyond the banal and the obvious. This is surely not our goal.

INDIVIDUAL DIFFERENCES

Because of the personal nature of autonomous interaction, the participation of a particular student will naturally be consistent with his personality. Some people are temperamentally incapable of interacting by means of a babble of words; to expect them to do so is to force them back into pseudo-communication and into mouthing memorized phrases. The quality of the interaction will be judged by other criteria: ability to receive and express meaning, to understand and convey intentions, to perform acceptably in all kinds of situations in his relations with others. The means by which the student attains these desirable goals will be a function of his personal learning strategies. We can allow these full play through the provision of a wide choice of activity options, but we cannot determine for him what they shall be.

THE INDIVIDUAL TEACHER

Some non-native teachers feel inadequate to the demands of autonomous interaction activities because of insufficiencies of training or a long period of time away from foreign-language teaching. Just like their students, such teachers grow in skill and confidence as they participate. In a non-authoritarian approach the teacher accepts and acknowledges his weaknessses, drawing on his strengths as an *animador* to compensate. The students then accept him as a member of a group which is learning together. From year to year his control of the language improves, especially if he uses tapes of authentic native speech regularly to supplement his teaching and seizes every opportunity to listen to the language on the radio or on the sound tracks of films and to speak it in his contacts with colleagues in the school, at professional meetings, and *especially in his own classroom.* He also reads for pleasure modern books and plays in the language to keep him in contact with its contemporary spoken form. What he does not know, he encourages his students to find out, or, better still, he and his students find it out together. He also makes every effort to join in professional visits to Spanish-speaking areas, or he goes on his own. If finances are the problem here, he organizes a group of students for such a visit and covers his expenses by accompanying them as guide and host. Many a poorly prepared teacher has overcome his inadequacies. The essential is the determination to do so.

3
Listening

Essential to all interaction is the ability to understand what others are saying. Even in the native language many people are poor listeners, whether through weak powers of concentration, egocentrism, or short auditory memory. Yet it has been estimated that, of the time adults spend in communication activities, 45 per cent is devoted to listening, only 30 per cent to speaking, 16 per cent to reading, and a mere 9 per cent to writing (and these data are from a pre-television, pre-talking-picture, pre-dictaphone era).[1] Apart from communicative interaction, much of the enjoyment in foreign-language use comes from listening activities—watching films and plays or listening to radio broadcasts, songs, or talks by native speakers. Even in class students learn a great deal from listening to their teacher, to tapes or records, or to each other.

It is noteworthy that some students who do not excel in other areas of foreign-language use achieve a very high level of success in understanding spoken messages. It has been suggested by some researchers that there is a special listening comprehension factor,[2] but this has not yet been fully characterized. Even in life situations many people become skilled, in their own or a foreign language, in understanding registers, dialectal variations, and complexities of structure which they cannot produce in their own speech. Troike[3] has called this a difference between receptive and productive competence. Students with special skill in listening comprehension should be encouraged and given opportunities to go beyond others in this

58

area, which is especially suitable for individualized work. They should also be rewarded in final grading with full consideration for this skill in which they excel.

Listening is a complex operation, integrating the distinct components of perception and linguistic knowledge in ways which are at present poorly understood.[4] Psychologists have tried to explain this phenomenon from several viewpoints, each of which can give us some clues to our students' problems in listening to a foreign language and suggest ways of structuring effective materials for practice and enjoyment.

The schema C1 brings out the cognitive nature of listening, which involves *perception* based on *internalized knowledge* of the rules of the language. Students have to learn to abstract from a stream of sound units which machines cannot as yet be programmed to identify, to assign these to categories, and to attribute to them functions in relation to other units, so that an intelligible message may be constructed from what they are hearing. While they are doing this, they are anticipating the import of the message, holding segments already identified in their immediate memory, and readjusting their interpretation of earlier segments in accordance with the final message *as they understand it*.

In this context the phrase "as they understand it" is basic, because listening is not a passive but an *active process of constructing a message* from a stream of sound with what one knows of the phonological, semantic, and syntactic potentialities of the language. Even in our own language we often "hear" what was never said. This becomes an even more frequent occurrence in a language we are still learning. It is this active process of message construction which has been labeled *reception* (or comprehension of the message) in C1. The two terms *perception* and *reception* represent the two levels[5] of practice required to improve systematically the student's skill in interpreting messages intended by speakers.

Models of listening processes

Some linguists[6] maintain that knowledge of the same system of grammatical rules of a language is basic to both listening and speaking. Some psychologists, on the other hand, believe the rules we apply are different and that we employ perceptual strategies[7] for surface scanning of what we are hearing, stopping to penetrate to underlying relations only to resolve ambiguities or untangle complexities. Despite their theoretical divergence, interesting insights can be derived from various linguistic and psychological schools of thought, each of which emphasizes a different facet of the complicated processes of listening and receiving messages.

In this section, we will discuss in detail (A) the role of uncertainty and redundancy in Cherry's theory of communication, (B) Neisser's active processing of a message, and (C) Bever's strategies of perceptual segmentation (with which we will link Schlesinger's semantic-syntactic decoding).

A. *The uncertainties of a spoken message*

Cherry[8] says, "Communication proceeds in the face of a number of uncertainties and has the character of . . . numerous inductive inferences being carried out concurrently."

He lists these uncertainties as:

1. Uncertainties of speech sounds, or acoustic patterning. Accents, tones, loudness may be varied; speakers may shout, sing, whisper, or talk with their mouths full.

2. Uncertainties of language and syntax. Sentence constructions differ; conversational language may be bound by few rules of syntax. Vocabularies vary; words have many near-synonyms, popular usages, special usages, et cetera.

3. Environmental uncertainties. Conversations are disturbed by street noises, by telephone bells, and background chatter.

4. Recognition uncertainties. Recognition depends upon the peculiar past experiences of the listener, upon his familiarity with the speaker's speech habits, knowledge of language, subject matter, et cetera.

Here we have in a nutshell many of the problems our students face in the comprehension of speech, each of these being compounded where a foreign language is involved. "Yet," Cherry continues, "speech communication works. It is so structured as to possess redundancy at a variety of levels, to assist in overcoming these uncertainties."[9] In C2 we examined some of the redundancies of spoken, as opposed to written, Spanish. It is time now to examine a specimen of completely unedited, authentic speech, uttered in a natural situation by a person who had no idea that what she said would ever serve any pedagogical purpose. (This passage will reinforce the impressions gained from C34.)

EDITED AND UNEDITED LISTENING COMPREHENSION MATERIALS

In preparing materials and activities for listening comprehension we do not give enough consideration to the differences between edited, or artificially constructed, messages and an authentic output of speech in natural interaction. As a result we make the listening comprehension materials we record, or present to the students orally in class, much more difficult to comprehend than we realize. The difference is like that between listening to a prepared and polished scholarly paper read verbatim and the free interchange of unprepared discussion which follows the paper and usually makes the speaker's ideas seem much clearer.

C35-37

The following edited and unedited discussions of the same subject will illustrate this difference. The unedited version is taken from an actual conversation.[10]

The speakers (*estudiantes españoles*) are discussing students' attitudes toward formal academic work in Spain and the United States. The following question was asked them:

"Hablando de la actitud de los estudiantes hacia los estudios, hacia su papel en la universidad y el papel de la universidad en la vida de ellos, ¿no?, ¿qué contrastes encontráis entre la universidad española y la americana?"

C35 Edited content of the remarks of a woman student:

La diferencia principal que yo veo, hablando en general, es que aquí se toman más en serio los estudios. Los primeros que se los toman en serio son los profesores, que exigen (y exigir quiere decir *exigir*) una serie de trabajos y cosas que, si no las haces, no puedes continuar. En España, todo es más fácil. Los profesores o no están tan organizados o no exigen tanto. Por ejemplo, muchas veces se planifica, para un curso, escribir tres o cuatro ensayos. Pero los dos últimos meses, los alumnos dicen que no se pueden hacer los cuatro, porque ha habido huelgas, y por eso se rebaja el número de los ensayos a solamente tres o quizás dos. Esto sucede bastante.

C36 The following passage, transcribed from the original tape, shows how the same ideas were expressed in authentic interaction. Slashes indicate the position of the pauses in delivery. With the exception of the interrogation marks in the question tag *¿no?*, no attempt has been made to insert punctuation, which is a convention of written language.

Pues / en principio / hablando en general / no España / creo que aquí se toma más en serio / me parece que se toma más en serio / esto es lo / lo principal ¿no? / y claro / los primeros que se lo toman en serio son también los profesores / eh / son los primeros y / exigen / y exigir quiere decir exigir ¿no? / una serie de / de trabajos y / y cosas que / que si no las haces no / no puedes continuar / mientras que en España / es todo / todo más fácil / no dudo / los profesores / o no están tan organizados o / no no fumo gracias / o no están tan organizados o / o no exigen tanto / muchas veces se planifica / por ejemplo / para un curso / escribir tres / eh / ensayos / o cuatro ensayos / digamos / y / los dos últimos meses /

los alumnos / oh / por favor / no se puede hacer / cuatro / ha habido huelgas / o / enfin / lo que sea ¿no? / solamente tres / y bien / tres / y quizá se rebajan a dos / esto sucede / bastante /

C37 If we set C36 and C35 out in parallel columns we see much more strikingly how much verbal redundancy has been eliminated even in such a colloquially expressed version as C35. For C36 a separate line has been allotted to each breath group.

C36	C35
Pues	La diferencia principal que yo veo
en principio	
hablando en general	hablando en general
no España	
creo que aquí se toma más en serio	es que aquí se toman más en serio
me parece que se toma más en serio	los estudios
esto es lo	
lo principal ¿no?	
y claro	
los primeros que se lo toman en serio son también los profesores	Los primeros que se los toman en serio son los profesores
eh	
son los primeros y	
exigen	que exigen
y exigir quiere decir exigir ¿no?	(y exigir quiere decir *exigir*)
una serie de	una serie de trabajos y cosas
de trabajos y	
y cosas que	
que si no las haces no	que si no las haces no puedes continuar
no puedes continuar	
mientras que en España	En España es todo más fácil.
es todo	
todo más fácil	
no dudo	
los profesores	Los profesores o no están tan organizados o no exigen tanto
o no están tan organizados o	
no no fumo gracias	
o no están tan organizados o	
o no exigen tanto	
muchas veces se planifica	Por ejemplo, muchas veces se plani-

por ejemplo
para un curso
escribir tres
eh
ensayos
o cuatro ensayos digamos

y

los dos últimos meses
los alumnos
oh
por favor
no se puede hacer
cuatro
ha habido huelgas
o
enfin
lo que sea ¿no?
solamente tres
y bien
tres
y quizá se rebajan a dos
esto sucede
bastante

fica para un curso escribir tres o cuatro ensayos.

Pero los dos últimos meses
los alumnos dicen que no se pueden hacer cuatro

porque ha habido huelgas

y por eso se rebaja el número de los ensayos a solamente tres o quizás dos.

Esto sucede bastante.

Commentary

Although the edited version of C35 retains the colloquial flavor of C36, it eliminates synonymous expressions which merely repeat the thought content or elaborate it in minor ways (*creo que aquí se toma más en serio / me parece que se toma más en serio*); function words indicating a direction of sentence structure which is not followed through (*no España, no dudo, oh / por favor*); hesitation expressions (*pues, eh, oh, y bien*); conversational tags (*¿no?*); parenthetical sentences which have nothing to do with the subject matter of the conversation (*no no fumo gracias*—said when someone offered the speaker a cigarette). It also regularizes syntax which does not observe the accepted constraints (*ha habido huelgas / o / enfin / lo que sea ¿no? / solamente tres / y bien / tres*). Thus, in a well-meaning attempt at improving the "disorderly" output of C36, the editor has provided in C35 a version which would demand much more concentrated effort in listening than the authentic speech of C36. As with speaking, we may well be demanding more of our foreign-language listeners in the exercises we present than is demanded in native-language listening.

Authentic materials of the type illustrated are unfortunately not easy for classroom teachers to obtain. The following suggestions should be implemented:

1. When Spanish-speaking guest speakers and exchange students are temporarily at hand, teachers should seize the opportunity to tape-record general conversation with the visitors. Suitable excerpts from the tapes should then be shared among groups of schools.

2. Spanish and Spanish-American cultural services should be asked to provide tapes of radio discussions, informal chats, and film sound tracks, so that an awareness is created that these are the types of materials our students need.

3. Exchanges of tapes should be encouraged between twinned classes in Spanish- and English-speaking schools. Both classes should be encouraged to send unedited tapes—not of prepared talks, but of free discussion among members of the class on aspects of their daily lives and their likes and dislikes. To obtain such tapes requires a change of attitude on the part of teachers who often expect a class exchange to be a perfectly orchestrated performance.

4. Individual students should be encouraged to begin tape exchanges with correspondents in Spanish-speaking countries, along the lines of the more conventional letter exchanges.

Listening to authentic tapes recorded by native speakers who are not teachers provides one of the best opportunities for students to have real contact with the life and thought of Spanish-speaking people, whether from Spain, or Spanish America, or Spanish-speaking areas in the United States. Through these tapes they encounter the normal and the natural, even the trivial, much more than in the reading of newspapers, magazines, novels, plays, and short stories, all of which tend to choose as subjects the exceptional, the sensational, the idealized, or the eccentric in order to arouse and maintain interest.

RECOGNITION UNCERTAINTIES

The listener constructs a message from what he is hearing according to certain expectations[11] based on:

—what he knows of the language, not only syntax and lexicon, but usage in these areas for different styles of language (see C5);

—his familiarity with the subject under discussion;

—the knowledge of the real world that he shares with the speaker (through which he can assume certain things which have not been expressed);

—his acquaintance with or assumptions about the personal attitudes and interests of the speaker;

—his observation and interpretation of the circumstances of the utterance, including what has preceded it;

—his understanding of the cultural context in which it occurs;

—his reading of paralinguistic cues (speed of speech, length of pauses, loudness, pitch, facial expressions), gestures, and other body language which differ from culture to culture.[12]

The listener imposes a syntactic structure on what he is hearing and this arouses further expectations about what is to come. Sometimes a succeeding segment proves to be incongruous with his syntactic expectations and this forces him to reconsider and project a different syntactic structure, in other words, to resolve the ambiguity.

For these reasons ability to receive messages aurally becomes more refined as knowledge of the potentialities of the grammatical system increases. Consider the following examples:

C38   1. *Oye, ¿cuántos libros le compró Juan a Herrera?*

Commentary

Taken out of any context, (1) is ambiguous, as it may be interpreted as a query as to how many books Juan bought either from or for Herrera. In the former case, (1) is semantically parallel to (2), and in the latter, to (3):

2. *¿Cuántas pólizas le compró Juan al vendedor?*

3. *¿Cuántos juguetes le compró Juan a su hijo?*

If the listener is unaware of the circumstances involving Juan and Herrera, he may initially hesitate between two possible semantic interpretations of the surface-structure adverb of interest *le . . . a Herrera.* In one case, *Herrera* is the semantic source (supplier, salesman), whereas in the other it is the beneficiary, that is, the recipient of a service or a set of objects. If the listener's extralinguistic knowledge informs him, however, that Herrera is a peddler who has been pestering Juan with recent bestsellers, he will interpret (1) as he would (2); on the other hand, if he knows that Juan has been trying to help a poor student named Herrera by buying some badly needed textbooks for him, the listener will be more likely to interpret (1) as he would (3).[13]

In these cases, the listener must hold the utterance in his immediate memory while comparing it with the context or the circumstances of the utterance before assigning it a disambiguating structure.

* Discuss the two possible syntactic structures of each of the following sentences:

C39 Ahora atacan los aviones.
Las muchachas se miraban atentamente.
Paco recibió el libro del maestro.
Se mataron los amantes.

Find other examples of ambiguities of structure in Spanish.

Ignorance of the cultural context can be an impediment

C40 (A) Javier Silva encuentra a Jaime Masdevall en la terraza del Canaletas.

JAVIER   ¡Hola, majo! No esperaba encontrarte aquí. ¿Por qué no estás en la facultad?

JAIME   ¡Hola! Porque el color gris me hace mal a la vista. ¿Qué hay de nuevo?

JAVIER   Pues, nada de particular. (Al camarero:) Lo de siempre, por favor.

JAIME   ¿Y tu libro?

JAVIER   Bueno, como vuestra *Sagrada Familia.* . . . Y el artículo ese que escribiste sobre la huelga universitaria, ¿cuándo se publica?

JAIME   Pues, mañana, en el diario en catalán.

JAVIER   Hombre, ¡qué mal andan las cosas!

Commentary

A student could well understand every word of this interchange without having any real idea of its meaning and its emotional overtones. Full comprehension of it requires knowledge in various domains:

1. *The setting:* Two students meeting in the very heart of Barcelona. Clues: *Canaletas* is the name of a well-known restaurant in Barcelona, located on Rambla de Canaletas, off Plaza de Cataluña. Jaime is Catalan, as indicated by his last name, Masdevall. *Tú* is commonly used among students. Javier (and probably Jaime as well) is a regular customer, as indicated by his way of ordering something (*lo de siempre* "the usual").

2. *The subject matter:* Several times in the early seventies there were student demonstrations in Barcelona and the university was closed down by government order. Jaime's remark about the color grey (*gris*) is an ironic reference to the presence of the grey-uniformed members of the *Policía Armada* (*los grises*) at the university.

3. Jaime inquires about Javier's forthcoming book, which remains unfinished. Clue: Javier's reference to *la Sagrada Familia,* the name of Barcelona's magnificent but unfinished cathedral by the Catalan architect Antoni Gaudí (1852–1926).

On the other hand, Javier's expression, *vuestra Sagrada Familia* indicates that he is probably not from Barcelona. Jaime's reply to the query about his article on the student strike means that it will not be published. Clue: Due to current governmental policies regarding regional languages in Spain, there is no daily newspaper in Catalan in Barcelona today (1974).[14]

4. *Syntax:* The style is conversational, with short sentences and colloquial expressions. In spoken form, tone of voice would contribute to comprehension of the dialogue. If the persons speaking were visible (on film, for instance), facial expression and movements would help in the interpretation of the participants' attitudes toward the subject matter of their conversation.[15]

C41 (A) *Noticiero*[16]

Son las siete y cuarenta y seis minutos. Más noticias locales y nacionales. Por resolución del Consejo de Quito, tomada en sesión del martes, hoy deben reanudarse las labores docentes en el Liceo Municipal Fernández Madrid, poniendo término a la suspensión de labores que se adoptó cuando un grupo de alumnas declararon una huelga en respaldo a una profesora y en contra de las autoridades del plantel. La resolución tomada por la comuna se debe, según se informó, a las múltiples peticiones de padres de familia, ya que la mayoría de estudiantes desean regresar al plantel para proseguir con los estudios. El alcalde, al dar la información, señaló que la medida fue consultada con las autoridades del liceo, que también están de acuerdo con la resolución del Consejo. Aclaró que no habrá retaliaciones contra las alumnas que declararon la huelga, ni contra ninguna de las estudiantes, decisión que también fue adoptada por las autoridades del plantel. La profesora continuará con sus actividades normales en el liceo y no se producirán cambios en los cargos directivos del establecimiento educacional.

(A) *Boletín de Noticias*[17]

Según afirma un diario norteamericano, el gobierno de Damasco ha invitado a Henry Kissinger a visitar nuevamente Oriente Medio para tratar de solucionar el problema de la retirada de las tropas sirio-israelíes en el frente de El Golán.

Commentary

1. The first excerpt exemplifies the *formal style* typical of many news reports. The listener is not addressed directly, but rather informed, in impersonal fashion, of the circumstances that led to the termination of a student strike in Quito. Although this is an item of local news, the report is worded in such a way that even a listener unfamiliar with the events has little difficulty in understanding the facts. The report begins with the substance of the news, i.e., the resumption of classes at a local school (*por resolución . . . Madrid*) and then tells the listener that there had been a strike going on, as well as giving the reasons thereof (*poniendo término . . . del plantel*). The source of the news item is mentioned (*el alcalde . . .*), as well as the consequences of the decision (*no habrá retaliaciones . . . del plantel*), and the situation of the personalities on whose account the students had struck (*La profesora . . . los cargos directivos del establecimiento*).

2. News broadcasts like these are more difficult to follow linguistically than the natural, informal speech of C36, because many of the rephrasings which provide redundancy of content are absent and a more specialized vocabulary is employed (e.g., *labores docentes, la medida fue consultada, retaliaciones, cargos directivos*). On the other hand, they are delivered in a more deliberate tone, with clearer enunciation, and distinct pauses at major syntactic boundaries.

3. Radio commentaries are often easier to follow than newscasts because they pursue a single subject for some time, whereas a complete newscast moves rapidly from one context to another.

4. In the case of news of international significance, such as that exemplified by the second excerpt in C41, knowledge of the international situation may provide a conceptual background for recognition, particularly if the news programs are made available within the week in which they were broadcast. It should be kept in mind that place and personal names given orally can hinder recognition considerably. Students should be given instruction in the recognition of names in the news. A sequence such as /orientemédio/ is not necessarily quickly identified by the student as the more familiar *Oriente Medio,* nor is /elfrentedeelgolán/ easily recognized as *el frente de El Golán,* which the average student may have some

difficulty in identifying as the Golan Heights front. World geography lessons with Spanish-language maps and guessing games with names of famous persons in the accepted Spanish oral form are helpful as associated activities when news broadcasts are being used as listening comprehension material. The students and the teacher should also keep a file of clippings from Spanish-language newspapers and magazines which give background information, with the requisite specialized vocabulary, for the current national and international preoccupations of Spain, Spanish America, and other Spanish-speaking areas.

5. The difficulties faced by the students on first hearing a newscast can be diminished by encouraging them to relisten to the recording of the broadcast until they have comprehended the gist of the discussion.

* What knowledge of history, contemporary Hispanic life and attitudes, and present-day international developments would a student need to have in order to fully comprehend the import of the news items in C41?

Equally important for the comprehension of radio broadcasts is *recognition of dates and numbers,* as in the following:

C42 (A) *Station identification*[18]

... 9.630 kilociclos, equivalentes a 31,15 metros, con antena dirigida a Cuba, Guatemala, El Salvador, Honduras, México y Nicaragua. Nuestro programa puede ser también escuchado de 11 de la noche a 5 de la madrugada, hora española, en las siguientes frecuencias y longitudes de onda: 15.145 kilociclos, equivalentes a 19,8 metros, y 9.530 kilociclos, equivalentes a 31,37 metros, con antena dirigida a Argentina, Bolivia, Chile, Paraguay, zona sur de Perú y Uruguay; y 11.775 kilociclos, equivalentes a 25,48 metros, con antena dirigida a Costa Rica, Colombia, Ecuador, Haití, Panamá, Perú, Puerto Rico, Santo Domingo y Venezuela.

Rapid recognition of numbers and dates is indispensable to modern communication. One has only to think of common situations like asking the operator for telephone numbers, requesting airline and train schedules, changing travel plans, and understanding prices, rates for service, final accounts, bank balances, exchange rates, current dates, dates of birth, times for performances, or document numbers. With the multiplication of computerized services, more and longer numbers are becoming a part of everyday life, the latter often involving also rapid recognition of the *names of letters of the alphabet.*

Practice in attentive listening to numbers is provided by games like *Lotería* (Bingo), in dictation of series of numbers of increasing complexity, and in competitions where events must be selected from lists of multiple-choice items to correspond with dates given orally. The alphabet should be learned early and students should become adept at recognizing the oral spelling of new words and names letter by letter—a skill which is also useful for a foreigner in many communication situations.

PRACTICAL APPLICATIONS

1. Activities to *prepare the learner conceptually* for the type of content in a listening exercise are valuable in helping students develop expectations and project possible meanings.

2. Listening comprehension materials should preferably be well *integrated thematically* with the rest of the learning program; otherwise, discussions of a related subject may be necessary to stimulate the student's thinking. For example, discussion of the differences in students' attitudes in Spain and the United States would prepare for listening to C36; a study of student life and attitudes in contemporary Barcelona would bring to life a listening tape of which C40 was a part; discussion of some aspects of the Spanish educational system makes comprehensible a conversation among students waiting for the *exámenes* of the *bachillerato;* at a more elementary level, practice in telling time in Spanish prepares for a tape where several prospective travelers are making enquiries at an airline counter.

3. Students may be encouraged to project, to think ahead to reasonable completions, by games which test their alertness in detecting tricks in the completion of sentences.

Controle Vd. al Narrador is a team game which forces the student to think of the meaningful use of learned phrases or facts by dislodging them from their familiar settings. It may be given orally or on tape.

At the elementary stage, simple narratives may capitalize on common errors in meaning which students are making in everyday phrases they have learned in dialogues or classroom conversation. (For instance, elementary students often confuse *¿Cómo está Usted?* and *¿Dónde está Usted?* or *¿Cuándo va Usted?* and *¿Adónde va Usted?.*) Groups of students can prepare these narratives to try out on other groups. The team preparing the narrative gets points for each item missed by the opposing team.

One, or two, narrators read the prepared narrative expressively, not pausing or indicating in any other way where there are anomalies. When a student interrupts to point out an anomaly and is able to give an appropriate replacement, his team scores a point.

C43 (E) With anomalies italicized:

Esta mañana salgo sola. Mi hermano *que me acompaña* me pregunta:
—*Señorita,* ¿cuántos años tiene *usted?*
—*Muy bien, gracias.* Y tú, *¿qué hora es?*
—*Tengo once años,* responde él.

Commentary

If each utterance begins, as in the last three utterances, with an inappropriate segment, the position of the error becomes predictable. Students preparing narratives should be alerted to avoid clues such as positional regularity, alternation of correct/incorrect, and so on.

(I) Attention to detail to overcome the lulling effects of expectation can also be encouraged in listening to factual material. In C44 below, some of the facts will be known to the student from a lesson in Spanish geography; the effect of this lesson will be to create expectations which may make it difficult for them to "hear" some of the discrepancies. Once again a point is awarded to the team of the student who detects a fantastic or incorrect fact and can supply a suitable replacement for the offending segment.

C44 (I)

Statements read	*Replacements*
Barcelona es un importante puerto marítimo situado *a cinco kilómetros* de Madrid.	a unos seiscientos kilómetros or a una larga distancia or muy lejos
Pocos barcos llegan cada día al puerto de Barcelona.	Muchos
Diariamente salen del puerto muchos *marcos* extranjeros.	barcos
Salen *de la puerta* de Barcelona para ir a todos los *riñones* del mundo.	del puerto rincones

Commentary

The narrator must be careful not to accentuate slightly the incorrect word or look for a response. Because of the phonetic similarity in some cases (*marcos/barcos*) and the fact that other words belong to the same semantic field (*muchos/pocos*) student expectations will often result in their thinking they have heard what makes sense in the context.

B. The active process of constructing a message: stages of perception[19]

1. PERCEIVING A SYSTEMATIC MESSAGE

In listening comprehension *we first learn to perceive that there is a systematic rather than accidental noise in a continuous stream of sound.* We learn to recognize a characteristic rise and fall of the voice, varying pitch levels, and recurrences of certain sound sequences which may seem some-what like those of our own language, yet strangely different. At this stage, we make an elementary segmentation of what we hear in order to retain it in our memory. Even with gibberish or an utterance in a completely unknown tongue, we must segment in some way in order to repeat or memorize it. Many of the amusing things little children say result from their idiosyncratic segmentation of what they do not fully understand. (This is the stage called *Identification* in the chart of activities for listening comprehension, C67.)

Prolonged listening as an introduction to language study

Students are often plunged into trying to produce utterances in a new lan-guage too soon. As a result, they approximate these to the phonological system of their own language without having any feeling for the distinc-tiveness of the new language.

It has been suggested by some that foreign-language learning should begin with a prolonged period of listening to the language without attempt-ing to produce it. Prolonged listening to a strange language which is not associated with visuals, action, writing, or some intellectual exercise to help in identification of meaning, can become boring and will not necessarily lead to advantageous results. A baby hears a great deal of language around him for a long time before he speaks, but always associated with persons, places, objects, and bodily needs so that he gradually focuses on segments of it which are functional in his living space.

The *total physical response* approach encourages early attentive listening with physical action to demonstrate comprehension, but with no attempt at production.[20]

C45 (E) In the form of the game "Simon Says" (*Simón dice*), this approach to teaching has always been with us:

TEACHER OR STUDENT   Alcen la mano.
Students do not react.
TEACHER OR STUDENT   Tóquense la cabeza.
Students do not react.
TEACHER OR STUDENT   Simón dice: Tóquense la cabeza.
Students touch their heads . . .

C46 In its more developed form, students learn to perform progressively more complicated series of actions, still without any attempt at production. This has been shown to produce a high rate of retention.[21]

Students move from simple imperatives (*escriban, levántense*) to short directions (*vaya Ud. a la ventana, escriba Ud. en la pizarra*), then to more complex directions (*vaya Ud. a la mesa del maestro y deje allá la tiza*), and finally to novel directions combining utterances already heard (*vaya Ud. a la ventana, tome su libro, póngalo sobre la mesa del maestro y siéntese en la silla*).

Some practice of this type should be included in all early lessons, no matter what approach is being used.

Discriminating sounds which change meaning

1. Gattegno, it will be remembered, encourages early listening to tapes and disks of different languages, so that the student gradually comes to *recognize characteristics of the language he is learning*. This is useful practice in identification. The classroom teacher can introduce this element without much difficulty by playing tapes of Spanish songs and readings of poetry as background in the elementary classroom—in intervals before classes begin, while students are engaged on projects, over amplifiers to set the atmosphere for the beginning of a language laboratory session, or in a listening room or a listening corner of the classroom. This strategy encourages individual students to listen for the pleasure of the sounds. Some students will pick up parts of the songs, particularly refrains, purely by imitation as some opera singers do, thus learning to segment what they are hearing. This is pure perception, not reception of a message. Documentary films may be shown with the original Spanish sound track, even before students can be expected to understand it, to familiarize the ear with the sound-aura of the language. After hearing a great deal of the language in this way, students will be far less inhibited about pronouncing words so that they really sound Spanish.

2. Various types of *aural discrimination* exercises are given in Chapter 5. Some of these exercises can be worked into aural discrimination games and into competitions which involve listening practice. They should be continued at the intermediate level to keep students alert to sound distinctions which affect meaning.

C47 *Corríjame, por favor*

The teacher or groups of students prepare stories into which they work words which are inappropriate in the context but could be confused with the appropriate word if the listeners were not paying careful attention to sound distinctions. The student who has the best pronunciation or the teacher tells the story orally. A point is awarded to each student who notices an inappropriate word and is able to give the appropriate substitute with correct pronunciation.

In the sample text below, incorrect words are italicized and correct words are given in parentheses.

(I) Hacía tres horas que caminábamos por el *parco* (parque), y como empezábamos a tener *hombre* (hambre), decidimos entrar en un bar a comer *alga* (algo). Mientras nos tomábamos una *capa* (copa) de vino y un bocadillo de *jabón* (jamón), se *sintió* (sentó) a nuestra mesa un viejo que apenas conocíamos. Con voz *pasada* (pausada) y *traste* (triste), dijo: —Os quiero *encontrar* (contar) una cosa muy extraña que me *corrió* (ocurrió) ayer, amigos.

2. IMPOSING A STRUCTURE

In the second stage of perception, we identify in what we are hearing segments with distinctive structure—segments which seem to cohere. These segments may not be distinguishable by machine because it is at this stage that *we impose a structure on what we are hearing according to our knowledge of the grammatical system of the language.* The more we know of a language the more easily we can detect meaningful segments, such as noun phrases, verb phrases, or adverbial phrases. Our experience with our own language makes us expect such structural segmentation. For this reason, we may segment incorrectly at first with a language with a very different structure. (It is interesting to note that in psychological experiments subjects rarely report hearing ungrammatical sentences, and when asked to repeat ungrammatical utterances they correct them, which indicates that they are imposing known structures in constructing a message from the sound signal.)

This early segmentation determines what we will remember of the actual sound signal. It is a process of *selection.* The identification of "chunks,"[22] or syntactic groupings, reduces the load on our memory. Just as it is easier to remember nine numbers in three groups (382 965 421), so it is easier to remember *Yo lo veo/en el jardín/de la casa roja* as three syntactic groupings, or meaningful chunks, rather than as nine separate words, even if we are not sure of the lexical meanings of some of the words.

If we have segmented incorrectly or heard inaccurately, we will retain what we think we have heard, because we will have no further access to the sound signal after echoic memory has faded. (Echoic memory is estimated to last a few seconds only. It is during this interval that we can still readjust our segmentation, as discussed in C38.)

Practical application

Except in specialized courses, listening comprehension is not usually practiced in isolation from other language-learning activities. Some common classroom techniques help students develop their ability to hear language in organized chunks (or to segment according to syntactic groupings).

1. The *backward buildup* technique is frequently used in the memorization of conversation-facilitation dialogues. Each utterance to be memorized is divided into syntactically coherent segments. Students learn the last segment with correct end-of-utterance intonation, then the second-last followed by the last, and so on.

C48 Utterance 7 of C20 would be memorized in imitation of the model as follows:

cerca de la estación.

muy bueno cerca de la estación.

Hay un restorancito muy bueno cerca de la estación.

In this way students move from a new segment to a segment they already know, making for more confident recitation.[23]

2. *Dictation* is useful when well integrated with other learning activities. Dictation also involves listening to language segmented in meaningful chunks. Students in the early stages should be encouraged to repeat the segments to themselves before trying to write what they think they have heard. This gives the student practice in imposing a construction on the segment before he writes it, thus increasing his short-term retention of the segment.

3. Oral exercises which require students to vary syntactic segments purposefully provide practice in "hearing" language in syntactically coherent chunks. (See Chapter 4: G9-G21.)

4. *Information Search* (*Busquen la información*), a kind of spot dictation, gives practice in detecting syntactic cues to segmentation. In this activity, students are asked to listen to a sequence of sentences, writing down only the segments which answer certain questions with which they are supplied beforehand. The passage is given orally several times, and students write down the segments which answer particular questions as they comprehend them, that is, after the first, the second, or the third hearing. This encourages attentive listening for specific segments that fulfill certain syntactic functions, e.g., who? where? what?

C49 (E) Es el día 20 de abril. Son las nueve menos cuarto. Pablo se encuentra en el restaurante de la universidad. El se desayuna mientras lee un periódico. Una amiga suya, María del Carmen, entra al restaurante y se acerca a la mesa de Pablo. Este alza los ojos y, poniéndose de pie, le ofrece una silla a la muchacha.

Questions supplied	*Segments to be written*
1. ¿Qué fecha es?	es el 20 de abril
2. ¿Qué hora es?	son las nueve menos cuarto
3. ¿Dónde está Pablo?	en el restaurante de la universidad
4. ¿Qué hace él?	se desayuna y lee un periódico
5. ¿Quién llega?	María del Carmen
6. ¿Quién es ella?	es una amiga de él
7. ¿Qué hace ella?	se acerca a la mesa de Pablo
8. ¿Qué hace él?	se levanta y le ofrece una silla

5. *Hacer o no Hacer.* Inexperienced students need practice in listening for certain *syntactic signals* which must be recognized automatically in rapid speech because their presence or absence crucially affects meaning. One of these is the signal of *negation.* Students need to recognize that *no . . . sino* merely modifies meaning, whereas *no, nunca, jamás* reverse it.

In this game, which can be devised at quite an elementary level, students listen to a narration and mime or do not mime actions according to whether they are described affirmatively or negatively. The narration is given at normal speed with the elisions and omissions of familiar style. Students who make the wrong movements are progressively eliminated until only one student remains.

C50 (E and I) Based on C15.

Por la mañana no me levanto temprano.
Duermo hasta las ocho.
Por fin me despierto y miro por la ventana.
No me lavo en seguida todos los días.
A veces me cepillo el pelo durante unos diez minutos.
Nunca me afeito porque no tengo barba.
No me limpio los dientes sino por la noche.
Termino de asearme en algunos minutos.
Entonces abro la ventana y miro los pájaros.

A variation of this game, *¿Hoy o mañana?*, draws attention to *signals of tense.* Students mime an action in the present tense, but clap or tap with a pencil when they hear the *r* of the future tense or the auxiliary use of *ir* to indicate futurity. Students making wrong reactions are progressively eliminated.

C51 (E and I) Based on C15 and C50.

No nos levantaremos temprano.
Dormimos muchas veces hasta casi las ocho.

Nos despertaremos y entonces miraremos por la ventana.
Yo voy a lavarme en seguida, pero no me cepillaré el pelo.
Me limpio los dientes por la mañana, pero no me afeito antes del desayuno.
Mi hermano también se afeitará más tarde.

✳ Work out a game to train for recognition of the various question forms and interrogative intonation patterns.[24]

3. RECIRCULATING, SELECTING, RECODING FOR STORAGE

At the third stage of perception we recirculate material we are hearing through our cognitive system to relate earlier to later segments and *make the final selection* of what we will retain as the message. In this way, we follow a "line of thought." We then *recode what we have selected for storage in long-term memory.*

Rehearsal or recirculation of material perceived

1. Unfamiliar language elements which are being held in suspension and recirculated while decisions are being made as to the composition of the entire message impose a *heavy load on the short-term memory.* Sometimes the short-term memory becomes overloaded and some of these segments have to be discarded in order to leave room for the absorption of new segments. It should not surprise us, therefore, if inexperienced listeners, at an elementary or even intermediate stage, declare that they understood everything as they were listening but are unable to recall what they understood. At this stage students may be able to recognize from multiple-choice items or true-false questions details of what they heard, whereas they would not be able to give a full account of the message without this help.

2. *Many different aspects of a listening text may be retained* by students, and these may not always be those elements the teacher expected. Students often need some guidance as to the facets of a message on which they should concentrate for the purpose of the exercise. This guidance in selection, which relieves the memory of some of the burden of detail, can be supplied by preliminary discussion or questions (given orally, or in writing).

3. At the elementary stage, students may be provided with questions with multiple-choice items *before* they begin listening. They should be encouraged to mark a tentative choice during the first hearing and confirm this on the second or third hearing. Teachers should remember that this method combines listening with reading. They should take care to see that the multiple-choice items supplied are short and expressed in language simple enough for the level of the students concerned. The items should not reproduce verbatim any sections of the material for listening practice, since this makes the task merely one of recognition, not comprehension.

4. Although some people consider that providing written questions is a *mixing of modalities* which raises doubts as to whether one is testing listening comprehension only, several other facts must be kept in mind.

a. *Oral questions* cannot be absorbed during the process of listening to other material. (Psychological studies show that we filter out competing oral stimuli when the material to which we are listening demands careful attention.)

b. Oral questions given before or after the listening material add a further aural exercise to the one being evaluated. (Students may have understood the exercise, but not the questions on it.)

c. Oral questions asked *after* a listening exercise of some length require the retention of details over a period of time. They therefore test not only immediate comprehension but long-term retention. The same observation may be made about oral questions asked *before* listening to an oral narrative, or dialogue, as a guide to selection. These will need to be repeated after the material has been heard. Otherwise, we are evaluating not only listening comprehension but also retention and recall. The use of oral questions is, therefore, more appropriate at the intermediate level. (For the special problems of short listening-comprehension items, see Designing Multiple-Choice Items for Listening Comprehension below.)

d. At the elementary level, the problem of oral versus written questions is often solved by the *use of pictures*. Students are asked to circle the letter corresponding to the picture which best represents what they are hearing. They may also be asked to complete a diagram, or picture, according to oral directions or to mime what they are hearing.

5. When the attention of students is directed to particular aspects of the listening task they will not retain in their memory material they do not require for this specific purpose, except incidentally. With C47, for instance, students may very well comprehend as they proceed and make correct decisions about the inappropriate items and appropriate replacements, yet still not be able to say at the end what the complete narration was about. After the C47 exercise has been completed, the passage should be read as a whole, with the appropriate replacements, as practice in comprehension of a complete narrative.

Note that since *the processes involved in fluent reading and in listening are similar,*[25] students will have the same problem in reading. A common test of reading has been to ask students to read a passage aloud with careful attention to diction, phrasing, and intonation. A student performing well on this task will not necessarily be able to answer questions on the content of what he has just read, without first being given the opportunity to reread the passage silently. With his attention concentrated on identifying meaningful segments, interrelating these in sentences distinguished by certain intonational patterns, and pronouncing individual words and groups of words comprehensibly, the student may have engaged his cognitive system in too much activity to be able also to recirculate segments and recode them for long-term storage.

6. When students have selected segments for the construction of the message they are extracting, they will no longer have access to the rejected segments (unless these were recirculated as alternatives and retained because the student was in doubt). If students have misunderstood the tenor of the message, the solution is not to question them further in an attempt to extract the correct message. They should be given some indication of where they misinterpreted the message and the opportunity to hear it again, so that they can construct a new version of it.

7. It is a mistake to make all listening comprehension exercises tests with strict limitations. Students should be *allowed to listen to material as often as they need to* until they are able to "hear" and retain the content. Relaxed conditions, with no feelings of apprehension, are essential, since emotional tension greatly affects our ability to "hear" a message. Students should have frequent opportunities to listen to material purely for the pleasure of comprehension without the threat of grading.

8. *The recirculation of material in the memory takes place during the pauses in speech,* so the pauses are vital. In normal speech, pauses are lengthened by hesitation expressions (*pues . . . bueno . . .* etc.), whereas in edited speech, or careful speech, these extensions of the pauses are missing. This allows less processing time for the listener. Speech which appears "too fast" to the inexperienced listener should be "slowed down" by lengthening slightly the pauses between segments, rather than by slowing down the delivery within the segments. The latter procedure distorts the natural sounds of the language by lengthening vowels, creating diphthongs, eliminating customary linking, and so on.

Recoding of material for storage in long-term memory

We store what we hear in long-term memory in a simplified form. In common parlance, *we retain the gist of what was said,* that is, the basic semantic information, rather than the actual statements with all their complications of structure.

C52 We may hear the following discussion of differences of formality in social relations in Spain and the United States.

CASTILLO   La cosa es muy complicada, porque, por otro lado, las relaciones entre profesores y alumnos son mucho más informales aquí que lo que son en España, porque el profesor allá es, como decía Unamuno, "su majestad el catedrático". Y yo te digo, de verdad, yo he tenido—casi ninguna relación con los catedráticos. Yo tenía un señor que me dirigía mis estudios, y sin embargo, con él era el señor don Tal y Cual, y siempre en una posición muy respetuosa. Cada vez que yo le iba a visitar a su oficina me sentaba así, y jamás me sentaría así, nunca, ¿no? Y siempre era así, señor Tal, señor Cual. Y por otro lado aquí, en cambio, hay una distancia enorme, que dentro de la informalidad ésta americana, de que uno puede poner los pies en cima de la mesa, no hay ninguna . . . ningún contacto verdadero. Parece que todo está legislado por una serie de normas no escritas, en las que uno nunca puede hablar, por ejemplo, de que mi esposa me engaña con otro—eso no se puede decir, ¿no? Mientras que allí se podría decir eso, con esta especie de forma tan . . . tan . . . circunspecta— con la forma circunspecta uno puede hablar de cosas más reales. Esa es la gran diferencia que noto yo entre las dos sociedades, que poniendo los pies encima de la mesa o viniendo en pantalones cortos, se mantiene una serie de distancias que se notan aquí después de cuatro o cinco años de convivir con gente. . . . Yo voy a casa del profesor Fulano y aquello es como un té en casa de mis tías, las de Burgos, en el cual nos sentamos así. . . . Eso es lo que yo noto, ¿no? Una . . . como si las dos cosas viajaran por su cuenta y obedecen a leyes totalmente distintas, ¿no?[26]

C53 If asked what this passage was about, a student might come up with a series of statements like these:

Castillo habla de las relaciones sociales en España.
Las relaciones sociales en España son muy diferentes de las relaciones sociales en los Estados Unidos.
En España los alumnos respetan mucho a los profesores.
Castillo mantenía una actitud muy respetuosa con su orientador.
En cambio, en los Estados Unidos, hay mucha confianza y falta de etiqueta.
Sin embargo, se mantiene la distancia social.

Commentary

1. In reducing what he heard to a set of factual statements, the student has produced *a series of simple active affirmative declarative sentences* (SAAD's to the psychologist). This is the basic type of sentence in most grammars. Facts in this form are the easiest to recall because all relationships are reduced to subject-verb-object, with some adverbial modifications.

2. A set of basic utterances like these is quite *redundant* in that much information is repeated from sentence to sentence, thus providing asso-

ciational tags which make it easier to retrieve all the information about any one aspect, as in the following questions:

C54 Cómo son las relaciones entre los alumnos y los profesores en España?

Las relaciones entre los alumnos y los profesores en España son más formales que en los Estados Unidos. Al visitar a un profesor, el estudiante español se sienta en una posición respetuosa y nunca pone los pies encima de la mesa.

Or: ¿No hay diferencias entre las relaciones que hay entre los profesores y alumnos, en España y en los Estados Unidos?

Sí, que hay muchas diferencias entre los dos países. En los Estados Unidos, las relaciones son menos formales. En España, por otro lado, el alumno tiene que tener una actitud más respetuosa.

3. Note that *a certain amount of the information in the original has been dropped.* Without looking back to check the details, our reader, like the student listener, will probably not recall, for instance, that the Spanish informant quoted Unamuno as referring to the professor as *"su majestad el catedrático"* or that the informant was proposing a comparison of relations between students and professors in Spain and the United States as a subject of discussion. In preparing questions which require retrieval of information from long-term memory, teachers should keep in mind how this information is stored and *focus on the central line of thought and the basic facts,* rather than on peripheral detail.

Where there is ambiguity, the listener, by reducing the message to its basic elements, clarifies interpretatively relationships between what he has assimilated and what he is hearing.

C55 The listener hears:

María del Pilar le sugiere a su prometido que se saquen unas fotografías en el jardín.

He recodes this information for long-term storage as
A. María del Pilar le sugiere algo a su prometido.
   El va a sacar unas fotografías en el jardín.
or B. María del Pilar le sugiere algo a su prometido.
   Ella va a sacar unas fotografías en el jardín.

If he has selected interpretation A for recoding for storage, this is what he will recall and he may even argue forcefully that this is what was said, as listeners often do in native-language situations. After he has constructed interpretation A from what he has heard, interpretation B will be accessible to him only if a contiguous segment forces him to readjust interpretation A while he is still recirculating what he heard through his short-term memory.

Since psychological experiments and empirical intuition seem to indicate that recoding is basic to long-term memory storage, *we can help our students develop efficiency in listening comprehension,* and in retention and recall, by:

1. presenting them with an outline of the main ideas in basic SAAD sentences before they listen to a structurally complicated version;

2. by asking them to state in basic SAAD sentences what they have retained of a listening comprehension exercise;

3. by asking questions on the text which require SAAD sentences as answers.

The teacher's expectations

We cannot expect students to extract and retain from foreign-language listening materials more than they do in the native language. Experiments have shown that average-ability adults recall a very low percentage of the possible information from broadcast talks (about 20 per cent when they were not aware that they were to be tested, 28 per cent when they knew they were to be tested). Other studies suggest that college students comprehend about half of the basic matter of lectures. The degree of listening efficiency on any particular occasion depends, of course, on the type of material and its organization, the interest the material holds for the listener, the way it is presented (speed, audibility, variations in tone of voice, situational relevance), and even such factors as the acoustics of the room and the emotional state or physical fatigue of the listener. Nevertheless, "evidence on the ability of people to be trained in listening makes it clear that many people listen below capacity"[27] in the native language. We may expect a higher degree of concentrated attention to a foreign-language listening exercise because students are aware of its difficulty for them, but *we must not look for total or near-total recall of detail.* In order to correct any unrealistic expectations, it is often useful to try a listening comprehension exercise out on a native speaker before giving it to foreign-language learners.

✻ Reduce the basic facts in the following text to SAAD's and write some questions which would extract from the listener this series of related facts, rather than a few isolated details.

C56

MILTON ¿Qué representa el tuteo en el contexto social español contemporáneo? ¿Cuándo empieza a tutearse la gente? ¿Quiénes se tutean?

MONTSERRAT Es muy complejo, esto. O sea, en principio, se tutean personas de la misma edad, hasta los veinticinco años. Después, se tutean compañeros de trabajo. Por ejemplo, los profesores, es normal que se tuteen, aunque uno sea recién licenciado y el otro compañero tenga sesenta años— normalmente. Ah . . . ¿Qué más? Y después el tuteo empieza, en otra escala, cuando una amistad—no sé—el tuteo empieza cuando se quiere romper una barrera social, quizá, o una barrera de amistad—no se cómo decirte cuando se podría romper . . . El *usted* . . .

MANUEL Como tú has dicho, hay dos barreras principales, la edad y la posición social, ¿no? A la diferencia de edad, me refiero. Porque dentro de la misma posición social un chico de veinte años, tú lo has dicho, claro, no tutea a una persona de cuarenta o cincuenta, ¿no? Un obrero no tutea, naturalmente, al patrón, ¿no?, o al jefe del taller, etcétera. . .

MONTSERRAT Sí, pero el patrón no puede tutear al obrero. . .

MANUEL Ah, sí, sí, bueno—ahí naturalmente hay un juego social . . . El patrón no lo hace.

RAFAEL Claro, hay un matiz estilístico en el *usted*—sobretodo en el uso del *usted*—o sea, que el término marcado en la oposición sería el *usted*. Cuando uno quiere mantener una distancia, como lo dices tú, entre el patrón y el obrero, puede haber el doble juego, o sea, si el patrón quiere mantener el respeto del obrero, le continuará tratando de *usted*. Yo, en las clases nuestras, yo—para mí me suena muy mal que los estudiantes entre sí se traten de *usted*— por eso les he dicho que la primera regla que tienen que aprender es que, entre los estudiantes, ellos tienen que tratarse de tú. Porque suena mal—a mí me suena mal. Así que yo creo que es mejor hacer ciertas caracterizaciones negativas del uso de *usted,* más que las positivas, porque depende, como ha dicho Montserrat, depende de muchos factores. Por ejemplo, cuando yo iba a la escuela primaria, yo fui tratado de usted desde el primer día. . .

MONTSERRAT   Yo también—tenía seis años—que me dijeran señorita. . .

MANUEL   Así es, siempre.

RAFAEL   Eso es . . . es . . . un matiz para instilar el respeto de la clase, el respeto del aula, ¿no? Yo recuerdo que cuando te decían: —¡Oye, tú!—era una cosa distinta—o resultaba una expresión cariñosa por parte del maestro, o si no, resultaba algo despectivo.

MONTSERRAT   Yo no he tratado a mis alumnos siempre de *tú* en el instituto, pero a estos los veo igual . . . y les trato de *tú* también. . . .

MILTON   Y ellos, ¿cómo te tratan?

MONTSERRAT   Ellos me tratan de *usted*. . . .

MANUEL   Para el estudiante norteamericano, aunque se le explique de todas maneras, es difícil, porque no tiene la vivencia de nuestra sociedad. Y yo aquí he visto a un estudiante graduado decirle al jefe del departamento *tú*—y yo me he quedado sorprendido, naturalmente, ¿no? Hablarle a alguien que . . .

RAFAEL   Muchas veces es porque no saben, o no se acuerdan de la forma del *usted*—recurren al *tú*, ¿no?

MILTON   . . . Creen muchos de nuestros estudiantes que con el nombre de pila automáticamente va el *tú*, ¿no?, lo cual no es verdad. Hay un matiz. . . .

RAFAEL   Eso es muy corriente en las relaciones entre patrones y obreros. Se dice a un obrero que se llame Pedro: —Oiga, Pedro, ¿a dónde va usted?—Sobretodo si el obrero es mayor de edad . . .

MILTON   Y el obrero, sin embargo, le dirá . . .

CASTILLO   . . . don Fulano.[28]

C. Strategies of perceptual segmentation

For the psychologist Bever, "the internal logical relations are a major determiner of perceptual segmentation in speech processing.[29] This view aligns well with that of the linguist G. Lakoff of the generative semantics group, that logical categories and logical classes provide the natural basis for grammar and, therefore, ultimately of language use.[30] In other words, since our experience of the real world has taught us to expect such functions as agents, actions, objects, and place, time, and manner modifications,[31] we identify these in what we hear.

Bever has identified four strategies[32] which we seem to employ in the perception of speech.

1. First of all, we tend to segment what we hear into sequences which could form *actor-action-object . . . modifier* relations. This segmentation strategy Bever calls Strategy A. Clearly, for this elementary segmentation, we need to be able to identify, at least approximately, syntactic groups. Fortunately, languages generally supply a certain number of surface indicators of function, or syntactic cues which we use to separate out different clauses within the sentence.[33] This aspect of perceptual segmentation has already been discussed as stage two of the active process of constructing a message, and exercises have been proposed for developing this ability in a foreign language.

2. In English at least, we learn to expect the first $N . . . V . . . (N)$ (that is, noun . . . verb . . . optional noun) *to be the main clause* (that is, to set out the overriding idea of the sentence) unless morphemes like *if, when,* or *before* warn us that we are dealing with a subordinate clause. This segmentation Strategy B carries over to Spanish, to a large extent, although this would not necessarily be so for all languages. The student needs to learn to interpret rapidly such cues as *si, cuando, antes que, aunque,* which indicate subordination, and, at the advanced level, to recognize such deviations from the usual pattern as the not uncommon sentence opening segment *past participle + noun phrase,* which he might encounter in more formal listening materials, e.g., *terminada la reunión, nos fuimos a cenar; arreglado el horario, vamos a la cuestión de los exámenes.*

3. In applying Strategy C, we seek the meaning by *combining the lexical items in the most plausible way.* Thus, *the dog bit the man* is easily comprehended, whereas *the man bit the dog,* not being consistent with our normal experiences of the real world, gives us pause. We may "hear" it as *the man was bitten by the dog,* but be forced to reprocess it as subject-verb-object when later segments make it clear that something unusual has happened. Alternatively, we may ask the speaker to repeat his statement.

4. Sometimes there is no specific semantic information to guide us in assigning relationships. We then fall back on a primary functional labeling strategy, based on the apparent order of lexical items in a sentence—Strategy D. We assume that any *noun-verb-(noun), NV(N), sequence* represents the relations *actor-action-object.* It is for this reason that we understand the active construction *the dog chased the cat* more quickly than the passive form *the cat was chased by the dog* which will often be heard as *the cat chased the dog,* especially by children. In the case of a passive of this type, which allows for reversal of roles, later information will cause us to pause and reprocess the utterance syntactically. We then search for cues (passive form of the verb, agent *by*-phrase) which indicate the order *logical object-verb-logical subject.*

SEMANTIC-SYNTACTIC DECODING

Schlesinger has called the process of relying at first on semantic expectations and resorting to syntactic processing only in doubtful cases *semantic-syntactic decoding*.[34] In summary, we perceive the semantic cues and rapidly assign these such roles as actor (or experiencer or instrument), action, object, or modifier according to our knowledge of the real world. It is when our initial interpretation does not fit into the developing message that we pause to analyze syntactic cues to function.

Because of this initial tendency in listening to take the easier road of semantic decoding, students with an *extensive vocabulary* can often interpret a great deal of what they hear by sheer word recognition and logical reasoning. A person listening to a news broadcast might identify the following lexical items:

C57 . . . según . . . trascendió . . . Lima . . . informes . . . Arequipa . . . setecientos . . . kilómetros . . . sudeste . . . capital . . . desde aviones . . . podido apreciar . . . habitantes . . . provincias . . . cuatro mil metros . . . empezado . . . emigrar . . . zonas . . . bajas . . . catastróficas . . . nevadas . . . nunca . . . vistas . . . región.

With this basic information, his knowledge of similar situations, and his powers of inference, the student might be able to deduce the essence of the following facts:

C58 Según se trascendió hoy en Lima, Perú, informes procedentes de la ciudad de Arequipa, setecientos cincuenta kilómetros al sudeste de esta capital, indican que desde aviones y helicópteros se ha podido apreciar que los habitantes de las provincias andinas a más de cuatro mil metros habían empezado a emigrar hacia zonas más bajas ante las catastróficas consecuencias de intensas nevadas nunca antes vistas en esta región.[35]

✻ As an exercise in introspection, try to remember which of Strategies A-D you employed in your perception of the meaning of C57.

AURAL RECOGNITION VOCABULARY

Since combining lexical items in a plausible way plays such an important role in listening comprehension, attention should be given to building an extensive aural recognition vocabulary.

For many students, particularly above the elementary level, the greater part of their vocabulary is acquired in association with reading and writing.

It is not surprising, therefore, that many of them have problems in recognizing by ear the words they already know in graphic form. They also have difficulty recognizing words derived from these, and even the cognates and the rapidly disseminated vocabulary of contemporary technology, science, politics, and social diversions (*el oleoducto, la ciencia-ficción, la cultura de masas, la discoteca y el fotorromance*). Many of these terms are pronounced in a sufficiently different fashion in Spanish to appear novel to the inexperienced ear. In C58, for instance, even /siudádearekípa/ when spoken at normal speed may not be obvious to a visually trained person, while phonemic groups like /seapodídoapresiár/ and /sónasmásbáxas/ elude recognition, and /prosedénte/ may not be recognized as a derivative of /prosedér/.

To develop confidence in aural recognition of words originally encountered in graphic form, students need to understand and apply constantly the rules of sound-symbol correspondence in Spanish. Although these rules may at times seem a little complicated (see R27), they are, on the whole, very regular. Knowledge of such rules often helps a student to visualize the probable spelling of a seemingly new word and so to relate it to what he knows. This is an ability which is important to a person who has been accustomed to learning the language graphically or who by modality preference is visually oriented.

All kinds of practice techniques and competitions can foster transfer from visual to aural recognition and from aural to visual.

1. Clearly *comprehensible pronunciation of all new words* should be expected as they are encountered, so that the students' ears are kept tuned to a high pitch. This is particularly important beyond the elementary level, where students and teacher often relax their efforts in this regard. It is no wonder that such students fail to recognize words pronounced so differently from the classroom norm.

2. Flashcards should be made of *groups of words which follow certain rules* of sound-symbol correspondence, and competitions organized with points allotted to the first person who gives the correct pronunciation for the series, e.g.,

llegué, pegué, seguí;
lado, dado, amado;
llora, llave, llanta.

Later, more rigorous competitions can be conducted with the words isolated from the series and presented in short sentences.

3. Conversely, students should hear words in short sentences and be asked to identify *which* of the *spellings* on two cards represents the word they heard, e.g.,

/kayó/   calló, cayó;
/kása/   casa, caza.

4. Students should be shown cards of words in *special problem groups* and drilled in their pronunciation, e.g.,

/sión/ or /θión/   nación, revolución, encarnación;

/k/   quedar, quitar, quemar.

5. Spelling bees (*concursos de ortografía*) may be conducted to arouse enthusiasm for a high level of performance. Words are given in sentences, then repeated in isolation, or in short word-groups, for the student to write down, e.g.,

El extranjero llegó al pueblo—*extranjero*

Se baila mucho en la plazuela—*la plazuela.*

Those making mistakes are progressively eliminated until a champion is found.

6. These may be paralleled by pronunciation bees (*concursos de pronunciación*). Sentences are flashed on the screen or wall by overhead projector, or are shown on flashcards, and elimination contests are conducted for acceptable pronunciation, e.g.,

No *habló* contigo. (Stress position: /abló/)

Note: Items for both 5 and 6 should be kept to words students may be expected to meet.

7. *Spot dictation* is useful at the elementary level (see R26); continuous dictation passages at higher levels.

8. If students are to understand radio news broadcasts and documentary films they should be given regular training in the aural identification of the *contemporary vocabulary for matters of international preoccupation*, e.g.,

/lakontaminaθiónatmosférika/   *la contaminación atmosférica,*

/laθienθiafikθión/   *la ciencia-ficción.*

Some people will object that the above recommendations relate the aural too closely to the graphic and that aural vocabulary should be learned only by ear. This may be advisable for specialized aural courses, although, even in this case, student modality preferences must be allowed some play. Most intermediate and advanced foreign-language classes have multiple aims. Students who have been trained to depend on visual information need the liberating realization that there are predictable relationships between the pronunciation of a word and its written form. In this way, what they have learned in one modality can become available to them in the other, and the students' limited processing capacity will be used more economically and efficiently.

Macro or micro?

With listening, as with all other aspects of language learning, we must keep in view the final goal of *macro-language use* (the ability to use language holistically for normal life-purposes). *Micro-language learning* (the learning of elements of language and their potential combinations) is only a means leading to this end.

In the macro context, listening can be evaluated only by response: How does the listener react emotionally? How does he respond—verbally or by action? Does he do what he has been asked or told? Does he use the information offered? Does he fill the supportive role of the listener? (In other words, does he utter, at appropriate intervals, agreeing or consoling interpolations, exclamations of surprise, or tut-tutting noises—such expressions in Spanish as *¿Sí? ¿Verdad? Así es. ¡Caramba! ¡Hombre!*) Does he laugh or smile at the right moments? Is he absorbed by what he is hearing?

Because micro-language learning is more easily assessed than macro-language use, there is a tendency to think of the evaluation of listening comprehension in terms of multiple-choice and true/false items. Certainly these play a useful part in directing the students' efforts in listening and helping them assess the accuracy of their comprehension. The importance of understanding fine detail at crucial points in some aural tasks cannot be ignored, since puzzlement can cause an emotional or cognitive block, which overloads channel capacity so that the student loses the thread. On the other hand, there are students who tackle aural comprehension almost heuristically with considerable success. Students who can cope with macro-language use practically from the start may be wasting their time on micro-tests of detail. Other students need the developmental, step-by-step approach and their needs should not be neglected. Even for the latter, however, functional comprehension in real situations must be the ultimate criterion.

For these reasons, listening comprehension is particularly suited to individualized arrangements, with students working at their own level and their own pace. Teachers should assemble all the materials they can find into *developmental listening kits,* each containing micro-training exercises for particular purposes, but culminating in a macro-activity. Students should be encouraged to work their way through a series of these kits in their own manner and at their own pace. Taking one's own time is important in listening, where individuals require differing lengths of time for processing. Students who are capable of doing so should be encouraged to jump from macro-activity to macro-activity, until listening to the foreign language becomes for them natural and effortless. Eventually most students will reach the stage where their listening is completely integrated with communication activities of the kind outlined in Chapter 2.

ASSESSMENT OF MACRO-LANGUAGE USE

We must place the student in a situation where listening comprehension plays an essential role, then see how he copes. Macro-language evaluation should be related to the normal uses of listening in life-situations:

1. as part of a purposeful communicative interchange;
2. for receiving direction or instructions;
3. for obtaining information;
4. for the pleasure of an activity like watching a play, a film, a TV show, or a fashion parade, or listening to a sports commentary, a newscast, or group discussion on the radio;
5. for participating in social gatherings (listening to small talk, listening to others conversing, and so on).

Any item in the B and D sections of the *Chart of Listening Comprehension Activities,* C67, is appropriate for macro-language assessment.

ASSESSMENT OF MICRO-LANGUAGE LEARNING

Many aspects of micro-language learning have already been discussed in this chapter (discrimination of sounds which change meaning; recognition of intonation patterns, syntactic segments, and word groups with high frequency of occurrence; aural vocabulary recognition). Any activity in the A and C sections of the *Chart of Listening Comprehension Activities,* C67, can be adapted to micro-language testing.

One of the commonest forms of assessment of this developmental phase of listening comprehension is the use of *multiple-choice questions,* yet the preparation of this type of test holds many pitfalls for the inexperienced.

The test items often consist of *short questions or comments in isolation,* like those in C59, for which students choose appropriate rejoinders (sometimes completions) from multiple-choice options.

C59 1. ¿A dónde vas ahora?
     2. ¿Qué hora es, por favor?
     3. ¿Qué pasa allí?

In natural interaction, there is a context for such short utterances which helps in the interpretation of the fleeting sounds, e.g., place, time, relationship of the person speaking to the person addressed, previous utterance, gesture of pointing or eyes turned in a certain direction, facial expression of exasperation, surprise, or expectancy. If the person addressed is taken off-guard, the interlocutor frequently makes a circumstantial comment before repeating the question, thus bringing it into focus, e.g.,

C60 A. ¿A dónde vas?
     B. ¿Cómo?
     A. Es demasiado temprano. ¿A dónde vas ahora?

Materials writers often seen not to realize that isolated short utterances are more difficult to "hear" correctly than longer, contextualized segments.

In real life, the responses which would actually occur to such short, non-contextualized utterances may well be some of the options considered "incorrect" by the writer of the multiple-choice exercise. Choosing the "appropriate" response then becomes a question of reading the mind of the item-writer or the corrector of the exercise.

C61 Circle the letter corresponding to the most appropriate response to the question you hear.

Recorded voice: ¿A dónde vas ahora?
  A. Acabo de pasar por el piso de Castillo.
  B. Al correo. ¿No quieres venir conmigo?
  C. Voy a escribir unas cartas.
  D. Espero a un amigo.

Any of the above is an "appropriate response" in a certain context.
  A. *Acabo de pasar por el piso de Castillo.* (I may be walking along the street, but I'm not *going* anywhere. I'm *coming back.*)
  B. *Al correo. ¿No quieres venir conmigo?* (The "appropriate response" anticipated.)
  C. *Voy a escribir unas cartas.* (I'm not going anywhere this morning. I've got far too much to do here at home.)
  D. *Espero a un amigo.* (I may look as if I'm waiting for the lights to change so that I can cross the road, but I'm not.)

As any experienced teacher knows, students who dispute the grading of such short multiple-choice items can often justify their choices quite logically. Some kind of context should be built into every listening item.

C62 (Cf. C59.)

  1. ¡Ya te pones el abrigo! ¿A dónde vas ahora?
  2. Tengo hambre. ¿Qué hora es, por favor?
  3. ¿Qué pasa allí? ¿Al otro lado de la calle?

Students should also be given opportunities from time to time to select more than one "appropriate response," adding a brief note indicating a possible context. This encourages projection of expectations of the kind provided also in *Situation Tapes* (C33).
The following fully contextualized passage for listening would actually be easier than a short, non-contextualized utterance (if we exclude clichés and sentences students have heard over and over again in class):

C63 (1) *Recorded voice:*

Hacía mucho calor y el agua estaba fresca. Por todas partes se veía a mucha gente bañándose. Pablo estaba acostado en la playa y parecía jugar con la arena. Lejos, un barco partía hacia la isla. ¿Qué hacía Pablo?

> *Choices supplied:*   A. Esperaba un barco.
> B. Se bañaba en el mar.
> C. Descansaba en la playa.
> D. Construía un castillo de arena.

The recorded passage contains a number of associated concepts which provide clues to the correct answer. The student who has understood some parts clearly, but not all, has more opportunity in a longer passage like this to reconstruct by conjecture those sections he did not comprehend fully.

DESIGNING MULTIPLE-CHOICE ITEMS FOR LISTENING COMPREHENSION

Many of the problems of multiple-choice items discussed in Chapter 7 in the section *Assisting and Assessing Reading Comprehension* (p. 217) apply also to multiple-choice items for assessing listening comprehension. There must be no ambiguity in the choices. The correct choice should not repeat word for word some sentence in the listening text. The correct choice should not depend on comprehension or non-comprehension of one unusual vocabulary item. Where there is a series of questions on one passage, the correct choices should not form an obvious sequence which students can detect without understanding the passage (a later item can sometimes supply the answer sought in an earlier question). Care must be taken to see that the items do not test powers of logical deduction, or ability to recognize exact paraphrases, rather than actual comprehension of the passage.

Apart from the general problems of preparing multiple-choice questions, items for listening comprehension present problems peculiar to this modality. The items have to be prepared in such a way that they give a clear indication of what the student "heard," that is, constructed personally from the sound signal. The item-writer must be able to imagine himself in the place of the neophyte and reconstruct what the latter may be "hearing." For these reasons, it is difficult for a native speaker to construct suitable choices for foreign-language listeners, unless he has had long experience with their particular problems.

It is useful to analyze the types of confusions one is anticipating on the part of the listeners by the choices one proposes. If there is no predictable rationale for a certain choice, it can be considered a "donkey item" which will be chosen only by a student who interpreted almost nothing of the sound signal. There should never be more than one "donkey item" in each set and this particular item must be very plausible, if it is to be selected at all. Unless it has some obvious relationship to the rest of the set, or re-echoes closely what was heard, even the donkeys will shy away from it.

C64 (E) *Recorded voice:* ¿Os acostasteis temprano anoche?

A. Sí, hoy cenamos a las siete.
B. Sí, nos acostamos siempre a las once.
C. Sí, ayer nos fuimos a dormir a eso de las ocho.
D. Sí, vosotros os acostáis muy temprano todas las noches.

Commentary

A. The student who chooses A identifies

1. the pronoun *os* and the verbal ending *-asteis,* requiring the answer *nosotros* (this eliminates D);

2. the adverb *temprano,* which does not match with the adverbial expression *a las once* (this eliminates B).

3. However, failure to recognize the verbal stem *acost-,* coupled with possible confusion between *anoche* and a hypothetical *hoy por la noche* leads to erroneous choice of A.

B. The student who chooses B identifies

1. the pronoun *os* and the verbal ending *-asteis,* requiring the answer *nosotros* (this eliminates D);

2. the verb stem *acost-* (this eliminates A).

3. However, failure to recognize the semantic similarity between *anoche* and *ayer* eliminates C. This may or may not be reinforced by failure to recognize the contrast between *temprano* and *a las once,* which would otherwise preclude choice of B.

C is the correct response.

It expresses the main concept in nearly synonymous terms (*acostarse— irse a dormir*), thus testing the apprehension of meaning, and contains a response element which is consistent with the question element (*temprano—a eso de las ocho*). This avoids the possibility that the student is not comprehending but selecting the choice with the most items in identical form.

D. The student has not understood the question, but the D response matches his audial image of parts he perceived (*os . . . acostasteis . . . temprano . . . noche . . .*) and seems plausible, so he chooses D, which is a "donkey item" in that it makes no pretense at answering the question.

C65 (I) La cocina española se halla situada bajo el signo del olivo. Este, por una parte, es alegoría de la paz, y por otra impregna todo el arte culinaria del Mediterráneo. El vino, como bebida, y el aceite de oliva, en calidad de condimento, son los dos líquidos que se hallan en permanencia en el arte del buen comer español.[36]

A. El vino y el aceite de oliva ocupan un lugar muy importante en la cocina española.

B. Todos los buenos platos españoles incluyen olivas y vino.

C. Como condimentos, el vino y el aceite se hallan en permanencia en la cocina española.

D. La cocina mediterránea se encuentra bajo el signo de la paz, y por eso emplea el aceite de oliva.

Commentary

An additional source of error in this example may be the student's lack of knowledge of the Spanish way of life.

A. The correct choice draws elements from different sentences and requires comprehension of a sequence of ideas.

B. The student who chooses B has a vague idea of what the passage he has heard is all about, but he makes an unwarranted generalization about the central point of that passage. Since this type of student has a rather elementary knowledge of Spanish, this choice is deliberately constructed by using only words commonly found in elementary courses. Furthermore, he confuses *olivo* "olive tree" and *oliva* "olive," which makes him ready to take the word *olivas* as further indication that B is the correct choice.

C. This choice echoes parts of the passage the student has heard (. . . *se hallan en permanencia, . . . la cocina española*). This may cause the student to disregard the crucial phrase, *como condimentos,* thus leading to selection of this item.

D. The student choosing D has not followed the line of thought but has recognized several words and phrases. His knowledge of Spanish, however, may not allow him to do anything more than to piece together parts of what he has heard so as to construct a meaningful reply.

✱ *Analyze* in similar fashion the anticipated reactions of the students who will choose the various alternatives in the following comprehension exercise.

C66 ¿Se han marchado tan temprano los oficiales?

A. Sí, les gusta marchar por la mañana.
B. Sí, van a marchar muy temprano.
C. Sí, tenían mucha prisa.
D. Sí, queremos marcharnos temprano.

C67 *Chart of listening comprehension activities*[37]
In the following chart, the activities are divided into four learning stages:

A. *Identification:* perception of sounds and phrases; identifying these directly and holistically with meaning.

B. *Identification and selection without retention:* listening for the pleasure of comprehension, extracting sequential meanings, without being expected to demonstrate comprehension through active use of language.

C. *Identification and guided selection with short-term retention:*[38] students are given some prior indication of what they are to listen for; they demonstrate their comprehension immediately in some active fashion.

D. *Identification and selection with long-term retention:* students demonstrate their comprehension, or use the material they have comprehended, after the listening experience has been completed; or they engage in an activity which requires recall of material learned some time previously.

Elementary Level (E)

A. IDENTIFICATION (E)
Macro
1. Listening to tapes of various languages to detect the language one is learning.
2. Listening to songs and poems for the pleasure of the sounds (in classroom, listening room, or listening corner).
3. Songs and poems amplified in language laboratory for atmosphere.
4. Hearing original sound tracks of documentary films before being able to understand them.

Micro
5. Aural discrimination exercises.
6. Short-phrase discrimination with picture.
7. Listening to segments of dialogue to be learned.

8. Responding with miming actions to segments from dialogue learned or from classroom conversation.

9. Responding with flashcards to names of letters of the alphabet.

10. Backward buildup in imitation of a model (C48).

B. IDENTIFICATION AND SELECTION WITHOUT RETENTION (E)

11. Games involving miming of words and phrases learned.

12. Listening to conversation-facilitation dialogues, songs, or poems already learned.

13. Listening to retelling of stories already read, reacting in some way to variations from the original.

14. Listening to a conversation which is a variant of a dialogue studied.

15. Listening to an anecdote based on reading material studied.

16. Teacher gives some background information on a topic, then tells an anecdote, or describes an experience.

With visual

17. Listening to description of pictures or slides.

18. Listening to an anecdote, story, or dialogue illustrated with a flannelboard.

19. Listening to a *Show and Tell* oral report.

With action

20. Total physical response activity or *Simón dice* (C45–C46).

21. Obeying classroom instructions.

22. Listening to simple narration, raising hands whenever a color (or occupation, or kind of food, etc.) is mentioned.

23. *Lotería Alfabética:* Letters of alphabet called randomly; each student checks against word in front of him; first student with complete word wins.

24. *Lotería:* Numbers called randomly; students check numbers on their cards; first student with all numbers correctly checked wins.

C. IDENTIFICATION AND GUIDED SELECTION
WITH SHORT-TERM RETENTION (E)
With visual

25. Discrimination of numbers, dates, and times of day by pairing with multiple-choice items, clockfaces, lists of famous events, or flight schedules.

26. Learning a dialogue with vanishing techniques (see *Dialogue Exploitation* in Chapter 1, p. 33).

27. True/false questions supplied beforehand; student listens to variation of dialogue or story read and checks answers.

28. Multiple-choice answers supplied beforehand; student listens to

dialogue or story using recombinations of vocabulary and structures learned, and checks appropriate answers.

With action

29. Miming the actions in story being narrated.

30. Obeying complex classroom instructions for class exercises and tests.

31. Completing a diagram according to instructions.

32. *Hacer o no hacer* (C50): miming affirmative, but not negative, statements.

With speaking

33. Directed dialogue (C24).

34. Group piecing together of a new dialogue from initial hearings.

35. Participating in Cummings device (C29).

36. Participating in Gouin series (C11–13).

37. Participating in verbal-active series (C15).

38. *¿Quién es? ¿Qué es? ¿Dónde está?* (guessing who, what, or which place is being described by teacher or student).

39. Intensive practice exercises varying syntactic segments (see Chapter 4).

40. Running commentary: listening to a story and giving the gist at the end of each sentence in SAAD's (see C52–53).

With writing

41. Writing down words which are dictated letter by letter.

42. Writing from dictation series of numbers of increasing length and complexity.

43. *Information Search* (*Busquen la información*, C49): writing down segments which answer particular questions.

44. Dictation: students repeat to themselves what they think they heard before they write it.

45. Spot dictation (R26).

D. IDENTIFICATION, SELECTION, AND LONG-TERM RETENTION (E)

46. Listening to a continuation of a story (with same vocabulary area, same setting, and same characters).

47. Listening to a story different from, but with similar vocabulary to, one already read.

48. Listening to a conversation similar to one studied.

49. Listening to skits prepared by other students.

50. Listening to dramatizations of stories read.

51. Listening without the text to the expressive reading (on tape, by the teacher, or by a student) of a poem already studied.

52. Listening to other students reciting poems in a poetry competition.

53. Checking answers to aural questions given before or after a passage for listening.

54. Checking appropriate choices for multiple-choice continuations (or rejoinders) given orally after a listening passage.

With speaking

55. Listening to a story, then giving the gist at the end in SAAD's (see C52–53).

56. Answering questions orally on a passage just heard.

57. Responding to others in spontaneous role-playing.

58. Listening to and discussing oral reports of other students.

59. Chain dialogue (C25).

60. Rubbishing the dialogue (C26).

61. Acting out learned dialogues with others (paraphrasing the sense rather than repeating by rote).

62. Learning and acting a part with others in a skit or original dialogue.

63. *¿Cuál es mi profesión?* student mimes a series of actions, others ask yes-no questions until they have guessed what the student does for a living.

With writing

64. Student answers questions in writing after he has listened to a story or conversation.

65. Student writes down what he has learned from another student's oral report.

66. Cloze test on content of what has been heard (W28).

Intermediate Level (I)

A. IDENTIFICATION (I)

1. Aural discrimination of small sound distinctions which change meaning of sentences.

2. Recognition of characteristics of familiar level of speech, with omission of consonants (e.g., in the ending -*ado*), replacement of vowels (e.g., of syllabic /e/ and /o/ by semivocalic [i̯] and [u̯], respectively, as in *teatro* and *ahorita*), through listening to authentic informal speech on tapes, disks, or film sound tracks.

With visual

3. Aural recognition of Spanish pronunciation of names of foreign personalities and places (supplied on scrambled lists).

4. Aural recognition of Spanish/English cognates from scrambled lists.

With action

5. Recognition of aural indicators of tense: *Hoy o mañana* (C51)— tapping for future tenses, miming present tenses.

With writing

6. Demonstrating recognition of Spanish equivalents of contemporary, international scientific, technical, political, and social vocabularies by writing these down.

B. IDENTIFICATION AND SELECTION WITHOUT RETENTION (I)

7. Listening to complete reading of story studied in sections.

8. Listening to dramatization of story read.

9. Listening to the acting out of scenes from play read.

10. Listening to disk or tape of reading by Spanish-speaking professional of short story, poem, or extracts from novel.

11. Listening to a version in SAAD's before listening to a more complicated version (see C52–53). No questions asked.

12. Listening to teacher or other student telling amusing incident which happened on the way to school or at school.

13. Listening to a news item told by teacher or another student.

14. Listening to teacher or another student give background information for news item.

15. Listening to teacher or another student give background information for reading or for a class or group project.

16. Following the line of discussion in a group conversation.

17. Listening to Spanish songs.

With visual

18. Listening to a presentation of slides of some aspect of Spain, Spanish history, or the arts.

19. Watching and listening to a documentary film on some aspect of Spain or Spanish life.

20. Watching and listening to a final showing of a scholastic film, with background of contemporary Hispanic culture which has already been studied in class.

21. Listening to a story as one is reading it silently, to improve fluent reading techniques.

With action

22. Following directions for classroom organization.

C. IDENTIFICATION AND GUIDED SELECTION
WITH SHORT-TERM RETENTION (I)

23. Selecting from aural choices completions for sentences heard.

24. Listening to oral compositions of other students.

25. Listening to skits and spontaneous role-playing of other students.

26. Students discuss news beforehand; then listen to newscasts to find answers to certain questions raised.

27. Students listen to exchange tapes and correspondence tapes.

28. *¿Qué describo?* (guessing object described by fellow student). Alternatives: *¿Dónde estoy? ¿Qué es?*

With visual

29. Student is provided with multiple-choice or true/false questions beforehand, then checks answers as he listens, or immediately afterwards.

30. Student chooses among written completions for sentences given orally.

31. Student practices reading aloud with tape model: student reads segment, listens to model reading, then rereads segment.

32. Students watch films of which they have previously studied sound track or synopsis.

33. Students watch films in which they are looking for specific cultural details, certain interactions of characters, or particular developments of the story.

With action

34. Following instructions for making something.

With speaking

35. Providing oral sentence completions at end of longer and longer sequences.

36. Student is asked questions aurally beforehand, hears passage, hears aural questions again, and gives oral answers.

37. Student gives spontaneous responses on Situation Tapes (C33).

38. *Corríjame, por favor* (C47): noting inappropriate words in story given orally and suggesting appropriate replacements.

39. *Veintiuna preguntas:* group asking of eliminative yes-no questions to discover name of famous person selected for the game. Alternatives: *Identificación, Animal-Vegetal-Mineral.*

40. *Ni sí, ni no:* group elimination game where students are asked all kinds of questions which they may answer in any way they can, so long as they never use *sí* or *no.*

41. Oral spelling bees (*Concursos de ortografía*).

42. Taking part in Lipson-type puzzle exercises.

43. Fulfilling the supportive role of the listener (*¿Verdad? ¿Y después?*).

With writing

44. Written spelling bees.

45. Spot comprehension: students are given incomplete statements about the content of what they will hear; after listening, they fill in the blanks with the missing details, expressed in short phrases.

46. Dictation: gradually increasing length of segment to be retained.

47. Taking dictations containing information on cultural matters discussed: e.g., famous sayings of leading historical figures, famous anecdotes most Spanish children know (e.g., *don Quijote y los molinos de viento, el general Moscardó*).

48. Taking from dictation notes on the lives and achievements of historical figures, painters, musicians.

D. IDENTIFICATION, SELECTION, AND LONG-TERM RETENTION (I)

49. Listening without a script to readings of plays studied.

50. Listening to a part of a play for which students will develop impromptu continuations later.

51. Listening to episodes of a mystery serial or interviews with native speakers.[39]

With speaking

52. Answering aural questions asked after a long listening passage.

53. Group conversations and discussions on an assigned topic.

54. Preliminary discussion for preparation of oral compositions.

55. Questions and discussion after listening to other students' oral compositions.

56. Participating in spontaneous skits and role-playing.

57. After listening, answering questions asked in SAAD's (see C52–53).

58. Listening to a passage, then giving the gist in SAAD's.

59. Listening to a mystery without hearing the conclusion; then discussing possible explanations.

60. Taking map journeys (C14).

61. *El culpado* (discovering crime of which one is accused and defending oneself).

62. Participating in simulated telephone conversations or authentic telephone conversations with monolingual, or presumed monolingual, Spanish speakers.

63. Interviewing a visiting native speaker of Spanish to find out who he is, what he does, what he thinks, and so on.

64. *Aquí no hay secretos:* discovering the secret a fellow student is concealing (can be pet peeves, career plans, weekend plans, etc.).

65. *¿Quién dice la verdad?* Three students pretend to be the person whose unusual experiences are recounted at the beginning; other students try to find out by questioning who is the real Señor Fulano (Señora Fulana).

66. *Charades:* see *Categories of Language Use* 10 in Chapter 2, p. 52.

67. *Pruebas de conocimientos generales:* students can choose such categories as contemporary Hispanic life, Spanish or Latin American history, institutions, current events, language, literature, art, music, sport, exploration, and famous men and women of the Hispanic world.

68. *Controle Vd. al Narrador* (C43–44) as a test of cultural information.

69. Listening to and discussing exchange and correspondence tapes.

70. Taking part in general conversation at Spanish clubs, Spanish tables, Spanish camps, Hispanic festivals, during summer abroad programs.

With writing

71. Listening to a passage and then writing the gist in SAAD's (see C52–53).

72. Listening to a mystery which stops before the conclusion, then writing an explanation.

73. Listening to a segment of dialogue, then writing a composition which gives it a context and a conclusion.

Advanced Level (A)

A. IDENTIFICATION (A)

1. Aural discrimination of features of rapid spoken style, regional accents, levels of language, through listening to authentic tapes, films, radio broadcasts, plays.

With writing

2. Transcribing and retranscribing tapes of unedited authentic speech until student has recorded it all (to learn, through personal observation, characteristics of unedited speech and tune ear to understand it).[40] Student plays back any sections of the tape as often as he wishes.

B. IDENTIFICATION AND SELECTION WITHOUT RETENTION (A)

3. Listening to a sequel to a passage read.

4. Listening to recordings of plays and poems already studied.

5. Listening to scenes from other plays by the same playwright.

6. Listening to other poems by the same poet.

7. Listening to debates and panel discussions by fellow-students.

8. Listening to Spanish-language newscasts for personal information and pleasure.

9. Listening to commercials recorded from short-wave broadcasts in Spanish or mock commercials prepared by fellow-students.

10. Listening to recordings of Spanish *cantantes*.

11. Continuing tape correspondence with Spanish-speaking friends.

C. IDENTIFICATION AND GUIDED SELECTION
WITH SHORT-TERM RETENTION (A)

12. Listening to student presentation of mock radio program, call-in program, or TV talk show.

With visual

13. Watching Spanish-language films.

14. Listening to student presentation of fashion parade.

With speaking

15. Listening to lecturettes by other students on aspects of Hispanic civilization, culture, or literature and asking questions.

16. Listening to an aural text and recording answers to questions on the text.

17. Group conversations with visiting native speakers.

18. Micro-texts: see *Categories of Language Use* 9 in Chapter 2, p. 51.

With writing

19. Students practice taking notes on classroom lecturettes, first with an outline of points to be covered, then without guidance.

20. Dictation: students are expected to listen to and retain whole sentences before writing.

D. IDENTIFICATION, SELECTION, AND LONG-TERM RETENTION (A)

21. Listening to lectures by Spanish-speaking visitors on aspects of contemporary Hispanic life.

22. Watching performances of Spanish-language plays by visiting actors.

23. Watching performances of Spanish plays by school Spanish club or on the invitation of other schools.

24. Listening to recordings of group conversations of Spanish speakers discussing subjects of interest.

25. Listening to readings of plays not studied previously.

With visual

26. Extracting different lines of thought from a listening passage: listening with one set of printed questions, then listening again with a different set of questions.

27. Visiting Spanish art show and listening to commentary in Spanish.

With action

28. Seeking information from documentaries, tapes, and records for group projects or class discussion.

29. Listening to lengthy instructions for a task one has to perform.

30. Learning Spanish or Latin American cooking from oral instructions.

31. Visiting a Spanish or Latin American restaurant, discussing menu with Spanish-speaking waiter, and eating a meal in company with other Spanish-speaking students.

32. Making preparations for a Hispanic festival with a Spanish or Latin American exchange student, or teacher, who explains what to do in Spanish.

33. Activities at Spanish club, Spanish camp, or during study abroad tour.

With speaking

34. As much of the lesson as possible is conducted in Spanish.

35. Listening to a passage and recording oral answers to questions about it.

36. Listening to recordings of plays, poems, and speeches and discussing them afterwards.

37. Learning Spanish or Latin American songs from recordings.

38. Learning a part for a play from a professional recording.

39. Group conversations and discussions on cultural subjects which students have researched, films they have seen, or books and journals they have read.

40. Discussion of newscasts from Spain or Spanish America.

41. Asking questions at lectures by Spanish-speaking visitors or exchange students.

42. Talking on telephone with native speakers of Spanish seeking information for projects or for reporting back to class.

43. Interviewing visiting, or local, Spanish speakers or exchange students to find out information on life, institutions in Spain or Latin America, and attitudes, for group project on contemporary Hispanic culture.

44. Watching Spanish or Latin American films and being able to dis-

cuss afterwards questions which require aural comprehension, rather than kinesic or visual interpretation.

45. Engaging in debates and discussions on controversial subjects.

46. Showing Spanish-speaking visitors around school or town.

47. Listening to a story which members of the class will dramatize spontaneously later.

48. Listening to tapes of radio discussions with Hispanic authors and civic leaders, or speeches by political figures, and discussing these in the context of contemporary Spanish or Spanish-American life.

49. Listening to newscasts in order to act as daily or weekly reporter for the class.

50. Taking part in such competitions as Intermediate activities 61, 64, 65, and 67.

51. *Reconstitución de un texto.*[41] As a preliminary study of the differences between spoken and literary language, leading later to *análisis literario* or *comentario de un texto literario,* students listen to a poem or short literary extract and, with the help of systematic questioning from the teacher reconstruct it orally.

With writing

52. Taking dictations containing information related to cultural subjects being researched.

53. While listening to a speech, lecture, or taped discussion, students take notes for use with a group project.

54. Listening to a speech, lecture, or taped discussion and writing afterwards a summary of main points for use with a group project.

55. *Reconstitución de un texto.* After having done 51, students reconstruct the text in writing, individually or as a group, and then compare their version with the original as an exercise in stylistics.

56. As an ambitious project for a class in which listening comprehension is a major objective, or as an independent study project: students listen to Spanish-language broadcasts to draw out information on cultural differences. They write up the results of their research in Spanish. (Much can be learned from the types of news reported and what this conveys about Hispanic interests and preoccupations; the types of goods advertised on Spanish-speaking commercial stations and the way they are advertised; the kinds of interviews conducted, and with whom; the types of music played on different stations; the subject matter of comedy hours, situation comedies, and *cantantes,* and the types of questions asked by listeners.)

4
Oral practice for the learning of grammar

Deductive or inductive?

At some stage students must learn the grammar of the language. This learning may be approached *deductively* (in which case the student is given a grammatical rule with examples before he practices the use of a particular structure) or *inductively* (the student sees a number of examples of the rule in operation in discourse, practices its use, and then evolves a rule with the help of the teacher; or he sees a number of examples, evolves a rule from these examples with the help of his teacher, and then practices using the structure). In either of these approaches, there is a phase wherein the student *practices* the use of grammatical rules in possible sentences. This subject is discussed in greater depth in Chapter 8.

Oral exercises

In many classrooms, the greater part of grammatical practice has always been in writing. Here, we are concerned with the contribution that can be made by oral practice exercises of many kinds. In this chapter, we shall:

1. examine types of exercises traditionally found in textbooks and see which ones are suitable for or can be adapted to oral practice;

2. study examples of more recently developed drills and exercises and discuss their features;

3. categorize, exemplify, and discuss six types of oral practice exercises

(repetition, substitution, conversion, sentence modification, response, and translation exercises).

Traditional types of exercises

To make the discussion of different exercises in this section comparable we will base a certain number of them on the expression of possession in Spanish, a structure which contrasts with English usage and is usually taught in the early stages. It involves a word order which is frequently different from English, and the contraction of the masculine singular form of the definite article *el* with a preceding *de* to form *del*.

The contraction *del* and the similar contraction of *a* + *el* to *al* are often taught first in their directional uses (*viene del museo, va al mercado*) because utterances containing these structures parallel their English equivalents in concept and in sequence of elements, and are, therefore, not difficult for English-speaking students. Expressions like these can also be practiced situationally (*Juana va al escritorio, María viene del laboratorio*) thus bringing more reality to oral practice.

1. GRAMMAR-TRANSLATION TYPE EXERCISES

(Although the examples in this section are taken from a book published many years ago, a number of the features we will discuss can still be found in books currently in use.)

If we examine older textbooks we find that many of them set out a *grammatical rule,* with some examples. The rule is often expressed in a traditional terminology with which the students may or may not be familiar. To practice the usage described in the rule the students are usually given sentences to translate.

G1 *Grammar rules from an older textbook*[1]

a. *Genitive case*—Possession is denoted by the preposition *de,* of.
   El libro de Juan   John's book
   Spanish nouns have one form for the singular and one for the plural; they have no ending that corresponds to the English *'s.*
b. *De* + *el* is contracted to *del;* but *de la, de los,* and *de las* are not contracted.
   Los libros del alumno.   The student's books.
   Los libros de los alumnos.   The students' books.

To practice the forms learned from the rules, the students are given *exercises* like the following:

G2 A. *Contéstese afirmativamente.* 1. ¿Tiene Juan el libro de María? 2. ¿Tiene María el libro de Juan? 3. ¿Son Vds. alumnos de la escuela? 4. ¿Tiene Vd. los libros de los niños?

B. *Escríbase.* 1. John has the teacher's book and is writing the exercise. 2. I have John's book and am studying the lesson. 3. All the students in the class are hard workers. 4. Do you have the mother's letter? . . .

The section ends with a summary of the grammar rules in Spanish.

G3 *Resumen Gramatical*

a. *Caso genitivo.* La idea de posesión se expresa mediante la preposición *de.*

Los nombres en español tienen una terminación para el singular y otra para el plural; carecen de una terminación análoga a la inglesa *'s.*

b. La preposición *de* y el artículo *el* se contraen en la forma *del,* pero *de la, de los,* y *de las* no se contraen.

Commentary

1. In this example, *grammatical terminology* which may, or may not, be familiar to the student is used (e.g., genitive case). Teachers can no longer assume that students have learned these terms in their language arts classes. (For further discussion of this question, see Chapter 8, p. 248.)

2. *Incomplete discussion of rules and limited and badly distributed examples.* Although English sentences are used for illustration of the rules, no mention is made of the fact that English also has a possessive form without *'s* which is similar to the Spanish form, as in: *the estate of Don Carlos.* If English-Spanish contrasts are used, the parallel concepts the student already possesses should be exploited.

Under rubric a. *Genitive case,* there are no examples in which the possessors are preceded by the definite article, e.g., *el libro de la hermana,* the sister's book. The one example given (*el libro de Juan*) could lead to the false assumption that **el libro de hermana* was a possible sentence. The rule under rubric b. would, therefore, seem rather puzzling to a beginning student in its present elliptic form. It may be noted further that under neither a. nor b. is the student given any examples of the use of *de la* or *de las.*

3. In the *exercises* in G2 the main problem discussed in G1, use of the *del* form, seems to have been *avoided,* depriving the student of oppor-

tunities to practice it. Yet, suddenly, *alumnos de la escuela* which, for an English speaker, seems to have no obvious connection with the rule for the genitive case (we do not speak in English of "the school's students") is introduced without any explanation that it is a similar structure in Spanish to those being practiced, even if in English it differs: In B3, "all the students in the class" will hardly appear to many students to require the application of the rule of the "genitive case" despite the earlier appearance of A3. Where grammar rules are presented in such explicit form, the materials writer should try to make them comprehensive and to arrange them in a logical sequence, with sufficient examples to make their application clear. The exercises should then reflect something of this logic.

4. Exercises like G2 A seem to provide the opportunity for a question-answer session in class. Yet closer examination shows that *improbable responses* are elicited as in A4. For the teacher to ask the students, "Are you students in the school?" and to receive the response, "Yes, we are students in the school" is the height of artificiality. Modern exercises, even when carefully constructed from the point of view of grammatical practice, often show the same disregard for probability and authenticity. As a result, students quickly develop the attitude that Spanish is an artificial classroom game which is irrelevant to real life and best forgotten as fast as possible, with other school nonsense.

5. *Stilted, unnatural use of language.* The English sentences in G2 B are modeled on the expected translation in Spanish, with the result that they do not sound like authentic English, e.g., "Do you have the mother's letter?" (In the same lesson we find "[we] must study a great deal in order to write the Spanish exercises," and "Few are lazy; many are industrious.") The students face a curious sort of English that is then converted into something stranger still. They are trained from the beginning to think from Spanish to English and from English to Spanish and to seek one-to-one equivalence of expression, even if it is necessary to distort the English sentence to achieve it. Sentence B4 could be made more realistic by giving it more context: "John is not in class. Do you have the mother's letter?"

5. *Translation of short sentences has its uses* (see G45–53 and W62), but only when they are ones which the student might conceivably use. The strongly moralizing tone of sentences like "All the students in the class are hard workers" does not appeal to the modern student.

6. *Unrealistic demands on the students.* The preface of the book from which these examples have been taken states (p. iii): "At the end of each Lesson the rules of grammar are repeated in Spanish, so that the students

may commit them to memory in either Spanish or English as the teacher prefers," hence the *Resumen Gramatical*, G3. Students are taught to analyze the grammar in an abstract fashion and then learn the rules by heart. There is no empirical evidence that students who learn rules by heart can apply them in active production. The old recommendation, "Learn the example, not the rule," comes closer to useful practice, but cannot be applied here because of the lack of examples with the rules, particularly in the case of the *Resumen Gramatical*.

The language of G3 is beyond the level of the language being practiced by the students in the exercises. Since the rule has already been given in English, this added chore of learning to mouth Spanish one could not use actively seems to be a futile imposition on the student.

7. The entire presentation is *teacher, or textbook, directed*. There is no place for student creativeness, for enjoyment, or even mild interest.

G4 *Paradigm*

Present Indicative of Tener, *to have*[2]

SINGULAR	PLURAL
yo tengo, I have	*nosotros* ⎱ *tenemos,* we have *nosotras* ⎰
tú tienes, thou hast	*vosotros* ⎱ *tenéis,* ye have *vosotras* ⎰
usted tiene, you have	*ustedes tienen,* you have
él ⎱ *tiene,* he ⎱ has *ella* ⎰ she ⎰	*ellos* ⎱ *tienen,* they have *ellas* ⎰

Commentary

1. This paradigm appears in Lesson 6 of an elementary level book (*yo* and *usted* have been introduced earlier). Suddenly the student is confronted with a great number of pronouns the uses of which are unfamiliar in English (*thou, ye*) or Spanish (*vosotros, vosotras; usted, ustedes*) and the absence of one familiar one (English *it*) without any explanation of its absence.

2. There is *no systematic practice* first of one aspect of the structure and then of the next (e.g., practice of *tú* as opposed to *usted;* of *vosotros* in relation to *tú* and of *ustedes* in relation to *usted;* of *nosotros* in relation to *nosotras,* and of these linked with *vosotros/vosotras, ellos/ellas*), and the all-pervading influence of grammatical gender in Spanish. The student, faced with this very complicated (and, for many, incomprehensible)

paradigm, is probably very relieved to learn in the next lesson that in Spanish the subject pronoun is usually omitted anyway.

3. A paradigm is useful as *a summary of what students have learned*. It can, however, become *an end in itself* if the students are presented with such tables before they have had experience with the elements they contain and are asked to memorize and reproduce them in tests and quizzes. Time is thus spent in memorizing what is only partially understood at the expense of practice in the language. After practice of subsections of the paradigm, the whole picture may be put together by the students themselves, with the teacher's help where this is needed. This approach clarifies confusions in the students' minds and provokes questions which come from experience in trying to use the language.

4. Practice exercises based on such paradigms usually take the form of artificial *series of sentences for translation* such as "We (f) are studying the lesson," "You (= thou) are writing the exercises." This may develop skill in producing Spanish-language forms on demand, usually in writing, but gives the students no opportunity to develop their ability to use Spanish for normal communication.

2. FILL-IN-THE-BLANK EXERCISES

These exercises are found in textbooks which profess to teach aural-oral skills as well as in texts oriented to written practice in grammar. They are discussed here because they are often used for oral practice in the classroom. (As written exercises they are examined in detail in Chapter 8.)

G5 Replace the English words in parentheses by the correct Spanish form (*del, de la, de los, de las*):

a. ¿Cuál es la fecha (of the) conquista de México?
b. La puerta (of the) tienda está cerrada.
c. La hermana (of the) ingeniero ha visitado el campamento.

Commentary

In most cases the student *jots down the Spanish replacement in isolation* in his exercise book. As a result he does not read, let alone hear or say, a complete Spanish sentence. The mixture of Spanish and English encourages the student to think of Spanish as disguised English, and language learning as essentially translation.

2. *Items are quite unconnected* and contain complications of unfamiliar

vocabulary and concepts which encourage the student to close his mind to all else but the blank to be filled.

3. When the exercise is completed orally, the student usually gives only the Spanish equivalent for the section in English only. For this, he does not even have to understand the sentence. He needs to recognize only the gender and number of the word following the blank. Then the exercise can be completed rather like a crossword puzzle. Since the student is "learning the rules" in isolation, it is unlikely that there will be any high degree of transfer to a spontaneous utterance, without further practice of a different nature.

G6 Include in the sentence the words in parentheses, making any necessary changes:

    a. El pañuelo está en el bolsillo (de el) profesor.
    b. La pizarra está en la pared (de la) sala de clase.
    c. Los papeles están en el libro (de el) alumno.
    d. Los lápices (de los) chicos están en el suelo.

Commentary

1. This exercise avoids the use of English but, even more than the preceding exercise, encourages students to find "answers" for segments. The words in the parentheses supply all the necessary information.

2. Students are confronted with an *incorrect Spanish* form (*de el*) which may be impressed on their minds more than the correct form, especially if they read out what is printed, thinking it is the correct form.

3. They are also encouraged to *think of de el first* and then transform it to *del,* instead of learning *del* directly as a Spanish form of expression and practicing it frequently in context.

4. Vocabulary in this case is connected with things in the classroom. The same task can be more effectively accomplished by a rapid oral exercise in which students are asked or ask each other questions like: Q: *¿Dónde está el pañuelo?* (R: *En el bolsillo del profesor*); Q: *¿Dónde están los papeles?* (R: *En el escritorio del alumno*); Q: *¿Qué está en el suelo?* (R: *El lápiz de María*). The teacher should make clear that all answers must contain a *de* phrase. This exercise can also be conducted with carefully selected pictures. (See also G12.)

G7 Fill in the blanks in the following sentences with the correct form of *de* + the definite article:

a. Enséñeme la foto _____ niño.
b. Deme los libros _____ profesor.
c. Entrégueme la lista _____ palabras.

Commentary

1. Here the student *must reflect more* than in G6 where gender and number were supplied.

2. The student *does not see incorrect forms* in print.

3. He may still *not see complete sentences* in Spanish since all the information he needs to complete the sentence correctly is supplied by the final segment.

4. This exercise is first of all a *visual* task (blanks cannot be spoken by the teacher). If the answers are read aloud in their full context, students at least articulate a complete Spanish sentence. Otherwise, they rush through, rapidly "filling in the blanks."

5. Items again are disparate and *uninteresting*. The imperative has been used presumably because students learned it recently. This fact could have been exploited more efficiently, allowing some place for student innovation, by devising a rapid oral exercise in which students ask each other to do various things, using extended phrases with *de* (e.g., *Enséñeme la foto del colegio*).

3. REPLACEMENT EXERCISES

G8 Replace the italicized word by the noun indicated, making any necessary changes.

a. El profesor cierra el cuaderno del *chico*. (chica)
b. ¿Ha visto Vd. la carta del *profesor*? (alumno)
c. No rompa Vd. los lápices de los *niños*. (niñas)

Commentary

1. The student sees or hears a *complete Spanish sentence* and responds in a complete Spanish sentence.

2. The exercise could be given orally. This is actually close to the substitution drill technique of G9. However, because of the continual changes in structural formation and lexical content in successive sentences, it would be difficult to hold the sentences in the memory while making substitutions orally. For this reason, it is *essentially an exercise for written*

practice. In the next section we will see how by observing certain restrictions it could be transformed into an oral exercise.

More recently developed oral practice exercises
1. PATTERN OR STRUCTURE DRILL EXERCISES

These types of exercises are found in most contemporary textbooks and on language laboratory tapes. They are designed for rapid oral practice in which more items are completed per minute than in written practice. Some teachers mistakenly use them for written practice, thus giving students a boring, tedious chore.

Pattern drill exercises are useful for demonstrating structural variations and familiarizing students with their use. They serve an *introductory function* and are useful only as a preliminary to practice in using the new structural variations in some natural interchange, or for consolidation of the use of certain structures when students seem in doubt.

When pattern drills are used, it is important that students understand the rationale of the variations they are performing. Sometimes a grammatical feature has been encountered in listening or reading material or in a dialogue. Its functioning has been experienced, or explained, and a rapid drill is conducted to familiarize the students with the feature in use in various contexts. Sometimes a demonstration pattern drill introduces the grammatical feature, which is then explained, before being practiced again in a drill sequence which requires thought.

Intensive practice exercises or drills are useful for learning such formal characteristics of Spanish as verb endings (not tense use), word order in statements and questions, the use of object pronouns before and after the verb, and so on. They can be of many types, as we shall see in this chapter.

Teaching series

G9 Repeat the model sentence you hear. In successive sentences replace the last word by the cue words given, making any necessary changes. You will then hear the correct sentence. Repeat it if you have made a mistake. (The modeled correction and the repetition of the correct response will be given here only for the first item, as a demonstration of the technique.)

a.	
MODEL SENTENCE	Es la hermana de Jorge.
CUE	María.
RESPONSE BY STUDENT	Es la hermana de María.
CORRECT RESPONSE CONFIRMED	Es la hermana de María.
REPETITION BY STUDENT OF CORRECT RESPONSE (IF DESIRED)	Es la hermana de María.
FURTHER CUES	(Juana, Pedro, Carlos, Ana).

b. Es el nombre del maestro.
   (director, jefe, muchacho, alumno . . .)

c. Es el nombre de la maestra.
   (niña, vecina, alumna, directora . . .)

d. Es la casa de los alumnos.
   (abuelos, ingenieros, maestros, directores, americanos, cubanos . . .)

e. Es el ruido de las niñas.
   (madres, alumnas, vacas, gallinas, olas, campanas . . .)

f. Es la foto de la familia.
   (Jorge, alumnos, director, niñas, americanos, casa, maestro, María . . .)

Commentary

1. This is called a *four-phase drill.* When the student does not repeat the correct answer after the model, it is referred to as a *three-phase drill.* The fourth phase is useful for the student who has made a mistake. The third phase (confirmation of correct response) is usually included on a laboratory tape, but it can become irritating in class when students are giving correct responses smartly. It should be used only when needed.

2. In this exercise there is a *fixed increment,* that is, a segment which is repeated in each utterance in a series. Here it is *es,* which makes the use of many different nouns with possessive phrases possible. The fixed increment reduces the memory load for the student and allows him to concentrate on the minimal change he is being asked to make. It is usually retained during *six or eight items,* especially when a new structure is being learned.

3. The sentences are *short,* thus lightening the memory load.

4. The *lexical content is restricted* to vocabulary with which the student is familiar so that he can concentrate on the structural rule he is applying.

5. Each sentence the student utters is one which could possibly appear in conversation.

6. There is *no ambiguity in the exercise.* The instructions are clear and each item is so composed that only one response will be correct. This makes it possible for the acceptability of the response to be confirmed by a correct response modeled by the teacher or the voice on the tape.

7. (f.) is the *testing phase* of the drill. It ranges over the five possibilities in eight (or more) items. Through it the teacher can tell whether the students need further practice of specific variations of the feature they have been learning.

8. It will depend on the age and maturity of the students and the intensiveness of the course whether this series is taught gradually over a period of days, or weeks, or taught in one lesson.

9. Since words are grouped according to gender and number, the operation of the drill can become mechanical and cease to be useful, because students are no longer concentrating on the grammatical point at issue. It should not be continued beyond the point where students have acquired familiarity with the forms.

Patterned response

The drill in G9 would be *less monotonous* and the students would be participating in a more realistic way if the response were not a simple repetition but required an answer form.

G10 a. Practice with the model (students repeat sentences demonstrating the structural model):

¿Gómez? ¿Es el profesor, entonces?
No, no es *el nombre del profesor.*
b. The drill continues, following the same pattern:
CUE   ¿Castillo? ¿Es el director, entonces?
RESPONSE   No, no es *el nombre del director.*
(Confirmation)
CUE   ¿García? ¿Es el médico, entonces?
RESPONSE   No, no es *el nombre del médico.*
(Confirmation)

Chain Drill

A *final practice* at the end of this series can be a chain drill on the following pattern: each student in turn invents his own contribution and produces a cue for his neighbor. Students should be encouraged at this stage to be as original as they can within the limitations of the pattern.

G11 STUDENT A TO STUDENT B   ¿Gómez? ¿Es el nombre del director?
STUDENT B   No, es el nombre de la maestra.
(TO STUDENT C)   ¿Juana? ¿Es el nombre de la chica?
STUDENT C   Sí, es el nombre de la chica.
(TO STUDENT D)   ¿Oyes el ruido de los animales?
Sí, es el ruido de los perros . . .

This chain drill can be a *team game,* each team gaining a point for each correct link in the chain (with a limit on the time for reflection to keep the game moving). The chain passes to the other team each time an error is made or a student fails to respond within the time allowed.

Patterned response in a situational context
A drill of this type is more interesting and has more reality if it is given a *situational* context.

G12 Context can be provided by the use of objects, pictures, or actions and the learning of a few simple cognates (*el interior, el exterior, la foto, el mapa, el Canadá, la capital*). The drill is conducted first in choral fashion with students describing things pointed out by the teacher. Then the drill moves to individual response, with students pointing things out to each other (*es el interior del coche; es el exterior de la casa*).

Finally a *game* develops.

1. Team points are awarded for correct answers to the question *¿Qué es esto?* Students understand that the answer must contain a possessive or *de* phrase; they respond with such expressions as *es la foto del profesor* or *es el mapa del Canadá*.

2. Alternatively, students gain points for correct descriptions of the actions of the teacher or other students. The teacher, or student, asks: *¿Qué hago yo?* Students reply: *Vd. abre el mapa del Canadá; Vd. mira la foto de la capital,* and so on.

With a little practice and some choral responses at the beginning, a game of this type can proceed as smartly as an oral drill. Swift response can be elicited by pausing a short time for one student to reply, then moving to another if the student is still hesitating.

Successful completion of an oral drill does not guarantee that the student will use the correct form in *autonomous production*. The student must try to express himself outside of a framework which forces him to produce certain answers.

G13 The lesson may conclude with the students asking each other questions: *¿Cuál es la capital de la Argentina? ¿De quién es la foto que está en el escritorio del maestro?* Alternatively, they may play a game such as *Estoy pensando en cierta cosa. ¿Qué es?* Students guess: *Es el mapa de la Argentina, es la foto del presidente* . . . until they find the right answer.

Suggestions for encouraging autonomous production are given in Chapter 2.

* Try to write a series of drills to teach and test the *contraction of the article* after *a*. Think of situational contexts in which these could be practiced and *games* which would produce the same types of responses as a drill. Then see if the types of games you have invented work smoothly by trying them out on other students.

2. SUBSTITUTION OR VARIATION TABLES

Oral drilling can also be performed with the use of *variation* or *substitution tables*[3] such as the following:

G14 *¿Quién es?*

Es	el hermano	de la	maestra
	la madre	del	vecino
	la tía	de los	chicos
	el primo	de las	muchachas

Commentary

1. This is a *mixed drill* and presumes some prior learning of the specific structural items either in dialogues, reading material, oral work in the classroom, or earlier more restricted drills on the different facets of the article with *de*. This drill serves a useful purpose in drawing together in a systematic way what has already been learned. (See also W1–3.)

2. The drill may be conducted with the complete table in front of the students in an initial *learning phase*. The teacher points to various items on a chart to elicit different combinations from the students, or the students respond to oral cues while looking at their books. In the second or *testing phase,* the students close their books and work from a chart where items have been jumbled and column 3 omitted.

G15

Es	el hermano		chicos
	la tía		vecino
	la hermana		muchachas
	el primo		alumno
	la madre		maestra

Finally, students move on to practice with items not on the original chart, and here suggestions from G12 for *applications in situational contexts* will apply.

3. If the items, as is usually the case, are related to dialogue or reading material already studied, the variations may be taught without books or

chart by using *flashcards or pictures* of characters familiar to the students. After considerable practice in this purely aural-oral fashion, students will then look at the chart in their books.

4. As with G9, this practice with variation tables is preliminary learning of grammatical structures. It must be accompanied by more extensive, and more spontaneous, applications of the variations in some form of *personal interchange* between students and teachers. (See G13.)

Six groups of oral exercises

For each type of exercise in this section a brief description with an example will be given, some comments will be made on common faults to be avoided in constructing such exercises, and some Spanish structural features for which this type of oral exercise would be useful will be listed.

Oral exercises fall into six groups: repetition, substitution, conversion, sentence modification, response, and translation drills.

1. REPETITION OR PRESENTATION DRILLS

In simple repetition drills, the instructor gives a model sentence containing a particular structure or form to be manipulated and the students repeat the sentence with correct intonation and stress. Repetition drills are not, in one sense, a special category of exercises which will be used for practicing certain types of structure; they represent, rather, a commonly used technique for familiarizing the student with the specific structure, with the *paradigm,* or with the *procedure for the practice.* For this reason they are sometimes called *presentation drills.* They are useful as *introductory material,* but it must be remembered that from mere repetition, no matter how prolonged, the student will learn little except the requirements of the drill.

G16   MODEL   ¿Dónde está el cine?   Ah, lo veo.
      STUDENT ¿Dónde está el cine?   Ah, lo veo.

      MODEL   ¿Dónde está la librería?   Ah, la veo.
      STUDENT ¿Dónde está la librería?   Ah, la veo.

      MODEL   ¿Dónde están las tiendas?   Ah, las veo.
      STUDENT ¿Dónde están las tiendas?   Ah, las veo.

Commentary

1. This example highlights one of the defects of many repetition drills: their unreality and lack of application to the students' situation. Unless the

students are looking at a picture showing the buildings in a town, G16 could become completely mechanical,[4] with students attending only to the cue words *lo, la,* or *las.* In this case, the structure could just as easily be presented with nonsense words: *¿Dónde está el dripo? Ah, lo veo,* a procedure which the students might actually find more amusing and which might focus their attention on the cues in the drill.

2. If students are to use in other situations the object pronouns being demonstrated, they should be concentrating on the meaning of what they are saying. Some reality can be introduced by referring to objects the students can see and having them point to them as they respond: *¿Dónde está el cuaderno? Ah, lo veo.*

2. SUBSTITUTION DRILLS

Commonly used types are simple substitution, double substitution, correlative substitution, and multiple substitution drills.

a. *Simple substitution drills* have been demonstrated in G9.

b. *Double substitution drills* are similar to simple substitutions in that the student has no other operation to perform apart from substitution of a new segment in the place of an existing segment, but they require the student to be more alert because they continually change the wording (and, therefore, the meaning) without changing the structure. They are *still mechanical,* however, because each segment is usually signalled in such a way that it can be substituted in the correct slot without the student's necessarily understanding its meaning.

G17 MODEL SENTENCE   Si lo encuentro / *te lo daré.*
              CUE   *Si tú lo quieres*
         RESPONSE   *Si tú lo quieres* / te lo daré.
              CUE   *él escribirá la carta*
         RESPONSE   Si tú lo quieres / *él escribirá la carta.*
              CUE   *Si yo se lo pido*
         RESPONSE   *Si yo se lo pido* / él escribirá la carta.
              CUE   *él saldrá*
         RESPONSE   Si yo se lo pido / *él saldrá.*

Commentary

1. The pattern of activity the student learns is "substitute in alternate slots, retaining the new segment for two responses (as in the sequence: AB, CB, CD, ED, EF . . .)."

2. If the instructor makes clear what elements are being manipulated (in this case "present tense in the *si* clause: future tense in the principal clause," the student will find this type of substitution useful for familiarizing himself with the correct tense form for the correct slot in the utterance. He will, however, need a more demanding type of activity later, such as an innovative *chain drill* (G11), a *game,* or a *structured interchange* (where he invents conditional statements himself) if the teacher is to be sure that he can really use the pattern in communication.

c. In *correlative substitution drills* each substitution requires a correlative change to be made elsewhere in the model sentence (see G9.f).

$G18$ MODEL SENTENCE   *Yo* no lo *comprendo.*
CUE   *Vd . . .*
RESPONSE   *Vd.* no lo *comprende.*
CUE   *María y Paco . . .*
RESPONSE   *María y Paco* no lo *comprenden.*

This type of drill is useful for learning such things as tense inflections, possessive forms, reflexive pronouns, irregular verbs, certain sequences of tenses in related clauses, and the agreement of the adjective with the gender and number of the noun. For example, a sequence like the following:

$G19$ MODEL SENTENCE   Prefiero *la casa blanca.*
CUE   *zapatos*
RESPONSE   Prefiero *los zapatos blancos.*
CUE   *coche*
RESPONSE   Prefiero *el coche blanco.*

should help the student familiarize himself with the fact that Spanish signals the plural through changes in the article as well as in the form of accompanying adjectives.

Correlative substitution can be made *more realistic* by designing the cue with a natural-sounding tag which elicits a response that completes a conversational interchange.

$G20$ CUE   Yo tomo café cada mañana. *¿Y José?*
RESPONSE   *José toma* café, también.
CUE   Yo tomo azúcar en mi café. *¿Y Vds.?*
RESPONSE   *Nosotros tomamos* azúcar, también.

This type of tag can also be used to elicit changes in masculine and feminine adjective forms:

G21   CUE   Aquel señor es viejo. ¿Y la señora?
    RESPONSE   La señora es vieja, también.
        CUE   Esta casa es nueva. ¿Y el coche?
    RESPONSE   El coche es nuevo, también.

d. *Multiple substitution drills* are a *testing device* to see whether the student can continue to make a grammatical adjustment he has learned while he is distracted by other preoccupations—in this case, thinking of the changing meaning of successive sentences so as to make substitutions in different slots. In order to make the substitutions in the appropriate slots, students have to think of the meaning of the whole sentence, which changes in focus with each substitution. For this reason, students need to be very alert to perform this exercise successfully.

After study and practice of the indefinite article or the preterite the following multiple substitution drill could be used:

G22 MODEL SENTENCE   Pepe me dio un regalo.
            CUE   *camisa*
        RESPONSE   Pepe me dio *una camisa.*
            CUE   *Tú*
        RESPONSE   *Tú* me *diste* una camisa.
            CUE   *guantes*
        RESPONSE   Tú me diste *unos guantes.*
            CUE   *compraste*
        RESPONSE   Tú me *compraste* unos guantes.
            CUE   *algo*
        RESPONSE   Tú me compraste *algo.*
            CUE   *nada*
        RESPONSE   Tú *no* me compraste *nada.*

The last response, requiring two correlative changes, provides a challenge for an enthusiastic class which enjoys showing how much it has learned.

3. CONVERSION DRILLS

The term *transformation* has long been applied to the types of exercises in which affirmative sentences are changed into negative sentences, statements are changed into questions, simple declarations are converted into emphatic declarations, active voice is converted into passive voice, or a present tense statement is changed into a past tense statement. Such exercises have been a staple of foreign-language classes for many years. Some of these processes happen to parallel what are known as "transformations" in transformational-generative grammar (e.g., negativization, passivization, and the interrogative transformation), and others do not; but when they do, this is more a coincidence than a derivative relationship. The term "transformation" is, therefore, misleading to some people because of a presumed connection with transformational-generative grammar. For this reason, the term "conversion drill" will be used for exercises in changing sentence type, combining two sentences into one, moving from one mood or tense to another, changing word class (e.g., replacing nouns by pronouns), substituting phrases for clauses or clauses for phrases (e.g., adverbial phrases for adverbial clauses, infinitive phrases for clauses), or substituting single words for phrases or phrases for single words (e.g., adverbs for adverbial phrases, adjectives for adjectival phrases).

These are conversions rather than substitutions in that they require the use of a different form (frequently with a correlative change), a change in word order, the introduction of new elements, or even considerable restructuring of the utterance. They are useful for developing flexibility in the selection of formal structures for the expression of personal meaning.

a. General conversion drills

In our discussion of the construction of common types of conversion drills and the weaknesses to be avoided, we will use examples based on the asking of *questions*. Interrogative forms are among the most frequently used in the language, and practice with them can easily be given a *situational context* and a *personal application*.

G23 Change the following statements into questions, using inversion whenever possible.

CUES   a. Nosotros también estamos en la clase.
         b. Yo soy americano.
         c. Los libros están en el escritorio.
         d. Yo tomo el desayuno a las ocho.
         e. La actriz y su marido están en Europa.
         f. Juana y yo estamos en el cine.

Commentary

1. This traditional type of elementary exercise *overemphasizes the inversion form* of interrogation. A sentence like *Los libros están en el escritorio* with its informal classroom content could most realistically be

converted into ¿*Los libros están en el escritorio?* (with rising intonation). This last form of interrogation is the easiest for the students to acquire and they can use it immediately without having to remember to invert the subject and the verb. (The fact that ¿*Los libros están en el escritorio?* and ¿*Están los libros en el escritorio?* presuppose different information, and will, therefore, be used with a different intent, requires separate treatment.)

2. When (a), (b), and (d) are converted into questions they produce questions which have close to zero probability of occurrence, yet such sentences can still be found in books in use at the present time. A better example for (b) would have been *Yo soy el líder del equipo hoy* and for (d) *Yo escribo las palabras correctamente,* both of which would produce probable questions of use to the students.

3. Statement (f) also results in an absurd question. Even with a probable theme for conversion into a question such as *Juana y yo hablamos demasiado,* a Spanish-speaker would be more likely to say *Juana y yo hablamos demasiado, ¿no?* or simply ¿*Juana y yo hablamos demasiado?* (with rising intonation).

4. Statement (e) illustrates the tendency for exercises of this type to range over any and all topics and into any vocabulary area, with no meaningful coherence. This may not appear to be a grave fault but it deepens the impression of many students that language study is mere manipulation of words and has no reality or relevance.

In these six sentences the student is *tested* for his knowledge of a number of aspects of the interrogation rules. The exercise should, therefore, come after a *series of learning exercises,* in which the student encounters the various aspects of the conversion and practices them step by step. Each exercise in such a series will consist of six or more sentences, with familiar vocabulary, which will produce after conversion questions formed on the same pattern and semantically related, as in the following:

G24 Convert the following statements into questions according to the model:

REPEAT Pedro tiene un coche nuevo.
        Pedro tiene un coche nuevo, ¿no?
  CUES a. Tú tienes un coche nuevo.
        b. El coche es rojo.
        c. Los jóvenes pasean en coche por el pueblo.
        d. Ellos paran el coche muy rápidamente . . .

A *complete series on yes-no question formation* would include a set eliciting questions in statement form with rising intonation, a set requiring interrogation with the tags *¿sí?, ¿no?, ¿verdad?,* and *¿no es verdad?,* a set with inversion of subject pronouns, a set with double pronoun subject, a set of questions with noun subjects without inversion (with rising intonation), the same set with noun subjects requiring inversion, a set with double noun subjects, and a set with mixed noun and pronoun subjects. Some review drills should be interpolated. Some study of all of these aspects although not necessarily all at once would normally precede a mixed exercise of the G23 type.

The great *advantage of oral exercises* is that so much more practice can be accomplished in the time available and this allows for step-by-step progression through a series of rules. The practice sets will normally be spread over several lessons. The amount of subdivision within these sets and the number of sets presented at any one time will depend on the level of instruction, the maturity of the students, and the intensiveness of the course. For elementary classes, the forms necessary for simple communication will suffice. For more mature students, discussion of the various possibilities can reduce the necessity to proceed by one-feature-at-a-time drills.

Earlier, examples were given of statements which after conversion produced improbable questions (see G23). This problem *of appropriateness of items after conversion* must be kept constantly in mind.

Situational and personal application. Another set of grammatical rules commonly practiced through conversion drills is the set determining the form, position, and order of pronouns as direct and indirect objects of the verb. All textbooks resort here to the replacement of nouns in sentences by pronouns: Pablo entrega los *papeles* a *su amigo* becomes Pablo *se los* entrega and ¡Escribe *una carta* a *tu hermano*! is rewritten as ¡Escríbe*sela*! Conversion exercises like the following are also used.

G25 For each negative sentence you hear give the affirmative form:

    a. ¡Pablo, no se lo des!
    b. Yo no les hablo.
    c. ¡No nos lo diga Vd.!

The question of the form and position in the sentence of pronoun objects is very complicated. The series of exercises necessary for assimilating these rules thoroughly would be very extensive. Once again, the series can be shortened by judicious explanations of grammatical functioning. Those conversion drills which are retained can be made more vivid by associating structure with action. Students may be asked to respond to instructions by making statements of their own invention, as in a normal conversational interchange, along the following lines:

G26 (I) ¡No de Vd. ese libro a Pedro! No se lo doy.
¡Déselo a él ahora! Ya se lo di.
¡Juana, dinos lo de tu novio en México! Pero ya se lo dije ayer.
¡Escriban Vds. los ejercicios! Ya los escribimos.

Commentary

1. If students prepare ahead of time they can come to class with instructions to give each other which will require quick-wittedness in responding and cause quite a lot of amusement for the class.

2. *A mixed practice* of this type presumes preliminary sequential learning, but it is very effective in providing for *review of a complicated set of rules*. Conducted orally, without hesitation, it enables the student to absorb the rhythm of the sequences. This is an aid to memory which is quite lost if the student constantly writes out his responses—editing and re-editing his first attempts as he "puts the objects in the right place" in a conscious, artificial way.

b. Combinations

Combinations are a form of conversion drill which has also been used for many years. It involves a process which reflects certain features of transformational grammatical analysis and can be very illuminating in differentiating some aspects of the rules. For instance, students often have difficulty in understanding the different uses of *que* and *lo que*. If we examine the sentence

Comí el postre que mi abuela preparó,
we find it combines two underlying sentences:

Comí el postre,
Mi abuela preparó el postre.

Asking students to combine these two underlying sentences by using a relative pronoun involves moving from a deeper level of structure to surface structure. The relative pronoun *que* replaces one occurrence of the element found in both sentences (*el postre*). On the other hand, the combining of two underlying sentences such as

Yo creo *A,*
Tú me dices *A,*

(where *A* refers to something not explicitly stated in either sentence) requires *lo que* to form the sentence
　Yo creo lo que tú me dices.
(Contrast with these the pair
　Yo creo el relato
　Tú me contaste el relato,
which combine as
　Yo creo el relato que tú me contaste.)
　The following oral exercises, G-27-28, require more active construction of sentences with relative pronouns than the traditional fill-in-the-blank exercise of the type:
　Allí está el professor ＿＿＿＿ conocimos en Sevilla.

G27 Combine the following pairs of sentences using *que*. In each case make the first sentence the main clause.
　a. Allí está el profesor. Conocimos al profesor en Sevilla.
　　(RESPONSE　Allí está el profesor que conocimos en Sevilla.)
　b. Allí está el lápiz. El lápiz se cayó de la mesa.
　c. Allí está el libro. Te enseñé el libro.

G28 Combine the following pairs of sentences using *lo que*.
　a. El profesor revisó *A*. Elena había escrito *A*.
　　RESPONSE　El profesor revisó lo que Elena había escrito.
　b. Luis me mostró *A*. *A* estaba en el patio.
　　RESPONSE　Luis me mostró lo que estaba en el patio.

　These sets of exercises would be expanded with sets using *a quien (-es)* and *de quien (-es)* as well as *el que* and its variations, and interspersed with mixed drills reviewing the various uses of the relative pronoun.
　This procedure of combining sentences to form one utterance can also be used for creating dependent phrases beginning with present or past participles (*tocaba la guitarra / se divertía mucho—Tocando la guitarra, se divertía mucho*), or with prepositions such as *antes de* and *después de* (*fue a Italia / antes empezó a estudiar italiano—Antes de ir a Italia, empezó a estudiar italiano*). It is also useful for situations which require a special sequence of tenses in successive clauses, e.g., conditional statements and dependent subjunctives. (Where one clause will be subordinate to another, it must be clear to the student which of the two sentences to be combined will be the main clause and which the dependent clause.)

c. Restatement
　Restatement is another useful type of conversion drill.

G29 One frequently used type of *directed dialogue* is a restatement exercise. (See also C24 c.)

      CUE   Dígale a Jorge que Vd. se llama Luis.
      RESPONSE   Jorge, me llamo Luis.
      CUE   Pregúntele a Pedro adónde va.
      RESPONSE   Pedro, ¿adónde vas?
      CUE   Dígale a Juan que lo espere.
      RESPONSE   Juan, espérame.

A series of this type is usually based on a dialogue which has been learned, but all kinds of restatements can be invented to practice different grammatical features. A realistic note is added if one student pretends to be giving directions to a third party by telephone, while a second student tells him what to say.

G30 A *running commentary* by one student on what another student or the teacher is saying softly gives practice in restatement of direct speech in indirect speech form.

  (I) STUDENT A   Acabo de llegar pero voy a salir pronto.
        STUDENT B   Ella dijo que acababa de llegar pero que iba a salir pronto.
        STUDENT A   ¿Por qué me miras así?
        STUDENT B   Ella me preguntó que por qué la miraba así.

Another type of restatement (sometimes called a *contraction*) consists of replacing a clause with a phrase, or a phrase with a single word, while retaining the basic meaning:

G31 Restate each of the following sentences replacing the adverbial clause with an adverbial phrase of similar meaning.

  a. *Después que él llegue,* invítelo a mi casa.
    RESPONSE   *Después de su llegada,* invítelo a mi casa.
  b. *Antes que ella salga,* yo le diré la verdad.
    RESPONSE   *Antes de su salida,* yo le diré la verdad.

G32 In each of the following sentences, replace the descriptive clause with an adjective of equivalent meaning. (This exercise can be used to practice the position of adjectives which convey different meanings when used before and after the noun.)

a. La iglesia *que es vieja* ha sido restaurada.

RESPONSE   La iglesia *vieja* ha sido restaurada.

b. La iglesia *que servía antes al culto* ha sido restaurada.

RESPONSE   La *vieja* iglesia ha sido restaurada.

c. El hombre *que es pobre* no tiene dinero.

RESPONSE   El hombre *pobre* no tiene dinero.

d. Ese hombre *que compadezco* no tiene dinero.

RESPONSE   Ese *pobre* hombre no tiene dinero.

✽ List for yourself other areas of Spanish grammar for which some form of restatement would be a suitable exercise and try to think of ways in which this restatement can be incorporated into a natural communication activity.

4. SENTENCE MODIFICATIONS

Sentence modification exercises are of three kinds: expansions, deletions, and completions.

a. Expansions

Expansions serve two purposes. Type A requires strictly grammatical manipulation and is useful for learning such things as the position of adverbs. It can be teacher- or student-directed. Type B is more spontaneous; it gives students the opportunity to create new and original sentences from a basic sentence, often in an atmosphere of competition.[5] Students should be encouraged to spice the drill with humorous items.

Type A expansions. In Spanish, adverbs generally follow the verb they modify. Compare:

Roberto cantaba *felizmente* y *en voz alta.*
Tú hablas *bien* el francés.
No estudio *nunca* los sábados.
Se despidieron *tristemente* los novios.

For emphasis, adverbs may occur at the beginning of a sentence. Compare:

Nunca estudio los sábados.
Tristemente se despidieron los novios.
Aquí no se permite fumar.

Adverbs such as *todavía* and *ya* may either follow or precede the verb without affecting emphasis. Compare:

¿Roberto viene *ya*?; ¿*Ya* viene Roberto?
No sé *todavía* si viene.; *Todavía* no sé si viene.

Adverbs precede a past participle, an adjective, or another adverb which they modify. Compare:

Esta novela parece *muy bien* escrita.
El maestro era *demasiado* severo.
Hable Vd. *más* despacio.

This set of rules can be practiced very effectively in an oral expansion drill of Type A:

G33 (1)

MODEL SENTENCE	El ha trabajado.
CUE	aquí
RESPONSE	El ha trabajado aquí. Aquí él ha trabajado. } both acceptable
CUE	mucho
RESPONSE	El ha trabajado mucho aquí. Aquí él ha trabajado mucho. } both acceptable
CUE	nunca
RESPONSE	El nunca ha trabajado mucho aquí. Aquí él nunca ha trabajado mucho. } both acceptable

Many other grammatical features can be practiced in a Type A expansion:

G34 Insert in the sentences you hear the expressions supplied in the cues, making any necessary changes:

a.	BASIC SENTENCE	El tiene amigos.
	CUE	muchos
	RESPONSE	El tiene muchos amigos.
	CUE	no
	RESPONSE	El no tiene muchos amigos.
b.	BASIC SENTENCE	Carlos compró una casa.
	CUE	gran
	RESPONSE	Carlos compró una gran casa.
	CUE	de ladrillo
	RESPONSE	Carlos compró una gran casa de ladrillo.
	CUE	rojo
	RESPONSE	Carlos compró una gran casa de ladrillo rojo.

Type B expansions provide students with the opportunity to create new sentences from a basic frame by expanding the frame as they wish as often as they wish. In this type of practice no two students would produce exactly the same answer.

G35

CUE El hombre cruzaba la calle.

STUDENT A El hombre viejo cruzaba la calle lentamente.

STUDENT B El hombre que tenía prisa cruzaba la calle sin hacer caso del tráfico.

A Type B expansion may be conducted as a *chaining activity,* with each student in succession adding a new element to the sentence until a limit seems to have been reached. At that stage, a new chain begins with another simple sentence.

b. Deletions

Flexibility in manipulating structures can be developed by reversing processes.

Type A deletions, which are the reverse of Type A expansions, provide further variety in practice.

G36 Delete the negative elements in the following sentences:

CUE Yo no estudiaba nunca la gramática.

RESPONSE Yo estudiaba la gramática.

CUE No le gusta nada la poesía.

RESPONSE Le gusta la poesía.

CUE Tú no lo conoces.

RESPONSE Tú lo conoces.

Type B deletions serve a less useful purpose than Type B expansions. Expansions require the student to decide at which point in the sentence to insert the additional information of his own choosing. Deletions of extra information usually require only formal changes, as practiced in Type A deletions. For this reason deletions are not creative.

c. Completions

In completions, part of the sentence is given as a cue and the student finishes the sentence either with a semantically constant segment in which some syntactic or morphological change must be made according to the cue (Type A_1), with a suitable segment which is to some extent semantically governed by the cue (Type A_2), or with a segment of his own invention (Type B).

Type A_1 completions

G37 (I) In the following exercise you will hear the model sentence: *Me alegro que él me haya escrito.* Throughout the exercise you will retain the concluding segment: *que él me haya escrito.* As the introductory segment

changes, you must decide whether or not to use the subjunctive in the concluding segment.

MODEL SENTENCE   Me alegro que él me haya escrito.
CUE   Yo siento . . .
RESPONSE   Yo siento que él me haya escrito.
CUE   Es posible . . .
RESPONSE   Es posible que él me haya escrito.
CUE   ¿Cree Vd . . . ?
RESPONSE   ¿Cree Vd. que él me haya escrito?

Type A₂ completions

G38 (I) In the following exercise you will hear the model sentence: *Ana me devuelve mi lápiz porque ella prefiere el suyo.* Throughout the exercise you will retain a concluding segment of similar meaning to *porque ella prefiere el suyo,* but as the introductory segment varies you will vary the person referred to in the concluding segment.

MODEL SENTENCE   Ana me devuelve mi lápiz porque ella prefiere el suyo.
CUE   Yo te devuelvo tu chaqueta . . .
RESPONSE   Yo te devuelvo tu chaqueta porque yo prefiero la mía.
CUE   Le devolvemos sus revistas . . .
RESPONSE   Le devolvemos sus revistas porque preferimos las nuestras.

Commentary

With an exercise involving a correlative change of this type, it is usually advisable for the student to repeat two, or even three, items with the instructor at the beginning in order to be sure of the type of manipulation required.

A Type A₂ completion is very useful for *vocabulary learning:*

G39 Complete the following statements with the appropriate occupational term, according to the model:

MODEL   El que conduce el taxi es el chófer.
CUE   El que trae el correo . . .
RESPONSE   El que trae el correo es el cartero.
CUE   El que vende la carne . . .
RESPONSE   El que vende la carne es el carnicero.

Type B completions. A Type B completion allows the student to make his personal semantic contribution within a syntactically fixed framewo₋.. It is useful for practicing such things as the governance of infinitives with *a, de, que,* and zero links, the use of the subjunctive, and the sequence of tenses where the dependent clause is in the subjunctive.

G40 (I) Invent a completion containing an infinitive construction for each sentence you hear, according to the following model: Vd. me ayuda . . .

Vd. me ayuda *a arreglar el asunto.*
      CUE   No se olvide . . .
   RESPONSE   No se olvide *de llamarnos cuando llegue.*
      CUE   No te permito . . .
   RESPONSE   No te permito *salir con mi hermana.*

Commentary

In a Type A_1 completion on governance of infinitives the concluding segment would remain the same throughout the exercise, except for the change of link: Yo empiezo / *a prepararlo;* Yo trato / *de prepararlo;* Yo tengo / *que prepararlo.* An exercise of Type A_1 may precede the Type B exercise above in order to familiarize the student with the required structures, or to refresh his memory. All practice should, however, move toward Type B exercises where the student supplies something of his own invention, and then beyond Type B to creative practice, like that described in Chapter 2: *Autonomous Interaction,* p. 45.

✻ Look for other areas of grammar for which sentence modifications would be useful and try to think of original ways of presenting them which draw close to the real purposes of communication.

5. RESPONSE DRILLS

All oral drills may, in one sense, be called response drills. In the particular type to which we are referring here, *question-answer* or *answer-question* procedures are used, or students learn to make appropriate conventional responses (*rejoinders*) to other people's utterances.

a. *Question-answer practice*

Ability to ask questions with ease and to recognize question forms effortlessly, so that one can reply appropriately, is of the essence of communication. It has always been a basic classroom activity. Unfortunately, much question-answer material is very stilted, questions being asked for the sake of the form, without attention to their real interest to the student. The structure of the question form itself can be practiced through conversion exercises. Question-answer practice is useful for such things as forms and uses of tenses, and interrogative and other kinds of pronouns. It is most frequently associated with a picture, slide, or film, reading material, some project or activity, or a game. It can, however, be carefully structured for language-learning purposes. Since the form of an appropriate answer is nearly always a reflection of the question, the teacher can elicit the forms and uses he wants by skillful construction of his questions. In the following series, for instance, successive questions elicit the use of different tenses from the student, yet the communicative interaction develops naturally.

G41 (I) The students have been reading about or viewing a film of the adventures of a group of young people in Mexico.

Q. ¿Por qué no volvieron los jóvenes a la hora convenida?
A. No volvieron porque hacía tan buen tiempo que querían continuar su paseo.
Q. ¿Vuelve Vd. tarde muchas veces por la noche?
A. No. Vuelvo temprano porque tengo que estudiar.
Q. Pero, cuando Vd. esté de vacaciones en junio, quizás volverá más tarde, ¿no?
A. Sí, es posible, porque no tendré clases y podré jugar al béisbol todas las tardes.
Q. ¿Qué haría Vd. si no tuviera clases durante todo el año?
A. Pues, ¡estaría muy contento!

Commentary

The development of this type of interchange is not predictable, but the alert questioner can keep on switching the conversation to a different time perspective. The same type of approach can be developed at the elementary level through discussion of an action picture.

Many *situations* can be created in the classroom for the asking of questions and the obtaining of answers.

G42 With a simulated telephone link, all kinds of situations can be invented which elicit questions and answers from students.

1. Student A calls student B on the phone. Student B asks questions until he is able to identify the person calling and his purpose.
2. Student C calls student D to get some information from him. Student

D has a Spanish-language brochure, menu, or a collection of advertisements from which he gives the information requested.

b. Answer-question practice

Frequently the teacher asks all the questions, yet in a foreign-language situation it is more commonly the language learner, or foreign visitor, who needs to be able to ask questions with ease. Certainly, in a natural conversation, each participant passes freely from the role of interlocutor to that of respondent. Answer-question practice occurs when the teacher, or some student, has the answer and the others must find out what it is. This type of exercise takes place naturally and interestingly in such games as *Veintiuna Preguntas, Animal-Vegetal-Mineral,* and *Identificación.*

G43 In *Veintiuna Preguntas* one person (A) thinks of someone or something. By asking eliminating questions to which A may reply only *Sí* or *No,* the players narrow the field of possibilities until they are able to guess the person or object in question. Only twenty-one questions may be asked before the game is lost.

Animal-Vegetal-Mineral is similar except that the first eliminations are in these three categories and the number of questions is not limited.

In *Identificación,* A thinks of a person and an object typically associated with this person. Forms of questions will be more varied than in the first two games because A may give information, although he tries to do this as ambiguously as possible. When the students have guessed the person, they must guess the object associated with this person (e.g., the school janitor and his keys; Sancho Panza and his *burro*).

c. Rejoinders

In every language there are conventional ways of responding to the utterances of others which ease social relations and make continued communication less effortful: ways of agreeing, disagreeing, expressing pleasure, astonishment, surprise, displeasure, or disgust, ways of responding to another person's monologue so that one appears to be participating, and ways of acknowledging replies to one's questions. These common responses are frequently not taught in any systematic way to foreigners, with the result that the latter often offend, either by not contributing as they should to an interchange, or by contributing too forcefully or pedantically. Some rejoinders will be learned incidentally because the teacher will use them frequently, others can be practiced in an oral exercise from time to time.

G44 Listen to the following sentences and respond to each with an appropriate exclamation or rejoinder:

CUE	¡Dios mío! ¡Se me rompió el reloj!
RESPONSE	*¡Qué lástima!*
CUE	¿Nos reunimos aquí mañana a las diez?
RESPONSE	*De acuerdo.*
CUE	Luis va a ayudarme hoy con la tarea.
RESPONSE	*¡Qué amable!*

Commentary

This mixed exercise is, of course, a review and presumes preliminary learning of appropriate rejoinders either through a series of exercises on particular rejoinders or through the teacher's continual use of them in class. Rejoinders learned artificially, out of context, are easily forgotten; students should be encouraged to intersperse them liberally through their communication activities.

* Begin keeping a list of rejoinders in Spanish which are frequently used so that you can use them yourself in class and teach them to your classes. Your list will certainly include such expressions as *es lástima* and *¡qué lástima!, de acuerdo, ¿verdad?, por favor, de nada, claro, ya lo creo, ¿cómo?, vale la pena, está bien, por supuesto, al contrario, tanto mejor, perdón, magnífico, ¡no me diga!, ¡qué barbaridad!, ¡caramba!, gracias, qué amable*, with many others.

6. TRANSLATION DRILLS

Translation exercises have slipped into disfavor in recent years. This is not because translation itself is reprehensible. In fact, it is a natural process with many practical uses. Unfortunately, for many teachers it became an end, rather than a means of improving the student's control of the structure of the language. As a result, many translation exercises became tortuous puzzles. (Try translating a sentence like: Didn't you wish the old woman had died before she knew about it?) The question of translation, and how it can be used most effectively, is discussed in depth in Chapter 9.

The habit of translating everything one hears or says (or reads or writes) can become a hindrance to fluency. Many students do not realize that it is possible to learn to comprehend and think in the foreign language directly; hence the need for procedures which encourage and develop this ability. For these reasons translation drills, if used at all, should be used sparingly, and then only for linguistic features which it is difficult to practice entirely in Spanish.

Oral translation drills differ from the older types of translation exercises in several ways:

1. Since the native language serves solely as a stimulus for the production of authentic Spanish utterances, only natural idiomatic utterances that the student could conceivably use in communication are introduced:

G45 *He went home early.* Se fue a casa temprano.

2. Stimulus sentences are *short,* centering exclusively on the grammatical feature being practiced:

G46 *I saw him.* Yo lo vi.
I didn't see him. Yo no lo vi.

3. Stimulus sentences remain within a *familiar vocabulary range* so that the student's attention is not distracted from the grammatical feature being practiced.

4. Translation drills do not encourage students to look for one-to-one equivalences between English and Spanish by distorting the English, as in the following example from a grammar-translation type textbook:

G47 *What did you let fall?*
¿Qué dejaste caer?

Instead they require students to produce a Spanish utterance which is *semantically equivalent* to the English stimulus.

G48 *Do you like it?* ¿A Vd. le gusta?

In this way, they encourage students to think in Spanish. They are particularly useful for practicing peculiarly Spanish idioms:

G49 *I feel like having something to eat.* Tengo ganas de comer algo.
Don't kid me. No me tomes el pelo.

5. Although stimulus sentences are short, they are not fragments but *complete utterances* providing a context which indicates usage. Instead of being asked to translate: *he came, she went, they left,* students are presented with more likely utterances, such as:

G50 *He woke up late.* Se despertó tarde.
He got up right away. Se levantó en seguida.
He got dressed quickly. Se vistió pronto.

6. As with other oral drills, translation drills provide practice of one grammatical feature consistently through six or seven items before the drill moves on to a related feature, or to a further complication of the same feature. (In G50, the use of the preterit tense of certain reflexive verbs is being practiced.)

G51 Set of stimulus sentences for practicing the *reflexive* and *non-reflexive* use of certain verbs in the preterite tense.

Diga en español:
a. He washed his child's face.
b. He washed his face.
c. She got up.
d. She raised her hand.
e. He put on his hat.
f. He put his hat on the chair.
g. She dressed her daughter.
h. She got dressed.

Commentary

This is a mixed practice exercise, to be conducted after other practices which have been limited to one aspect of this complex feature. Here, the student is expected to decide rapidly to which category the different verbs belong, as he would have to do in communication.

7. After several drills developing familiarity with a certain feature, a mixed drill may be given (as in G9).

8. Translation drills provide a stimulus for quick production of verb forms for particular tenses as in G52 (but not for the use of these tenses which is more complicated), and for irregular verb forms as in G53:

G52 *He'll arrive tomorrow.* El llegará mañana.
They'll arrive tomorrow. Ellos llegarán mañana . . .

G53 *He has it.* El lo tiene.
He had it. El lo tuvo.
He'll have it. El lo tendrá.
He used to have it. El lo tenía . . .

It would be difficult to change G53 into a substitution drill, or even a conversion drill, yet such rapid checking of knowledge of irregular forms is useful and necessary.

7. Translation drills are *useful for quick review*—for refreshing students' memories and pinpointing persistent inaccuracies. Conducted orally, at a brisk pace, they do not give the students time to pore over the Spanish equivalents and edit them, as they do with written exercises.

Simultaneous interpretation

When some grammatical features are well learned, oral translation drills for review may be placed in a more realistic setting by giving individual students the opportunity to act as Spanish simultaneous interpreters for the poor monolingual English-speaking teacher or a fellow-student. With classroom-laboratory facilities, an authentic simultaneous interpreting situation can be staged. The passage for interpretation will be carefully prepared by the teacher so that it is possible for the student to interpret successfully. (It can also be designed to elicit certain features, for instance, specific tenses.) Other students will be asked to comment on the success of the interpreting and have the opportunity to improve on it. This type of activity is also suitable for recording in the language laboratory.

✳ Form small groups of students interested in different types of oral exercises.

1. Find examples of the selected type of oral exercise in textbooks, workbooks, or laboratory manuals, and discuss whether or not they are well constructed.

2. Try writing an exercise of this type for a structural feature for which it is appropriate.

3. Try your exercise out on the class to see if it is effective.

4. Take some poorly constructed oral exercises of this type, rewrite them in a more effective form, and then try them out on other students.

5
Teaching the sound system

Understanding descriptions of phonological systems: a little terminology[1]

In order to follow the discussion in this section, the reader needs to be familiar with certain commonly used terms. The sounds we make are *phones*. Although the number of phones that can be produced by any individual speaker is practically unlimited, only certain sounds are recognized by the speakers and hearers of a particular language as conveying meaning. The smallest unit of significant or meaningful sound is called a *phoneme*. A phoneme is actually an abstraction rather than a concrete description of a specific sound. Any particular phoneme comprises a group or *class* of sounds that are phonetically similar but whose articulations vary according to their position relative to the other sounds which precede or follow them. The environmentally conditioned variants of any particular sound occurring in complementary distribution are *allophones*. "In complementary distribution" means that these sound variants are regularly found in certain environments where they do not contrast with each other, e.g., variant A may occur only in medial position between vowels, whereas variant B always occurs in initial or final position.

In *articulatory phonetics,* we study the positions of the organs of speech, e.g., the tongue, lips, or vocal cords, in the production of different sounds. These articulatory descriptions are intended to help us to form unfamiliar sounds. In speech, however, the organs are in continual motion, so that

140

sounds may vary slightly as they are produced in association with other sounds or are given differing degrees of stress. This variation must remain within a certain band of tolerance if it is not to hinder comprehension (that is, if the phonetic variants are still to be recognizable as manifestations of the same phoneme to a listener familiar with that language).

The concepts mentioned above are useful for the teacher in understanding and defining problem areas which speakers of one language encounter when attempting to learn another. For example, the Spanish /l/ is phonemic, as shown by the fact that *lodo* and *modo* have different meanings which are signalled only by the change of the element /l/ to /m/. In English /l/ is also phonemic, as witness *it's a lot, it's a pot*. The phoneme /l/ in English, however, has two allophones, the so-called clear (alveolar) *l* [l] and the so-called dark (velar) *l* [ɫ] which occur in different environments ([l] before vowels and /j/, and [ɫ] after vowels) and are, therefore, in complementary distribution.

In Spanish, the /b/ phoneme is expressed quite differently in initial position and in intervocalic position, with different points of articulation, that is, as [b] in *bolo* [bólo] and as [ƀ] in *lobo* [lóƀo]; yet both manifestations are heard as /b/ by native speakers. These varying /b/ sounds always appear in certain environments and are, therefore, allophones of the phoneme /b/. The fact that they do not alternate with each other in the same position, but rather, have a clearly defined distribution, means that they are not merely accidental or dialectal.

The recognition of the phoneme is basically a psychological process which results from experience with a particular language. Most English speakers do not notice the difference between [l] and [ɫ] in their own language, because these sounds are non-distinctive in English, that is, they do not differentiate one word from another. Students need to be helped to hear differences to which they are not accustomed but which may be phonemic in a new language; otherwise, they may unwittingly transfer their English speech habits to the new language. Naturally, teachers of Spanish need to be very familiar with the significant differences between the Spanish and English sound systems if they are to help their students acquire a pronunciation acceptable and comprehensible to the native speaker.

In *generative phonology*,[2] sound systems are described not in terms of phonemes, but of *distinctive features*. These features are *binary*, that is, either present (+) or absent (−), which enables the phonologist to represent the phonological system of a language by a feature matrix. Features are described in terms which may be *articulatory* (taking into account such things as place and manner of articulation), *acoustic* (referring to information detectable by technical instruments), or *perceptual* (e.g., syllables or stress). Generative phonologists are attempting to establish a set of *universal* distinctive features which may be used to characterize the sounds of all languages. To the generative phonologist the pronunciation of a word is the spoken (surface) realization of an abstract underlying form, which results from the application of a set of rules to this abstract form. This approach has brought to light some interesting relationships between surface (phonological) representations and traditional spelling systems.

Languages change: how many phonemes are there in modern Spanish?

The number of Spanish phonemes is variously given as 24 or 25: 19 or 20 consonants and 5 vowels. The number of consonants depends on whether /r̄/ is classified as a phoneme or a variant of /r/. In this text it will be considered to be a separate phoneme, because even though it contrasts with /r/ only in intervocalic position, in that position it meets the criteria for defining a phoneme. There are many minimal pairs in which the only distinction lies in the /r/: /r̄/ contrast, e.g., *pero/perro; caro/carro; fiero/fierro; coro/corro,* to mention a few.

The consonant phonemes include two, namely Castilian /θ/ as in *vez* and /ḷ/ as in *allá,* which have effectively been lost for most Latin American speakers of Spanish. On the other hand, the vowel system of both Peninsular and Latin American Spanish shows signs of the continual pressure to change to which all spoken languages are subject.

Although the five vowel phonemes are considered to be very stable, with no significant differences between open and close articulations and with no diphthongization, Navarro Tomás has observed what he calls the "beginning of an important modification"[3] in the vowel system of Spanish. This, he believes, is the result, first, of a regular change from word final alveolar [s] and interdental [θ] (orthographic *z*) to an aspirated allophone [h]. This aspiration, in turn, has been lost in certain regions of Spain and Latin America, resulting in such forms as *dio* (verb) and *dio(s)* (noun) seemingly being pronounced the same. However, according to Navarro Tomás, there is a distinction between these forms due to a difference in the quality of the vowel—*dio* with mid-back [o] and *dio(s)* with a more open [o]. He finds this process of differentiation especially notable between singular and plural forms such as *boca/boca(s); casa/casa(s),* and in verb forms such as *viene/viene(s); pierde/pierde(s).* Navarro Tomás also finds a tendency to lengthen the final vowel.[4] The probability, over the course of time, of the inclusion of a new set of distinctive vowel sounds in the Spanish vowel system remains, of course, conjecture at present. But this observation does allow a glimpse of what may prove to be part of the continuing evolution of spoken Spanish. For a complete discussion of these matters, see Navarro Tomás, *Studies in Spanish Phonology,* pp. 36–39.

Languages contrast: major differences between the Spanish and English phonological systems

In his careful analysis of the sound systems of English and Spanish, Delattre summarized the phonetic characteristics of the vowels of the two languages:

Comparatively, English vowels are predominantly low, back, unrounded, with a strong tendency to center the short and unstressed (except when very low). Duration contributes to vowel distinctions. All English vowels are more or less diphthongized. Most characteristic series: the somewhat back-unrounded / u, ʊ, ɔ, ʌ/ .[5]

... Comparatively, Spanish vowels are predominantly high and peripheral. They are distinct from each other. The open/close difference of mid-vowels is negligible. Differences of duration are not distinctive. There is no diphthongization. Most characteristic series: the mid-open/mid-close vowels /e/ and /o/, which are midway between the ... English close and open vowels.[6]

A major characteristic of the English vowel system lies in the tendency for unstressed vowels to become centralized. Delattre points out that "about 90% of unstressed vowels turn to some sort of schwa (neutral vowel)"[7] symbolized as [ə]. Although the stressed vowels are distinctive, the same vowels in unstressed syllables may occur as either [ɨ] or [ə]. This is altogether different from Spanish where the same five vowels occur in both stressed and unstressed positions, as habla [ábla]; poco [póko], and where the contrast between vowel phonemes is maintained in unstressed syllables, as in hablo [áblo]; habla [ábla]. This feature and the need to learn to produce vowels which are not diphthongized may pose particular problems for the English speaker learning Spanish.

It is lack of recognition of basic contrastive differences such as these which results in a marked "foreign accent" as the student tries to make a few new sounds influenced by his native-language phonological system. The teacher will not explain these differences to his students in scientific terms (except at an adult level), but he will need to understand them himself if he is to help his students form correct Spanish sounds. Slight distinctions in sound which can hinder comprehension of a message are made by movements of the tongue and other organs in the teacher's mouth and throat which the students cannot normally see. Consequently, merely making Spanish sounds which are different from English sounds and urging students to imitate these, without giving some indications as to how they can be produced, may not be sufficient to ensure accurate production, particularly where a specific phoneme does not exist in English, as with

/r̄/ and /ñ/, or where it varies in some way from a familiar English sound as does the Spanish /l/.

Articulatory descriptions and empirical recommendations

Articulatory descriptions for the production of a particular sound, using terms like those in the previous section, are useful for the preparation of the teacher. They make clear to young teachers what they themselves have been doing, perhaps intuitively rather than consciously, in the pronunciation of Spanish. They highlight the types of articulatory difficulties English speakers may be expected to encounter. The teacher does not usually give such descriptions to the students at the introductory stage (although they may be helpful for remedial work and of interest to older students or to students learning a third language). Instead, from their knowledge of the articulatory data, teachers develop empirical recommendations to help their students produce sounds they do not seem to acquire easily by imitation.[8] (This subject is discussed in more detail below under *Remedial Training,* p. 158.)

TEACHING SPANISH /r/ AND /r̄/

We may take as an example of a sound which often proves difficult for speakers of English, the Spanish /r/ *vibrante simple.* (The *vibrante múltiple* /r̄/ is also a problem and its production should be discussed also by the class.)[9]

In teaching students to produce a Spanish /r/, it is often useful to begin by drawing their attention to the way they produce their native language /r/. Many students have never thought about this.

Prator's advice for the production of an American /r/ is as follows:

S1 "Pronounce the vowel [a]. As you do so, curve the tip of your tongue up and slide the sides of the tongue backward along the tooth ridge, and you should have no difficulty in producing a perfect American [r]."[10]

Armstrong describes the production of the British English fricative /r/, usually transcribed [ɹ], as follows:

"1. The tip of the tongue is raised to the back part of the teeth-ridge.
"2. The passage is narrowed at that point, but not sufficiently to cause much friction.
"3. The sound is voiced."[11]

Next we consider the formation of the Spanish /r/. Stockwell and Bowen give the following articulatory information:

S2 "The pronunciation of /r/ that appears in most dialects—and that is un-questionably the standard variety—is an alveolar FLAP, produced by a rapid motion of the tongue tip upward from behind the lower teeth across the alveolar ridge with no stop-phase between, merely touching against the alveolar area in passing on to the next sound. When a consonant follows the flap, there may or may not be a slight friction during part of the flap. Before a terminal-rising or a terminal-falling juncture the friction is much more noticeable, the /r/ is generally voiceless, and there may even be several voiceless flaps together, especially if the syllable is stressed."[12]

Interesting and helpful though this information may be to teachers and advanced students, the beginning student needs more practical advice like the following from Bull:

S3 "Most American students fail to hear [r] correctly and so have no notion of what to imitate. They can be helped by putting Spanish [r] in English words spoken with a strong Spanish accent: *very, pardon, partake, sorrow,* etc.
   "The closest American approximation is [d] when this sound follows a stressed syllable: *ladder, shudder, biddie.* The tongue position is the same but in making the Spanish [r] less of the tongue touches the roof of the mouth, the tongue is considerably more tense, and the contact is shorter. A fair imitation of *para* can be gotten by contracting *pod of* to *poda* and having the students say this rapidly. 'Pot o'tea' is fairly close to *para ti.*"[13]
   S3 does not provide a full articulatory description of the production of Spanish /r/, but rather endeavors to induce the correct articulatory posi-tions through the production of familiar movements which lead to the un-familiar movement required. The following instructions for the production of the *vibrante múltiple* /r̄/, or /rr/[14] are also empirical recommendations.

S4 "Have the student say *had* and hold the tongue tensely in the position for the final sound of *d*. This is the proper tongue position for [rr]. Now relax the tongue just enough so air can be forcefully blown out between the tongue and the alveolar ridge. A little experimentation with variations of tenseness will produce a proper degree at which the tongue will begin to flutter or flap. When the student can do this, the addition of voicing produces [rr]."[15]

* From your knowledge of English and Spanish articulatory movements, work out in similar fashion empirical recommendations for inducing students to make correct /o/ and /p/ sounds.

Teaching Spanish sounds as a system

Teachers often concentrate on correct articulatory production of those distinctive Spanish sounds which are very different from English sounds (the so-called "difficult" sounds) while allowing students to produce English near-equivalents for the rest. Unfortunately, incorrectly articulated consonants affect the production of adjacent consonants and vowels, just as incorrect vowel production affects the contiguous consonants.

Politzer points out that once the /r/ is mastered in intervocalic position, its occurrence after most other consonants (e.g., *pr, br, cr, gr*) is not difficult to learn. However, the groups *tr* and *dr* may present some difficulty if the student starts off from wrong assumptions. "If the learner fails to place the tip of the tongue against the upper teeth, that is, if he starts off with an English alveolar /t/ or /d/, he will have difficulty making the tap /r/ at the same point of articulation, and a fricative sound somewhat like [ʃ] will be produced. This mispronunciation is annoying to Spanish-speaking people."[16]

EFFECT OF INCORRECT PRODUCTION OF FINAL *l*

Many students do not realize that in English they are using two *l*s: the so-called *clear l* as in *leaf* and *lack,* which is different from the so-called *dark l* of *bull, fell* or *table.* The *l* used in initial position in English is not very .different from the Spanish *l*. According to Rodriguez-Castellano, "Para pronunciar la /l/ española se apoya la punta de la lengua contra los alvéolos de los incisivos superiores. La /l/ inicial inglesa se articula en el mismo lugar que la española, pero cuando es final de sílaba o va seguida de consonante la lengua adopta una posición más cóncava, esto es, el dorso de la lengua no se eleva tanto. . . . (La mala pronunciación de esta consonante no impide el ser entendido, pero acusa marcado 'acento estranjero.')"[17] When the student, unwittingly, uses in Spanish an English *dark l* in final position or for *l* + consonant, he distorts and tends to diphthongize the preceding vowel, as in *mal* [máəł], *el sol* [eəłsóəł] or *saltar* [saəłtar], because the general tongue position for the English *final l* is close to the position of /ʊ/ in *pull.* Stockwell and Bowen comment, "The mispronunciation of /l/ marks the English accent in Spanish more clearly than any consonant but /r/."[18] Though a mispronunciation will not usually cause misunderstanding, it is still very important to try to improve the /l/, since pronouncing it incorrectly will always call attention to the way you say it and away from what you are saying. Any efforts the teacher may have made to teach students to pronounce correctly /a/ and /o/ will thus be negated by failure to teach the correct pronunciation of /l/.

One of the characteristics of connected speech in English is open or plus /+/ juncture which, by its presence or absence or change of position, can indicate word boundary, as for example, *an aim* /ən+éɪm/, *a name* /ənéɪm/; *great ape* /gréɪt+éɪp/, *gray tape* /gréɪ+téɪp/. A number of phonetic features may account for the presence of /+/ juncture, such as the aspirated allophone of /t/ occurring in [tʰéɪp] as opposed to the unaspirated final allophone in [gréɪt]. A very frequent indicator of /+/ juncture is the insertion of a glottal stop before an initial vowel across word boundary: *an iceman* [ənʔáɪsmæn]. This glottal stop does not occur before a vowel in an identical internal sequence: *a nice man* [ənáɪsmæn]. This kind of indicator does not occur in Spanish. Thus *helado* is indistinguishable from *el hado:* the vowels of h*e* and *e*(l) are both open; the consonant is articulated as the syllable initial allophone [l] in both instances; and the onset of the vowels -*a*do and -(l)*ha*do is the same.

Therefore, the characteristic of close or internal juncture, i.e., the normal transition from one sound to the next within words, is important in Spanish since this will, in most cases, occur *across word boundaries* as well. There are several ways in which close juncture across word boundaries affects the final and initial allophones of successive words. One of these is the change in articulation of the voiced stops /b,d,g/ from their initially occurring allophones [b,d,g] to those of medial position [b,d,g]: *boca* [bóka] vs. *la boca* [labóka]; *dichoso* [dičóso] vs. *fue dichoso* [fu̯eđičóso]; *gusto* [gústo] vs. *qué gusto* [kegústo].

An exception to the regularity of occurrence of close juncture across word boundary is found in the change of /n/ in word final position to [ŋ] when followed by an initial vowel or pause. In many Latin American and Peninsular areas [ŋ] is an allophone of /n/ denoting open (+) juncture, as in *con amor* [koɲamór], *está bien* [estabi̯éɲ]. Students should know that this feature is sufficiently widespread, particularly in Latin America, not to be considered dialectal or an undesirable speech habit.

＊ The above discussion of the differences between the English and Spanish sound systems is illustrative only and by no means exhaustive. Be sure you are aware of and able to help students with such other problems as the unaspirated [p,t,k], the elusive difference between the pronunciation of the English *ni* of "onion" and the Spanish *ñ* of *niño,* and between the English *lli* of "million" and the Spanish *ll* of *silla;* the joining of vowels across word boundaries (ella está aquí), the aspiration of word or syllable final /s/; and differences in stress and in patterns of intonation.

Aural discrimination

Students confronted with strange sounds will at first tend to perceive them as variants of the categories of sounds with which they are familiar in their native language. If this continues, it may, of course, not only affect comprehension, but will also hinder the development of a near-native pronunciation. The student who is not aware of certain distinctions between sounds is unlikely to produce unfamiliar sounds correctly, except by chance on random occasions. When he is able to "hear" the differences, that is, discriminate aurally between sounds, he can work toward achieving these distinctions in his own production.

Spanish sounds which have no counterpart in English will at first be difficult for speakers of English to distinguish. They will tend not to perceive the difference between /r/ and /r̄/ as in *caro/carro*. A failure to hear the aspirated allophone of final /s/ may result in a failure to recognize common forms like *los* [loʰ]. English speakers may have trouble distinguishing unaspirated [p,t,k] from /b,d,g/.

Certain allophones may not be recognized as positional variants of a single Spanish phoneme and therefore may be confused with two different English phonemes. Students may associate the unvoiced allophone [s] of Spanish /s/, as in *es su padre* [ésupádre], with English /s/ in *east* [í:st], but may confuse its voiced allophone [z], as in *es mi padre* [ézmipádre], with English /z/ as in *easy* [í:zi]. They may, therefore, not recognize the form *es* as being the same word in both cases.

AURAL DISCRIMINATION PROBLEMS

Exercises may be designed to help students discriminate sounds which are causing them difficulty, once the problem involved has been identified. Particular Spanish sounds should be differentiated both from closely related Spanish sounds and from English sounds that may be interfering with the student's perception.

Just how much difficulty a particular English-speaking student may have in distinguishing one sound of Spanish from others depends on a number of factors, such as his individual sensitivity to distinctions of sound, the pronunciation of the teacher, and how carefully the student happens to be listening on that day. As a rule, students are first taught to discriminate a problem sound from a similar Spanish sound or from an interfering similar sound in English. If the students' inability to distinguish the sound persists because of confusion with other sounds, then the number of discrimination exercises is increased to cope with this complexity. Problem areas in Spanish which involve one or more discriminations are illustrated in examples S5–9. In the diagrams accompanying these examples, the sounds to be discriminated are connected by arrows. The various discriminations involved in each example are numbered.

1. A simple Spanish-English discrimination.

S5

$$\text{Sp. } [t] \longleftrightarrow \text{Eng. } [t^h]$$
$$(1)$$

The student learns to discriminate between the Spanish unaspirated *t* and the English aspirated *t*.

2. Distinguishing two *similar* Spanish sounds from each other and each of these from an *interfering* English sound.

S6

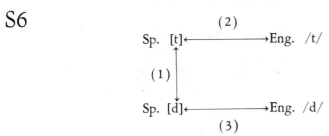

The student learns to discriminate Spanish unaspirated [t] of *temor* from [d] of *demora* and these from English phonemes /t/ and /d/ in *team* and *deem* respectively.

3. Distinguishing two *different* Spanish sounds from each other and one of these from an *interfering* English sound.

S7

$$\text{Sp. } [k] \longleftrightarrow \text{Eng. } /g/$$
$$(2)$$
$$(1)$$
$$\text{Sp. } [g]$$

The student learns to discriminate the Spanish [k] of *coma* from Spanish [g] of *goma,* as well as distinguishing the former from the English /g/ of *gum.*

4. Distinguishing two Spanish *variant* sounds from each other and one of these from an *interfering* English sound.

S8

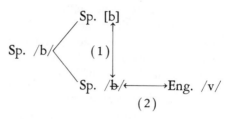

The student learns to discriminate between the Spanish [b] of *bola* and
[b] of *lobo,* and the latter from English /v/ of *love.*

The student learns to discriminate between the Spanish [b] of *bola* and
[b] of *lobo,* and the latter from English /v/ of *love.*

S9

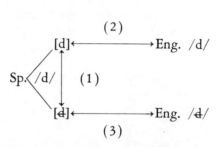

The student learns to discriminate Spanish [d] in d*ora* from Spanish [đ]
in a*dora,* and to recognize further that Spanish [đ] is different from
English /đ/ in th*is* and that Spanish [đ] is different from English /d/
in a*dore.*

* Show diagrammatically the discrimination problems an English speaker
can encounter in learning to distinguish *caro* and *carro, parata* and *barata.*

TYPES OF AURAL DISCRIMINATION EXERCISES

These exercises are necessary only when discrimination problems become
evident. Often they serve remedial purposes. Which types of exercises and
how many are used at one time and how these are interspersed with
production exercises will vary according to the needs of a particular group
of students at a particular time. Usually, after some aural discrimination
exercises, students will be encouraged to produce the sounds themselves to
demonstrate what they have observed. If confusions are still evident, more
aural discrimination exercises may be tried.

The Spanish /r/ and /r̄/, which are easily confused by English speakers,
will be used for demonstration purposes in the following examples. These
sounds may be identified and practiced individually, discriminated from

each other and from interfering English sounds, and finally produced in close proximity, as demonstrated below.[19]

Type 1: Identification of the sound, e.g., /r/

The sound will have been encountered in dialogue or conversational narrative, or in oral work in the classroom, in an utterance like: *Es para María,* or *Mañana sí, pero ahora no.*

    1. The sound in a *familiar context*.

S10 Listen carefully to these sentences:

    a. ¿Para quién es?
    b. Es para María.
    c. Es para Teresa.

    2. The sound in *single words of vowel + consonant + vowel construction*.

S11 Listen again to the sound /r/ in the following words:

    d. hora, aro, era . . .

    3. The sound in a *larger context*.

S12 How many times do you hear the sound /r/ in the following sentences?

    e. Es para Teresa.
    f. Pero ahora no está.
    g. María hablará como un loro.

Type 2: Minimal pair technique

    1. Discrimination between *similar sounds in Spanish and English.*

S13 Listen to the difference between the Spanish /r/ and the English /r/.

    a. *aroma* / aroma
    b. *moro* / morrow
    c. *aro* / arrow

    2. Discrimination between *similar sounds within the Spanish phonological system.*

S14 The sound /r/ is not the same as /r̄/. Listen carefully to the differences between the following pairs:

    d. caro / carro

e. coro / corro
f. pero / perro
g. moro / morro
h. Es un moro. / Es un morro . . .
   Si la amara . . . / Si la amarra . . .

Type 3: Same-different exercises

Listen carefully to the following sounds in these pairs of words and tell me (or: mark on your answer sheet) if the two words in each pair are the same or different.

1. Spanish / English

S15 (For Spanish /r/ vs. English /r/):

a. *toro, toro*   (same)
b. *cera,* Sarah   (different)
c. *mero, mero*   (same)...

S16 (For Spanish /r̄/ vs. English /dr/):

d. *rey,* dray   (different)
e. *corría, corría* (same)
f. drama, *rama*   (different)...

2. Spanish / Spanish

S17 (For /r̄/ vs. /dr/):

g. reno, dreno   (different)
h. Roma, Roma   (same)
i. drogar, rogar   (different)
j. draga, draga   (same)...

S18 (For /r/ vs. /r̄/):

k. Son carros. Son caros.   (different)
l. ¿Para qué?, ¿Para qué?   (same)
m. Es un cero., Es un cerro. (different)

(With Spanish/Spanish discriminations it is possible to use a few examples in larger contexts than single words as long as the only difference in sound is the change of the consonant. See also Type 2, h.)

Type 4: Differentiation exercises
You will hear three words numbered 1, 2, and 3. Write down (or: tell me) the number of the one which is different from the others.

1. Spanish / English

S19 (For Spanish /r/ vs. English /r/):

a. 1. *cera*	2. *cera*	3. Sarah	(3)
b. 1. chorus	2. *coros*	3. chorus	(2)

S20 (For Spanish /r/ vs. English /t/ or /d/):

c. 1. photo	2. photo	3. *foro*	(3)
d. 1. *oro*	2. auto	3. *oro*	(2)

2. Spanish / Spanish

S21 (For /r/ vs. /r̄/):

e. 1. ahorra	2. ahora	3. ahora	(1)
f. 1. Si lo amarra	2. Si lo amarra	3. Si lo amara	(3)

S22 *Variation.*

In the following groups of words, one does not have the same sound as the others. Make a check mark for each word as you hear it, crossing the mark you have made for the one which has a different sound from the others (e.g., / / ≠)

g. oro, moro, *codo,* loro, toro
h. ahorra, amarra, perro, *cera,* torre

Type 5: Rhyming exercise (combining aural discrimination and production)

S23 Listen to the following word and give me as many words as you can think of which rhyme with it:

TEACHER   foro
STUDENTS   oro, coro, moro;   loro, toro.
                        corro, morro,

✱ Construct items similar to those in Types 2, 3, and 4 of this section to help students discriminate:

1. unstressed Spanish vowels;
2. Spanish /e/ from English /ɛɪ/
3. Spanish [b] from Spanish [ƀ]

Production
INTRODUCTION OF THE SPANISH SOUND SYSTEM

Should the learning of a language begin with a series of lessons on the sound system? This is the approach of some textbooks. Usually, when this is done, little attention is paid to the usefulness of the words in which the sounds are produced or whether they will be used in classwork in the early lessons. In a quick check of several such textbooks the following words were found for practice: *soso, engero, pompo, porche, ducho, pira, galgo, serete, seronda, quío, neme, tongo, baqueta, zurro, quijo,* and *áloe.* None of these words appears in the five thousand words listed in the *Frequency Dictionary of Spanish Words.* This approach may be acceptable for highly motivated adult learners to whom the rationale of the teaching has been explained but it is unwise for elementary, junior high school, or senior high school classes. It can become boring and its relevance is not understood by the students who are anxious to be able to say something practical in Spanish.

In the early lessons the students can be introduced to the whole array of Spanish sounds which they try to repeat after the teacher before being drilled carefully in particular problems of pronunciation. Sentences like the following are frequently the first the student learns:

Buenos días, Carlos. ¿Cómo estás? /buenosdíaskárlos/ /kómoestás/

These five words contain fourteen different sounds, of which only five /e, o, a, s, k/ are repeated and only six /b, u, n, s, k, m/ pose no difficulty for English speakers. A normal reply: *Muy bien, gracias. ¿Y tú?* /muibiengrasiasitu/ introduces three more, making a total of seventeen distinct sounds. This shows the impracticality of trying to keep early material within the limits of certain sounds if natural, usable utterances are to be learned. Sentences such as *Enrique quería que Quintana se quedara en Quito* which are artificially constructed to introduce only one or two sounds at a time may have some place in laboratory drill, particularly of a remedial nature, but their utility is limited in developing conversational interchange. Tongue-twisters like *Erre con erre cigarro, erre con erre barril. Rápido corren los carros, por la línea del ferrocarril,* for practicing /r̄/, may be used for relaxation in the classroom and to focus attention on a particular problem. Repetition of such concentrated conglomerations of one sound gives some practice in the correct articulation of the sound. This, of itself, does not ensure equally successful transfer to utterances where the sound is more sparsely distributed. The sound will need to be practiced in many contexts if it is to reappear correctly articulated in spontaneous utterances.

EARLY TEACHING OF THE SOUND SYSTEM

Language learning usually begins either with the simple dialogue, useful expressions for classroom interchange, or a conversational narrative in the textbook. As the student listens to the teacher or model, his ear becomes attuned to the overall system of sounds of the language and its characteristic rhythm, stress, and intonation or melodic patterns. *Approximations to correct pronunciation* are sought in everything the student reproduces, without insistence on perfection at every point since this is too discouraging for the students at this early stage.

Problem sounds are singled out at intervals in the first few weeks and practiced with attention to acceptable and comprehensible production.

1. The teacher begins with *short phrases* from current work, then, if necessary, isolates *specific words,* gives practice in *a specific sound,* returns to practice of *words* and then to *the complete phrase,* moving, e.g., from *muy bien, gracias* to *muy bien,* to *muy,* and if absolutely necessary to [ųi], then rebuilding to *muy, muy bien,* and finally *muy bien, gracias.*

Students may be asked to produce the sound in isolation a few times if they are having trouble with it, but not for long. Most sounds are rarely heard in isolation, and students must become accustomed to the slight variations which occur when sounds are made in association with other sounds.

2. Where possible, the sound is practiced first in *strong stressed* position, and then in *weak stressed* position, with the students being trained to retain in weak stressed position the full quality of the Spanish sound as a counteraction to their English language habits.

S24 Está con Tomás. (strong) *or* él habla (strong/weak)
Voy con esta chica. (weak) él hablaba (weak/strong/weak)

3. When the teacher senses that students would profit from intensive practice in specific pronunciation problems, the training should move from *identification* of the sound (associated with aural discrimination of similar sounds, where necessary, as in S6–19), to *imitative production.* When imitative production is well advanced, the practice moves to *guided non-imitative production* (where the exercise is so structured that the student is induced to produce the sound without first hearing the model). The goal must be *autonomous production* of the correct sound in non-structured contexts.

During intensive training in the production of a certain sound, it is helpful for the student to hear a correct model after he has produced the sound himself. He needs to be sensitized to the differences between his own production and the desired pronunciation if he is to improve in unsupervised practice. Where his own production has been faulty he should correct it immediately, while he still retains the auditory image of the model. (The four-phase format of G9 is often employed for this reason.)

1. Identification. Student listens.

S25 MODEL   Esta mujer está con Pepe . . . Esta . . . está . . . Esta mujer está con Pepe. . . . Esta mujer . . . está con Pepe. . . . Esta mujer está con Pepe.

2. Imitative production (strong vs. weak stress).

S26 MODEL   Esta mujer está con Pepe; STUDENT   Esta mujer está con Pepe;
MODEL   Esta mujer está con Pepe.
Student repeats after the model to correct his production or confirm it.

A similar four-phase format continues while the student imitates *Esta . . . está . . . Esta mujer está con Pepe,* thus practicing the sound in reduced contexts and then producing it once more in the larger context.

The practice moves on to such expressions as:

S27 Esta señora es mi mamá; sí, ésta es mi mamá.
Está con mi papá. Esta noche está con Papá.
Tomás, ¿tomas champaña? ¿Tomas champaña con Tomás?

3. Guided non-imitative production.

S28 TEACHER   ¿Cuál de ésas es tu mamá?
STUDENT   Esta es mi mamá. (weak/weak/strong)
TEACHER   ¿Dónde está Pepe esta noche?
STUDENT   Esta noche está con Papá. (weak/strong/weak/strong)
TEACHER   Pregúntele a Tomás si toma champaña con Papá.
STUDENT   Tomás, ¿tomas champaña con Papá? (strong/weak/weak/strong/weak/weak/strong)

4. Autonomous production.

S29 An interchange takes place between students, with the students themselves selecting the way they will ask the question or answer it.

¿Dónde está Tomás?
Está en casa.

¿Quién es esta señora?
   Es mi mamá.
¿Qué toma Tomás?
   Toma champaña.
¿Con Mamá?
   No, con Papá.

If the interchange is truly autonomous, students will occasionally produce sentences which do not contain the sound being practiced.

In the early lessons it is not only particular sounds which are practiced, but also smooth production of vowel onset (*ataque suave*), the contraction of two vowels or syllables into one (syneresis or *sinéresis*), and the linking of words across word boundaries (synalepha or *sinalefa*).[20]

WHAT DEGREE OF PERFECTION SHOULD BE EXPECTED IN THE EARLY STAGES?

Practice should concentrate on errors of pronunciation which would hinder comprehension and errors which force students into other errors (like those discussed above under *Teaching Spanish Sounds as a System*). The teacher will need to return again and again, in an unobtrusive fashion, to certain persistent faults which are crucial to comprehension or acceptability, while continuing to improve the overall standard of pronunciation.

Remedial training

A distinction must be drawn between the types of exercises suitable in the very early stages when the student knows only a little of the foreign language and appropriate exercises for remedial training at a later stage. At first, emphasis is laid on phonemic distinctions which hinder comprehension. Later, advanced students often need intensive training in the production of certain sounds or sequences of sounds to correct a "foreign accent."

Remedial work at an advanced level usually takes the form of a *systematic review of the Spanish sound system*. At this stage, students have a wide-ranging vocabulary and considerable knowledge of grammatical structure. After a certain number of retraining drills (see S35–38), exercises can be used which exploit the students' knowledge of the language, eliciting from them the sounds being reviewed while they are concentrating on grammatical conversions and manipulations (see S39).

REMEDIAL PRODUCTION EXERCISES

Exercises of this type are usually constructed on a contrastive basis, highlighting problems of interference from English sounds which are close to the Spanish sounds being practiced, and from other Spanish sounds which to an English ear appear similar to the particular sound to be produced (see S5–9). The remedial exercises in production may be preceded by *aural identification exercises* in which the sound is used in short utterances which are meaningful.

1. Remedial production exercises are frequently preceded by *articulatory instructions* for the correct production of the sound, with warnings about English habits which interfere with correct articulation. These are sometimes accompanied by photographs or diagrams showing the recommended position of the speech organs. (Articulatory information, can, of course, be supplied without the use of technical terms. In the instructions below, *dental, alveolar,* and *aspirated* can be omitted and the explanations of these terms used instead.)

S30 *Articulatory instructions for the production of a Spanish t*

Spanish *t* is *dental,* that is, it is produced with the tip of the tongue down and the tongue pressed against the upper teeth, whereas English *t* is *alveolar,* that is, it is produced with the tip of the tongue raised and touching the gums or tooth ridge. The Spanish *t* sound is *unaspirated* [t] whereas the English counterpart is usually *aspirated* [tʰ] (that is, when it is articulated a puff of air is emitted) except when it follows English [s] as in s*t*op.

These articulatory instructions are often accompanied by *empirical recommendations* for achieving the correct articulation or for testing whether the sound is being correctly produced.

S31 *Empirical recommendations: Spanish t—English t*

Hold a piece of paper (or a lighted match) in front of your mouth as you say English *t*op and notice how the paper (or flame) is blown by the puff of air emitted with the [tʰ]. Now say s*t*op and observe that the paper (or flame) does not move very much at all. This is because the English *t* is aspirated in initial position and unaspirated after [s]. Try to say s...top, s...top, s...top without aspirating the *t*; now try to say s...top with your tongue against your upper teeth with the tip down and no aspiration. You will now have made a Spanish [t].

S32 *Articulatory instructions for the production of a consonant: Spanish [y]*

As pointed out by Navarro Tomás (1971, pp. 129–30), Spanish [y] is a voiced palatal fricative. Lip position is that of contiguous vowels; the tip of the tongue rests against the inner surface of the lower front teeth; the tongue is arched, touching the palate on both sides and forming an elongated opening.

S33 *Empirical recommendations: Spanish* [y]

In order to achieve the correct consonantal quality of this sound, the student needs to practice raising and lowering the tongue, gradually increasing and decreasing the distance between tongue and palate. After he can feel the difference in position ranging from complete closure to complete opening, he needs to identify that tongue height that enables him to approximate the tenseness and friction produced by the model—his teacher or a recording.

2. Production exercises *should not begin with the sound in isolation.* This is useful only when articulatory movements are being practiced. (No Spanish phoneme occurs normally in isolation, except in a few exclamations and tags, e.g., ¡ah! ¡oh!) The various relationships into which a sound enters modify it slightly and it is these natural sequences which must be learned. Production exercises begin, then, with the *sound in single words or short phrases* which demonstrate the various environments in which it can occur, although often with a slightly different pronunciation. For instance, a voiced stop (/b/, /d/, or /g/) may be practiced in the following environments (a) after a pause (#), after a nasal sound, and in the case of /d/, after /l/; (b) in utterance final position; and (c) elsewhere. A vowel may be practiced in strong stress and in weak stress positions. This is the stage of *imitative production.* The words in which the sounds are practiced should be words which students can use rather than nonsense words.

S34 *Relationships in which the consonant* /d/ *may occur* (as above)

a. Di ... #, Del ... #, Dan ... #, Drama ... #; un dios, andar; falda, sueldo
b. ... sed #, ... Cid #, ... virtud #, ... libertad #
c. a Dios, adiós, las doce, tarde, padre

S35 *The vowel* /o/ *in various stress positions.*

a. es español, me la vendió, sí les habló (strong stress)
b. él teléfono, tengo mucho gusto, horizontal (weak stress)

3. The sound is then practiced in short sentences, also in various environments and intonation patterns. This is still imitative production.

S36 *The consonant /r/ in short sentences in various environments*

a. Era para María. b. Era verde. c. Eso me parece curioso. d. Pero a Carlos no. e. ¿Es hora de salir? f. Sí, ahora mismo.

g. ¿Prefieren el periódico? h. ¿Por qué no se compran uno?

4. Remedial exercises often *practice two similar sounds at the same time,* or some other contrasting feature, in order to highlight auditory and kinesthetic differences, since it is oppositions and contrasts within the sound system which make a language meaningful.

S37 *Vowel contrasts* are demonstrated in such pairs as:

a. son franceses: son francesas;
b. me gusta el color: me gusta el calor;
c. lo han sabido: lo han subido.

S38 *Differences in the position of stress* distinguish the meaning of the following pairs:

a. hablo despacio: habló despacio;
b. Sí, habrá: sí, abra;
c. no lo busque: no lo busqué.

5. Exercises are next introduced which, through some form of *grammatical manipulation,* encourage the student to *produce the sound unmodeled.* This is *guided non-imitative production.*

S39   a. A change from singular *él habló poco* to plural *ellos hablaron poco* requires the student to produce bilabial nasal [m] before the bilabial [p] while concentrating on the grammatical manipulation he is asked to perform.

b. A change from *no hay más* to the expanded *no hay más manzanas* requires the change from an unvoiced [s] to the voiced [z] across a word boundary.

6. The sound is then practiced in *longer utterances,* in mixed environments, or in sections of discourse. In this way the effects of proximity to other sounds in characteristic sequences, of intonation, stress, *sinéresis,* vowel onset (*ataque suave*), and *sinalefa* are more fully experienced. This practice need not be purely repetitive and imitative. It can take the form of a question and answer series, so designed as to induce the student to produce certain sounds.

S40 *The diphthong* /ai/.

a. Yo ba*i*lo con Marta. ¿Y tú?
   Ba*i*lo con Elena.
b. ¿Cuántos estudiantes ha*y* aquí?
   Ha*y* muchos.
c. ¿Qué me traes en esa bolsa?
   Te tra*i*go un regalo de cumpleaños.

In the application practice of this type, there is no need to concoct sentences loaded with a particular sound like: No tra*i*gas esa ga*i*ta al ba*i*le. Such artificiality makes the student overconscious of what the exercise demands of him and the resulting production is no real indication of what he will produce autonomously.

7. Sounds may finally be practiced *in a formal context* such as the reading of *poetry or literary prose,* since much of the language in earlier exercises will have been informal. It is important that students learn the differences between the formal and informal style of spoken Spanish.

If the passage is read after a model, this is merely imitative production. If it is later read by the student alone, this is guided non-imitative production.

8. There is a place for some *anticipation practice*. The student reads each section first before hearing it read by a model. He then has the opportunity to reread this section and continue reading the next section before again hearing the model. This can be done as spaced reading on tape, provided that the natural pauses between word groupings are as obvious as in the following passage of simple conversation.

S41 [b] vs. [ƀ] *contrasts.*

STUDENT ¿Con quién *v*as al *b*aile el sá*b*ado?
MODEL ¿Con quién *v*as al *b*aile el sá*b*ado?
STUDENT ¿Con quién *v*as al *b*aile el sá*b*ado? preguntó E*v*a.
MODEL ...preguntó E*v*a.
STUDENT ...preguntó E*v*a. Creo que con *V*icente, pero toda*v*ía no me ha in*v*itado.
MODEL Creo que con *V*icente, pero toda*v*ía no me ha in*v*itado.
STUDENT Creo que con *V*icente, pero toda*v*ía no me ha in*v*itado. ¿*V*erdad? ¿Y si no te in*v*ita él?
MODEL ¿*V*erdad? ¿Y si no te in*v*ita él?

STUDENT   ¿*V*erdad? ¿Y si no te in*v*ita él? Entonces *v*oy con el primero que
                   me in*v*ite.

MODEL   Entonces *v*oy con el primero que me in*v*ite.

9. The goal of this type of remedial practice is for the student to
demonstrate control of the sound he has been practicing when he is engaged in autonomous production in conversation.

✻ *Questions to discuss* in class or with other teachers.

1. Should remedial production exercises be conducted with book open
or with book closed? (What has been your own experience?)

2. Why do you think nursery and counting rhymes, like S42[21] are
often used for pronunciation practice?

S42   a.   Se murió Lola.
                  ¿Qué Lola?
                  Lolamento.
                  ¿Qué mento?
                  Mentosán.
                  ¿Qué san?
                  San Germán.
                  ¿Qué man?
                  Manatí.
                  ¿Qué ti?
                  Tiburón.
                  ¿Qué ron?
                  Ron Don Q.
                  ¿Qué Q?
                  Cubo de agua.
                  ¿Qué agua?
                  Agua de rá.
                  ¿Qué rá?
                  Rabo de mono.
                  ¿Qué mono?
                  Monopolio.
                  ¿Qué polí?
                  Policía.
                  ¿Qué cía?
                  Se acabó.

        b.   Uno, dos, tres, cuatro, cinco.
                  Cogí un conejo de un brinco.

Seis, siete, ocho, nueve, diez.

Se me escapó otra vez.

3. How would you help a student to correct the following faults? Aspiration of /p/; pronouncing Spanish *tú* the same as English *two;* reducing weak-stressed vowels in such a way that words like *estos* and *estas* are both pronounced /estəs/; misplacing strong stress on words such as *teléfono* (mispronounced: *télefono* or *telefóno*), *telegrama* (mispronounced: *télegrama*), and *policía* (mispronounced: *policia*).

4. Which do you consider the most useful for practicing sounds: poems or prose extracts? Why?

* *Find some short poems* which would be useful for practicing certain types of sounds. They must be attractive and simple in content, with vocabulary and structures appropriate for the level at which you propose to use them. A certain amount of repetition of lines, or segments of lines, will make them more useful, particularly if this involves alliteration of a feature to be practiced or assonance involving vowels requiring special attention. Short lines are an advantage if you wish the poem to be memorized.

STIMULATING INTEREST IN REMEDIAL PRONUNCIATION PRACTICE

If students need corrective training but have become bored with the usual sound production exercises, this remedial work can be associated with the study of a system of symbols for Spanish sounds like that in the Appendix. As students concentrate on learning which sounds are represented by which symbols and as they endeavor to write down dictated passages in phonetic symbols, they become more sensitive to fine distinctions of sound. The reading aloud of passages in phonetic symbols can be a useful remedial production exercise. The transcribing of passages in phonetic symbols into normal written Spanish draws the students' attention to the relationships between the Spanish sound and spelling systems. These new intellectual interests often stimulate motivation to improve pronunciation where "more pronunciation exercises" would fail.

Similarly the organization of a poetry recitation competition, the production of some short one-act plays by different groups for a festival or an inter-school social gathering, or the exchange of letter-tapes with Spanish-speaking correspondents will make students conscious of the need to improve their pronunciation and intonation.

MONITORING ONE'S OWN PRODUCTION

When working with tapes on their own, students have difficulty in detecting their errors of pronunciation. Aural discrimination exercises help the student refine his ability to perceive distinctions.

To make them more conscious of these distinctions in their own production, students may be asked to read on to tape a series of aural discrimination exercises of Types 3 and 4 (S15–21) and then, later, to use this recording as an exercise, comparing their final discrimination decisions with the original script from which they recorded the exercise.

Students can be encouraged to evaluate their progress in perfecting their pronunciation by marking their weaknesses and their successes on a *pronunciation checklist* (S43).

1. When *working with tapes,* students should keep the checklist beside them as a guide to the features of the Spanish sound system to which they should be attentive.

2. If the practice session is monitored, students should mark on the checklist the weaknesses in pronunciation which the monitor has drawn to their attention, so that they may concentrate on improving their production of these features.

3. The monitor should keep a cumulative record on a pronunciation checklist for each student, so that at each session he may refresh his memory of the weaknesses he has already drawn to the attention of the particular student to whom he is listening. In this way he will be able to emphasize some faults at one session and others at another, thus making maximum use of the short time at his disposal.

4. If pronunciation tapes are checked from time to time by the teacher, comments may be entered on a duplicate pronunciation checklist for the student's consideration when recording.

S43 *Sample Pronunciation Checklist*

Features for Attention	Estimate of Quality (E, A, or U) *	Monitor's Comments and Notes on Progress
General Features		
1. Vigorous lip movement (rounding, unrounding, opening).		
2. Division of syllables.		
3. Stress: word, sentence.		
Vowels		
4. Purity of vowels (no diphthongization).		

	Estimate of Quality (E, A, or U) *	Monitor's Comments and Notes on Progress
Features for Attention		
5. Preservation of vowel quality of un-stressed vowels (no reduction).		
Consonants		
6. [b;b̶]‡		
7. [d;d̶]‡		
8. [g;g̶]‡		
9. [l]		
10. [l̩] or [y]		
11. [ñ]		
12. [p/b]†		
13. [t/d]†		
14. [r/r̄]†		
15. [s;z]‡		
16. semi-consonants [y,w]		
17. aspiration of final *s*: [h]		
Intonation		
18. Statements.		
19. Yes-no question.		
20. Information question.		
21. Exclamation and interjections.		
General Fluency		
22. Vowel onset (*ataque suave*).		
23. *Sinéresis.*		
24. *Sinalefa.*		
25. Grouping of words in meaningful units.		

* E = Excellent (near-native); A = Acceptable (but not perfect); U = Unacceptable (needs attention)
‡ ; indicates grouping because of similarity of articulation (e.g., [b;b̶]).
† / indicates that sounds must not be confused in pronunciation (e.g., [r/r̄]).

❊ *Use this checklist to evaluate a recording of your own speech in Spanish.*

You will have to ask another student, a fellow teacher, or your instructor to evaluate point 1 for you by watching you. Later, discuss in class how the list can be improved. Is it too long for practical use? Could certain categories be evaluated together?

❊ Sometimes teachers (and students) use for initial or final evaluation of pronunciation a recording of a *passage* such as the following which *includes most of the features in the sample checklist.* Try to evaluate a recording by one of your fellow students of this passage.

S44 *Evaluation Passage*

Study the following passage carefully for three minutes to see that you understand the development of the dialogue, but do not make any marks on the paper. Read the passage clearly and expressively into the microphone with your tape recorder set at Record. Do not read the names Adela and Amador.

ADELA	—Por curiosidad. ¿Quién es usted?
AMADOR	—¿Quién? ¿Yo?
ADELA	—¡Sí! ¡Usted!
AMADOR	—¡Je! Leonardo Amador Ramírez, soltero, treinta y dos años, natural de Vitoria . . .
ADELA	(*Muy impaciente*) —¡No me importa todo eso!
AMADOR	(*Francamente defraudado*) —¡Vaya! Pues si . . .
ADELA	—Lo que quiero saber es algo muy diferente. ¿Qué hace usted aquí?
AMADOR	(*Estupefacto*) —¿Cómo?
ADELA	—¿Con qué derecho entra usted en este apartamento? ¿Por qué tiene usted la llave?
AMADOR	—Pero, señorita, eso está clarísimo . . .
ADELA	—¿De veras?
AMADOR	—¡Claro! Esta mañana he comprado este apartamento.[22]
ADELA	—¿Está seguro de que es este mismo?

II
THE WRITTEN WORD

6
Reading I:
purposes and procedures

Most students learning Spanish expect to be able to read the language sooner or later. Their personal desires and expectations vary from wanting to be able to read a play by Lorca or a scientific journal to being able to read a menu, a tourist brochure, or posters advertising the Pamplona corridas. Fortunately, reading is a completely individual activity, and students in the same course may be reading at very different levels of difficulty in Spanish just as they do in English.

To be able to read in Spanish in the sense of extracting meaning from a graphic script is not an aim in itself. The student's aim is to be able to extract something specific—something of interest to him—and this must be kept in mind from the beginning. Many a Spanish textbook started the student reading with such inanities as:

R1 Soy un alumno. Estoy en la sala de clase. El profesor está al frente de la clase. El empieza la lección. Abre el libro. Yo soy inteligente. Abro el libro también. El libro es verde. Es un libro de español.

Reading activities should, from the beginning, be directed toward *natural uses of reading*. Normally, we read:

1. because we want information for some purpose or are curious about some topic;
2. because we need instructions in order to perform some task for our

work or for our daily life (we want to know how an appliance works, we are interested in a new recipe, we have forms to fill in);

3. because we want to act a play, play a new game, do a puzzle, or carry out some other activity which is pleasant and amusing;

4. because we want to keep in touch with friends by correspondence or understand business letters;

5. because we want to know when or where something will take place or what is available (we consult timetables, programs, announcements and menus, or we read advertisements);

6. because we want to know what is happening or has happened (we read newspapers, magazines, reports);

7. because we seek enjoyment or excitement (we read novels of all kinds, short stories, poems, words of songs).

Activities for developing reading skill should exploit these natural desires and impulses, preferably by supplying something which cannot be readily obtained in the native language: something which is interesting, amusing, exciting, useful, or leads to pleasurable activity.

R2 A quick check of one commonly used textbook reveals as reading material:

Long *dialogues,* introduced by a few narrative sentences, which are stilted, dull, and too obviously contrived to illustrate particular points of grammar to be taught in that unit (e.g., agreement of many adjectives; question forms of various types; the future tense; comparisons). These dialogues are strained to include an unrealistic number of items of vocabulary related to one particular theme (animals, or eating utensils, or parts of the body).

Lengthy *prose passages* about Spain or Latin America, packed with geographical and historical detail which cannot be absorbed in such density and is therefore tedious.

Long, detailed *descriptions* of people, the small actions they perform from day to day, and the places where they live and work, with no unusual, exciting, or amusing happenings to relieve the monotony.

Anecdotal or descriptive passages about people and places introducing innumerable *unfamiliar vocabulary items* which are translated in footnotes at the bottom of the page, so that the eye is continually skipping back and forth, and interest very quickly lost.

✻ Look at the reading material in several elementary and intermediate textbooks and class this material according to the normal uses of reading. Mark in each case whether it is interesting in content, amusing, exciting, useful, or promotes some activity.

There are various ways of approaching the teaching of reading. The approach will be selected according to the objectives of the students. Teachers now realize that students must be attracted to the learning of a foreign language by the assurance that they will be able to attain the kind of competence they themselves are interested in, rather than being "put through the mill" according to someone else's preconceptions of the ideal foreign-language course.

Five possible objectives for a reading course are: reading for information; reading of informal material; fluent, direct reading of all kinds of material; literary analysis; and translation of texts.

A. Reading for information

Some students may wish to learn merely to *extract certain kinds of information from Spanish texts* (scientific, historical, political, philosophic, economic, sociological). They wish only to learn to *decipher,* to break the code sufficiently for their purposes. Courses of this type appeal particularly to students in the senior years of high school (especially those who are anxious to acquire some knowledge of a third language), and they fulfill the needs of some undergraduate and graduate students.

Courses (and materials) can be designed to teach the students to extract information from texts with only a recognition knowledge of basic grammatical relations[1] and of the commonly used function words (determiners, prepositions, conjunctions, common adverbs, interrogative and negation words)—words which commonly emerge among the first two hundred words in frequency lists. The students can then achieve their purpose with the help of specialized dictionaries of terms used in their particular fields of interest. Students can be taught to guess audaciously at the content. They then discuss the reasons for their guesses and reasons for the inaccuracy of some of these guesses.[2] From the beginning, students read texts of interest to them, carefully selected to provide a gradation of difficulty. In a course of this type the students do not want, nor expect, to learn fine points of pronunciation or aural-oral or writing skills, nor do they want to learn to read directly and fluently in the foreign language for pleasure. They gain their pleasure from their ability to draw the information they want from the text rapidly, without attention to style.

These students need the following skills:

1. *Complete control in recognition of points of grammar which impede comprehension of written Spanish.*

R3 One such point is the pronoun insertion that occurs when the subject-verb-direct object construction is inverted. Unaware of this process, the student may interpret differently the following semantically equivalent sentences:

El cazador más joven mató el tigre. (Normal order)

El tigre lo mató el cazador más joven. (Inverted order)

* List five other points of *recognition grammar* which could cause problems for the English-speaking reader.

  2. *Knowledge of word formation* which will help them to recognize the functions and nuances of meaning of words derived from the same radical.

R4 They should be able to separate *prefixes and suffixes* from the radical and recognize the part of speech indicated by the suffix.

Traer, extraer

ver, prever

cansar, descansar

tener, detener, retener

casa, casita

carne, carnicería

monte, montaña, montañoso, montañés, montañuela

pobre, empobrecer, pobreza, empobrecimiento

rico, enriquecer, riqueza

diez, décimo; ciento, centenares

sano, sanidad; bueno, bondad

rojo, rojear, rojez, rojura, rojizo

verde, verdear, verdoso, verdura, verdín

R5 They should be able to infer the meaning of compounds like the following: tocadiscos, abrelatas, guardarropa, quitamanchas, cochecomedor, boca-calle, pluma fuente, madre patria, sinvergüenza, anteayer, contradanza, anteojos

* Make up some word games which would develop sensitivity to word families, e.g., competitions in listing derivatives, in constructing as many words as possible from letters supplied, in extending radicals with affixes to make new words.

  3. *Practice in recognizing Spanish-English cognate radicals.* Since many of these cognates are learned words in English, because they are derived from Latin rather than Germanic roots, we often overestimate the student's ability to recognize them. The area of meaning they cover and the way they are used in the two languages, that is, their distribution, often do not exactly coincide, which creates a further difficulty.

R6 *El es muy célebre.* We would not expect in English, "He is very cele-brated." "Celebrated" in English in the sense of "famous" is always used with a noun or noun phrase: "a celebrated opera singer," or "He was celebrated for his operatic voice."

R7 *Con práctica se perfecciona en hablar español.* In English we do not have a verb "to perfection." With the radical "perfec" smothered by the affixes *-ion* and *-a* on one side and the *se,* which does not correspond with any-thing in the English version, on the other, the inexperienced student is likely to seek the help of his dictionary.

R8 *La Sagrada Escritura.* The student who has no knowledge of the relation-ship between English initial *s* and Spanish *es* + consonant (cf. *espíritu, estado*) will look upon *escritura* as a new word, despite his knowledge of *escribir/escrito.* He will associate *sagrada* with English *"sacred"* rather than with "holy" and will look in his dictionary to find "Holy Scripture."

Many Spanish/English cognates are disguised by historical change, but some of these disguises are systematic enough to be useful to the reader.

R9 a. Sp. *es/ex* + *consonant* frequently equals Eng. initial *s* + *consonant,* as in:

extranjero,	*stranger*
esclerosis,	*sclerosis*
escándalo,	*scandal*
escénico,	*scenic*
esfera,	*sphere*
esponja,	*sponge*
estúpido,	*stupid*

b. Sp. *gu-* sometimes equals English *w-.*

guerra,	*war*
guerrero,	*warrior*
Guillermo,	*William*

c. Sp. endings *-dad* and *-tad* always correspond to English *-ty.*

calidad, or cualidad,	*quality*
cantidad,	*quantity*
sociedad,	*society*
necesidad,	*necessity*
ciudad,	*city*
libertad,	*liberty*

✴ Share notes within the class on other regular features of Spanish/English cognates and disguised cognates that you have observed or can discover.

4. *Recognition knowledge of the most frequent "falsos amigos"* (that is, cognates whose meanings have diverged in the two languages). Students should begin a self-constructed cumulative list of *falsos amigos* which should contain for each item a short sentence illustrating its use.

R10 *Falsos amigos:*

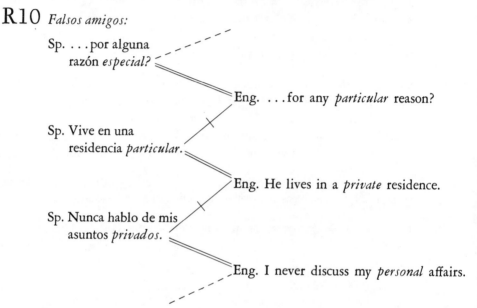

Sp. . . . por alguna
    razón *especial?*

Eng. . . . for any *particular* reason?

Sp. Vive en una
    residencia *particular.*

Eng. He lives in a *private* residence.

Sp. Nunca hablo de mis
    asuntos *privados.*

Eng. I never discuss my *personal* affairs.

✴ Add to this list by sharing with others in your class the *falsos amigos* which have caused you trouble.

WHAT DO WE DO ON THE FIRST DAY?

As with all teaching, the way the students are oriented toward the course at the beginning can be crucial to their progress. In a course where students are reading for information they should be *given confidence* from the first lesson that they will be able to read Spanish without difficulty in a very short time. Because of the many cognates in Spanish and English this is possible very early with carefully selected texts. The teacher should *explain to the students the techniques* that will be employed to extract meaning from the text and impress on them that they must acquire rapidly a *recognition knowledge of basic grammar* and an automatic recognition knowledge of *common relational words,* like prepositions, conjunctions, adverbs, and pronouns, so that these no longer impede their extraction of meaning. They must also learn thoroughly the *most frequently used nouns and verbs* so that these can provide a framework for guessing the meaning of new words from the context. Very early, they must begin a *personal list of words* which often cause them to pause as well as of specialized vocabulary of interest to them (their *vocabulario disponible*, which will be discussed later in this chapter).

A PLAN FOR THE FIRST LESSON

1. Begin with all the Spanish words you and your students can think of which are commonly used in English:

R11 plaza, canyon, corral, patio, adobe, vista, rodeo, siesta. . . .
As you write each word on the chalkboard, pronounce it in Spanish and ask students to repeat it after you. The length of the list will impress the students with the number of Spanish words they already know.

2. Have a short discussion on the history of the English language with its intertwined Anglo-Saxon (Germanic) and Romance (Latin) origins (and many subsequent borrowings). Show how we tend to use the strands in parallel:

R12 *Informal* Germanic strand: start; leave; end.
Formal Latin-derived strand: commence; depart; terminate.

3. Ask the students to think of as many English parallels of this type as they can. Write these on the chalkboard with their Spanish equivalents and use them as a further incidental introduction to Spanish pronunciation.

R13
East	Orient	oriente
reward	recompense	recompensa
land	nation	nación
smell	perfume	perfume
show	demonstrate	demostrar
easy	facile	fácil
stop	arrest	arrestar

By this time students should begin to see that differences in spelling are a thin disguise for cognates.

4. Give them sentences to read based on cognates, like:

R14 El actor es inteligente y creativo.
El presidente termina la discusión.

Design these sentences so that you can point out incidentally simple Spanish function words like: *el, la, los, un, una, a, de, en, por.*

5. Give some further sentences which show that determiners and verbs vary more in form in Spanish than in English, and that this helps to make the meaning clear:

R15 The sheep in the park.
Is there any way of knowing how many sheep there are?
    Compare: *La oveja del parque; las ovejas del parque.*
Note that these Spanish phrases include information as to the number. (In the second Spanish phrase, the agreement rules tell you twice that it is plural, so you cannot miss this information.)
    Las ovejas blancas
Here the Spanish expression tells you three times that it is plural so only a very inattentive person could miss it.

6. At this point, the position of the adjective may be discussed, using as examples well-known English expressions and place names:

R16 (las ovejas blancas)
Palo Alto,
Sierra Nevada,
Río Grande,
Mesa Verde,
Puerto Rico
In this context Baja California would need explaining.

7. Students may volunteer such names as Los Angeles and Eldorado. These contributions should be followed up by linking them with the earlier discussion of *los* and *el* in 4.

8. The first lesson should end with a group deciphering of a short passage with a great number of cognates, so that the students can leave the class "knowing how to read Spanish already."

A passage like the following would be suitable:

R17 Geográficamente, México pertenece a la América del Norte. Culturalmente, es una de las naciones que . . . se formaron de lo que antiguamente eran colonias españolas en el Nuevo Mundo. México, la nación más al norte de ese vasto territorio . . . posee una rica tradición cultural. . . .

De España heredó México la lengua, la religión, la organización social, las diversiones y buena parte de su psicología. . . . Como la fusión de las . . . culturas es casi perfecta, podemos hablar de una cultura mexicana, que ya no es . . . ni española ni azteca o maya. ¿Cuáles son las características predominantes de esa cultura? Trataremos en las páginas que siguen de dar una idea de los elementos que han moldeado el carácter de esa cultura.[3]

9. As preparation for the next lesson, ask the students to make a list of expressions, slogans, trade names, hotel names, quotations, inscriptions, and proper names in common use which are borrowed from Spanish. Use these in the second lesson for pronunciation practice and further incidental teaching.

ACTIVITIES IN THE READING FOR INFORMATION CLASS

As soon as students have acquired some skill in extracting information from a Spanish text they may begin to work in small interest groups, in pairs, or individually, according to temperament, as a supplement to large group guidance on aspects of written Spanish. Gradually, large group activity is reduced to those occasions when students feel the need for further help in specific areas. Only in this way will the students become autonomous readers.

Every possibility for encouraging autonomous activity should be explored. One such avenue is the preparation of group projects centered around special interests. Students in the project group may fan out in exploratory reading for a certain period in order to report back and establish a list of what is worthwhile reading for all members of the group. Alternatively, students may assign each other specific articles or sections of books on which the readers will report back to the group for a sharing of the information gathered.

Eventually, students should become interested in seeking out information in the foreign language to enhance research projects in other subjects and thus develop the habit of using their newly developed skill purposefully.

B. *Reading of informal material*

Some students, more interested in Spanish for interpersonal communication, may want only to be able to *read correspondence, notices, newspaper headings, and advertisements.* For these a course emphasizing listening and speaking will be complemented with practice in reading informal Spanish materials and in writing informally, with some study of the clichés of officialese and popular journalism. For these purposes, it would be enough for the students to be familiar with the *presente* (*hablo*), the *pretérito indefinido* (*hablé*), the *préterito imperfecto* (*hablaba*), and the *pretérito perfecto* (*he hablado*), as well as the *presente* and the *pretérito perfecto* of the subjunctive (*hable, haya hablado*). They may ignore for the time being other tenses, such as the *pluscuamperfecto* of the indicative (*había hablado*), as well as the *pretérito imperfecto* (*hablara/hablase*) and the *pretérito pluscuamperfecto* (*hubiera/hubiese hablado*) of the subjunctive, among others. They will use more freely the immediate future (*voy a hablar/hablo*) than the more distant future (*hablaré*), although the latter will be useful at times. They will feel at home with the formulas for the immediate past (*acabo de comer*) and action in progress (*estoy escribiendo*). In other words, they will read Spanish written in the informal style they use in speech rather than in a formal literary style. Their reading will thus reinforce their speech patterns.

The earlier stages of reading training described later in this chapter will prepare this group for their objectives.

C. Fluent, direct reading of all kinds of material

Students who want to learn to use Spanish flexibly in all modalities, who hope to be able to pick up a novel, a biography, a newspaper, or a magazine (light or serious) and read the contents fluently for pleasure as well as being able to communicate orally and in writing, will require a course which provides balanced development of all language skills. It is to this group that the six stages of reading development described in this chapter and the next apply. This is the group which aims at attaining the stage of reading directly in Spanish without mental translation and without constant recourse to a dictionary.

D. Literary analysis

Some of Group C will wish to develop also the skill of in-depth analysis of literary material, which requires considerable refinement in perception of nuances and choices in language. For this they require special training.

Teachers interested particularly in the preparation of this group are referred to: "The Times and Places for Literature," F. André Paquette, et al., in *Foreign Languages: Reading, Literature, Requirements,* ed. T. E. Bird (*NEC,* 1967), pp. 51–102; *The Teaching of Foreign Literatures,* theme of *MLJ* 56, 5(1972), and Harold K. Moon, *Spanish Literature: A Critical Approach* (Lexington, Mass.: Xerox College Publishing, 1972).

E. Translation

Other students may want to *translate Spanish texts* accurately into English. This is an art which requires a sophisticated knowledge of English as well as Spanish. A course with finesse of translation as its objective will concentrate on fine distinctions of syntax and vocabulary and contrastive aspects of sentence and paragraph formation. The perfecting of pronunciation, fluency in oral communication, and composition in Spanish will not be emphasized. Translation for scientific and industrial purposes requires a more than superficial acquaintance with many fields and much experience with the many dictionaries available for the specialized vocabularies of medicine, physics, engineering, chemistry, electronics, business, and so on. Translation of literary works requires a sensitivity to nuances and subtleties of meaning, speech registers, and levels of style in Spanish and a perceptive awareness of the flexibility and potentialities of the English language. Such a course can be engrossing for those with a special fascination for language but tedious and frustrating for any who are not in the course of their own volition. Translation is discussed more fully in Chapter 9.

Each of these five objectives is, of course, legitimate. In designing or selecting reading materials and learning activities, the teacher needs to keep clearly in mind the specific purpose toward which the course, or a particular student's interests, are directed.

The remainder of this chapter will concentrate on the needs of Group C (which covers in its earlier stages the needs of Group B, and from which Group D and some of Group E will later emerge). Some of what is said about this program for progressive development of reading skill can be adapted also to certain aspects of courses for Group A. The teacher of the latter course will extrapolate what seems to him to be appropriate.

Lexical, structural (or grammatical), and social-cultural meaning

The reader must learn to extract from the graphic script three levels of meaning: lexical meaning (the semantic implications of the words and expressions), structural or grammatical meaning (which is expressed at times by semantically empty functional words, but also by interrelationships among words, or parts of words), and social-cultural meaning (the evaluative dimension which Spanish-speaking people give to words and groups of words because of their common experiences with language in their culture). When we consult a dictionary we find an *approximation of lexical meaning,* usually in the form of a paraphrase. Where a synonym is given, this frequently has a non-matching distribution of meaning, e.g., for *escrupuloso* the synonym *cuidadoso* may be given. However, all who are *cuidadoso* are not necessarily *escrupuloso* which is a far more restrictive term.

A study of grammar rules and experience with language in action help us to apprehend *structural meaning.* It is *social-cultural meaning* which is most difficult for a foreigner to penetrate. This is meaning which springs from shared experiences, values, and attitudes. When this type of meaning is not taken into account, or when the student interprets a Spanish text according to his own cultural experiences, distortions and misapprehensions result. Living among Spanish-speaking people for a long period will give a teacher or student an insight into this aspect of meaning, but the average student will need to depend on footnotes and his teacher's explanations. As his vicarious experience of Spanish or Latin American life and attitudes increases through much reading, he will come to a deeper understanding of the full meaning of a text.[4]

R18 In the following passage, the tribute to the Spanish social institution of the *tertulia* and its close association with the *café*, can be appreciated by anyone who knows the American institution of the "cocktail hour," or of any informal convivial gathering. The comparison between the local *café* and the imported *cafetería* or *coffee shop* may be less comprehensible to those who know only the latter.

Y de pronto, un día, se murió la tertulia. ¿De qué enfermedad? ¡Ah! pero no lo sé. . . .

Sus más fieles la lloramos como se merecía. Cada vez la echamos más de menos . . . ¡Era tan buena la pobre! No nos dió un solo disgusto. Y cuidado que esto es difícil. Desfilaron por ella infinidad de gentes, muy heterogéneas, de muy diversas profesiones y aficiones. Y nada, ni un roce, ni la más leve disputa, ni una voz más alta que otra. Se discutía, pero nunca con destemplanza.

Mala época la que atravesamos para las tertulias. Se están acabando los cafés, su lugar natural y propicio. ¿Desaparecen los cafés porque ya no hay tertulias o ya no hay tertulias porque desaparecen los cafés? Dicen por ahí que los cafés perecen por causas económicas. Porque se han visto obligados a elevar sus precios considerablemente. No lo creo. Por una razón. Las cafeterías, que son sus herederas ilegítimas, son mucho más caras. Y ahí están proliferándose como una plaga.

En las cafeterías priva el mostrador, la "barra" que dicen sus habituales. Las mesas están relegadas a un rincón, como de prestado, como una concesión. Ante estas mesas nos podemos sentar, pero nos sentimos incómodos, como si estuviera allí de visita de cumplido. ¡Qué diferencia con el café, en donde estábamos como en nuestra casa! El ruido de las cafeterías es insoportable. En el café había ruido, ¡ya lo creo que había ruido!, pero cuán distinto. Era un ruido familiar, apacible, íntimo, grato de percibir, que nos acompañaba, que envolvía nuestra charla, separándola, tamizándola de las otras conversaciones. El de las cafeterías es un ruido caótico, confuso, estridente. En las cafeterías entra y sale sin cesar el gentío que apura sus consumiciones en el mostrador como el viajero en la fonda de una estación, rápidamente, con prisa inexplicable, con el absurdo afán de largarse cuanto antes.

Las cafeterías parece ser que han venido de los Estados Unidos. Y también parece ser que en los Estados Unidos sus habitantes no tienen tiempo para nada y necesitan comer en cinco minutos y beberse un batido de fresa en cinco segundos. ¡Desgraciados!

¿Tertulias en una cafetería? ¡Ni pensarlo! Sería tanto como pretender celebrarlas en el Polo Norte, pongo por lugar inhóspito.[5]

Tertulia and *café* have *lexical meanings*. The *Diccionario de la lengua española* of the Real Academia Española, 19th edition, 1970, gives the following meanings: *tertulia:* "reunión de personas que se juntan habitualmente para discurrir sobre alguna materia, para conversar amigablemente o para algún pasatiempo honesto"; *café:* "casa o sitio público donde se vende y toma esta bebida" (i.e., coffee). These have been translated in the widely used *Velasquez New Pronouncing Dictionary of the Spanish and English Languages,* 1967, as: *tertulia:* "club, assembly, circle, coterie, evening party"; *café:* "cafe, coffeehouse."

To a person from a country other than Spain or Latin America, neither the Academy nor the Velasquez rendering conveys the full connotational meaning of *café* as the *lugar natural y propicio* for the *tertulia*. They may even convey quite a different connotational meaning in countries where the coffee shop is a snack-bar and the cafeteria a self-service restaurant. The Spaniard or Latin American reading these terms sees a gathering place, open to the public, but attracting a particular clientele, generally centering around a prominent figure, literary or political, who presides over the *tertulia* and its ongoing discussions of current affairs. (Unamuno was the leader of such a group.) The famous café Pombo near the Puerta del Sol was the meeting place of the "new modernists" who revolved around Rubén Darío, the early 20th century Nicaraguan poet who had a profound influence on contemporary Spanish writing. As the author of the above excerpt describes it, ". . . era el café, admirable invención para ir tumbando las horas una a una y que un café con leche nos durara media tarde o toda una noche, ayudándole con infinitos vasos de agua."

Yet, the conviviality of the *tertulia* is by no means limited to the literary or political intelligentsia or to the physical locale of the *café*. It may be found, according to Díaz-Cañabate, in the local taverns, in casinos, on street corners and small plazas, in the summer in the large public gardens, at refreshment stands—or at any place where congenial people can comfortably meet to talk and pass the time.

The social-cultural meanings of *tertulia* and *café* can be understood only by a student who has learned something of the way of life of the average Spaniard or Latin American.

Structural meaning

R19 ". . . se han visto obligados *a* elevar sus precios . . ."
". . . como si estuviera allí *de* visita . . ."

In these sentences, neither *a* nor *de* can be assigned a precise lexical meaning, yet they are essential if the sentence is to be understood; they show structural relationships between elements of the sentences and may therefore be said to have *structural* or *grammatical* meaning.

Word counts and frequency lists

Several lists of the most frequently used words in the Spanish language have been published. Two of the word lists used most often in the editing of texts for students are Milton A. Buchanan, *A Graded Spanish Word Book* (Toronto: University of Toronto Press, 1927) and Hayward Keniston, *A Standard List of Spanish Words and Idioms* (Lexington, Ky.: D. C. Heath & Co., 1941).

Buchanan's list (GSWB) was established from a corpus of over 1,200,000 running words in 40 excerpts from 7 types of written texts. The list comprises approximately 6,700 words (if the 190 very common words listed separately are included). The words are set out in order of merit and identified by "credit-numbers," i.e., a combination of range (how many of the 40 texts contained occurrences of any particular word) and absolute frequency of occurrence. The list includes all words that occurred at least 10 times or in at least 5 kinds of text materials. *Parte,* for instance, occurs in all 40 texts, being found 950 times, and therefore heads the list with a credit-number of 135. At a lower point in the list, *restaurant* and *oso* both have credit-numbers of 3, although *restaurant* is found to occur 20 times in one text, while *oso* occurs 10 times in 2 texts.

The words in the Buchanan list have proved useful for students learning to read texts found in traditional school reading materials because the "40 categories of words were chosen to represent Spanish in all its 'bookish phases.' "[6] This usefulness reflects the fact that the Spanish taught in the classroom has, until recently, been primarily literary. The Buchanan list has often been used for establishing levels of reading difficulty in Spanish texts for classroom use.

Keniston's list (SL) incorporates in a *Composite List* the words of

Buchanan's GSWB, C. W. Cartwright's "A Study of the Vocabularies of Eleven Spanish Grammars and Fifteen Spanish Reading Texts," *MLJ* 10 (1925), 1–14, and Keniston's own earlier "Common Words in Spanish," *Hispania* 3 (1920), 85–96. The Composite List provides a corpus of 3,060 words of which the first 1,500 were considered by Keniston to be those words basic to any kind of text material. Beyond this core of 1,500 words, according to Keniston, the content of any word count is probably influenced by the kinds of materials used. Keniston makes no claim that the SL gives any useful information concerning the informal spoken language. But he does maintain that "all these words are of general value, basic to any use of Spanish, whether for comprehension or for expression. They may properly form the foundation for elementary grammars, readers, syllabi, and tests in Spanish; they are the words which students must know as a preparation for any subsequent use of the language."[7]

The 1,500 Basic Words were arranged in three groups of 500 each, according to credit-numbers assigned to the words of the Composite List. *Group 1* includes 122 fundamental and structural words (e.g., articles, pronouns, days of the week, numerals, etc.) plus the first 378 words of the Composite List. *Group 2* contains "essential words" (numbers 379–878 of the Composite List), and *Group 3* contains "indispensable words" (numbers 879–1,378 of the Composite List). An additional group of 500 "useful words" was included to cover special vocabulary needs such as conversational and travel words, informational material for writing elementary texts, words for dictionary definitions, words with a high functional load (i.e., which yield a high number of derivatives), words equivalent to high frequency words in English and other language vocabulary lists, and words numbered 1,379 to 1,878 of the Composite List. The 500 "useful words" were selected primarily on the basis of their range of usage. Special vocabulary items dealing with technical subjects were omitted, since Keniston felt that "these, and other special 'environmental' words, are most effectively learned by experience or from special lists compiled to meet a particular need."[8]

R20 As an example of such special "environmental" words, on reading the sentence: Mi hermano menor, quien ha desaparecido detrás un arbol, me contesta "He encontrado unos hongos," a student is more likely to be interested in the word *hongos* (which does not appear in either Buchanan or Keniston) than in words such as *mi, un,* or *contesta* (all in SL Group 1). *Mi, un,* and *contesta* belong to the fundamental and structural words of Group 1; *hongos* would be added to the student's "special words," his personal vocabulary which is available to him when in a situation where toadstools are relevant.

In another interesting attempt at vocabulary analysis, Victor Garcia Hoz examined about 240,000 words for his *Vocabulario Usual, Vocabulario Comun y Vocabulario Fundamental* (1953).[9] He drew 60,000 words from each of four sources which he considered representative of the *vocabulario usual* that people in a speech community share. These sources were *private letters* (reflecting family life), *periodicals* (representative of social life in general), *official documents* (representing regulated social life—political, religious, etc.), and *books* (as the embodiment of the cultural sphere). From this corpus, he derived some 13,000 general vocabulary words. Those which appeared in all four sources, he called the *vocabulario comun* —nearly 2,000 words. Just over 200 words appeared with high frequency in all sources, not just as individual tokens but very often in association with other words: these he called the *vocabulario fundamental,* that is, such words as *y* (15,254 appearances), *de* (27,585), *a* (9,131) and *un* (6,305). These 200 or so words are duplicated in the high frequency lists of each of the standard counts.

In 1964, A. Juilland of Stanford University and E. Chang-Rodriguez of City University of New York published a *Frequency Dictionary of Spanish Words* (The Hague: Mouton & Co., 1964) as the first part of a much larger collection, *The Romance Languages and Their Structures.* This work, presenting the result of investigations since 1956, was undertaken to develop computer techniques for "the descriptive, comparative and historical study of the various aspects of natural languages," specifically to enable an "exhaustive study of the phonological, grammatical, and lexical structuration of the five major Romance languages,"[10] including, of course, Spanish. The original plan for this work was to include data from previously published frequency dictionaries and graded word lists, such as GSWB, but methodological considerations and differences in sampling and data collection made this impractical, and the Juilland study therefore was made *de novo.*

The *Frequency Dictionary* (FDSW) is derived from a corpus of approximately 500,000 words selected from about 25,000 sentences divided equally amongst text materials from five types of literature. The representative texts were taken from those written in Peninsular Spanish and published between World Wars I and II. These give a more recent sampling of the language than either GSWB, SL, or Garcia Hoz.

The FDSW ranks its words by usage, which it defines as a measure of prediction of occurrence in the language outside the sample, by frequency of occurrence within the sample, and by dispersion, or range over the sample. Like Keniston's SL, the first 500 words include the very common words excluded from Buchanan's count.

Knowledge of a basic vocabulary will ensure that the students know the most widely used words, which provide the framework of any sentence, revealing to them a set of relationships that will serve as a basis for "intelligent guessing" or "inferencing" when they encounter unfamiliar content words. (R24 demonstrates this process.) Students will need, then, to build their own *personal vocabulary* (their *vocabulario disponible*) from their reading, and for this they should be encouraged to keep individual notebooks into which they copy words they wish to remember, setting them out in short sentences which demonstrate their use in context.

How an unfamiliar text appears to a student

In the following discussion, an excerpt of some paragraphs from "La Gitanilla" by Miguel Cervantes[11] will be used for demonstration. The full text is given at the end of this section (R25). Our readers should refrain from referring to it until they have worked through this section, in order to get the feeling their students may have on being confronted with this text for the first time. The discussion in this section will be based on the *Frequency Dictionary of Spanish Words* (FDSW) and the *Graded Spanish Word Book* (GSWB).

R21   Text from "La Gitanilla" as it would appear to a student knowing only the first 250 words of FDSW, based on written language. On the right are shown additions and deletions to be made to the text if the student has learned the first 250 words of GSWB. Numbers refer to the order of blanks in the line.

Una ____ ____ ____ a una ____ como ____   (2) add *vieja*
                                                          (4) add *muchacha*

suya, a quien puso por nombre (Preciosa), y a
quien ____ todas sus ____, sus ____, y sobre
todo a ____. La tal (Preciosa) salió la mejor
____ y la más ____ de todas las ____. Ni el   (2) add *hermosa*
____, ni el ____, ni todas las ____ del tiempo   (1) add *sol*
                                                          (2) add *aire*

pudieron ____ ____ la ____ de su ____ ni de   (1) add *jamás*
sus manos. A ____ del modo en que ____ ____,   (1) add *pesar*
____ haber ____ ____ ____ y bien hablada. Es   omit *hablada*
verdad que sus ____ eran ____ ____, pero ____   (2) add *algo*
                                                          (4) add *jamás*

____. Al ____, era tan ____ que en su ____
ninguna ____, ____ ni ____, ____ ____ a   (2) add *vieja*
                                                          (3) add *joven*

____ ____ malas ni a decir palabras no buenas.

La _____, pues, conoció el _____ que en la _____   (1) add *vieja*
tenía, y así _____ _____ de ella todo el _____   (2) add *sacar*
posible, y _____ a vivir por sus _____.   omit *posible*

R22 Text from "La Gitanilla" as it would appear to a student knowing only the first 250 words of FDSW and GSWB and recognizing certain cognates. Notes on cognates appear in the correspondingly numbered sections of the commentary following the passage.

Una _____ vieja _____ a una muchacha como _____ suya, a quien puso por nombre (Preciosa), y a quien _____ todas sus _____, sus _____, y sobre todo a _____. La tal (Preciosa) salió la mejor bailarina[1] y la más hermosa de todas las _____. Ni el sol, ni el aire, ni todas las inclemencias[2] del tiempo pudieron jamás _____ la _____ de su _____ ni de sus manos. A pesar del modo en que se _____, demostraba[3] haber _____ naturalmente[4] cortés[5] y bien hablada. Es verdad que sus _____ eran algo _____, pero jamás deshonestos[6]. Al contrario[7], era tan honesta[8] que en su presencia ninguna _____, vieja ni joven, se _____ a _____ _____ malas ni a decir palabras no buenas. La vieja, pues, conoció el tesoro[9] que en la _____ tenía, y así decidió sacar de ella todo el _____ posible, y _____ a vivir por sus _____.

Commentary

1. *Bailarina:* saying this aloud should help students recognize it as *ballerina,* or dancer.

2. *Inclemencias:* combined with the weather words, *sol, aire,* and *tiempo,* this should be recognizable as *inclemencies.*

3. *Demostraba:* if students have already learned the regular imperfect tense ending *-aba,* they would probably not have much trouble guessing the meaning *demonstrated* or *showed.*

4. *Naturalmente:* if the adverb ending *-mente* is familiar, this word should be obvious.

5. *Cortés:* this may not be recognized by all students as a cognate of *courteous,* although saying the word aloud may give some clue.

6. *Deshonestos:* a *falso amigo* since it means *immodest,* not dishonest. However, even if misinterpreted, it gives the student the sense of a negative attribute, confirmed by the affirmative form *honesta* in the next sentence.

7. *Al contrario:* although this is an idiom, the form, plus the opposition

of *deshonestas/honesta,* would probably be recognized as a cognate of *contrary.*

8. *Honesta:* see 6 above.

9. *Tesoro:* the fact that the English word *treasure* is a cognate might not be apparent to all students because of the considerable deviation in spelling.

R23 This passage shows how the text from "La Gitanilla" would look if the 250 most frequent words from FDSW and GSWB were omitted.

_____ gitana _____ crió _____ _____ _____ _____ nieta _____, _____
_____ _____ _____ _____ Preciosa, _____ _____ _____ enseñó _____ _____
gitanerías, _____ engaños, _____ _____ _____ _____ hurtar. _____ _____
Preciosa _____ _____ _____ bailarina _____ _____ _____ _____ _____
_____ gitanas. _____ _____ _____, _____ _____ _____, _____ _____
inclemencias _____ _____ _____ _____ marchitar _____ belleza _____ _____
rostro _____ _____ _____ _____. _____ _____ _____ _____ _____ _____
criaba, demostraba _____ nacido naturalmente cortés _____ _____ _____.
_____ _____ _____ _____ modales _____ _____ libres, _____ _____ deshonestos. Al contrario, _____ _____ honesta _____ _____ _____ presencia
_____ gitana, _____ _____ _____, se atrevía _____ cantar canciones _____
_____ _____ _____ _____ _____ _____. _____ _____, _____, _____ _____
tesoro _____ _____ _____ nieta _____, _____ _____ decidió _____ _____
_____ _____ _____ provecho posible, _____ enseñarla _____ _____
_____ uñas.

Commentary

Here we have a clear demonstration of the *indispensability to meaning* of function words (like *de, a, por, la, ni, en*); common verbs (*ser, decir*); adverbs (*más, tan*); prepositions and conjunctions (*pues, y*); and pronouns (*ella, suya*).

R24 This passage shows how the text from "La Gitanilla" would look to a student knowing the 750 most frequent words of FDSW and GSWB. The obvious cognates not in the first 750 words are given in parentheses. (In the right margin are indicated words not included in the first 750 words of GSWB.)

Una _____[1] vieja _____[2] a una muchacha como
_____[3] suya, a quien puso por nombre (Preciosa),

y a quien enseñó todas sus gitanerías[1], sus ____[4],
y sobre todo a ____[5]. La tal (Preciosa) salió la
mejor (bailarina) y la más hermosa de todas las
____[1]. Ni el sol, ni el aire, ni todas las (incle-
mencias) del tiempo pudieron jamás ____[6] la
belleza de su rostro ni di sus manos. A pesar del
modo en que se ____[2], demostraba haber nacido   omit *demostraba*
natural(mente) ____[7] y bien hablada. Es verdad   omit *hablada*
que sus ____[8] eran algo libres, pero jamás (deshonestos). Al contrario, era tan (honesta) que
en su presencia ninguna ____[1], vieja ni joven,
se atrevía a cantar ____[9] malas ni a decir palabras no buenas. La vieja, pues, conoció el ____[10]
que en la ____[3] tenía, y así (decidió) sacar de
ella todo el ____[11] posible, y enseñarla a vivir
por sus ____[12].

Commentary

Once the reader is familiar with the function words and common verbs,
adverbs, pronouns, prepositions, and conjunctions and has a recognition
knowledge of some basic vocabulary, he can usually work out the meaning of most of the remaining words in a passage by intelligent guesswork
or inferencing. We will presume that the title "La Gitanilla" has been
explained (by translation or by a visual representation). This disposes of
1. (specialized vocabulary). Inferences will be indicated with an asterisk.

  1. See explanation of title (*gitanilla*). The student not knowing
gitanerías will be able to associate this word with the title through the
radical *gitan-*.

  2. The exact meaning of *criar* ("to raise, bring up") is not important
here. It could just as well be *amar* or *considerar*—as long as the reader
realizes that the old gypsy felt or acted or related in some way to the girl
as if she were her own (suya).

  3. In context *nieta* would probably be understood as some *kinship
term. The meaning of the story would not be greatly altered if the student
guessed niece instead of "granddaughter."

  4. and 5. By analogy with *gitanerías,* the student might infer that these
are *questionable activities generally associated with gypsies—"cheating"
and "stealing."

  6. What would exposure to the sun, air, and rigors of the weather be

expected to do to the beauty of one's face and hands? Dry it, most likely (*marchitar:* "to wither, to fade").

7. In spite of her upbringing as a gypsy, she showed that she had been born naturally good in some way. Even if *cortés* is not recognized as "courteous," it should be apparent that it refers to a *positive quality—especially since it is combined here with *bien hablada.*

8. Continuing with her upbringing, a student might logically infer that *modales* has to do with how she behaves, her *manners.

9. Even if *canciones* is not recognized as a derivative of *cantar,* a student should not have much difficulty in guessing that *songs is a reasonable object of *cantar* ("to sing").

10. Some more sophisticated readers will probably recognize *tesoro* as a cognate of "treasure" in view of the general tenor of the text.

11. Recognizing her treasure, the old gypsy decided to take all possible "something" from it: use? advantage? benefit? (*provecho:* "benefit").

12. To get the most benefit from Preciosa's attributes, the old gypsy would teach her how to live most advantageously—by her *wits.* The idiomatic use of *uñas* ("nails," "claws") in this sense is closely akin to the English expression "to claw one's way."

R25 Excerpt from "La Gitanilla" (Novelas Ejemplares, Miguel de Cervantes Saavedra).

Una gitana vieja crió a una muchacha como nieta suya, a quien puso por nombre Preciosa, y a quien enseñó todas sus gitanerías, sus engaños, y sobre todo a hurtar. La tal Preciosa salió la mejor bailarina y la más hermosa de todas las gitanas. Ni el sol, ni el aire, ni todas las inclemencias del tiempo pudieron jamás marchitar la belleza de su rostro ni de sus manos. A pesar del modo en que se criaba, demostraba haber nacido naturalmente cortés y bien hablada. Es verdad que sus modales eran algo libres, pero jamás deshonestos. Al contrario, era tan honesta que en su presencia ninguna gitana, vieja ni joven, se atrevía a cantar canciones malas ni a decir palabras no buenas. La vieja, pues, conoció el tesoro que en la nieta tenía, y así decidió sacar de ella todo el provecho posible, y enseñarla a vivir por sus uñas.

Six stages of reading development

To help the student develop progressively his ability to read more and more fluently and independently materials of increasing difficulty and complexity, six stages of reading development are recommended. Materials in Spanish of an appropriate level of difficulty for each stage are presented and discussed, and suitable activities are suggested for reinforcing the developing reading skill and for ensuring a clear grasp of the meaning of what is read. More detailed discussion will be found in *Teaching Foreign-Language Skills* (Rivers, 1968), pp. 221–37.

The six stages do not represent six levels of study (in the sense in which Brooks used this term).[12] Stage One may begin after the first oral presentation of a short dialogue, or after some active learning of simple actions and statements in the classroom context or in simulated situations. Should teacher and class prefer it, Stage One may be postponed to allow for two or three weeks of entirely oral work. This is often the case with younger students. As soon as students acquire some familiarity with sound-symbol correspondences in Spanish and the word order of simple sentences they pass from Stage One to Stage Two (reading of recombinations of familiar material). For a while Stage Two may alternate with Stage One. A more mature group of students, already adept at native-language reading, may pass rapidly through Stages One and Two and move on to Stage Three (reading of simple narrative and conversational material which is not based on work being practiced orally). Some textbooks plunge the student directly into Stage Three at the beginning, particularly if development of reading skill is the primary objective. Progress through Stages Three, Four, and Five becomes a largely individual matter as students outpace one another in ability to read increasingly more complicated material.

Stage One: Introduction to reading

The introduction to reading will be very short or longer depending on the age of the students and the intensive or non-intensive nature of the course.

Students learn to read what they have already learned to say either in short dialogues in informal classroom conversation, or through the oral presentation of the initial conversational narrative. Questions require only recognition of material in the text.

The major emphasis is on the identification of *sound-symbol correspondences* so that the student perceives in graphic form the meaning with which he has become familiar in oral form.

Reading is an integrated part of language study, not a specialized activity. At this stage:

Reading is linked with listening.

Students learn to segment an oral message[13] (that is, to identify its phrase structure groupings) and then try to recognize these groupings in graphic form.

Reading is linked with speaking.

Students learn to say a few simple things in Spanish and then to recognize the graphic symbols for the oral utterances they have been practicing. The script helps them to remember what they were saying, to see more clearly how it was structured, and to learn it more thoroughly. It also provides further variations of these utterances for them to use orally.

Reading is linked with improvement in pronunciation and intonation.

Students practice correct production of sounds and appropriate phrasing as they learn to associate symbols with sounds.

Reading is linked with writing.

Students consolidate sound-symbol associations through dictation or spot dictation exercises. They confirm this learning by copying out, with correct spelling, sentences they have been learning. They write out sentences associated with pictures and use, as practice in reading, what their fellow students have written. Teacher or students write out instructions which others read and then put into action.

R26 *Spot Dictation*

Spot dictation enables the teacher to focus the attention of the students on the correct spelling of certain words and on slight differences in the spelling of near-homographs. It is a testing device to encourage the mastery of the spelling system, as contrasted with word recognition. Sometimes students write the words separately, sometimes in blanks on a partial script.

The teacher reads a complete sentence to the class so that the students hear the word in context.

TEACHER   Pedro tiene un amigo que se llama Roberto.

The teacher then repeats a particular word or group of words which the students write down.

TEACHER   *que se llama* . . . (Students write que se llama.)
TEACHER   Pedro tiene un amigo que se llama Roberto.
           A Roberto no le gusta la música.
           la música . . . (Students write.)
TEACHER   A Roberto no le gusta la música, pero le gustan mucho los estudios.
           mucho . . . (Students write.)
TEACHER   Pero le gustan mucho los estudios.
           los estudios . . . (Students write.)
TEACHER   El habla bien el español.
           el español . . . (Students write.)

Reading is linked with the learning of grammar.

Students see in written form what they have been learning orally and consolidate their grasp of grammatical structure.

Reading is linked with learning about language.

Students become conscious of differences in the surface structure of
Spanish and English. Students take language universals for granted because they are universals, e.g., the fact that sentences consist of noun
phrases and verb phrases. They tend to expect other features to be universals too. Many surface differences which students often do not discern
until they have full control of pronunciation are more clearly observable in
written language, e.g., number agreements and some manifestations of gender in Spanish.

Reading is linked with learning about Hispanic culture.

The written script in textbooks should be accompanied by illustrations
and photographs which elucidate many aspects of the life and customs of
the people and add new meaning to even the simplest of exchanges in the
foreign language. Even culturally neutral material (see Rivers, 1968, p.
275) becomes more alive when the student sees how everyday situations
vary in other cultures and have a different import. Some time should be
spent from the earliest lessons in arousing the students' interest in Hispanic
life and attitudes. (As reading skill develops and students read more
widely, this particular link becomes more and more important.)

RECOGNITION OF SOUND PATTERNS REPRESENTED BY THE GRAPHIC SYMBOLS

The student beginning to read Spanish will find that /b/ has two variants,
[b] and [b̄], depending on its distribution, and that both variants are represented orthographically by both *b* and *v*.

R27
1.	vamos	[bámos]
2.	no vamos	[nob̄ámos]
3.	bien	[bi̯én]
4.	muy bien	[mu̯ib̄i̯én]
5.	un vaso	[umbáso]
6.	mi vaso	[mib̄áso]
7.	un beso	[umbéso]
8.	tus besos	[tuzb̄ésos]
9.	un vestido	[umbestíd̄o]
10.	este vestido	[esteb̄estíd̄o]
11.	vámonos	[bámonos]
12.	no nos vamos	[nonozb̄ámos]

R28 A speaker of English will also find that some words spelled like English
words (and even in some cases having a meaning similar to that of their
English counterparts) have a distinctly different pronunciation in Spanish:

e.g., *horrible* will now be pronounced [oríble];
   general will now be pronounced [henerál];
   cordial will now be pronounced [kordiál].

R29 Similar problems arise when students encounter words whose spelling is close to that of their English counterparts but which are pronounced quite differently in Spanish:

e.g., presidente   [presidénte]
   sensacional   [sensasionál]
   automóvil   [automóbil]

The student will become more conscious of variations of the types described if, instead of merely repeating after the teacher as he reads or is corrected, he also constructs lists from his reading of different letters which are pronounced the same, of letters which have more than one possible pronunciation, and of troublesome "look-alike" words which deceive by their very resemblance to English.

✳ Compare notes in class on other sound-symbol areas which you yourself have found particularly confusing.

MATERIALS FOR STAGE ONE

If a dialogue-learning approach is being used, an early dialogue the student will read after having practiced it orally may resemble the following:

R30 *Unit Five: Basic Dialogue "Los problemas de Pedrito"* [14]

MADRE   ¿Adónde vas con tanta prisa? ¿Al partido de fútbol?
PEDRITO   Sí, juega el Santos, campeón del mundo. A propósito, mami . . . este . . .
MADRE   Ajá, ya sé. No tienes dinero. ¿Cuánto cuestan los boletos?
PEDRITO   No recuerdo. Creo que cinco pesos.

(Construction of suitable dialogues is discussed in detail in Chapter 1.)

Commentary

1. The subject matter is of interest to high school students.
2. The utterances are authentic.
3. The speech patterns are typical of informal Spanish (e.g., use of familiar verb forms *vas, tienes;* use of *mami*).

4. The sentences are short or break into short semantically and structurally replaceable segments (e.g., *No tienes dinero; ¿cuánto cuestan?; con tanta prisa*), thus providing opportunities for variation and recombination practice.

5. Useful expressions and idioms are provided (e.g., *a propósito; este; ajá*).

6. Provision is made for the study of basic grammar (e.g., contractions *al* and *del;* interrogation with *¿adónde?, ¿cuánto?;* adjective-noun agreement: tant*a* pris*a*; possession with *de: campeón del mundo*).

7. With additional vocabulary supplied, this dialogue provides a natural stepping stone to the recombinations for reading practice of Stage Two. The forms provided permit interesting recombinations.

8. Sound-symbol correspondences: every vowel and consonant in Spanish is represented in this passage, except /č/ and /ñ/. There is ample material for practice in the contrasting Spanish syllabification, *sinalefa;* contrasts with English phonic values for certain symbols, e.g., f*ú*tbol, *j*uega, q*u*e; and two diacritics are represented: *puntos de interrogación* and *acento*.

When dialogues are not used, the first reading material consists of a graphic representation on the chalkboard, in the textbook, on the overhead projector, or on flashcards of the Spanish sentences being learned orally in the classroom context or in simulated situations. (These are often associated with pictures.)

R31   —¿Qué es esto?
—Eso es un reloj despertador.

—¿Qué hace Ud. cuando su despertador suena?
—Cuando mi despertador suena yo me despierto.

—¿A qué hora suena el despertador de Raúl?
—El despertador de Raúl suena a las seis y media.[15]

Stage Two: Familiarization

Students read rearrangements and recombinations of material they have been learning orally. These recombinations may be situational dialogues, conversations that can be acted out in class, or take the form of interesting narratives.

The recombinations may be written by the students themselves, thus linking writing practice with reading. All material will be written in informal style. Students may write out such things as directions from the school to their home; these may be passed out to the class and other students asked to identify the address. Students may write down things they are presumed to be doing while other students try to identify the time of day or place associated with these actions. Many other realistic activities can be invented which use the vocabulary and structures the students have learned at this particular stage.

MATERIALS FOR STAGE TWO

R32 When dialogues like R30 have been used in Stage One, a *recombination conversation* like the one below[16] may be used for Stage Two.

(The previous occurrence of a similar item in the book from which this passage has been taken is indicated by the following symbols: S—supplement; BD—basic dialogue; R—a previous recombination.)

EL CHICO   Buenos días. ¡Qué bonita es esta corbata (S 4)! ¿Cuánto cuesta (BD 5)?
EL SEÑOR   Muy barata, mi amigo, muy barata (BD 2, S 5, and BD 1): diez pesos (S 3 and BD 5).
EL CHICO   ¡Diez pesos (S 3 and BD 5)! Adiós (S 4).
EL SEÑOR   ¿Le gusta la corbata (S 4 and R 4)? Ocho pesos (S 3 and BD 5).
EL CHICO   No (BD 1 and 2), gracias (S 5). Muy cara (BD 2 and S 5) todavía (BD 2 and R 2).
EL SEÑOR   ¡Siete (S 3)!
EL CHICO   Muy cara (BD 2 and S 5). Cinco (S 3), tal vez (BD 2).
EL SEÑOR   ¡No no no no no no y no (BD 1 and 2)! No puedo (BD 3 and R 3). ¡Seis pesos (S 3 and BD 5)! Un regalo (BD 3 and R 4).
EL CHICO   Cinco (S 3 and BD 5).
EL SEÑOR   ¡Ay caramba (BD 5)! Está bien (BD 4): cinco (S 3 and BD 5).

R33 When classroom conversations like R31 are used, recombination readings like the following[17] are appropriate. (In this example, all segments have been practiced either in the current lesson or in previous ones.)

En mi casa, mi madre se despierta cuando suena el despertador y se levanta inmediatamente. Mi padre se despierta a la misma hora, pero no se levanta. Yo me despierto más tarde y me levanto inmediatamente. Mis hermanos menores no se levantan temprano.

R34 Sometimes a little humor can help. The teacher (or students) can deliberately construct absurd sentences using only words which have appeared in
previous lessons in the textbook or the workbook. (The following sentences are constructed from words typical of a first-year Spanish course.)

1. Cuando hace calor me pongo el abrigo y los guantes y me levanto para
   sentarme.
2. Para el desayuno comemos platos y mesas con nuestros exámenes.
3. El profesor quiere dormir porque tiene hambre.
4. Hay una silla y un coche en el sombrero de mi biblioteca.
5. Ellos saben mucha prisa porque salen y hablan fácilmente.

It is certain that the student who could read and understand these sentences would not be depending on recollection of memorized material.

R35 *Recombinations in narrative form*

As a further step away from dependence on what has been learned in
conversational form, the following recombination narrative reintroduces
words, phrases, and structures previously learned and practiced, but extends
the vocabulary range by the use of cognates (indicated by an asterisk),
and creates a completely new and entertaining narrative which is nevertheless conversational in tone. For a few words marked with ° an English
equivalent is given in the margin.

El teléfono (Unit 10)[18]
Ese aparato* feo y de color negro, de figura* poco
artística*, frío de personalidad*, ese instrumento* que un
señor con uniforme* de la Compañía* Nacional* de
Electricidad* colgó en una pared° de la cocina de mi casa,   pared f: wall
ése es nuestro° indispensable* y sincero* amigo, el telé-   nuestro: our
fono.
Si de todos los aparatos eléctricos* que la técnica* moderna ha creado*, alguien me dice que solamente uno
puedo tener en mi casa, y me ordena* eliminar* todos los
otros, yo inmediatamente selecciono* el teléfono y elimino
el refrigerador*, el radio, y todos los otros que tenemos
en la casa, inclusive* la televisión* en colores que es tan
bonita.

At Stage Two, students learn to recognize meaningful segments of thought
and read in coherent word groupings. The familiarity of the structure and

of most of the lexical items enables students to relate segments of meaning in what they are reading to what has preceded and to keep all of this in their immediate memory while processing what follows. Students are acquiring reading habits basic to fluent direct reading. For this reason reading practice at this stage is best done in class, where the teacher can guide the student in techniques, rather than being set as homework. Questions require answers which force students to recombine known elements in new combinations.

Stage Three: Acquiring reading techniques

Students read simple narrative and conversational material with an uncomplicated and entertaining theme. They are introduced to written style and more complicated structure. Vocabulary remains largely in the area of the known, with some unfamiliar words whose meaning can be deduced from illustrations, from cognates, or from the context. (See examples of inferencing in comments on R24.) Reading materials are a step behind what is currently being learned in order to encourage direct reading in Spanish, a process which becomes exceedingly difficult when too many novelties of vocabulary and structure are encountered at the same time.

A recombination narrative like R35 bridges the gap between Stages Two and Three.

MATERIALS FOR STAGE THREE

R36 This passage is accompanied by five amusing drawings which illuminate the meaning of each of the italicized sentences. The words marked ° are explained with small sketches or Spanish glosses in the margin.

Cómo defenderse de las mujeres[19]

Todos los periódicos tienen artículos para las mujeres que buscan un esposo. Estos artículos les ofrecen ideas para atrapar fácilmente a los hombres. ¿Puede un hombre hacer algo contra eso? ¿Tiene él que ser la víctima inocente de los planes de una mujer? ¡No! El hombre debe defenderse. Aquí están unas ideas muy prácticas:

1. *Cambie con frecuencia.* Es necesario ver a muchas chicas, porque cuando un hombre ve a una misma todo el tiempo, está en el camino del matrimonio.

2. *Sea cruel con los niños y los animales.* Si una señorita ve que usted es sentimental, nunca va a dejarle escapar.

3. *Muestre a la chica, y más importante a su padre, que usted tiene muy poco dinero.*

4. *Trate muy mal a la madre de la chica y también a sus amigas.* Cuando estas mujeres dicen cosas malas de usted, la chica no sabe qué hacer.

5. *No demuestre cortesía.°* No le abra la puerta del coche a la señorita. No la ayude con el abrigo° ni le diga cosas dulces.

Si la señorita todavía le sigue a usted después de un mes de esta fórmula, ¡hombre, usted ha perdido!

Adaptación de un artículo de *Meridiano* (Barcelona)

Commentary

1. The passage was written by a native speaker but has been simplified and adapted without destroying its authentic flavor. The language is contemporary.

2. Vocabulary and structures are of the type commonly taught in elementary courses, or else are easily recognizable cognates.

3. The segments are short and uncomplicated.

4. The extract shows a nice balance between familiar situations in the native culture of the learner and situations in the foreign culture. Because of its theme it is more suited to high school or college students, since the humor springs largely from situations which would not be grasped fully by younger students.

5. The level of difficulty of the vocabulary is defined: words which do not occur in the 1000 words most likely to be familiar to American students, which Pimsleur established by correlating with the word lists in *Recuento de vocabulario español* (Rio Piedras: University of Puerto Rico, 1952) the vocabulary of six widely used high school and college Spanish textbooks, are glossed in the margin on their first appearance or otherwise explained or simplified.

When fluent reading is considered the primary objective,[20] Stages One and Two are frequently omitted and simple, entertaining narrative and conversational material with much repetition of vocabulary and structures, sometimes profusely illustrated, is used from the beginning. These passages are often written in such a way that they can be used for dramatic readings or role-playing; in this they resemble the dialogues of Stage One. An example of such material is given below. The meaning of the italicized expressions is made clear in the book by footnotes and idiom lists.

R37   Prohibido Fumar en el Tranvía[21]

Un tranvía va por la calle Cangallo en Buenos Aires.

Un viejo con una pipa en la boca lo detiene en una *esquina* y sube. Paga sus diez centavos al *cobrador* y se sienta.

Se sienta directamente bajo un letrero que dice:

PROHIBIDO

FUMAR

EN EL TRANVÍA

Sigue con la pipa en la boca.

El cobrador lo nota y se acerca.

—Perdone Ud., señor,—dice el cobrador,—pero está prohibido fumar en el tranvía.

—Lo sé—responde *el de la pipa.* —Aquí tenemos un letrero que lo anuncia.

Y señala el letrero.

—Muy bien,—continúa el cobrador—pero si Ud. insiste en fumar, *tengo que* hacerle bajar del tranvía. Es *el reglamento.*

—No insisto en fumar—dice el viejo, que todavía tiene en la boca la famosa pipa, de *la cual* sube el humo en espiral.

—Luego *deje Ud. de* fumar—responde el cobrador.

—No estoy fumando—*vuelve a* decir el pasajero.

—¿Pues, no tiene Ud. la pipa en la boca?—pregunta el cobrador.

—Claro que tengo la pipa en la boca.

—¿Y no tiene tabaco en la pipa?—vuelve a preguntar el cobrador.

—*Por supuesto,*—responde el otro.—Pero no estoy fumando.

—¿Y no sale humo de la pipa?

—Claro,—vuelve a decir el viejo—pero digo que no estoy fumando.

Y luego añade, extendiendo un pie delante del cobrador:

—¿Ve Ud. mis pies? Llevo zapatos, un zapato en cada pie, pero eso no significa que estoy caminando *a pie.*

Ante la lógica del pasajero el cobrador tiene que retirarse y no le molesta más.

Commentary

The cultural background in this passage is basically neutral. Verb tenses are limited to the present indicative and present progressive, plus one occurrence of the formal imperative. Cognates are used liberally, and structures to be practiced orally and in writing are repeated several times.

For students who have passed through Stages One and Two, material for reading at Stage Three will be more demanding than the extract just quoted. In the following passage, specially written by a native speaker, new words, beyond the usual vocabulary of classroom texts, are introduced at the rate of about one word in every hundred running words. These words, marked °, are glossed in the margin on their first appearance. Easily recognizable cognates are also used and marked with an asterisk to encourage the student to think first before rushing to a dictionary or vocabulary list.

Details of rail travel in Europe are introduced in a narrative of two students, an American and a Venezuelan, who are enroute from Barcelona, Spain, to Italy (thus providing an opportunity for the American student of Spanish to identify himself in his reading with people of his own age and interests).

R38 — *En el Expreso de Barcelona*[22]

En esta ciudad Johnny y Guillermo habían visitado a Gloria Berenguer, una muchacha catalana graciosa y entusiasta que era compañera de ellos en la universidad, en los Estados Unidos. Durante sus cinco días en Barcelona ella les había servido de guía y ahora que se marchaban a Italia, vía* el sur de Francia, venía a despedirlos.

—Mira, Gloria, sube con Johnny a ver si encuentran un compartimiento*[1] desocupado. Yo me quedo aquí para cuidar el equipaje.

Los dos entraron en el vagón y pronto llamaron desde el pasillo.[2]

—Parece que todos están desocupados. No hay nadie en todo el vagón.

—¡Caramba!—dijo Johnny—. Espero que éste sea nuestro tren. Me extraña que no haya nadie aquí.

—No te preocupes—le contestó Gloria—. Es temprano todavía. Pero por si acaso, mientras vosotros vais[3] arreglando las cosas, yo voy a averiguar° a qué hora sale el   *to find out* tren para estar segura que no han hecho ningún cambio. . . . Tenéis suerte. Este vagón es limpio y nuevo.

—Ya lo creo, y qué° cómodos son los asientos. Oye, al   *how* averiguar lo del horario, averigua también si este vagón va hasta Italia—le pidió Johnny.

—Claro que no.° Tenéis que cambiar de tren en la   *of course not* frontera* de Francia.

---

[1] Most European trains have first-, second-, and third-class coaches. The first- and second-class coaches have enclosed compartments for six or eight people respectively.

The third-class cars are more like American coaches, though the seats are often made of wood.

² A narrow *pasillo,* or "passageway," runs along one side of the coach. Each compartment has a narrow sliding door which opens onto the passageway.

³ Remember that in Castilian Spanish the plural form of *tú* is *vosotros,* rather than *ustedes,* and has its own set of verb endings. Thus in the plural, *tú vas* becomes *vosotros vais, tú tienes* becomes *vosotros tenéis,* and so forth.

RECOGNITION OF STRUCTURAL CLUES

For fluent reading, the student must be able to detect rapidly meaningful groups of words, even when their lexical content is not clear to him.

Through Stages Three and Four, students will be learning to detect effortlessly the indicators of word classes (parts of speech), and of persons and tenses of the verb; the words which introduce phrases (*dentro de, en, después de, antes de*) and clauses (*después que, mientras que, antes que, porque, si*) and the particular modifications of meaning they indicate; the adverbs and adverbial expressions which limit the action in time, place, and manner (*mañana, muchas veces, allí, aquí, bien, demasiado, bastante, vigorosamente*); and the indicators of interrogation (*¿Qué?; ¿Cuándo?; ¿Dónde?; ¿Cómo?; ¿Por qué?*) and negation (*no, nunca, nada, nadie*). Questions will be designed to attract the students' attention to these structural clues.

R39 For rapid comprehension, students should be trained to recognize such features as the *-r-* which is always present as an indicator of future time or of some type of hypothetical or unrealized action:

Ella llega*r*á (contrast: ella llega);
Ella vend*r*á pronto;
Ella ya hab*r*á salido (where this is the speaker's presumption—he has no certain information);
Si yo lo vie*r*a se lo paga*r*ía.

R40 Students should be made aware of the role played by the preposition *a.* When not used as a directional particle meaning *to(wards),* the preposition *a* precedes nouns standing for people or things directly or indirectly acted upon by others. Being aware of this role of *a,* the student will readily recognize that *a los jóvenes no los conocen* means that the young people are not known, whereas *los jóvenes no los conocen* means that the young people do not know others.

R41 Knowledge of the following fact will help the reader of a Spanish text whenever he comes across a reflexive form: except for cases of reciprocal or joint action, the reflexive construction signals lack of participation of an external human agent. Thus, the following sentences express processes which come about without any external human agency:

Carlos se murió;

Se han sorprendido mucho los estudiantes;

A Pedro se le cayó la taza.

* Discuss other structural clues on which you depend to clarify the meaning of what you are reading.

7
Reading II:
from dependence to independence

Stage Four: Practice

Students now practice their reading skill with a wider range of language. Reading is of two kinds: *intensive,* where reading is linked with further study of grammar and vocabulary; and *extensive,* where the student is on his own, reading for his own purposes or for pleasure. In both cases texts are authentic writings by Hispanic authors, but they are carefully selected to be accessible to the student at this stage of his development; that is, difficult or complex style or esoteric vocabulary is avoided. As the student progresses through this practice stage he reads material of increasing complexity with a wider and wider range of vocabulary. The first 3,500 words of the Juilland and Chang-Rodríguez *Frequency Dictionary of Spanish Words* (FDSW) as a recognition vocabulary seems a reasonable limitation. This will, of course, be augmented by cognates and some specialized vocabulary associated with a specific topic.

INTENSIVE READING

This provides material for close study of problem areas.

1. The systems and subsystems of the language[1]

English-speaking students always have difficulty understanding the Spanish system for expressing time relationships and particularly the subsystem for expressing action in the past.

R42 Through reading, the student becomes aware that Spanish verb forms convey not only a notion of time but also one of aspect.[2] For example, although both the *pretérito* and the *imperfecto* refer to past time, these two tenses differ from each other in the manner whereby they focus on past events. The *pretérito* emphasizes the perfectivity of the event, thus describing it as conceptually finished: *Pablo me llamó.* On the other hand, the *imperfecto* stresses the on-goingness of the event, regardless of its inception or end: *El taxi avanzaba lentamente por la calle.*

El accidente ocurrió el 3 de noviembre. Ella no pensaba en otra cosa. El suceso la preocupaba tanto que quería suicidarse. Por fin su marido pudo distraerla . . .

Commentary

In *ocurrió* and *pudo* [*distraerla*], the events are seen as accomplished, that is, as expressing perfective aspect. In *pensaba, preocupaba, quería,* on the other hand, the aspect is imperfective. We look at the woman's predicament, her state of mind, as they develop in time; we live through the situation with her for a short interval as the story continues.

R43 Compare the variations of aspect and time value in the following:

De pronto un hombre sintió que le tiraban de una manga insistentemente. Balbuceó preguntas al que así lo tenía, mas como no le contestaban, encendió un fósforo y descubrió el grotesco y velludo rostro de un mono grande que con ojos aterrorizados parecía interrogarlo acerca de lo que pasaba. El desconocido, de un empujón, apartó la bestia de sí, y muchos que estaban próximos a él se fijaron en que los animales estaban en libertad.[3]

R44 In formal style:

¡Pum! . . . ¡Pum! . . . ¡Pum! . . . Y ¡nada! ¡No respondía nadie! ¡No abrían! ¡No se movía una mosca! Sólo se oía el claro rumor de los caños de una fuente que había en el patio de la casa. Y de esta manera transcurrían minutos, largos como eternidades. Al fin, cerca de la una, abrióse un ventanillo del piso segundo.[4]

Commentary

To make students more aware of this important distinction in the use of past tense forms, they may be asked questions like the following:

1. Discuss the reasons for the use of the *imperfecto* in the section: "¡No respondía nadie . . . largos como eternidades."

2. In the last sentence could *abrióse* be replaced by *se abría* and still convey the same effect as in the present text? Explain the reasons for your answer.

Focusing the students' attention on the tense choices of Hispanic writers who wish to convey certain effects will make the Spanish way of expressing past action, and specifically the distinctive uses of the *pretérito* and the *imperfecto,* appear more rational and meaningful. Many other problems of contrastive Spanish-English usage are also more efficiently studied through the thoughtful analysis of a text than through the study of a rule, illustrated by examples detached from the wider context of interacting rules. Nor is translation of sentences from English to Spanish particularly effective in such areas of contrast just because at these points English does not make a particular distinction in parallel fashion.

* Look for passages in Spanish which show clearly the use of the subjunctive for expressing a subtle nuance in meaning, as in such statements as: *Quiero trabajar con un profesor que sabe español* and *Quiero trabajar con un profesor que sepa español.* In the first sentence, the speaker either knows about or at least has some reason to assume the existence of a professor who knows Spanish; in this case, *profesor* is characterized as *specific.* In the second sentence, however, *profesor* is marked as *unspecific:* the speaker makes no assumption about the existence of a person with such characteristics. (See also the discussion in Chapter 8, p. 266.) For an explanation of the feature specific as used here, see Roger L. Hadlich, *A Transformational Grammar of Spanish* (Englewood Cliffs, N.J.: Prentice-Hall, 1971), p. 190.

2. *Contrastive problems of meaning*

It is in functioning language that students will begin to assimilate the differences in coverage of semantic space of Spanish words which seem to be equivalent in meaning to certain English words.

R45 The concept of the English verb "to leave" does not coincide with Spanish *dejar,* nor with Spanish *partir.* Sometimes it would be rendered in Spanish by *abandonar* or *salir.*

El *dejó* el libro en la mesa. He *left* the book on the table.

El *salió* del cuarto. He *left* the room.

El acaba de *partir.* He's just *left.*

En la *abandonó* por otra. He *left* her for someone else.

¡*Deje* eso en paz! *Leave* that alone!

R46 Similarly, a familiar concept like "to take" becomes a problem for English speakers.

El *cogió* el libro. He *took* the book (= picked it up).
El *llevó* el libro a la biblioteca. He *took* the book to the library.
¡El me *quitó* el libro! He *took* my book!
El *dio* un paseo. He *took* a walk.
El *hizo* un viaje. He *took* a trip.
El *tomó* dos aspirinas. He *took* two aspirin.

Such uses as these must be encountered in context on many occasions if they are to be used spontaneously.

Students come to appreciate the resources of the Spanish language when they *listen* to the plays, poems, and prose they have studied intensively being acted, recited, or read by Hispanic actors and sometimes by the writers themselves.

This is the stage for intellectually challenging ideas and the cultivation of aesthetic values. Material for Stage Four should be selected for the literary, informational, or provocative value of its content, not merely as a language vehicle. Questions should go beyond Who? What? When? Where? How (manner)? and yes-no questions, to considerations of implications, that is, Why? If . . . then what? and How (explanation)? questions.[5]

EXTENSIVE READING

This gives the student the opportunity to use his knowledge of the language for his own purposes. It is an individualized or shared activity as the student prefers. With some help from the teacher in selection as he needs it, the student reads for his own pleasure short stories, plays, short novels, newspapers or magazines specially written for schools, or selected articles and advertisements (particularly those profusely illustrated) from Spanish or Hispano-American sources. He may read for information about a topic which interests him or prepare a project, a report, or a debate with a friend or a group of friends. He attempts to increase his reading speed; setting timed goals may help him in this. He learns to tolerate a certain vagueness, reading whole sections at a time in order to establish the general meaning so that he can develop his ability to deduce from semantic and syntactic clues the meaning of unfamiliar words and phrases.

MATERIALS FOR STAGE FOUR

Passages like "En el Expreso de Barcelona" (R38) may be read and discussed in class at Stage Three to supplement the steady diet of the intermediate level textbook or used for the *extensive reading* of Stage Four, which should always be at a lower level of difficulty than material for intensive reading.

R47   A book published in 1942 gives the following passage for an "elementary course in college." We may hope that "elementary" in that period meant at least "intermediate" (whether at secondary or college level) in modern terms. In this passage all words, except cognates, not in the first 3,500 words of FDSW have been italicized.

> Lejos de que le fuese de algún provecho esta ingeniosa explicación, vió que el amo *fruncía* las *cejas* y hacía una *mueca* cual si no *cupiera* en sí de *ira*. Y de veras le hubiera *reñido* severamente, si el respeto a los *comensales* no le detuviera; pero no pareciéndole conveniente que *controvirtiese* con el cocinero o le *zahiriese* delante de los convidados, sólo le dijo con cierta sonrisa *burlona*, que quería que fuera con él a cazar para que le hiciera el favor de enseñarle tan extraño fenómeno. Si las *grullas*, dijo el amo, no tuvieren más que una pata sola, será muy fácil que demos al *traste* con las ideas aceptadas desde hace muchos siglos sobre ese asunto. Añadió que, en tal caso, convendría que se corrigiesen las falsas aserciones de los que hasta entonces habían pasado por sabios, de modo que el mundo no anduviera errado por más tiempo, sino que se convirtiera a la doctrina del cocinero, etc., etc.[6]

Commentary

1. Of the words italicized, *ira, comensales,* and *burlona* could be considered cognates, but it is unlikely that all students would recognize them as such.

2. Presuming that students know all of the first 3,500 words of the FDSW (which is not at all certain at this stage), this passage contains 11 new words in 160 running words, a rate of one new word in 14. Scherer recommends a rate of one new word in 35.[7] He also recommends that the new words be spaced evenly, that the new vocabulary be useful, that cognates be signaled in some way, and that new words "be surrounded by contextual clues so that it is possible to infer the meaning."[8]

3. The sentences in the passage are also long and complicated, placing a strain on the memory of the student who is making any attempt at direct reading of the extract.[9]

We may say that this passage was intended for intensive reading and therefore extension of vocabulary and knowledge of structure. The words italicized are hardly likely to be encountered in further reading or in communication (*mueca, comensales, controvirtiese, zahiriese, traste,* and so on).

In contrast to R47, the following passage, selected from a current reader, controls both vocabulary and structural content while treating an authentic, contemporary theme.[10]

R48   *La emigración sigue*

Viajo en tercera clase en un tren que va de España a Francia. Veo hombres de caras tristes y trajes con años de uso. Veo pocos niños y mujeres. Las manos de los hombres son duras y de color oscuro. Hablan español con acento de las provincias de Andalucía y Galicia.

Me hago amigo de Pedro, un fuerte campesino de la provincia de Andalucía, quien me presenta a sus compañeros. Todos ellos son emigrantes que van a Francia. Algunos saben adonde van a trabajar. Otros no saben adónde van a dormir la próxima noche. Pero todos esperan tener mejor vida. Son muchos. Veo tres vagones del tren llenos. Todos los años, todos los meses, todos los días salen españoles para el extranjero. Tres millones y medio cada año.

In case it should be objected that this passage is mainly in the present tense, with fewer structural complexities than R47, the reader can compare the following passage which was selected from the same book as R48 and which presents a greater variety of verb tenses and vocabulary.[11]

R49
Casi cada día en los periódicos de Madrid o Barcelona se pueden leer artículos como éste: "Ha desaparecido° de la casa de sus padres el chico de dieciséis años, X. Y. Lleva pantalones y suéter azules, y es alto y robusto. Si puede identificar al muchacho por esta foto, llame por teléfono a sus padres."

    salido sin
    dar razones

En el pasado, esto occuría poco, y además era siempre en serio.° El adolescente iba a otro país, a otra ciudad, se hacía un hombre, y cuando tenía una posición, una mujer, y a veces unos hijos, volvía a la casa de sus padres feliz de haber realizado estas cosas "por sus propios medios."

    en . . . de carácter
    grave; sin frivolidad

Pero ahora hay una diferencia fundamental. Hoy día,° los adolescentes no quieren escaparse a otro país ni a otra ciudad. El objetivo es vivir en

    Hoy . . . hoy

la misma ciudad de sus padres, pero en otro
apartamento. El año pasado la mayoría de los
jóvenes alemanes° que entraron en la Universidad   gente de Alemania,
de Berlín tenían su residencia aparte de sus pa-   país al este de Francia
dres, aunque en la misma ciudad. En Francia, el
periódico *Triunfo* dice que este año casi 10.000
adolescentes huyeron de sus padres.

Commentary

Here in 188 running words there are two words, apart from recognizable
cognates, which are not in the first 3,500 words of FDSW. Even if we
do not consider these two (*pantalones* and *alemanes*) as comprehensible
through their context, there is at most, then, about one new word per 100
running words.

* Examine some reading passages in textbooks in common use for Stage
Four to see how they measure up to the criteria discussed; then find in the
library some suitable passages in novels and short stories from various
parts of the Spanish-speaking world and share them with your fellow students, before adding them to your personal file.

Stage Five: Expansion

At Stage Five, students can read without becoming discouraged a wide
variety of materials in their original form. At most there will have been
some judicious editing to eliminate occasional paragraphs of excessively
complicated structure and rare vocabulary. Once again the material that
the student is encouraged to read entirely on his own, his extensive reading,
will be more readily accessible in language and content than that which is
being studied intensively. Reading is now a technique, not an end, and
language is a vehicle and a model. Students are expected to be able to
discuss not only the content but the implications of what they have been
reading.

Material for intensive reading is chosen with a view to developing the
student's aesthetic appreciation, imagination, and powers of judgment and
discriminative reasoning. Students learn to scan for information, to read
with careful attention, and to extract the major ideas and arguments.
Attention is paid to matters of style in writing, and students are given some
experience in exact translation from Spanish to English to make them
more conscious of the choices involved in literary writing and the potentialities of their own language, as well as the Spanish language. Reading is

still linked with *listening* (to plays, poems, readings, speeches), with *writing* (of reports, summaries, commentaries, and, for self-selected students, even poetry), and with *speaking* (discussion of ideas, themes, and values). Students seek to penetrate the mind and heart of the Spanish-speaking people and compare and contrast their attitudes and aspirations with their own. They continue to read widely on subjects which interest them personally (political, social, scientific, artistic, practical) and prepare presentations in which they share what they have enjoyed with their fellow students.

Teachers need not feel at a loss in providing widely diversified reading for their Stage Five students, since material now being made available by publishers is much more varied than in previous decades.

* Examine advertisements in recent journals and publishers' catalogues to see how many areas of interest you can identify in recently published books of readings.

Students at Stage Five still need help with more difficult aspects of Spanish written style. Many students, for instance, never grasp the essential differences between the common logical connectives such as *sin embargo, no obstante, por eso, entonces, por fin, luego,* and *además,* yet words such as these are indispensable for understanding the development of thought and for drawing implications. A situational technique may be used to familiarize students at this level with their meaning.

R50 A key sentence is selected, such as:

El no ha pagado sus deudas.

A situation is described in Spanish and the student is asked to link this key sentence with the idea: tú le vuelves a prestar dinero, in some such way as: El no ha pagado sus deudas; *sin embargo* tú le vuelves a prestar dinero.

Other possibilities are:

El no ha pagado sus deudas. No piensa hacerlo.

El no ha pagado sus deudas; *además* no piensa hacerlo.

El no ha pagado sus deudas; se siente avergonzado cuando nos encontramos.

El no ha pagado sus deudas; *por eso* se siente avergonzado cuando nos encontramos.

El no ha pagado sus deudas. Yo me he negado a salir con él.

El no ha pagado sus deudas; *luego* yo me he negado a salir con él.

Important clue words like these are frequently omitted entirely from the Spanish course, with the result that students continue for years to express themselves in simple sentences, or link sentences only with *y* and *pero*, and are incapable of recognizing the significance of the logical connectives in modifying the meaning of what they are reading. A careful study should be made of the way an argument is developed in Spanish through a succession of such connectives.

READING WITH WRITING

A class which is reading for information would find practicing these connectives orally very difficult. A written exercise which requires analysis of the logical development and choice among possible connectives may be used instead.

R51 Write out the following passage as a paragraph, selecting from the logical connectives supplied those which will provide the most natural development of thought.

Yo te doy este libro del cual no he tratado de leer más que unas cuantas páginas. (Entonces; además; por eso) no comprendí casi nada de lo que leí. (Sin embargo; por consiguiente; luego) se trata de un tema que me interesa, y me gustaría encontrar otro libro de la misma serie. (Porque; en efecto; no obstante) ésta no es la primera vez que trato de informarme sobre la estadística. (Pero; entonces; por eso) no renuncio a él. (Además; sin embargo; luego) no tengo la intención de perder mucho tiempo con eso.

MATERIALS FOR STAGE FIVE

Some textbooks may propose for intensive reading in a general course at this level material like the following excerpt from a poem by Francisco de Quevedo (1601):[12]

R52 *Letrilla*

Poderoso caballero
es don Dinero.

Madre, yo al oro me humillo;
él es mi amante y mi amado,
pues de puro enamorado,
de contino anda amarillo;
que pues, doblón o sencillo,
hace todo cuanto quiero,

poderoso caballero
es don Dinero.

Nace en las Indias honrado,
donde el mundo le acompaña;
viene a morir en España,
y es en Génova enterrado.
Y pues quien le trae al lado
es hermoso, aunque sea fiero
poderoso caballero
es don Dinero.

Naturally enough nearly every line of this poem requires a footnote.
Important, and clever, as the poem is, it is not clear how the average
intermediate-level student could do more than decipher it, whereas he
would be able to read easily and with enjoyment certain poems of
Bécquer, Lorca, or Jiménez. For a general textbook, then, this poem is un-
suitable, whereas it would fascinate Group D which has chosen to specialize
in literary analysis.

Verses which have delighted many non-specialized students and made
Spanish poetry accessible to them are these *Rimas* by the noted nineteenth-
century poet Gustavo Adolfo Bécquer.[13] They have been reprinted in many
textbooks and anthologies for students of Spanish for many decades, but
poetry is timeless in its appeal to new generations.

R53 *Rimas*

"¿Qué es la poesía?," dices mientras clavas
en mi pupila tu pupila azul;
"¿Qué es la poesía? ¿Y tú me lo preguntas?
Poesía . . . eres tú."

Los suspiros son aire y van al aire.
Las lágrimas son agua y van al mar.
Dime, mujer: cuando el amor se olvida,
    ¿sabes tú adónde va?

Por una mirada, un mundo;
por una sonrisa, un cielo;
por un beso . . . ¡yo no sé
qué te diera por un beso!

These verses, in contrast to R52, are easily understood by most, if not all,
intermediate students. Their theme is universal, yet immediate, calling forth
an emotional response with little need for explanation.

Many works by twentieth-century poets are equally accessible to the general student. As an example we may take the following poem of Juan Ramón Jiménez:[14]

R54 *El Viaje Definitivo*

. . . Y yo me iré. Y se quedarán los pájaros cantando,
y se quedará mi huerto, con su verde árbol,
y con su pozo blanco.

Todas las tardes, el cielo será azul y plácido,
y tocarán, como esta tarde están tocando,
las campanas del campanario.

Se morirán los que me amaron,
y el pueblo se hará nuevo cada año;
y lejos del bullicio distinto, sordo, raro,
del domingo cerrado, . . .
en el rincón secreto de mi huerto florido y encalado,
mi espíritu de hoy errará, nostáljico. . . .

Y yo me iré; y estaré solo, sin hogar; sin árbol
verde, sin pozo blanco,
sin cielo azul y plácido . . .
Y se quedarán los pájaros cantando.

Again, the theme is universal and appealing to modern students. The poem could be learned by heart with pleasure by many and added to their store of treasured literary memories. In this way poetry becomes a personal experience, not another arduous classroom assignment.

With prose readings, similarly, care must be exercised in the selection of materials for Group C. (Group D, as we have noted, is a self-selected group of specialized interests with a declared desire to explore literature.) Some books offer selections like the following where the language is not inaccessible and there are many cognates, but the content is very difficult for the average student of Spanish.

R55 Las nubes nos dan una sensación de inestabilidad y de eternidad. Las nubes son—como el mar—siempre varias y siempre las mismas. Sentimos, mirándolas, cómo nuestro ser y todas las cosas corren hacia la nada, en tanto que ellas—tan fugitivas—permanecen eternas. A estas nubes que ahora miramos, las miraron hace doscientos, quinientos, mil, tres mil años, otros hombres con las mismas pasiones y las mismas ansias que nosotros. Cuando queremos tener aprisionado el tiempo—en un momento de ventura—vemos que han pasado ya semanas, meses, años. . . .

Siglos después de este día en que Calisto está con la mano en la mejilla, un gran poeta—Campoamor—habrá de dedicar a las nubes un canto en uno de sus poemas titulado *Colón*. Las nubes—dice el poeta—nos ofrecen el espectáculo de la vida. La existencia, ¿qué es sino un juego de nubes? ...

Las nubes son la imagen del Tiempo. ¿Habrá sensación más trágica que aquella de quien sienta el Tiempo, la de quien vea ya en el presente el pasado y en el pasado lo porvenir?[15]

A passion for the chronological presentation of literary masterpieces must be curbed at this stage if students are to become fluent in reading and using contemporary language. If the oral skills are to be kept at a high level, reading material must be such that the students can discuss its content and implications with ease and confidence. This does not mean that the content must be of little literary or philosophical value as the following extract from a contemporary Spanish short story demonstrates.

R56 The story is set in contemporary Spain in a small town. Mariana is a young woman whose husband Antonio travels occasionally on business. She is threatened by the insinuations of an old tramp that he knows about her lover Constantino. In exchange for the tramp's silence, Mariana provides him with free food and lodging, which arouses Antonio's curiosity for a time. However as time passes and Antonio's questions about the tramp's presence diminish, Mariana's anxiety increases and she is tormented by the fear that somehow Antonio knows her secret.

Mariana sentía un temblor extraño. Hacía cerca de quince días que el viejo entró en la posada. Dormía, comía y se despiojaba descaradamente ... , junto a la puerta del huerto. El primer día Antonio preguntó:
—¿Y ése, qué pinta ahí?
—Me dio lástima—dijo ella, apretando entre los dedos los flecos de su chal—. Es tan viejo ... y hace tan mal tiempo. ...
Antonio no dijo nada. Le pareció que se iba hacia el viejo como para echarle de allí. Y ella corrió escaleras arriba. Tenía miedo. Sí: tenía mucho miedo. ... "Si el viejo vio a Constantino subir al castaño, bajo la ventana. Si le vio saltar a la habitación, las noches que iba Antonio con el carro, de camino. ..." ¿Qué podía querer decir, si no, con aquello de *lo vi todo, sí, lo vi con estos ojos?*"
Ya no podía más. No: ya no podía más. El viejo no se limitaba a vivir en la casa. Pedía dinero, ya. ... Y lo extraño es que Antonio no volvió a hablar de él. Se limitaba a ignorarle. Sólo que, de cuando en cuando, la

miraba a ella. Mariana sentía la fijeza de sos ojos grandes, negros y lucientes, y temblaba.[16]

Commentary

This story deals with human problems which should stimulate discussion of interest to the students, yet in language it is within the reading scope of Stage Five. Scherer suggests a vocabulary of at least 5,000 words for the last stage before liberated reading.[17] All the words in R56 occur within the 5,000-word limit of FDSW except *temblor, apretando, fijeza,* and *lucientes* (all of which are very near cognates of words that do occur within the limit); *chal* which is a recognizable cognate, especially if spoken; *flecos* and *castaño* which are comprehensible in the context; and *despiojaba* and *descaradamente* which are probably the only words which would be completely beyond the grasp of Stage Five students. There are at most, then, nine unfamiliar words in 197 running words and for many students only two.

✱ Look for suitable poems, stories, essays, scenes from plays, and short novels which you think would appeal to Stage Five students and which are accessible in vocabulary range and complexity of structure. (Keep careful notes of bibliographic details and page references.) Share your discoveries with others in your class and add them to your file for future reference.

Stage Six: Autonomy

Students who have reached this stage should be encouraged to develop an independent reading program tailored to their special interests. They should be able to come to the teacher on a personal basis at regular intervals to discuss what they have been reading and share the exhilaration of their discoveries.

Their reading may be in some special area of literature which interests them, or they may be reading widely with the aim of finding out as much as they can about the cultural attitudes or the civilization of the Hispanic people. On the other hand, they may have some specialized interest they wish to pursue: a contrastive study of Spanish and American advertising, or of the content of popular magazines; the theories behind modern Mexican architecture; urban problems; or folklore. An independent reading unit becomes more purposeful if it leads to some form of display: a one-man show at a Spanish club festival, an illustrated presentation to interested Spanish classes, an article for the school magazine, or the elaboration of a plan for study abroad in the area of the student's interest.

Independent study of this type for advanced students stimulates self-disciplined motivation and is an excellent preparation for autonomous intellectual exploration in later life.

Ordering the reading lesson

The reading lesson is not a quiescent interlude as some teachers seem to think. Because students have learned to associate sound and symbol in their native language, it does not follow that they know how to extract the full meaning from what they see in print. For the teacher the reading lesson or reading assignment has six parts.

1. *Selection* of suitable material at an appropriate level of reading difficulty for this particular group of students; selection of the right amount of material for the time available and for arousing and maintaining interest in the content of the text.

2. *Preparation* by the teacher, who checks on: the necessary background information; words which need explaining (and how best to explain them—by visual, action, Spanish definition or synonym, or translation); structural complications; the obscurity of meaning or allusion; and the most effective way to arouse interest in this particular text.

The teacher who has prepared the material ahead of time can often slip some of the unfamiliar vocabulary into class discussions and exercises in a preceding lesson, or can center an oral lesson on a semantic area germane to the reading text, thus not only introducing useful vocabulary but also preparing students unobtrusively for intelligent guessing when they are face to face with the text. A review of certain grammatical features may refresh the students' memory so that comprehension is not impeded by structural complexity.

3. *Introduction* of the material to the students. This introduction may take the form of the provision of background information or some explanation of cultural differences, either directly—visually or orally—or indirectly, during some other activity when the students may have been given the opportunity to find out information which will be useful for a later reading lesson. Sometimes the introduction will take the form of a provocative discussion on a question which is raised in the reading text, with the students then reading more alertly as they find out how the author has viewed the problem or whether the outcome is as they had anticipated. This approach is particularly valuable at Stage Five when a writer is developing difficult concepts or setting out a complicated discussion of ideas. Stimulating the student's own thinking about the central issue or problem helps him to anticipate the probable meaning of unfamiliar vocabulary and to perceive disguised cognates in the matrix of the development of ideas.

4. *Reading.* Throughout this section, and particularly in the discussion of the different stages, many practical suggestions have been given as to ways to approach the actual reading of the passage. These should be exploited on different occasions to ensure that the reading lesson does not fall into a set pattern. Individualized reading assignments also should be designed with a variety of activities in mind. The cardinal principle for each approach (except for Group E: *Translation*) is that it should encourage students to keep looking ahead for meaning, rather than stopping at each word to seek an exact English equivalent.

5. *Discussion.* It is at this point that the teacher is able to gauge and increase the student's overall comprehension of the passage, not by explaining and restating, but by encouraging the student to go back to the passage and look into it more carefully. Suggestions for improving this part of the lesson are developed in the next section.

6. *Application.* Reading is not an isolated activity. In a language class it should lead to something and thus be integrated with the improvement of all skills. This idea is developed below in the section: *Integrating the Language Skills,* p. 232.

* From all the indications scattered throughout this section, draw up three different lesson plans for the reading of R57 below.

Assisting and assessing reading comprehension

The following passage will be used as a basis for demonstration and evaluation of various methods for assisting and assessing the student's comprehension of reading material. In each example, items given are for illustration only and in no case represent a complete set.

R57

El Gato que Nunca Murió

Nuestro gato se llamaba Chiche. Era muy bonito—completamente negro 1
con una pequeña estrella blanca en la frente. Chiche era precioso. Toda la 2
familia lo amaba. Cuando era pequeño, nuestros tres hijos jugaban con él 3
días enteros. Algunas veces lo ponían en una pequeña caja, suspendida 4
entre dos sillas por medio de una cuerda, y Chiche pasaba muchas horas 5
durmiendo con la cabeza sobre una de las patas puesta en el borde de la 6
caja. De esta manera, Chiche tenía una hamaca perfecta; estaba conten- 7
tísimo. 8

A cada hora del día siempre era lo mismo—todo el mundo pensaba en 9
Chiche: 10

—¡Chiche tiene sed, mamá!—decía mi hijo. 11

—¿Por qué no das de comer a Chiche, Juana?—preguntaba mi marido. 12

—¡Qué mono está Chiche sentado en esa silla!—exclamaba yo.   13

Como es fácil de comprender, todo lo mejor era para Chiche. Com- 14
prábamos sardinas varias veces por semana, porque a Chiche le gustaban 15
mucho. Comprábamos también queso, porque a Chiche le gustaba mu- 16
chísimo el queso. Se bebía una botella de leche todos los días.   17

Nos agradaba mucho ver a Chiche durmiendo cerca de la chimenea o 18
sentado delante de la puerta pidiendo permiso para entrar.   19

Se dice que un gato tiene siete vidas. Estoy segura de que esto es verdad, 20
porque nuestro amado Chiche tuvo muchas más; tuvo un sinnúmero de 21
vidas. Cuando apenas tenía un año comenzó a salir mucho de la casa, y con 22
frecuencia se halló al borde de la tumba. Muchas veces Chiche corría 23
debajo de los automóviles que pasaban velozmente enfrente de nuestra 24
casa, y cada vez que esto sucedía, creía yo verlo muerto en la calle; pero 25
siempre salía al otro lado de los coches sin ningún daño.[18]   26

Commentary

All the words in this passage are in FDSW except *hamaca,* which is a
cognate whose meaning can be easily inferred; *mono* which is comprehensible from the context; *sardinas* which is an obvious cognate; and
queso which is commonly learned along with other foods in beginning
classes. *Sin, número,* and *velocidad* are in FDSW, so *sin/número* and
veloz/mente should not pose problems.

1. *Content questions,* that is, Who? What? When? Where? How
(manner)? and yes-no questions, are most appropriate at Stage Three.

R58   a. ¿Cuándo jugaban los niños con el gato días enteros?
Los niños jugaban con el gato días enteros cuando era pequeño.
b. ¿Dónde ponían el gato algunas veces?
Algunas veces lo ponían en una pequeña caja.
c. ¿Qué compraban varias veces por semana?
Compraban sardinas varias veces por semana.

Commentary

Questions of this type are too simple for Stages Four and Five. Answers
to the questions can be copied directly from the text with a little infusion
of words from the question itself. They do not necessarily require comprehension of the text; once the student has identified the place in the text

where the answer can be found he responds to structural clues—
¿cuándo? . . . cuando . . . cuando era pequeño; ¿dónde? en . . . en una pequeña caja; compraban . . . compraban sardinas . . .

2. *Implication questions,* that is, Why? If . . . then what? and How (explanation)? questions, should be asked at Stages Four and Five.

R59   a. ¿Por qué pensaba todo el mundo siempre en Chiche?
Todo el mundo pensaba siempre en Chiche porque toda la familia lo amaba (o: porque Chiche era precioso y la familia lo amaba).
   b. ¿Cómo sabían que un gato tiene siete vidas?
Sabían que un gato tiene siete vidas porque Chiche siempre se escapaba de los peligros sin ningún daño (o: porque Chiche corría debajo de los automóviles en la calle y siempre salía bien, o alternativamente: porque Chiche se halló al borde de la tumba, pero no murió).

Commentary

Question (a) requires the student to answer from line 2 a question based on line 9. Question (b) is based on lines 20–21 and requires an answer from a whole section of the text (lines 23–26). Some teachers insist that students copy out, or repeat, the relevant part of the question and thus always answer with a complete sentence. If the aim is to evaluate degree of reading comprehension, this is really busy work at this point and can become laborious for the student, with no particular gain in skill. The student who has not done so should not be penalized. Note that with questions of this type there will be a number of possible answers, depending on the way the student chooses to express the idea.

The problem arises: If one is evaluating reading comprehension, should one require skill in composition, written or oral, at the same time? If the student has demonstrated quite clearly that he has understood the passage by giving the right facts in answer to the questions, should he be penalized for writing or phrasing his answers in incorrect Spanish, since this has nothing to do with reading comprehension? At Stage Five one should expect students to be able to express themselves in simple correct Spanish. For some students at Stage Four, and certainly at Stage Three, it may be better to try other methods of eliciting information gained from reading. If the method outlined is used because students are seeking to attain a high level in all skills, a form of dual credit be adopted: allowing some credit for comprehension and some for the way the answer is formulated.

3. *Multiple-choice questions* are frequently used.

a. At Stage Three, *sentence completions* requiring only discrimination among several short alternative phrases may be used. The choices are usually set out in written form; if they are given orally, they also test listening comprehension and auditory memory.

R60 Choose a completion for each of the following sentences according to the information you have just read:

Cuando Chiche era pequeño dormía _____.

A. en una silla
B. en una hamaca
C. en una caja
D. junto a la chimenea

Commentary

The choices are designed so that the correct answer (C) is quite clear to the student who understood the text. (A), (B), and (D) pick up expressions in the text which may attract students who did not understand completely. (A) points to line 13: . . . *sentado en esa silla*. (B) could attract a student who interpreted literally the phrase . . . *tenía una hamaca perfecta*. (D) could attract a student who failed to perceive the fact that the action described in line 18 (. . . *durmiendo cerca de la chimenea* . . .) refers to a habit of Chiche's when he was older. Multiple-choice selections must always be designed so that they reflect some element in the text which may have been misunderstood, but the correct version should never reproduce word for word some sentence in the text. The choices should also be plausible completions—in this case (A), (B), (C), and (D) all describe the kinds of places a cat might choose to sleep. There must be no ambiguity in the choices which would cause an intelligent student to hesitate between possibilities. If students are warned in advance, there can occasionally be more than one correct choice in a set.

Variation: Sometimes single word completions are used.

R61 Chiche era un gato _____.

A. muerto
B. amado
C. viejo
D. agradecido

Commentary

With single word completions, once again, it is important that the correct completion does not parallel a sentence the student can identify in the text without understanding its meaning. Since the purpose of this exercise is to assess comprehension of the passage, it is important that the choices contain words whose meanings the students may be expected to know.

b. At Stages Four and Five, multiple choice sets will consist of *longer statements* which the student must be able to comprehend as well as the original text.

R62 La familia pensaba constantemente en Chiche porque _____.

A. tenía sed
B. Juana no le daba de comer
C. tenía miedo de la cuerda
D. todos lo amaban mucho

Commentary

Once again, each of the choices is plausible in the context. (A) draws attention to line 11 ("¡Chiche *tiene sed,* Mamá!"), (B) points to line 12 but puts a wrong interpretation on the sentence ("¿Por qué *no das de comer* a Chiche, Juana?"), (C) could attract a student who carelessly reads "por *medio* de una cuerda" as "por *miedo* de una cuerda," and (D) is correct.

Variation: In an expository text, one sentence important in the comprehension of the development of ideas may be chosen and students asked to select a correct paraphrase for the idea in the sentence from several alternatives.

DIGRESSION

In "How to Pass Multiple-Choice Tests when you Don't Know the Answers," Hoffman[19] sets out for ambitious but indolent students a few rules based on common faults of multiple-choice tests. Below are seven which are applicable to reading comprehension tests.

1. With five alternatives the correct answer tends to be the third, with four alternatives the second or third.

2. An alternative which is much longer or shorter than the others tends to be the correct answer.

3. With a sentence to complete: if the alternative when added to the stem does not make grammatical sequence, that alternative is not the correct item.

4. Look for clues in other questions.

5. If two alternatives are exactly the same except for one word, one of them is usually the correct answer.

6. "None of the above" is usually wrong.

7. Find out before the test if there is a penalty for guessing the wrong answer.

* Apply these rules to some tests you have constructed to see if a wily student could have "guessed" his way to an A.

4. *True-false-don't know checks.* True-false checks are useful as a quick assessment of reading comprehension, particularly for extensive-reading assignments. If students are given two points for a correct answer, lose a point for an incorrect answer, but do not lose a point for answering don't know, they will be less likely to make wild guesses and the score will more truly reflect their comprehension of the passage.

R63 Read the following statements and check whether each is T (True) or F (False) according to the information in the passage you have just read. If you are not sure circle D (Don't Know). (If the instructions are written in Spanish the terms *Verdad, Falso* [or *Mentira*], and *No Sé* will be used.)

1. T F D Algunas veces los hijos jugaban con Chiche en una hamaca.
2. T F D Chiche no comía más que sardinas.
3. T F D Chiche tenía la costumbre de correr debajo de los coches para atravesar la calle.
4. T F D Una vez la mamá vio a Chiche muerto en la calle.

Commentary

As with multiple-choice items, all statements must be plausible in the context and must be based on possible misunderstanding of specific phrases in the text. Care must be taken not to develop a pattern of correct responses, e.g., TFTFTF, or TFFTTFFTT. There is no need for an equal number of T's and F's: students are quick to discover that this is usually the case will adjust their answers accordingly. Correct statements should not be so phrased that they repeat exactly the words of the text. True-False questions provide a good opportunity to test the student's attention to structural clues, e.g., "Chiche *no* comía *más que* sardinas."

5. *Questions in Spanish requiring answers in English.* We have discussed the particular problem of reading comprehension questions requiring written or spoken answers in Spanish. Some teachers avoid this problem by asking questions in Spanish to which the students respond in English. This makes it impossible for a student to frame a response using words from the question or the text without knowing their meaning. It also requires comprehension of the questions which are in Spanish.

R64 ¿Por qué dice la mamá que Chiche tuvo muchas más de siete vidas?

Because from the time Chiche was a year old he went outside a lot and would often cross the street by running underneath the fast-moving cars that went by in front of the house. The mother always expected Chiche to be killed, but he never got hurt.

Commentary

Many students who have understood the text perfectly would have trouble saying all this in correct Spanish. This method enables the teacher to dig more deeply into the student's comprehension of what he has read. If this approach is used, questions should not move methodically through the text so that the student can pinpoint the particular sentences in which the answers can probably be found, but should require the student to think about and interpret the content of large sections of the text.

6. *Questions in English to be answered in English* are not advisable. The questions in English often solve problems of vocabulary and structure for some of the students, and the very sequence of the English questions sometimes supplies a kind of résumé of the meaning. *Questions in English to be answered in Spanish* would be pointless. Students capable of answering the questions in Spanish would also be capable of understanding the questions in Spanish, and once again the questions would supply the students with clues to the meaning of many sections of the text.

7. *Anticipatory Questions.* With a difficult text the student may be supplied with questions before he begins to read. These questions are designed to lead the reader to seek for certain information which will make the passage clearer to him. Anticipatory questions are more appropriate for expository and informational passages than for a narrative like R57. How-

ever, questions like the following would make the student look carefully at
the text.

R65   a. ¿Cómo manifestaba la familia su amor por Chiche?
       b. ¿Por qué tenía miedo la mamá de ver muerto a Chiche?

8. *Résumé with key words omitted.* After the student has read the text
and put it away, he may be supplied with a résumé in Spanish of the content, with certain words omitted. He then shows by the way he completes
the résumé how well he understood the text and how much attention he
paid to the vocabulary.

R66 La familia de este cuento tenía un _____ que se llamaba Chiche. A Chiche
le _____ mucho las sardinas y el _____. Chiche tuvo un sinnúmero de
_____, porque _____ debajo de los coches en la _____, pero siempre salía
al _____ lado _____ ningún _____.

9. *Assessing overall comprehension.* Depending on the content of the
passage students may be asked to do such things as:
a. supply in Spanish a suitable title for a film of the story and subtitles
for the main sections into which it could be divided;
b. make a chart of the relationships of the persons in the story;
c. sketch (or describe) a suitable stage setting for a dramatization of
the scene;
d. draw a map showing the various areas in which the action took place;
e. write a brief day-to-day diary of the hero's adventures;
f. outline the plot under the headings: presentation of characters, development, climax, dénouement (or unraveling of the complications).

10. *Assessing comprehension of expository reading.* (Exercises of the
types below would be suitable for R67.)
a. Give the passage a suitable title. (In this case no title would be
supplied with the text.)
b. For each paragraph, give the main gist in one sentence, then set down
the important details related to the central idea, showing clearly their
relationships in the development of this idea. (Exercises a. and b. would
be given and completed in English for Group A who are reading for information, but in Spanish for Groups C and D.)
c. Below are four sentences for each paragraph in the text. Select from
the four choices in each case the one which best sums up the central idea
of that paragraph. (Choices are given in Spanish.)
d. Rearrange the following statements to form a simplified but con-
secutive account of the development of ideas in the passage you have just

read. (The student is presented with a jumbled set of paraphrases of statements made in the text. The statements are in Spanish, but are so worded as not to be identifiable by simple matching with the text.)

e. For Group A: In which paragraphs are the following ideas discussed? (Paraphrased summaries of the ideas in the passage are given in Spanish, care being taken to see that they are so expressed that they cannot be matched from the text without being fully understood. To give practice in reading rapidly to extract the main ideas, the student is set a time limit within which to complete the exercise.)

* Below is a reading passage suitable for Stage Four or Stage Five. Develop some questions of the different types which have just been described and discuss in class their effectiveness.

R67 *Los Melenudos Envidian a la Mujer*[20]

Después de Freud hemos hablado mucho de la envidia que los hombres inspiran en la mujer. Pero la moneda tiene otra cara. Y según el psicoanalista mexicano Armando Barriguete, ya es hora de hablar de eso. (Y seguramente los partidarios del movimiento para la liberación de las mujeres estarán de acuerdo.) Dice el doctor Barriguete que hemos descubierto que un enorme sector del género masculino desearía pertenecer al sexo débil. Y nada hay de anormal en estos sujetos.

Las envidias, dice él, son restos de resentimientos infantiles. Desde temprana edad los niños descubren que los padres no les tratan igual que a sus hermanas. Miman a las niñas y las cuidan de los peligros a los que ellas están expuestas. Dicen a los muchachos: "Tú eres hombre; debes valerte por ti mismo."

Y esta envidia que el niño siente por sus hermanas se alimenta y fortalece con los años. Cada nueva experiencia acentúa el complejo. Cuando un muchacho va por la calle con su hermana, las atenciones y los piropos son para ella. También a él le gustaría ser elogiado. . . .

De tal manera, las melenas y los vestidos estrambóticos, según el doctor Barriguete, son una protesta, individual o social, consciente o subconsciente, contra formas de vida que los muchachos no aprueban y contra un sistema cada día más mecanizado que no aceptan.

Adaptación de un articulo de *Contenido*

Building and maintaining an adequate vocabulary (Stages Four and Five)

Moulton gives foreign-language students three practical recommendations for acquiring vocabulary: "First, never 'look a word up' until you have read the whole context in which it occurs—at least an entire sentence. . . . Second, don't be afraid of making 'intelligent guesses.' . . . Third, make a special list of your 'nuisance words'—the ones you find yourself looking up over and over again. Put them down on paper and memorize them."[21] These recommendations may well be passed on to students as an essential form of personal discipline. Going beyond this, however, the teacher may develop exercises to help the student "increase his word power" in Spanish through focusing on form, focusing on meaning, expanding by association, and recirculating the vocabulary he has acquired.

FOCUSING ON FORM

Often students are not given guidelines for multiplying the vocabulary they already know through recognition of related forms.

Many are not familiar with simple facts about the Spanish language such as those exemplified in R4 and R5.

They have never been taught to recognize the many *nouns formed from the masculine or feminine forms of the past participles of verbs.*

R68
comer	la comida
lavar	el lavado
hacer	el hecho
decir	el dicho
llegar	la llegada
salir	la salida
pasar	el pasado
ver	la vista
venir	la venida

They do not know how to discover the meaning of *words prefixed by common prepositions or adverbs* with which they are familiar:

R69
contra	contradecir
por	el pordiosero
sobre	sobrecargado
bien	el bienestar
	bienvenido
mal	un malhechor

Recognition of common *changes due to phonetic environment* will help them to see *in-/im-/il-/ir-* as the same negative prefix, and *co-/con-/com-* as variations of the familiar English co-worker, compatriot.

R70 incapaz, inolvidable
      imposible, imparcial
      ilegítimo, ilegal
      irrazonable, irregular
      colaborador, cohabitar
      compatriota, compañero

* Think of words which can be deciphered through recognition of *re-* as meaning "again" or "back" and *de-/des-* as indicating the opposite meaning to that of the radical (or the lack of something).

Common *suffixes* also give clues to the meaning of seemingly "new" words.

R71 *-i(s) quear* diminishes the action of well-known verbs:

      morder (to bite): mordisquear (to nibble)
      llorar (to weep): lloriquear (to whine)

Teachers who are not familiar themselves with these formal indications of meaning variation will find much of interest in Chapter 32: "Word Making," in M. M. Ramsey, *A Textbook of Modern Spanish*, rev. by R. K. Spaulding (New York: Holt, Rinehart and Winston, 1956).

Exercises

1. Students may be asked to give nouns corresponding to adjectives (*blanco, el blancor*), adjectives corresponding to nouns (*pobreza, pobre*), verbs corresponding to nouns (*comienzo, comenzar*), adverbs corresponding to adjectives (*alegre, alegremente*), verbs corresponding to adjectives (*alegre, alegrar*), and so on.

2. Students may be asked to change the meaning of sentences by the addition of a prefix to a word underlined (ese día me sentía *contento;* ese día me sentía *descontento*) or to complete sentences with a word with a different suffix (No va a *llover* mucho. Sólo va a *lloviznar.*).

FOCUSING ON MEANING

Valuable practice in vocabulary building is provided when students are asked to do exercises like the following:

1. To supply paraphrases of definitions for words in the text they have just read (él viaja: él hace un viaje);

2. To identify from multiple-choice items the correct paraphrases or definitions for certain words in the text (in R57: *mono* = [A] *cómico,* [B] *pequeño,* [C] *precioso,* [D] *serio*).

3. To find words in the text to match paraphrases or definitions supplied (in R57: Find the words in the text which mean [A] *durante todo el día,* [B] *con rapidez*).

4. To complete sentences, based on the text, with certain words on which they will need to focus their attention. These sentences should not reproduce the original text exactly and should usually require the student to reuse the vocabulary in a different form, e.g., in a different person, number, or tense.

R72 Complete the following sentences with words from the text you have just read (R57).

    a. Los padres y los hijos pensaban constantemente en Chiche porque lo _____ mucho.

    b. La hamaca de Chiche era, en realidad, una _____.

    c. A Chiche le gustaba _____ leche todos los días.

5. *Exercises may be unrelated to a known text,* e.g., students discover for themselves, through dictionary search, synonyms and antonyms (*amable, simpático, bueno, malo*). They may compete to see who can find the largest number of synonyms and antonyms in a given period of time. Learning to enjoy a purposeful search for information in dictionaries and grammars is an important preparation for autonomous progress. (See also W68-75.)

6. Students complete an unfamiliar text in a plausible way by supplying for each blank a word carefully selected from multiple-choice alternatives. This type of exercise can be developed with simple texts or more complex texts, functioning as an amusing and challenging exercise right through to the advanced level.

R73 Anteriormente, las (flores, aguas, calles) del (lago, centro, jardín) tenían un (aspecto, olor, color) desagradable por estar contaminadas por la suciedad de los (pantanos, turistas, coches) que (circulaban, caminaban, desembocaban) en ellas.

Commentary

A passage such as this teaches the student to pay attention to distinctions of meaning, but it is also an exercise in reading comprehension. The student should write out his completed version as a coherent paragraph, rather than merely circling choices. In this way he can read his version through to see that it makes sense and then read it aloud to his fellow students. With a little ingenuity, passages can be designed to have several final versions, and students can be encouraged to reconstitute the several possibilities. Advanced students may like to prepare such passages for the other students to complete. (A teacher or student who does not feel confident in constructing a passage in Spanish himself can easily adapt paragraphs from books or magazines.)

* Find in various composition and reading texts other types of exercises which focus on meaning distinctions and discuss their effectiveness.

EXPANDING BY ASSOCIATION

We tend to recall words through meaningful associational bonds, and words tend to appear in texts in collocations, that is, in relation to centers of interest or semantic areas (*pan* is likely to appear in a text in which *panadero* appears; *llantas, frenos,* and *coche* are very likely to occur together). It is for this reason that learning vocabulary in context is much more valuable than learning isolated words.

Exercises

Many possibilities suggest themselves, and each teacher can think of his own once he understands the necessity for developing chains of associations and for expanding nuclei. Many of these exercises can take the form of games or team competitions which can be directed by the students themselves. Three come immediately to mind.

R74 What action do you associate with the following objects? Follow the pattern:

¿El pan? Se lo puede comer.

In each case give as many alternatives as you can find. The team gains points for every alternative its team members can discover.

¿Las flores?   Se las puede mirar.
Se las puede coger.
Se las puede plantar.

¿El libro?   Se lo puede leer.
Se lo puede abrir.
Se lo puede cerrar. . . .

R75 As each object is named, give the Spanish word for a person you associate with it. You must answer in three seconds.

¿papel?   estudiante
¿tiza?   profesor
¿avión?   piloto
¿correo?   cartero

Alternatively: As each person, animal, or object is named, give the Spanish word for a place you associate with it. You must answer in three seconds.

¿panadero?   panadería
¿chocolates?   dulcería
¿caballo?   establo/corral

R76 Intelligence-test series can be adapted as follows. This exercise can be used from elementary to advanced levels and, again, students may be encouraged to make up further exercises themselves.

In the following lists underline the word which does not seem to belong with the others in the series;

azul, rojo, frío, verde
árbol, flor, piedra, hierba
calor, frío, fresco, honor (This item can be answered in two ways: by form or by semantic area.)

RECIRCULATING VOCABULARY ACQUIRED

Students learn new words with every passage they read. Often they forget them rapidly because they do not encounter them again for a long while. All kinds of games and exercises can be introduced to enliven the class while giving students the opportunity to retrieve words they have learned in the past and recirculate them through their conscious minds. In this way the ease with which these words can be retrieved, when required, is increased. The following suggestions will bring to mind other possibilities. They are arranged in approximate order of difficulty.

R77 From the parallel lists of words given select pairs which have a natural association:

mar   pan
panadero   tinta
pluma   ola . . .

Students working in teams may make their own parallel lists to try out on members of the other teams.

R78 Begin with the words *un árbol* (or . . .) and write down rapidly any ten Spanish words which come to your mind. Write whichever word you think of. Do not try to develop a logical series. (With each word, include some form of the definite or indefinite article.)

The lists, when completed, may be read aloud for amusement. Series may come out like the following:

un árbol, una flor, el perfume, la mujer, un vestido, un traje, una tienda, la calle, el policía, la cárcel.

un árbol, un pájaro, un nido, un huevo, el desayuno, la mañana, el colegio, la sala de clase, un libro, la biblioteca.

R79 *Semantic areas.* Write down as many words as you can think of which have a natural association with *el árbol* (or . . .). Points will be given to the team having the largest number of different words. (Include some form of the definite or indefinite article with each word.)

el árbol, la cáscara, la hierba, el jardín, las flores, las ramas, las hojas . . .

Or: Write down all the words you know which have a similar meaning to *la casa.* (Include some form of the definite or indefinite article with each.)

la casa, el palacio, el castillo, el apartamento . . .

R80 Make as many words as you can from the letters in "es un árbol." No letter may be used more times than it appears in the sentence. Accents may be added or deleted, as necessary.

es, un, árbol, se, su, sol, lo, los, la, las, no, son, rosa, una, unas, beso, luna . . .

R81 Write down all the idiomatic expressions you can think of which contain the word *vez* (or . . .) and make up a sentence to show the use of each:

a la vez   en vez de
otra vez   de vez en cuando
tal vez . . . .

R82 List any five words on the chalkboard and ask students to make up a brief story incorporating all five, e.g.:

beca, río, iglesia, brazo, carpintero

R83 *Crucigramas.* Simple crossword puzzles may be constructed by the students as exercises, then tried out on their fellow students. These provide practice in recalling words from their definitions or by association. Students may use definitions they find in monolingual dictionaries, thus giving them a purposeful familiarity with such dictionaries. One source of Spanish crosswords in published form is *Crucigramas para Estudiantes* by Jane Burnett (Skokie, Ill.: National Textbook Co., 1973).

Scrabble sets geared to the letter frequencies of particular languages are also available.

Vocabulary enrichment and retrieval should be woven into the lesson fabric or the learning packet as an important and purposeful activity, not dredged up to fill in time on the day when the teacher and the class are sufffering from end-of-the-week fatigue. By encouraging the students to play with words, the teacher can help to increase their interest in words in relation to concepts and in association with other words, and to refine their appreciation for nuances of meaning.

* Think of further ideas for vocabulary expansion and retrieval and develop these into possible classroom or individual activities.

Integrating the language skills at Stages Three to Five
READING AND WRITING

Students may be asked a series of questions which, when answered in sequence, develop a summary or résumé of the material read. They may write an ending to a story or play of which they have read part or develop a different ending from the one in the book. They may write letters which one character in the story might have written to others. Completed compositions may be passed around, with the writer's consent, to be read by other students. Students may create their own stories on similar themes to those they have been reading. They may write *sainetes* based on some parts of the narrative which will be acted in class or at the Spanish club. Comprehension of extensive reading undertaken on an individualized basis will often be demonstrated in activities of this kind.

After reading a play, students may write the story as it might appear in a theater program, adding short descriptions of the characters. Should opportunity arise to act parts of the play before other classes, the best synopsis will be printed in a program for distribution.

Further suggestions for integrating reading and writing will be found in Chapter 9.

READING AND LISTENING COMPREHENSION

Students may listen to a story, play, poem, or speech by a famous person and then read it, or they may read first and then listen to a worthwhile reading or dramatic presentation of what they have read. The aural element adds vividness and life to the reading unit. Students may take turns listening to tapes of news broadcasts from a Spanish-speaking source (Spain, Mexico, Central and South America, and certain areas of the United States) and then write summaries of the news which will be posted for other students to read, thus integrating listening, writing, and reading in a purposeful activity. Before listening to a Spanish play, students may read a synopsis of the action. In this way they are better prepared to comprehend because they have some expectations to help them project meaning.

In some ways the processes of fluent, direct reading for meaning appear to parallel the processes of listening comprehension. We recognize in a quick, impressionistic way, meaningful syntactic units, interrelating those we have selected and are holding in our memory with what follows, then rapidly revising expectations when these are not supported by the later segments we identify. Practice in direct reading of a text which is readily accessible to the student at his level of knowledge, while listening to a tape model reading it in meaningful and expressive segments, can help the student develop useful habits of anticipation and syntactic identification in both of these skills. Later he can practice rapid reading of a text to which he has already listened without a script.[22] (For further suggestions, see Chapter 3.)

READING AND SPEAKING

Students should be provided with frequent opportunities to give in Spanish the gist of what they have been reading. They may be encouraged to prepare their own questions to ask of others in the class. When small groups are engaged in similar extensive reading projects they should discuss together what they have discovered. Students reading individually may share what they have been reading with others. Some of the material read will serve as a basis for oral presentations of projects; some will be dramatized in the original form or through extempore role-playing; and some will provide ammunition for discussions and debates. Many other ideas can be gleaned from Chapter 2.

READING AND PURPOSEFUL ACTIVITY

At all levels students should be encouraged to do research reading in an area which interests them in order to find the information necessary to

carry out some activity. A few indications are outlined below, but at Stages
Three through Five students should be expected to propose their own.

1. Students read advertisements for a particular type of product in
magazines in order to prepare a commercial for a class television or radio
show.

2. Students find out information about a popular Spanish singer in order
to introduce a session of records of his songs.

3. Students read a play carefully in order to design a stage setting for a
class performance or play-reading.

4. Students seek out information on events, people, costumes, or social
customs at a particular period in Spanish history in order to produce a
pageant for some historical anniversary.

5. Students study tourist brochures, guide books, geography, history,
and art books in order to give an illustrated lecture or slide commentary on
some part of Spain or the Spanish-speaking world.

6. Students read through Spanish cookbooks in order to prepare some
Spanish dishes for a Spanish club festivity.

7. Students undertake tasks set out by the teacher or another student in
the form of detailed instructions which lead to the collecting or making of
something which can later be brought back as proof of the completion of
the task.

At Stage Three, the well-known Scavenger Hunt game (*En Busca del
Tesoro*) can be adapted to the Spanish class. Students work in pairs to
find and bring to the class next day a series of strange objects which are
described in Spanish on instruction cards. They win points for their team
for each object they find.

R84 One list might be: un abrelatas, dos huevos pasados por agua, un sello
español, una moneda mexicana, un anuncio de boda, un pelo rojo, una
pistolera de cuero negro, medio boleto de cine, un cordón de zapato, diez
presillas encadenadas.

While students are looking for these things they read and reread the
list so that the words become impressed on their minds. Then, when showing the objects in class, they must state what each one is and how they
came to acquire it.

Improving reading speed

The reading speed of different students varies considerably in their native
language. The teacher must, therefore, expect considerable variation in the
reading of the foreign language. To become fluent readers, however, the
students must acquire the skill of reading whole word groups and whole

sentences in Spanish and of holding material in their memory over larger and larger sections as they move on with the developing thought.

1. At Stages Two and Three an overhead projector can be used to encourage continuity of reading. The text is moved slowly upward on the roll, so that the slower reader is encouraged to keep his eyes moving forward while the faster reader is not impeded, as would be the case if only one line were shown at a time. This is the process frequently used in films or on television where there is a long introduction to, or explanation of, the story. This procedure will be associated with silent reading for information, rather than reading aloud, since the aim is to help each student to improve his own reading rate.

2. At Stages Three and Four, students may be timed in reading a certain number of pages to a pre-established comprehension criterion level. Mere pace without adequate comprehension is pointless. Since this is an individual endeavor, students should be encouraged to improve their own rate rather than compete with others in number of pages read.

3. As an encouragement to practice *scanning,* which is a very useful reading skill, students may be given questions to which they are to find as many answers as possible in a given time.

4. Students will increase their reading speed in a natural way if they have set themselves the clearly defined goal of reading in a stated period of time a certain amount of material selected by themselves because of the interest of the subject matter.

8
Writing and written exercises I: the nuts and bolts

What is writing?

The Soviet psychologist Vygotsky draws our attention to the fact that all the higher functions of human consciousness, that is, those which involve more than mere physical skill, are characterized by *awareness, abstraction,* and control.[1] For example, learning to pronounce the allophones of /d/ by a process of successive approximations in imitation of a model may be relatively easy. Learning to say /d/ in response to various graphic combinations in a script and in a variety of graphic contexts is already more complicated. It demands the recognition of abstract representations and their conversion from a visual to a phonic form, before the skill acquired in the simpler act can come into operation in the new situation. In short, it requires awareness of the relevance of the graphic symbol, recognition of what it stands for in the phonic medium, as well as control of the production of the sound. It also requires awareness of what other graphic symbols stand for, since the phonetic realization of the phoneme represented by the letter *d* will be [d] if that letter comes after a pause (e.g., *¿Dudas?*) or after /l/ (e.g., *soldado*) or after a nasal consonant (e.g., *sendero*), but it will be [đ] in other environments. Abstract processes such as those described above are in operation when one writes the letter *d* in response to the sounds [d] or [đ].

That a graphic representation of sound combinations is an abstraction with an arbitrary relationship to that which it represents is frequently overlooked. Convention alone makes the relationship between sound and written

236

symbol predictable. The abstract quality of a written communication is intensified by:

1. its *complete detachment from expressive features,* such as facial or body movement, pitch and tone of voice, hesitations or speed of delivery, and emotional indicators such as heightened facial color or variation in breathing;

2. its *lack of material context:* surroundings, feedback from interlocutors, relevant movement (hence the attraction of the comic book for modern readers);

3. its *displacement in time:* a written communication may be read as soon as it is written (like a note slipped to a companion) or months, years, or centuries later. It is interesting that we often do not understand a note we ourselves wrote when we find it years later.

The operation of writing, unlike speaking, must be performed as it were in a void, in response to a personal internal stimulus. Consequently, the writer must compensate for the absence of external contextual elements by the deliberate inclusion and elaboration of explanatory details which the speaker would omit.

For reasons such as these, Vygotsky suggests that the comparative difficulty for the child in acquiring facility in speech and in writing approximates that of learning arithmetic and algebra. All children learn to speak and express themselves effectively in speech at about the same age, even though some by personality and temperament may be more articulate than others. On the other hand, many people never learn to express themselves freely in writing. Even with careful instruction, there is a considerable lag between the achievement of an expressive level in speech in one's native language and a similar level of expressiveness in writing—a gap which, for many, widens as their education or life experience progresses. Certainly, many learn quite quickly to "write things down," if these are not too complicated, but this is the least demanding aspect of writing. Many who know how to "write things down" in their native language avoid expressing themselves in writing almost completely, even in personal letters. To write so that one is really communicating a message, isolated in place and time, is an art which requires consciously directed effort and deliberate choice in language. The old saying, "If you can say it, you can write it," is simplistic in its concept of the communicative aspect of writing. On the other hand, "He talks like a book" emphasizes the elaborations and comprehension explanations of written messages which are quite unnecessary in face-to-face communication.

WRITING AND OTHER LANGUAGE ACTIVITIES

We must not be surprised, then, that a high level of written expression is so difficult to attain in a foreign language. It cannot be achieved by chance, as a kind of by-product of other language activities, although it draws on what has been learned in these areas. Good writing implies a knowledge of the conventions of the written code (the "good manners" of the medium); to be effective, it needs the precision and nuances which derive from a thorough understanding of the syntactic and lexical choices the language offers; to be interesting, it requires the ability to vary structures and patterns for rhetorical effect. So good writing will not develop merely from practice exercises in grammar and vocabulary choice. Experience in speaking freely seems to facilitate early writing, which often parallels what one would say. For the development of a writing style, however, much acquaintance with the practical output of native writers in all kinds of expressive styles is essential. Familiarity with the great variety of expression to which the language lends itself gives the neophyte writer an intuitive feel for an authentic turn of phrase which he can acquire in no other way.

Included in this chapter are activities which associate writing with experiences in listening, speaking, and reading. (Further suggestions are to be found in Chapters 3 and 7.)

WHAT ARE WE TEACHING WHEN WE TEACH "WRITING"?

As with oral communication, we can classify writing activities as either skill-getting or skill-using (see model C1), with the same need for bridging activities which resemble the desired communicative activity to facilitate transfer from one to the other. *Interaction through the written message* is the goal: what is written should be a purposeful communication, on the practical or imaginative level, expressed in such a way that it is comprehensible to another person. Otherwise, we are dealing with hermetic or esoteric writing of purely personal value which can be set down in any idiosyncratic code.

Skill-getting, for oral or written communication, is based on knowledge of the way the language operates (*cognition*). Many grammatical rules are the same for speech and writing, e.g., the agreement of subject and verb in certain conventional ways: *nosotros hablamos* /nosotrosablámos/; the position and form of the relative pronoun: *quien* or *quienes* for the subject of a relative clause, in close proximity to the expression for which they are acting as a substitute, with the choice between the two forms depending on whether the referent is singular or plural (e.g., *Mi padre, quien vive en Madrid* . . . vs. *Mis padres, quienes viven en Madrid* . . .). Other rules vary according to the degree of formality of the spoken or written communication (e.g., formal writing or speech: "Tenga Ud. la bondad de llamarme a las siete, por favor," informal speech: "Llámame a las siete, ¿quieres?")[2] Note that a personal letter may retain many of the features of an informal chat, whereas a scholarly lecture given on a formal occasion adheres in the main to the same rules as a written paper or scientific report. In an orally oriented course, early writing will consist of the writing down of what one would say, moving further away from oral forms as knowledge of the rules of written language advances.

Learning the rules and conventions of written language is reinforced by writing out examples and applying the rules in new contexts, thus developing *awareness of the abstraction and control of its graphic manifestation.* For written language, this activity parallels the oral-practice exercises which help students develop flexibility in structuring their oral expression. Writing things out helps with the organization of material to be held in memory and clarifies rules at points of uncertainty. It gives concrete expression to abstract notions. All of this is, however, merely preliminary activity which is pointless unless it is serving some clearly understood purpose of meaningful communication.

Considerable disappointment and frustration will be avoided if the nature and purpose of any particular writing task are clearly understood by student and teacher alike. In this chapter and the next, we will discuss writing under four headings. These do not represent sequential stages but, rather, constantly interwoven activities. They are:

I. *Writing down:* learning the conventions of the code.

II. *Writing in the language:* learning the potential of the code (we shall include here grammatical exercises and the study of samples of written language to develop awareness of its characteristics).

III. *Production:* practicing the construction of fluent expressive sentences and paragraphs.

IV. *Expressive writing or composition:* using the code for purposeful communication.

Finally, *translation* will be discussed at some length as a separate activity.

I. Writing down

Activities of this type, although apparently simple, contribute to awareness. The student either copies or reproduces without the copy in front of him. To do this accurately, he must focus his attention on the conventions of writing: spelling, capitalization, punctuation (¿ ?, ¡ !), digraphs (*ch, ll*), special letters (*ñ*), diacritical marks (such as the accent ´ and diaeresis ¨), number conventions (W6), abbreviations (*pág., v.g.*), indicators of direct discourse and quotation (*la raya, las comillas*), and so on.

This activity prepares for eventual expressive writing. It is, however, useful in itself. Language users need to be able to interpret and copy down printed schedules, timetables, records, details of projects, charts, formulas, prices, recipes, new words and phrases they wish to remember. They should be capable of writing down accurately and comprehensibly oral arrangements and instructions for themselves and others. As students studying in the language they may need to copy accurately diagrams, details of experiments, and quotations from literary works.

COPYING

1. (E) Students are given dittoed sheets with simple *outline illustrations,* or stick figures, suggesting the lines of a dialogue or parts of a narrative they have been studying. They transcribe from the text sentences which are appropriate to each sketch.

2. (E) Each student copies a line of dialogue and passes it to his neighbor who copies out an appropriate response. This operates like a *chain* dialogue (C25), with students selecting utterances and appropriate responses from any material they have studied.

3. (E) Students copy the initial part of an utterance and pass it on to their neighbors for a *completion,* or students choose and copy completions for parts of utterances supplied on a dittoed sheet, trying to make as many different sentences as they can with each opening phrase.

4. (E) Students make new sentences by copying segments from *substitution tables.* This activity familiarizes the students with the logical segmentation of sentences into subject, verb, object, and adverbial extensions.

W1 (E) Make six different sentences by selecting one segment from each column in the following table:

Juanita	vio	a Pablo	delante del monumento
El sereno	buscó	al niño	en la oficina
La florista	encontró	a la pareja	detrás de la escuela
El profesor	abrazó	al ladrón	cerca del teatro

Note: If pronoun subjects of different persons and numbers are used, it is advisable to keep subject and verb in the one column to accustom elementary-level students to the correct combination of pronoun subject and verb ending:

W2 (E)

Nosotros buscamos	a la madre de Juan	en la iglesia
Ellos encontraron	a los urbanos	delante de la escuela
Vosotros visteis	al cura	en la plazuela

Developing sentences from a substitution table becomes a more thoughtful process when only some subject items can be appropriately used with some of the verb items, some of the objects, and so on. This can be done by means of a combination table such as the one below:[3]

W3 (E)

Un	avión	pasó		el niño		vio
	gato	entró		Juanita		sintió
	autobús		pero	ellas	no lo	notaron
	pájaro	ladró		tú		visteis
	perro	cantó		vosotros		escuchaste
						vieron

New tables of this type can be developed as a writing exercise by groups of students for use by other students, thus moving into the second activity: writing in the language.

5. (E) Students copy from the chalkboard a simple poem they have been learning orally. Lorca's *Canción de Jinete* is a useful copying exercise with its short, concise sentences. Machado's delicate metaphor about the reality of life, *Parábola I* is also a good copying exercise because of its segments of interpolated speech. Its use of the *pretérito anterior* in the lines

> *Apenas lo hubo cogido*
> *el niño se despertó*

can be explained as a feature of the literary language and should not worry the students unduly, since poetry is often unusual in any language. Its presence alerts them early to the fact that formal written language in Spanish has distinctive characteristics.

* Find for your personal file some suitable short poems for elementary classes. Share these with other members of the class and discuss their appropriateness.

REPRODUCTION

Copying activities 1, 2, and 3 above may also be reproduction exercises, with students writing the utterances, or completing them, from memory.

6. (E) *Scrambled sentences* are sometimes used as a stimulus to the reproduction of a dialogue or narrative. This technique forces students to think of the meaning of what they are reproducing. Credit should be given for ingenuity in working out novel but possible recombinations.

7. (E) Students write down from *dictation* utterances they have learned or recombinations of familiar segments, or they may concentrate on the spelling of more difficult words in *spot dictation* (see R26).

(E and I) The spot dictation may focus on subjects and verb (tense endings, irregularities, past participle agreements), or on noun and adjective agreements.

8. (I and A) *Dictation of unfamiliar material* as an exercise in auditory recognition and accurate reproduction has been a standard classroom technique for centuries. The passage to be dictated should normally have some thematic relationship to something already read or discussed. It can often provide supplementary material worth keeping on some subject of cultural interest. The standard procedure is described below. There are also several possible variations which are useful language-learning aids.

a. *Standard procedure.* The material is read in its entirety at a normal, but unhurried, pace. It is then dictated in meaningful, undistorted segments, each segment being read twice. After students have looked over what they have written, corrected obvious mistakes, and tentatively filled in gaps according to semantic or grammatical expectations, the passage is read again at a normal pace to enable students to check on doubtful segments. After opportunity for a final check, students correct their own versions from a model. If one student has written his dictation at one side of the chalkboard or for projection on the overhead projector, the correction process is facilitated: students suggest corrections and the teacher is able to comment on errors probably committed by other students as well or answer questions about problem segments. Each dictation should be regarded as an opportunity for learning, not as a test. For this reason, immediate correction is desirable, before students have forgotten which segments they found difficult and why they solved the problems as they did. Since it is difficult for students to detect all the errors in their work, they should exchange papers for a final check by a classmate.

b. *Variations.*

i. (E) *Students are encouraged to repeat the segment* to themselves before writing it. This forces them to make identification decisions before they begin writing and strengthens their memory of what they have heard.

ii. (E and I) If interpreting the aural signal and writing the message down accurately is a valuable exercise, there is no reason why students should be limited to an arbitrary number of repetitions of the segments. The dictation may be taped and *students encouraged to keep playing the passage over* until they have been able to take down the complete message.

iii. (E and I) Students are asked to *hold longer and longer segments in their immediate memory* before beginning to write. In this way they are not working with echoic memory, but are forced to process the segments, that is, interpret them and situate them syntactically in the structure of the sentence, before reproducing them. Dictation then becomes more challenging and more meaningful.

iv. (I) *The speed of the dictation is gradually increased* as students become more adept at making the various morphological adjustments, particularly those which are not apparent in the spoken signal.

v. (I and A) *The repetition of segments is eliminated* and students are expected to listen carefully, retain the segment they have heard only once, and write it down without expecting further help. This forces students to concentrate on the message and the semantic and syntactic expectations it arouses.

vi. (A) Finally, students should be able to *take down a dictated letter or report,* with their own set of abbreviations, and write it out, or type it up correctly, as they might be expected to do in a business situation. This activity can be practiced individually with tapes.

FOCUSING ON SPELLING AND ACCENTS

1. (E and I) This goes beyond the initial stages. The teacher can focus the students' attention on spelling conventions by asking them to work out for themselves, from reading passages or dialogues they have studied, *probable rules of spelling* like the following:

W 4 /k/ is spelled *c* before *a, o, u: casa, comer, cuidado.*

It may also be spelled *qu* as in *querer, quiso.*

/s/ is spelled *s* before *a, e, i, o, u: saber, sed, si, sobre, supe.*

If the dialect being learned does not have the phoneme /θ/, then /s/ can also be represented by *c* before *e, i* (*empiece, ciudad*) as well as by *z* (*caza, zeta, zigzag, zoclo, zumo*).

This is a suitable small group activity. It can be undertaken whenever particular spelling problems emerge in dictation or writing practice.

2. (E and I) Students are frequently bothered unnecessarily by indecision about whether to use the acute accent in writing familiar words. Such uncertainty is sometimes reinforced by the fact that—the Spanish Academy's rules notwithstanding—one often finds discrepancies in different publications as regards the use of the accent. For example, one can find *fuí, vió, dió, fué,* as easily as *fui, vio, dio, fue.* To relieve this uncertainty they may be given a research project to find out from printed texts regularities in the positional occurrence of the accent. Through personal observation they will easily discover facts like the following:

W 5 1. Certain words are written with an accent when used with an interrogative function, but not if used as relative pronouns or adverbs:

    a. *¿Dónde está él?*
    b. *El parque donde se halla el monumento es muy hermoso.*

2. Demonstrative pronouns (*éste, ése, aquél*) are often written with an accent, even though the Spanish Academy's norms prescribe such prac-

tice only in order to avoid ambiguity. Students should follow the Academy's ruling, but they should not be surprised to find that writers vary in their practice in this regard.

3. Words stressed on the third-from-the-last syllable take the written accent: *cómodo, idéntico,* etc.

4. The diaeresis is used to indicate that *u* is pronounced in the groups *güe* and *güi,* as in *bilingüe, lingüística.* Such groups contrast with *gue* and *gui,* in which the *u* is not pronounced, as in *guerra* and *guitarra.*

When students have discovered that the positions in which the accent occurs follow regular patterns, they find the rules easier to remember. (I and A) This project may be continued to discover pronunciation rules reflected by accents.

Note: Correct use of accentuation rules should not be so emphasized that it becomes an important element in the grading or evaluation of writing. Many educated speakers of Spanish are often inconsistent, not to say careless, in their use of accentuation marks. Particularly at the elementary levels, the teacher should only insist upon the use of written accents where they are essential to avoid serious ambiguity (e.g., *llego* vs. *llegó, hable* vs. *hablé,* etc.). Emphasis should be placed where it belongs: on fluent, idiomatic writing comprehensible to a native speaker, not on incidental graphic features.

LEARNING NUMBER CONVENTIONS

Misunderstandings can result from the use of English numerical conventions in Spanish writing.

W6 (E) Students should be familiar with such differences as the indicators for decimals and for thousands, e.g., English 21.5 = Spanish 21,5; English 3,365,820 = Spanish 3.365.820; abbreviations like 3,65 m. and 11.000 Km.; N° 2 or núm. 2; 1.° or 1.ª; Cía; 4 CV and ways of writing times (15 h.45m.) and dates (31.12.75). It is also useful for students to learn the handwritten forms for numbers, particularly 1 and 7.

These special features can be practiced in projects such as *describing a trip from Barcelona to Seville,* in which the student studies timetables, route maps, and area maps, and gives full details of times of departure and arrival, distances traveled, and heights of surrounding mountains. Prices of rooms and meals can be found in travel guides or information sheets obtained by writing to the *Spanish National Tourist Office,* which has branches in many countries, or to the *Ministerio de Información y Turismo, Dirección General de Promoción del Turismo,* in Madrid.

PROOFREADING

It is a commonly held opinion that students should not be shown incorrect Spanish because they will learn the errors in the text and these misapprehensions will be difficult to eradicate. This assumption does not seem to have been scientifically tested. It is clear that young teachers improve in their control of the syntax and spelling of the language as they teach it, yet they see a great deal of incorrect Spanish in the process. The difference, in the latter case, is that these young teachers are looking for errors and check facts in grammars or dictionaries whenever they are uncertain about correctness of usage or form in the exercises they are grading. This attitude of alertness to erroneous forms, and pleasure in finding the facts when in doubt, needs to be developed in students so that they will take an interest in proofreading their own work before submitting it for checking or grading by the teacher. It can be cultivated by an occasional problem-solving competition along the following lines.

W7 (E and I) *Preparemos el texto final*

1. The teacher takes a text of a level comprehensible to the students and types it out, double- or triple-spaced, with a certain number of spelling errors (*faltas de ortografía*) of the type the students themselves tend to make (e.g., *peresoso, apartmento*), a few typing slips (*faltas de mecanografía*) which do not change pronunciation (e.g., *aier* or *ombre*), and some other typing slips which constitute morphological or syntactic inaccuracies in written language (e.g., *los libros verde, la primer ocasión*).

2. The students work in pairs or small groups to prepare a perfect text for the final typing. Each group has a different text, a pencil of a distinctive color, and a group symbol which they put beside each correction they make. Students may check in dictionaries, grammars, or their textbooks.

3. Points will be awarded for every correction made and deducted not only for errors not detected but also for miscorrections.

4. After a time, corrected texts are passed on to the next group for rechecking. Groups gain further points for discovering miscorrections and undetected errors in the texts from other groups, but they lose points for wrongly challenging another group's corrections. (In this second round, it is essential that groups remember to put their group symbol beside their corrections and recorrections.)

5. Final results in points for each group will usually have to be de-

ferred till the next day, to allow the teacher time to sort out the different corrections and challenges. The perfected texts, with corrections still visible, are then retyped on dittoes by those students who are learning business skills. The final text is then used for some class or individualized activity.

6. When the next composition is due, students are given some class time to proofread each other's work and write suggested improvements in colored pencil.

＊ The regular *relationships between many noun endings and the gender* of the noun are frequently not made clear to students, yet they can provide a considerable shortcut to the mastery of this troublesome feature. It is also reassuring to students to know that the gender of a new noun is not completely unpredictable.

Make notes for your teaching file on these regularities, with lists of words of high frequency in each of the categories and the common exceptions.[4] Work out an interesting activity students could undertake to discover many of these regularities for themselves (e.g., *-eza* f. abstract qualities: *belleza, tristeza, rudeza; -or* m. agents: *comprar—comprador, matar—matador, admirar—admirador; -ción* f. abstract nouns: *admiración, civilización, degeneración, reacción*). Whenever possible, the teacher will point out structural correspondences between Spanish and English (e.g., Span. *-ción, -dad*, Eng. *-tion, -ty*).

II. *Writing in the language*

Writing down words from a Spanish dictionary inserted into native-language patterns in native-language syntax is not "writing in the language."

W 8 ＊ El día de mi cumpleaños fui dado un regalo muy bonito por mi papá.
＊ Mi padre me quiere ir a la universidad.

Commentary

This extract from a student's composition about her experience during Freshman Orientation Week at college is clearly Spanglish (English structure dressed in Spanish lexicon—a form of fractured Spanish which may, or may not, be comprehensible to a speaker of Spanish, depending on his patience and imagination, or his knowledge of English. Our students will want to go beyond this stage. Unless they can eventually write so that their meaning is immediately comprehensible to a Spanish-speaking person, they are wasting a great deal of precious time on this demanding activity.

To acquire an adequate foundation for autonomous writing the student studies the potential for diversity of meaning of the Spanish syntactic system. He seeks to understand how it works (*cognition* in model C1) and essays the expression of a variety of meanings in written exercises (thus learning *production* through the *construction* of fluent, idiomatic sentences). This controlled micro-practice, like limbering-up exercises, is useful for developing the linguistic flexibility needed to communicate specific meanings.

PRESENTING THE GRAMMAR: COGNITION AND ABSTRACTION

Students must not only understand the grammatical concepts they encounter, but also appreciate how each, like a link in a coat of chain mail, interrelates with all the others in one fabric—the Spanish language system. They may practice a concept in isolation, e.g., the subjunctive: *Quiere que el muchacho salga,* becoming familiar with its form and primary function. No concept, however, is fully assimilated until it can be used, or its specific meaning recognized, in a matrix of other grammatical concepts (e.g., *sale cuando llega el padre* as contrasted with *sale cuando llegue el padre*). The student must be able to select, with conscious differentiation of meaning, what he needs from this matrix (e.g., is *llega, llegue,* or *haya llegado* the most appropriate?).

It is this need for our students to comprehend grammatical concepts in relation to, or in contrast with, other grammatical concepts which guides us in selecting among the *various ways of presenting the grammar.*

1. The teacher, or more usually the textbook writer, decides, for example, that the students should now learn the future tense (or the subjunctive or negation or the relative pronoun). This decision is an arbitrary one, and the next lesson is designed accordingly. The forms of the future tense are set out in a paradigm, and the way it is used explained and demonstrated in some example sentences. Students are then asked to write out the future tense forms of some verbs and to use them in written (or oral) exercises or translation sentences.

This is the standard *deductive approach.*[5] It highlights aspects of the grammar extracted from the matrix. The new forms being learned then need to be incorporated into reading or oral activities, where their relationships with other aspects of the grammar may be observed; otherwise, the students will tend to think of them as separate "rules" rather than elements in an interacting system. This deductive approach is incorporated, in a non-arbitrary fashion, as part of 3 below.

2. The students may encounter a new aspect of the grammar in a matrix of language and become curious about its function. This is the initial stage of *inductive learning.*

a. The student may hear a form which is unfamiliar to him as he is listening to oral Spanish. He may look puzzled or ask about it. In response, the teacher explains that this is a way of expressing future action and discusses its use. Opportunity is then provided for the student to hear other examples of the use of this future form in further oral work.

b. The future form may be encountered in reading material. Its function may be inferred from the context and then discussed in relation to other expressions of time relations. The forms and use of the future tense are then practiced orally in other contexts or in written exercises.

3. The student may need an expression of futurity for something he wishes to say or write. He asks for the form he needs. The teacher tells him briefly how to create future tenses from known verbs and explains the difference between expressions for the immediate and for a more distant, less certain, future. The teacher then encourages the student to use other future forms in what he is trying to say or write. This is a *deductive approach in response to a felt need.*

Each of these approaches has its use for specific age-groups or for particular aspects of the language. The deductive approach is most useful for mature, well-motivated students with some knowledge of the language who are anxious to understand the more complicated aspects of the grammatical system; students who have already learned one foreign language and are interested in the way this language deals with certain grammatical relationships; and adult students in intensive courses who have reasons for wishing to understand how the language works as fast as possible. The inductive approach is very appropriate for young language learners who have not yet developed fully their ability to think in abstractions[6] and who enjoy learning through active application; students who can take time to assimilate the language through use; and those studying the language in an environment where they hear it all around them. Most classroom teachers use a mixture of inductive and deductive approaches according to the type of student with whom they are dealing and the degree of complication of the problem being presented.

What about grammatical terminology?

Grammatical terminology has long been the bugbear of foreign-language teachers. Even switching from traditional terms to those used by any of the several competing systems of contemporary grammatical study does not seem to solve the problem. Students learn new terms and a schematic apparatus readily enough without coming to grips with the concepts they represent.

Ultimately, foreign-language teachers must take the responsibility themselves for teaching the student as much, or as little, abstract grammar as seems to be needed by each particular group for the specific language they are learning. Teachers must feel free to adapt or invent terminology which they find helps their students grasp the concepts and use the language effectively. In Spanish, for instance, it is often more useful in the early stages to talk about *el* and *la* words and the ramifications of their behavior, rather than about masculine and feminine nouns. The latter concept, in its Spanish form, seems extraordinary to the average English-speaking student and causes him to hesitate about such usages as *Pablo le habla a* la *hermana* and *¿Dónde están* las *maletas vuestras?* The concept of *el* and *la* words, augmented by *los* and *las* words, carries the student from definite articles to indefinite articles (*un* and *una* words), and demonstrative adjectives (*este, esta,* etc., words). The same concept helps elucidate adjective agreements (*Todavía no tengo listas las pruebas*). Each teacher should experiment with his own non-traditional ways of talking about grammar and continue with those that work.

How do written exercises for learning grammatical concepts differ from oral practice?

1. Oral exercises provide the opportunity for many more examples of the rule to be practiced, immediately corrected, and repracticed in a given time.

2. When exercises are practiced orally, the observant teacher can judge more accurately when to skip some exercises which performance indicates are not needed, and when to add further exercises to ensure assimilation of the rule.

3. Oral exercises can be used to prepare students for written exercises by allowing opportunity for questions and comment on obvious areas of misunderstanding and a rapid repracticing of the point at issue.

4. Written exercises provide useful reinforcement of what has been practiced orally; they help to build in concepts through the abstract process of thinking out the written forms.

5. Written exercises have an individual diagnostic function, revealing what sections of the work have not been thoroughly assimilated by a particular student and where their application in wider contexts is not fully understood. It is in written exercises that one focuses the student's attention on specific problems, rather than in expressive writing where the student is attempting to do a number of things at the same time.

6. Because they allow time for editing and re-editing, written exercises are less likely than oral exercises to reflect slips due to inattention or momentary distraction, and are often better indicators of genuine misunderstanding of the functioning of the system.

7. Certain aspects of the language are best practiced in writing because they are more fully expressed in the written code, e.g., agreement of adjectives and past participles, and certain verb inflections for person or tense.

8. It is easier for the student to submit in writing several possible versions, in which he can show how one rule parallels, interacts with, or contrasts with other rules.

9. Written exercises allow time for consulting references (dictionaries, grammars, or the textbook) and can, therefore, take on problem-solving characteristics.

10. Written exercises allow students with physical or emotional aural difficulties, or with slow response reactions to demonstrate what they know through a medium in which they feel more relaxed.

COGNITIVE EXERCISES

Whether the grammar has been presented deductively or inductively, a time comes when the students need to try for themselves whether they can use the various parts of it in novel contexts to express specific meanings. Through cognitive exercises they explore its possibilities and become more conscious of the constraints it imposes. They also clarify for themselves their individual areas of vagueness and miscomprehension.

Several very commonly used types of exercises may be termed cognitive, in the sense that they require of the student an abstract comprehension of the workings of the grammatical system. It is not surprising, therefore, that in form some of them resemble various well-known tests for estimating intelligence and ability to undertake abstract learning tasks. Success in these types of exercises does not necessarily mean that the student will be able to think of the appropriate rule at the appropriate moment when he is composing sentences himself. Nevertheless, it is a step on the way, since this basic knowledge is indispensable for effective language use. Students must, however, clearly understand that such exercises mark only a beginning—a foundation on which to build the all-important structure of personal meaning.

Under this heading we will consider multiple-choice exercises, fill-in-the-blank and completion exercises, the cloze procedure, and exercises in living language for the inductive exploration of particular problems of grammar. Conversions, restatements, expansions, and combinations will be considered under *Production*.

Some of these types of exercises are also dealt with in Chapter 4 and occasional reference will be made to the discussion in that section. Most of these exercises are also commonly used as *tests*.

Multiple-choice exercises

A *typical multiple-choice grammar exercise* will look like the following:

W9 (E or I) Circle in the margin the letter corresponding to the correct form to complete the following sentences when

A = el   D = las
B = un   E = no extra word
C = los

1. Hemos leído pocos _____ libros esta semana.   A B C D E
2. A Manolo no le gustan _____ corbatas baratas.   A B C D E
3. ¿Dónde está _____ catalán de quien me hablaste?   A B C D E
4. Quiero comprar _____ coche como el tuyo.   A B C D E
5. ¿Dónde hay _____ buen hostal en este pueblo?   A B C D E
6. Tengan la bondad de quitarse _____ zapatos.   A B C D E
7. Hay demasiados _____ problemas en todas las
   grandes ciudades.   A B C D E

Commentary

1. This exercise forces the student to think over carefully the various aspects of the interrelated rules for the use of the definite and indefinite articles in specific grammatical and semantic contexts. He must understand the whole sentence and the implications of each part to be able to select successfully.

2. The number of choices is too great for a student to succeed through guessing, except by a fluke. The fluke probability is also reduced by the fact that the student thinks he knows at least some of the items and so is not depending on pure guesswork for the complete exercise.

3. If a separate computer answer-sheet is used, the exercise may be machine-scored as a test. The answer format of W9 can be rapidly checked with an easily constructed punched-stencil key (with holes punched to mark the positions of the correct answers).

4. The W9 format provides a useful mechanism for students in individualized programs to check their mastery of certain concepts and their readiness to move on.

5. It is easy to construct from a basic model several equivalent versions of an exercise of this type by changing the lexical items, and thus the semantic context, while retaining the grammatical context. The following three items are equivalent in grammatical difficulty and test the same rule:

W10

    a. Hemos leído pocos _____ libros esta semana.
    b. Hay muchas _____ muchachas en la playa.
    c. Todavía no hemos conocido a mucha _____ gente.

From the point of view of knowledge of the rule, the following items are also equivalent:

    d. Mi hermana ya tiene muchos _____ libros.
    e. La sirvienta no ha ido al mercado, pero de todas maneras tenemos mucho _____ pan y _____ jamón serrano.

Note, however, that (e) contains expressions and vocabulary of a level of difficulty above the level of the grammatical item sought. *De todas maneras* is intermediate level; *jamón serrano* is a culturally linked noun phrase which may disconcert an elementary-level student—the only one who would normally be working through exercises like those exemplified above.

6. It is essential in this type of exercise or test that each of the items be unambiguous. Students should not have to hesitate over possible interpretations while they try to decide what the instructor had in mind.

W11   a. No tenemos _____ revistas inglesas.
       b. No tenemos revistas inglesas.
       c. No tenemos las revistas inglesas.

Both (b) and (c) are possible Spanish sentences in the appropriate context. Clearly the constructor of item (a) had the particular problems of the article after a negation in mind and, therefore, expected (b). With more context, as in W12, the correct choice is clear:

W12   a. Le puedo vender periódicos franceses, pero no tenemos _____ revistas inglesas.

       b. Lo siento, pero todavía no hemos recibido _____ revistas inglesas a que se refiere Ud.

This multiple-choice format can be used for a number of aspects of grammar, even the *use of tenses:*

W13 (I) Read the following sentences carefully. Circle in the margin the letter corresponding to the tense and mood of the verb that you would use to complete the sentence when

A = present indicative
B = conditional
C = present subjunctive

1. Me dijo que me _____ ayer. (pagar)	A B C
2. Siento que él no _____ ir con nosotros manaña. (poder)	A B C
3. Te lo cuento para que _____ lo que dicen. (saber)	A B C
4. Nosotros _____ tarde los domingos. (levantarse)	A B C
5. Yo lo _____ mañana si tuviese dinero. (comprar)	A B C

6. Si no puedes hacerlo, lo _____ yo por ti.   A   B   C
                     (hacer)

7. Si yo hablara inglés, _____ un empleo mejor.   A   B   C
                     (tener)

8. Cuando _____ dinero, te lo prestaré.   A   B   C
         (tener)

Commentary

1. This is clearly a review exercise since it requires comparative knowledge of the use of three tenses in two different moods.

2. The exercise tests knowledge of the functioning of the language system, not ability to produce the forms required. As it is constructed, it is useful as an objectively corrected test of cognitive assimilation of the rules. When using W13 as an exercise, students would, of course, also fill in the appropriate forms of the verbs in the blanks.

3. In constructing items to test ability to select correct tenses, sufficient indicators of time relationships must be given to make the appropriate choice clear. In most of the above examples, tenses and moods required in the blanks are either syntactically constrained by other tenses in associated clauses (as in 7: *Si yo hablara inglés, tendría un empleo mejor*), semantically and temporally constrained by a superordinate verb (as in 2: *Siento que él no pueda ir con nosotros mañana*, or clearly indicated by an adverbial phrase of time (as in 5: *Yo lo compraría mañana si tuviese dinero*).

4. Other factors which have been kept in mind in constructing the items are:

   a. that the sentences should be of a type that the students might encounter or wish to use;

   b. that the vocabulary and general construction of the sentence should be of a level that the students can easily comprehend, so that they are not distracted from the real task of deciding on tense and mood.

The same format can be used for practice in *distinguishing among expressions* whose precise usage is often confusing.

W14 (I) Circle in the margin the letter corresponding to the most appropriate completion for the following sentences when

A = se pone de pie   D = se sienta
B = está de pie   E = está sentado
C = se queda de pie   F = está sentándose

1. A Pablo no le gusta viajar sentado. El _____ aun
   cuando hay asientos desocupados en el autobús.   A B C D E F
2. —¿Dónde está Carlos?
   —_____ en el sillón, leyendo los periódicos.   A B C D E F
3. Alguien debiera cederle el lugar a ese señor. Hace
   media hora que el pobre _____ y ya empieza a
   dar muestras de cansancio.   A B C D E F
4. La gente siempre _____ para aplaudir al presidente.   A B C D E F
5. Cuando se siente cansado, el mendigo _____ en
   un banco del jardín.   A B C D E F

Commentary

In this example, the number of items is not equal to the number of choices. This is one way to avoid selection by pure elimination procedures. Another way is to write the items so that some of the choices are appropriate for more than one item.

The novice multiple-choice item constructor should not be misled by the final product into underestimating the difficulty of constructing unambiguous, useful test items in this format. The first step is to make a careful list of exactly which items it is desirable to include. After the test has been constructed and carefully scanned for ambiguities, inappropriate vocabulary, unintentional comprehension difficulty or obscurity, stilted expressions, unlikely meanings (e.g., *Mi abuelita nunca lleva _____ ropas*), and a regular pattern order of correct choices (e.g., A B C A B C),[7] it should be passed on to another person to be read and checked for these weaknesses. Even an experienced test constructor is sometimes temporarily blinded by the knowledge of his intentions.

A similar format may be used for testing the students' understanding of the *meanings of words*.

W15 (E or I) Circle in the margin the letter corresponding to the phrase which correctly completes the sentence:

1. En una carnicería Ud. puede comprar   A B C D
   A. carne
   B. legumbres
   C. galletas
   D. frutas

2. "Serrano" es el nombre que se da a una clase de   A   B   C   D
   A. queso
   B. jamón
   C. jabón
   D. pescado

3. En una bodega se puede comprar   A   B   C   D
   A. pan ＇
   B. vino
   C. mantequilla
   D. tabaco

Commentary

1. Items 1 and 3 are based on traditional, but still existing, Spanish shopping patterns. (Teachers will keep up, through reading and visits, with the changes taking place in Hispanic countries, e.g., the rapid spread of *supermercados*.)

2. These items would not be given to students out of the blue. The exercise is obviously based on material in the students' textbook.

3. This type of exercise can be fun to make up and groups of students may be asked to construct exercises for other groups of students. Another format, which is not suitable for a test because of the fifty-fifty chances it provides, but which is very amusing to construct and to answer, is as follows:

W16 (I) Some of the following statements are sensible and some are ridiculous. Circle in the margin
   A: if the sentence is sensible,
   B: if the sentence is ridiculous.

1. Un escaparate es una salida de emergencia.   A   B
2. El panadero vende pan.   A   B
3. Una olla sirve para guisar.   A   B
4. El inodoro es un animal doméstico.   A   B
5. El sastre hace chaquetas y pantalones.   A   B
6. El peatón es un animal salvaje.   A   B

The multiple-choice format can be used also to test appreciation of *appropriate rejoinders, responses, or comments* as in the following:

W17 (E) Circle in the margin the letter corresponding to the most appropriate response to the following questions:

    1. ¿Tendría Ud. cambio para quinientas pesetas?   A B C D
      A. De nada, caballero.
      B. Me parece que sí.
      C. Quinientas pesetas valen diez dólares, más o menos.
      D. Muy bien, señor. Pase usted.

Alternatively, the student may be asked to select the appropriate response in a particular situation.

W18 (E) Circle in the margin the letter corresponding to the appropriate response in the situation described.

    1. Caminando por la calle, Ud. encuentra al director de   A B C D
      su escuela y le saluda:
      A. Hola, ¿qué tal?
      B. Hasta la vista, señor director.
      C. ¿Qué hay de nuevo, viejo?
      D. Buenos días. ¿Cómo está usted?

* Construct a multiple-choice test for the forms of the relative pronoun or the uses of *hay, son,* and *están.* Try the test out on other members of the class. Discuss the strengths and weaknesses of the various tests contructed by the class members.

Fill-in-the-blank exercises

Some weaknesses of this format have already been discussed in Chapter 4, particularly the type of construction which makes these exercises mechanical busywork. To earn a place as a cognitive exercise, the fill-in-the-blank activity must demand of the student *understanding of the complete sentence and careful thought.* W13 meets this criterion as a fill-in-the-blank exercise when each verb has to be written in with the correct form for the tense and mood selected. The purpose of W13 can also be achieved in the format of W19.

W19 (E or I) Read the following sentences carefully and write in the blank the most appropriate past tense form of the verb in the margin.

acostarse 1. Yo estaba muy cansado anoche y por eso _____ temprano.
comprar   2. La semana pasada mi padre le _____ un coche a mi hermana.

esperar	3. María _____ el autobús cuando yo llegué.
mirar	4. Papa leía el periódico mientras mamá _____ la televisión.
trabajar	5. Le dije que hacía tres años que yo _____ aquí.
ver	6. Sí que los _____ ayer en la fiesta.
bailar	7. Cuando vivíamos en Barcelona, _____ la sardana todos los domingos.

Commentary

1. In this exercise, the student must first look carefully at all indicators of time relationships in each sentence. Then, having selected an appropriate tense, they must make decisions about this particular verb: Is it regular? If so, which type? Has it any peculiarities? What kinds of agreements are required?

2. If items are written in, the exercise cannot be mechanically scored.

3. The student's choice here is between the *pretérito* and the *imperfecto*. Each item should be allotted at least two points so that credit may be given to the student who chooses the correct tense, even if he makes some mistake in the spelling of the verb.

4. Students may be asked to write out the whole sentence. This depends on whether W19 is used as a practice exercise in writing or as part of a test with a large number of items to be covered in a restricted amount of time. If students do write out the whole item, points should not be deducted for slips in copying other parts of the sentence when the fill-in item is correct. If the copying is careless throughout, a penalty of two or three points may be deducted from the total for this specific fault.

5. Note that in sentence 1, a reflexive construction is used. The problem would then arise as to whether to withhold partial credit from the student who either omitted the correct pronoun (*me*) or used an incorrect one (thus yielding, e.g., **se acosté*). In this and similar cases, depending on the level of study of the student, one would either expect him to use the correct pronoun as a matter of course, or one would allot more points to this item.

At the intermediate and advanced levels fill-in-the-blank exercises can become very demanding as in a *mixed, overall structure test* with no guides to the blanks:

W20 (I and A) Complete the following sentences appropriately as indicated by the clues in the sentences.

1. Si yo _____ ser rico, no habría estudiado para maestro.

2. No le daría el empleo aunque _____ correctamente todas las preguntas.
3. En Andorra _____ aparatos eléctricos a precios bajísimos.
4. Aunque _____ mañana, iremos a la quermese.
5. ¿La manzana? Juanita dijo que _____ a dar a la maestra.
6. El mendigo _____ pidió una limosna y no _____ pude negar.

The fill-in-the-blank format is also useful for *testing irregular verb forms in context.*

W21 (I and A)

Write in the margin the correct form of the verbs on the left, as indicated by the clues in the sentences.

1. saber   Eso no es novedad. Nosotros lo _____   1. _____
            anoche por la radio.
2. querer   Si no lo invitamos, no _____ venir mañana.   2. _____
3. caerse   Tenga cuidado al bajar del coche. No que-   3. _____
            remos que usted _____.
4. hacer   Yo lo _____ cuando venga el jefe.   4. _____

Commentary

1. In a complete exercise more items would be given for each verb.

2. The format with blanks in the right-hand margin provides for rapid correction of the test, since all the answers are in one column. As a class exercise, it would be preferable for students to write in the blanks within the sentences so that they could read over the complete sentence as they checked the appropriateness of their choice of tense and mood.

3. A set of such exercises, with alternative versions covering all the common irregular verbs is useful in an individualized program. Students can then check regularly their control of this troublesome area.

The fill-in-the-blank exercise may take the form of a *connected passage* of prose. This is a common way of giving practice in, or testing, choice between the *pretérito perfecto absoluto* or the *imperfecto*.

W22 (A) Write out the following passage, putting each verb either into the *pretérito perfecto absoluto* or the *imperfecto* as would be most appropriate in such a narrative context. Underline each verb in your answer.

Cuando _____ pequeña, Luz María _____ en un pueblecito
      (ser)   (vivir)

en las montañas. _____ cada día a la escuela, _____ mucho y
      (ir)   (estudiar)

siempre _____ buenas notas. Al terminar los estudios primarios, le
    (sacar)

_____ a su padre que _____ estudiar en la capital. Allí la
 (decir)   (querer)

muchacha _____ a un teniente del ejército y _____ de él. A los
      (conocer)   (enamorarse)

dos meses _____ y _____ a vivir en las afueras de la capital.
       (casarse)   (ir)

La pareja _____ diez hijos en diez años. Los varones _____ a
     (tener)   (ir)

estudiar a la Academia Militar y las muchachas _____ una a una.
                                      (casarse)

Un día, Luz María _____ atropellada por un camión y _____
            (ser)   (morirse)

en un hospital. El marido la enterró y luego _____ con una viuda
                                 (casarse)

que _____ mucho dinero.
  (tener)

Clearly, this format is also useful for other areas of grammar, e.g., the recurrent problem of which preposition to use after different verbs when they are followed by an infinitive. This is a more natural way to practice this feature than by writing out lists of verbs which require a preposition such as *a, de, en,* or *con.*

W23 (I) Cuando mi padre decidió ____ comprar un coche, nos apresuramos ____ contárselo a nuestros compañeros de escuela, pero eso no contribuyó ____ aumentar nuestra popularidad. Al contrario, muchos muchachos se valieron ____ la noticia ____ que íbamos ____ tener coche para alejarse aún más ____ nosotros.

Uses for fill-in-the-blank exercises are limited only by the imagination of the instructor, as witness the following miscellany:

W24 (E or I) With English translation stimulus.

(what)   1. ¿_____ desea usted?
(which)   2. Conozco un café _____ se queda abierto toda la noche.
(who)   3. Sus hermanos, _____ viven en Barcelona, ya se consideran
            catalanes.

Commentary

The indications in English are unnecessary for any of these items. In item 1, for example, one can expect *qué,* but it would be possible to have other interrogative words as well, depending on context. However, the teacher can limit the possibility of choice to *qué* by providing an appropriate context, e.g., —*Buenas tardes, señor. ¿_____ desea Ud? —Un vaso de vino tinto, por favor.*

W25 (E or I) With Spanish paraphrase as stimulus.

Esa noche Juan no _____ estudiar.
(Juan no tenía ganas de estudiar)

Commentary

Presumably *quería* is sought. With this type of exercise care must be taken to see that the paraphrase is not in less familiar language than the item sought. Here also *tenía ganas de* could distract the student into thinking that a similar expression, such as *tenía tiempo de* was expected, especially as this would make a possible sentence. On the other hand, a different lexical item could be used (e.g., *deseaba*), which would also yield a possible sentence for which credit should be granted.

W26 (I) With grammatical indications given.

Juan y María _____ de dirección.
(equivocarse, pluscuamperfecto)

Commentary

This would be a more cognitive type of exercise if a suitable context were given for the item rather than the precise tense reference (see W13, W19, and W20). In this example, only the form for the tense is being tested, not the use. Both would be tested in:
Juan y María me telefonearon para decir que _____
(equivocarse)
de dirección al salir del metro.

W27 (E or I) With information given in associated sentences to show what is required.

1. Alberto es buen violinista. Enrique no toca muy bien.
   Alberto es _____ violinista que Enrique.
2. Juan es alto. Francisco no es muy alto.
   Francisco no es _____ alto _____ Juan.

The cloze procedure

If we combine the idea of W20 with the sequential format of W22, we arrive at the cloze procedure. Strictly speaking, the cloze procedure, as developed for native speakers, was a test of reading comprehension. It consisted of giving the student a passage to complete in which every *n*th word was deleted. In one passage it could be every fifth word, in another every tenth word, or whatever the examiner chose. This will immediately recall the discussion in Chapter 3 of Cherry's uncertainties of a spoken message and Schlesinger's semantic-syntactic decoding. In a cloze test, the native speaker projects expectations about the development of the message. The foreign-language learner has also to think carefully about grammatical detail. For the foreign-language learner, then, the blanks need not be kept rigidly to a set pattern. The cloze procedure provides an interesting and thought-provoking exercise which trains the student to look carefully at all structural clues and to range around within a semantic field for related concepts. It is good preparation for careful reading and a useful overall written test.

W28

(E) Hace dos días que Juan y Ana están _____ Barcelona. Llegaron _____ la noche, _____ el tren _____ París. Desgraciadamente, _____ encontraron _____ taxi, porque llovía _____ y _____ muy tarde. Trataron _____ telefonear _____ algunos hoteles, _____ estaban todos _____. Por eso, tuvieron _____ pasarse la noche _____ la estación.

Commentary

1. Any completion which makes sense in the context and fits into the grammatical structure is acceptable. Passages can be constructed which are more ambiguous than W28, thus allowing more scope for student ingenuity. (See also W47.)

2. (I and A) After a reading passage has been studied intensively, the students may do a cloze test on it to see how much of the vocabulary and grammatical structure they have retained.

✻ Prepare a cloze test from one of the passages in Chapters 6 or 7.

✻ Look at fill-in-the-blank exercises in various textbooks and suggest ways to make them more intellectually stimulating.

Beyond the elementary level

    Inductive learning need not be limited to a few early lessons of patterned oral practice of the type discussed in Chapter 4. At the intermediate and advanced levels, the students' curiosity can be channeled into discovering for themselves quite complicated sets of rules which they tend to remember better because they themselves have worked them out.

The Rosetta procedure[8]

    (I) The student can improve his understanding of certain grammatical structures through methodic study of their occurrence in written script. Suppose, for example, that several uses of the pronoun *se* have been presented and drilled at different points in the program and the students express curiosity about differences they have observed and hazard guesses as to the rules governing these divergencies. The teacher then gives them passages like those below, and asks them to develop coherent, mutually exclusive rules which will explain each occurrence of *se*.

W29   1. Aquí en Andorra se vive bien, sobretodo si se tiene la suerte de vivir en una pensión situada lejos de la carretera principal. Si se está en La Masana, por ejemplo, entonces puede levantarse uno tranquilamente, despertándose cuando lo determine el cuerpo y no las bocinas de los turistas que invaden el país en el verano. Después de lavarse y afeitarse, sale uno a sentarse en el café, donde se toma en sosiego el desayuno.

    2. Al encontrarse en el café, la gente se saluda sin prisa y se pone a charlar. Se habla de la familia y de los negocios, quejándose de estos, más por hábito que por otra razón. Si llega al café un forastero como yo, no se le ocurre a nadie dejar de saludarle. Si él les pide alguna información sobre cómo llegar a algun sitio, se la dan cortésmente y a veces se toman el trabajo de acompañarle hasta donde quiera ir, para que no se pierda. ¡Qué gente más simpática, estos andorranos!

Learning from living language

    Even at the advanced level, English-speaking students find the subtleties of the use of the verb *deber* difficult to grasp. Instead of telling students all over again, with demonstration sentences, about its use to indicate inference, moral duty, obligation, necessity, etc., the teacher may give advanced students extracts of living language in which the context clarifies the nuance supplied by *deber* (or *deber de*) followed by an infinitive. Through an exercise of this type, the students focus on the variable semantic contribution of this verb and the formal indications of its role (that is, the tense in which it appears). Moreover, they also become familiar with certain facts which, the rules of normative grammar notwithstanding, are part and parcel of native speakers' normal use of Spanish. For example, the students should learn that *deber de* is often used to indicate obligation (e.g., *No puedo ir con vosotros proque debo de hablarle al jefe dentro de diez minutos*), even though some grammars insist on assigning to that construction only the semantic value of inference or supposition (e.g., *María debe de estar en su habitación. ¿No oyes la música?*).

W 30   (A) Examine the following extracts carefully, and identify the nuance of meaning of *deber* in each. Does it indicate a probable or supposed situation, an intention or arrangement, a constraint or necessity for the person concerned, or a moral obligation? From your answers, work out which tenses of *deber* are used to convey particular meanings. Do any tenses of *deber* seem to be ambiguous, that is, capable of bearing two different meanings?

1. —¿Cómo aparecieron las comadronas?
    —Ya existían desde los tiempos prehispánicos. Debe considerárselas como un elemento muy valioso.
    (From an interview in *El Nacional,* México)

2. —¿No te parece que es así como se debería programar el curso, para obtener los resultados que queremos?   (From a recorded dialogue.)

3. —Pero, ¿debo o no escribir el informe ése a que te refieres?
    —Sí que debes.   (From a live conversation.)

4. —Perdóname, yo debía haberte dicho que no nos íbamos a reunir el viernes, pero se me olvidó hacerlo.   (From a live dialogue.)

5. —Y el decano ése, ¿ya te ha llamado?
    —Debía haberlo hecho, pero hasta ahora, nada.
    (From a live dialogue.)

6. —Esos informes deberán entregarse en la oficina del departamento antes del viernes, día cinco de enero.   (From a departmental memo.)

7. —¿No quisiste almorzar con nosotros ayer?
    —No es que no lo haya querido, es que debí participar en una reunión de doce a una.   (From a live conversation.)

8. —¿Llegaba ayer su mujer?
    —Debía de llegar. Le telefoneó diciendo que iba a salir de Nueva York ayer por la tarde.   (From a recorded dialogue.)

9. —Debo de haber dicho algo sobre eso, puesto que ahora ya lo saben todos o casi todos. Tú, ¿qué piensas de eso?
    (From a recorded dialogue.)

10. —Es inútil correr porque ellos deberán haber salido del edificio antes que llegues. Creo que lo mejor es tratar de telefonearles.
    (From a live dialogue.)

11. —Lo siento, pero el jefe ha debido ir a la biblioteca. ¿No quiere esperar? El debe de volver pronto.   (From a conversation.)

Commentary

1. These examples are not sufficient to cover all aspects of this subject, but they provide enough material to alert students to the subtleties of meaning of *deber,* to stimulate their curiosity to identify nuances of *deber* in what they are reading, and to help them to use it in a more versatile fashion in speech.

2. There is enough material in W30 to draw together the following information.[9]

Inference or supposition:	presente, *debe de,* 12; *debo de,* 9;
	imperfecto, *debía de,* 8.
	futuro, *deberán,* 11.
	pretérito perfecto actual, *ha debido,* 12.
Necessity or obligation:	presente, *debo,* 3;
	pretérito perfecto absoluto, *debí,* 7;
	imperfecto, *debía,* 4.
	condicional, *debería,* 2.
	futuro, *deberán,* 6.

Notice, furthermore, that *El debe de volver pronto,* in No. 12, is somewhat ambiguous, as it may signify either inference (the secretary assumes that her boss will return from the library) or obligation (the secretary knows that, for one reason or another, her boss *has* to come back to his office).

(I and A) The *imperfecto* continues to be a particular problem for successive groups of English-speaking language-learners. They have great difficulty in using it correctly in association with the *pretérito.* Many scholars point out that the *imperfecto,* besides showing the time value we associate with a tense, also indicates an *aspect*[10] of the action. This notion of aspect is unfamiliar to most of our students. Consider the following example.

W31 Dejamos el coche en la carretera y nos pusimos a escalar la montaña. Al cabo de media hora, llegábamos al sítio donde todavía se levantaba la capilla de campanar cuadrangular. Vacilamos un poco sobre si valía o no la pena echarle un vistazo al interior, pero la idea de que teníamos que caminar muchos kilómetros en terreno montañoso para llegar al lago de Tristaina antes del atardecer nos hizo proseguir. El sol iba alto en el cielo y nos quemaba ferozmente los brazos, el cuello y la cara, cuando llegamos por fin a la cumbre de un monte, desde donde se veía, no muy lejos, lo que buscábamos. Nos quedamos allí diez minutos, fumándonos un cigarrillo y tomando aliento, y luego reanudamos la caminata. El pavoroso accidente tuvo lugar mientras bajábamos la cuesta.

Commentary

This short passage demonstrates what a deductive explanation of the use of the *imperfecto* rarely makes clear to students—the way in which that tense brings the reader into the action as though he were there, observing the details as in a picture. Traditional explanations such as "the *pretérito* is used for a series of actions in the past, the *imperfecto* for an action seen as having no beginning and no end," simply do not explain a passage like this one. On the one hand, the very notion of "action" or "verbal action" is a rather nebulous one. For example, even in *dejamos el coche* and *nos pusimos a andar* can be interpreted as referring to actual actions, how are we to interpret the semantic concept of the verb in *se levantaba la capilla* or in *si valía o no la pena?* Is *se levantaba* a state verb? And what about *valía?* If it expresses an action, who or what is the agent?

On the other hand, the concepts involved in the notion of aspect (e.g., perfectivity vs. imperfectivity, termination vs. continuation) are helpful in explaining and understanding the contrast between, say, *entrábamos en la ciudad* (the entry considered in its development and *cuando entramos en la ciudad* (the entry seen in its totality, almost in retrospect, as it were). In *iba alto, nos quemaba,* and *buscábamos* we have a series of parallel events which take place during the period of time which reaches its culminating point with *llegamos.* On the other hand, *se veía* denotes a certain possible action (which might be expressed in English as *could be seen*) rather than an actual one (which might have been expressed as *desde donde vimos, no muy lejos . . .*). Only through living language can we really assimilate differences like these which are fundamental to the effective use and understanding of Spanish. (See also R42–44.)

Teachers who wish to retain and improve upon the level of Spanish they attained on graduating will seek opportunities to visit Spain and Spanish-speaking countries. Meanwhile, they will read widely and constantly in Spanish for pleasure. Material of the type used in W30 and W31 can be collected by teachers from their own reading of newspapers, magazines, plays, novels, or books of general information.

* Find other material of this type to clarify the uses of the tenses in contemporary written Spanish. Remember that there must be sufficient context in each item to establish the particular meaning conveyed by the use of one tense, or aspect, rather than another.

Deductive learning also has its place at the advanced level. Because of the subtlety of the distinction and the paucity of comparable examples in any one text, it would be very time-consuming, for instance, to try to work out inductively the way the subjunctive mode[11] is used in Spanish to convey the distinction between specific and non-specific reference as in the following examples:

　　a) *Buscamos una muchacha que habla portugués.*
　　b) *Buscamos una muchacha que hable portugués.*

The speaker of a) has a specific referent in mind (*una muchacha* that he knows exists) and consequently he uses the indicative mood *habla* in the subordinate clause. On the other hand, the speaker of b) does not have a specific *muchacha* in mind, but is looking for any one who might meet the requirement; he, therefore, uses the subjunctive *hable*. These sentences could occur in similar contexts without any clear contextual clues as to why the author selected one rather than the other. Yet the intention of the author in selecting (a) over (b) would be basic to the interpretation of the text.

For these reasons, the particular problems of the subjunctive would normally be explained deductively, with demonstrations in passages of living language of the various ways in which it is used. Students would then be encouraged to explain why an author had used a subjunctive whenever an interesting example was encountered in texts for intensive study. They would also be expected to have a reason for using a subjunctive in their own writing.

* Begin a collection of suitable extracts for the advanced level demonstrating interesting uses of *negation forms* and share them with other members of the class.

GRAMMAR AND WRITING SKILL

However grammatical concepts are introduced and demonstrated, it is essential that the students' activity be directed as soon as possible to *the concept in use*. Understanding the operation of the grammar, observing its functioning, or practicing the effective use of it in exercises will not ensure that the student can use it efficiently in writing.

Experiments in the writing of English by native speakers have shown specifically that the formal study of grammar and of grammatical terminology does not improve skill in writing.[12] Native speakers who can control the grammar of their language in speech and have been taught in elementary and secondary school how it operates still write ungrammatical and incomplete sentences. Formal grammar is an abstract study. After foreign-language students have been shown how the various parts of the language system operate, they seem to benefit more from discussion of the types of errors they are making in their writing in relation to what they were trying to say, with opportunity provided to correct their errors in context, than from a second (third, fourth, fifth?) exposition of the workings of the Spanish pronoun system.[13] In this way they focus on the details they partly know or do not know, rather than having their attention dispersed over a wider area of abstract concepts.

9
Writing and written exercises II: flexibility and expression

III. Production: flexibility measures

Cognitive exercises of the types described, despite their usefulness in clarifying grammatical concepts, do not require students to construct their own sentences to express their personal meaning, nor to develop their ideas in logical and coherent paragraphs within a larger discourse. "Knowing about" is not "knowing how." *Practice is needed in actual sequential writing.* Having learned about the various parts of the machine, and parts of parts, and how these synchronize in action, the student needs to set the machine in motion with the different parts active in weaving the intricate pattern of meaning. Here guidance is helpful in learning which parts will operate together to form new patterns. Student aptitudes vary widely in writing. Some need considerable help in developing a smooth and effective operation; others seem intuitively to take off and create interesting patterns of their own. The teacher needs to distinguish these types early and *individualize writing activities* so that each benefits to the maximum, according to his preferred style of activity.

Although writing within a framework and expressive writing will now be discussed in sequence, it must be emphasized that opportunities for expressive writing should be provided as soon as possible. Even the elementary-level student should have opportunities to experiment with the potential for expression of his rudimentary knowledge of the language. Students should not, however, be left to sink or swim in such a difficult area. Most

268

students need some guided practice in using new combinations and exploring possibilities of expression, if they are to go beyond simple, uncomplicated sentences; they need resources other than Spanglish when they wish to express more sophisticated ideas in the new medium.

Expressive writing experiments with all the possibilities of syntax and lexicon. If there is to be transfer from guided practice in using this potential, then the practice itself must be recognizably purposeful and applicable.

This section will concentrate on measures for developing flexibility in the construction of sentences and paragraphs within the shelter of a framework.

CONVERSIONS AND RESTATEMENTS

The problems of single-sentence conversions have been discussed at length in Chapter 4. Since they are to be found in any textbook, examples of all the different kinds will not be given here. Some will be examined in detail to show ways in which they can be made to serve the ultimate purpose of developing ability to write clearly, comprehensibly, and expressively.

Conversions are cognitive exercises in that they require the student to think through the rules and select the ones applicable to the particular case under consideration. Two of the commonest types are the following.

W32 (E) Rewrite the following sentences, replacing the italicized nouns with feminine nouns, and making all necessary adjustments.

1. Mi *hermano* mayor se marchó de vacaciones ayer con su *amigo* catalán . . .
   (Expected conversion: Mi hermana mayor se marchó de vacaciones ayer con su amiga catalana.)

W33 (E) Answer the following questions according to the indication given, replacing the italicized words with appropriate pronouns.

1. ¿Verdad que tu hermano le dio *un coche* a *esa muchacha?*
   Sí . . .
   (Expected reply: Sí, se lo dio.)
2. ¿Ha comprado *tu padre la casa?*
   No . . .
   (Expected reply: No, él no la ha comprado.)

Students may learn to complete exercises like W32 and W33 accurately, without there being any necessary transfer of what has been learned to expressive writing. Some items of this type may be useful for familiarizing students with the mechanics of these operations, but, as soon as the students seem to have grasped the idea, they should be given a more interesting and imaginative task like W34, which requires of them the same types of operations in a simulated, possible situation. (After completing the writing, they may act out the short scene they have created.)

W34 (E or I)

1. Usted acaba de comprarse una radio, pero desgraciadamente el aparato no funciona bien. Usted vuelve a la tienda donde la ha comprado para que se la sustituyan por otra. El vendedor no quiere creer que usted la haya comprado allí, y por eso ustedes empiezan a discutir. Escriba el diálogo que resulta de esa situación.

This subject should elicit sentences like the following:

CLIENTE   Buenos días. Le traigo esta radio que compré aquí la semana pasada. Desgraciadamente, no funciona muy bien.

VENDEDOR   Lo siento, pero creo que usted está equivocado. Aquí no se vende esa marca de radio. Si usted quiere que se la cambien, debe llevarla adonde la compró.

CLEINTE   Pero sí que la compré aquí. Fíjese, aquí tiene usted el recibo de venta.

2. Usted ha comprado un diccionario y, a los dos días, se da cuenta de que le faltan algunas páginas. Vuelve entonces a la librería para que se lo cambien por otro. La vendedora dice que nunca le ha vendido semejante libro. Escriba el diálogo que resulta de esa situación.

CLIENTE   Buenos días, señorita. Quizás pueda usted ayudarme. Se trata de este diccionario que me vendió usted hace dos días. Le faltan unas cuantas páginas, y quisiera cambiarlo por otro.

VENDEDORA No es posible, caballero. Este diccionario, no se lo he vendido yo . . .

* Take from a textbook an exercise for converting conditional clauses from one tense to another (e.g., *Si lo veo, le doy una paliza* for conversion into *Si lo viese le daría una paliza*) and work out a more imaginative exercise which would elicit these types of conversions in a creative framework.

A conversion becomes a *restatement* when it retains the general form of the original, but the changes made are more than mere switches from tense to tense, gender to gender, or sentence type to sentence type. W35 below is a conversion and W36 a restatement using the same basic material.

W35 (I) Según Julio Camba,[1] el turista yanqui siempre se interesa en saber lo que valen las cosas que ve. Al hallarse ante una catedral, pregunta cuánto cuesta,—en millones de dólares, por supuesto. Al visitar unas ruinas, se interesa por lo que vale, no como monumento histórico, sino por su valor comercial. Y al ser presentado a un noble de sangre azul, la primera pregunta que hace tiene que ver con lo que tendría que pagar para conseguirlo como yerno.

Reescriba Ud. el párrafo de arriba, en forma de discurso directo, empleando las preguntas directas que hace el turista yanqui. Ejemplo: —¿Cuánto cree Ud. que pueda valer esta catedral?

W36 (I) En *El turista yanqui,* Julio Camba describe la actitud del turista yanqui ante los objetos de arte, los monumentos, y aún las personas importantes. Según aquel autor, esa clase de turista lo valora todo sobre la base de lo que cuesta, y sólo le interesan las cosas que valgan muchos miles de dólares.

Suponga que Ud. se haya pasado una semana viajando en España en compañía de un turista yanqui como el que describe Camba. Escríbale una carta a un amigo, relatando sus impresiones sobre su compañero de viaje.

The restatement comes closer to *composition or expressive writing,* when W36 is followed by W37.

W37 (I) Según el modelo del artículo de Camba, escriba una descripción del turista español en Nueva York.

SENTENCE MODIFICATION

Flexibility in writing means being able to make a sentence say what you want it to say and to say it vividly, humorously, poignantly, obliquely, or succinctly.

W38 The simple notion: *Quiero acompañarle* can be expressed with all kinds of nuances:

Tendré el máximo gusto en acompañarle, señor.
Por supuesto que le acompañaré.
Le acompañaré, no cabe duda.
Bueno, le acompaño.
Voy con usted, ¡qué remédio!

Or the notion *No puedo ir con usted:*

> Tendría el máximo gusto en acompañarle, pero desgraciadamente . . .
> Quisiera acompañarle, pero desgraciadamente . . .
> No es que no quiera acompañarle, pero . . .
> No voy contigo, y ¡se acabó!

Practice in types of sentences

Students should learn early to try to express similar ideas in different forms from various points of view. One amusing way to do this is to take a particular situation and ask the students to express the reactions of a number of people to it.

W39 (E or I) Al salir del hospital, un joven médico atraviesa corriendo una estrecha calle, llena de coches, en hora de intensa circulación. Su acción suscita diferentes reacciones y comentarios. Escriba lo que dirían las personas siguientes:

> Un guardia urbano (pregunta)
> Un peatón al guardia urbano (pregunta)
> Un niño a su madre (pregunta, comentario)
> Un conductor de autobús (exclamación)
> La mujer del médico (exclamación, pregunta)
> Un joven en motocicleta (exclamación)
> Una vieja al niño (pregunta negativa)
> Un comerciante a la puerta de su tienda (comentario)

Since what is written is intended to be read, students may copy down the comments in W39 as one side of a dialogue, exchange papers with other students, and complete the dialogues for acting out.

One side of the dialogue might read:

W40 GUARDIA URBANO   ¿Quién es ese hombre que atraviesa la calle?

. . . .

EL PEATÓN   Bueno, si puede cruzar él, también puedo yo, ¿no le parece a Ud.?

. . . .

EL NIÑO A SU MADRE   ¿Se puede cruzar la calle, mamá?
Fíjate, acaba de cruzarla aquel señor.

. . . .

EL CONDUCTOR DE AUTOBÚS   ¡Cuidado, imbécil!

. . . .

LA MUJER DEL MÉDICO   Pero, Francisco, ¡qué loco eres! ¡Vuelve, que te vas a matar!

Combinations

If students are to write well they must be shaken out of the shelter of the simple sentence and the compound sentence with *y* and *pero*. One way of eliciting complex sentences from students has been the combination exercise.

W 41 (E) Combine the following pairs of sentences into one by using relative pronouns.

1. Fuimos a visitar a un artista madrileño.
   El tenía cinco hijos.
   (Expected combination: Fuimos a visitar a un artista madrileño que tenía cinco hijos.)
2. La criada preparó los bocadillos.
   Comimos los bocadillos.
   (Expected combination: Comimos los bocadillos que preparó la criada.)

or (E) Combine the following sets of sentences into one sentence without using *y* or *pero*.

3. El guardia urbano hizo parar los coches.
   El deja pasar a una viejecita.
   La viejecita llevaba un paraguas azul.
   (Expected combination: El guardia urbano hizo parar los coches para dejar pasar a una viejecita que llevaba un paraguas azul.)

Too many of these become busywork exercises. After a few examples, the students know what is expected of them and their energies are taken up with "completing the set."

A more interesting approach which challenges the students' ingenuity is as follows.

W 42 (E) Students are asked to think of simple sentences—any simple sentences. These are written on the chalkboard in the order in which they are supplied. Students are then given time, singly, in pairs, or in groups, to combine these sentences in any way they like to make a sensible paragraph.

No simple sentence may be used and only one *y* and one *pero* for joining clauses are permissible in each paragraph. Adverbs, adjectives, and a few phrases may be added to improve the narrative.

Below is an example of how the procedure might work.

Sentences provided by the students:

La pipa huele mal.
Nosotros vamos a la playa.
Todo va muy mal.
El viejo pegó al muchacho.
El periódico es de ayer.
La criada es española.
El tocadiscos estaba descompuesto.

Possible paragraph:

Hoy todo va muy mal. El viejo portero pegó al muchacho de los periódicos. Por eso, nuestra criada española tuvo que comprar un periódico, pero compró el de ayer. El tocadiscos de mi hermana está descompuesto y mi pipa huele mal. Por eso, vamos a la playa, de vacaciones.

Contractions

Writing in Spanish can be made more concise and succinct if certain clauses are reduced to phrases (*ante que partan—antes de su partida; porque tenían hambre—debido al hambre* and some phrases reduced to single words (*el que manejaba el taxi—el taxista; el hombre que mató al presidente—el asesino*). Instead of giving students a series of disconnected sentences to contract in specific ways, the teacher may provide a complete passage and ask students to use their ingenuity to reduce its length by at least a third.

Expansions

Students should have many opportunities to expand simple statements by using all the variations they have been learning—to flex their writing muscles as it were. Most textbooks provide a number of expansion exercises, but these are usually very dull affairs. Sometimes, a list of adjectives is set down beside a series of simple sentences and students are asked to insert before or after the nouns appropriate adjectives from the list. In other cases, the student is given a series of adverbs or adverbial phrases and asked to expand a set of simple sentences by inserting these at the appropriate places. Students may complete these exercises dutifully, but it is doubtful whether they thereby improve their ability to write in the language, since they contribute nothing of their own to the task. Much of the cognitive learning involved in these tasks can be accomplished as effectively or at least more briskly in the types of oral exercises described in Chapter 4.

Even if staid exercises like those described above appear in an imposed textbook, teachers should be prepared to think up more imaginative ways of presenting the same material. Writing assignments should be interesting, amusing, or useful—never boring or trivial.

Below are some suggestions for creative approaches to the same problems.

Expanding with adjectives. Students can be handed part of a passage like W43 (based on C58) and asked to describe the situation from several points of view.

W 43 (E or I) Según informes procedentes de Lima, Perú, un gran número de habitantes de las provincias andinas, situadas a más de cuatro mil metros, han empezado a emigrar hacia zonas más bajas, debido a las catastróficas consecuencias de intensas nevadas. En los helicópteros y aviones que ha enviado a la región el gobierno, con el fin de obtener informaciones sobre la situación, se encuentran, además de oficiales de la Fuerza Aérea y del Ejército, algunos representantes de la prensa y de la Cruz Roja.

Escriba usted cuatro descripciones de las escenas de la emigración, empleando tantos adjetivos y locuciones adjetivales como sea posible. En esas descripciones, adopte los siguientes puntos de vista:
1. el del piloto de un helicóptero que ha volado sobre la región;
2. el de un reportero radiofónico que habla a sus oyentes, directamente del helicóptero;
3. el de uno de los emigrantes, al llegar a un campo de refugiados;
4. el de un reportero que ha acompañado a los emigrantes.

Expanding with adverbs.

W 44 (E or I) Mientras se baña por la mañana, su vecina suele cantar en voz muy alta, pero eso no les gusta a los que la oyen. Escriba lo que dicen de ella las personas siguientes. (Tomando como base la frase *ella canta* y expandiendo el pronombre (*ella*) y el verbo (*canta*), indique los diferentes puntos de vista usando frases adverbiales, que expresen dónde, cuándo, cómo, por qué.)
1. En la oficina, el marido de la vecina le habla a su jefe.
2. Su hijo le habla a un compañero de escuela.
3. Usted le habla a su peluquero (o peluquera).

4. La sirvienta de la vecina le habla a una de sus amigas.

5. El cartero le habla a su mujer.

Possible answer No. 5: La señora de la calle Primo de Rivera, número quinientos, canta tan alto que la oigo desde la esquina. Y ¡qué mal canta, Jesús!

Expanding frames. Sometimes students are asked to expand what have been called *dehydrated sentences.*

W 45 (E or I) Write out the following outline in the past tense in complete sentences, supplying any words missing and making all necessary changes. Capital letters indicate new sentences and proper names.

Andorra / pequeño / país / situar / los Pirineos / Francia / España / Tener / superficie / 452 kilómetros cuadrados / diez y siete / mil / habitantes / La visitan / anualmente / miles / turistas / todas / partes / Europa / Ese / país / tener / sistema / gobierno / especial / Haber / dos / co-príncipes / Obispo / la Seo de Urgel / Presidente / Francia / quienes / ejercer / su / autoridad / a través / sus / representantes / país / Andorra / conservar / costumbres / muy antiguas / pero / modernizarse / aspectos / muy / diversos / sobretodo / relacionar / turismo.

W 46 Unraveled, the passage reads as follows:

Andorra es un pequeño país situado en los Pirineos, entre Francia e España. Tiene una superficie de 452 kilómetros cuadrados y diez y siete mil habitantes. La visitan anualmente miles de turistas de todas las partes de Europa. Ese país tiene un sistema de gobierno especial. Hay dos co-príncipes, el Obispo de la Seo de Urgel y el Presidente de Francia, quienes ejercen su autoridad a través de sus representantes en el país. Andorra conserva costumbres muy antiguas pero se ha modernizado en aspectos muy diversos, sobretodo en los relacionados al turismo.

This format can be useful for testing ability to introduce grammatical features at required points in the sentence, although the same kinds of demands are made by the cloze procedure within a framework which is much closer to normal language. (Cf. W28)

W 47 Andorra _____ un pequeño país situado _____ los Pirineos, _____ Francia _____ España. Tiene _____ superficie _____ 452 kilómetros _____ y diez y siete mil _____. La visitan anualmente miles _____ turistas _____ todas

—— partes de Europa. Ese país —— un sistema —— gobierno ——.
Hay dos co-príncipes, —— Obispo de la Seo de Urgel —— el Presidente
—— Francia, —— ejercen su autoridad a través —— sus representantes
en —— país. Andorra conserva costumbres muy —— pero —— ha
modernizado —— los aspectos relacionados —— turismo.

Commentary

A few more grammatical features are supplied for the student in W47
than in W45 and there are several places which allow for more than one
possibility, but these are not necessarily undesirable features. In W45,
students may become confused by the number of decisions they have to
make.

Because of their artificiality, dehydrated sentences can become something of a chore, and therefore counter-productive. A note of reality is
added if the dehydrated frame is presented in the form of *news headlines*
or *telegrams* for expansion.

Fortunately, there is available in the real world a type of script which
resembles the dehydrated sentence but which gives students authentic contact with many aspects of Hispanic life, namely, the *anuncios clasificados*
in the daily newspapers (*los diarios*). One copy of *La Vanguardia Española*,
for example, will supply the teacher with from three to four thousand items
from which to draw, dealing with everything from positions vacant, apartments to let, cars and animals for sale, lost property, or vacation opportunities. The less abbreviated classified advertisements supply useful clues
for the interpretation of the more abbreviated.

W48 (I) Write out in full the following advertisements from *La Vanguardia*,[2]
for apartments for sale. Study their location on the map, then write a
letter in Spanish to a friend telling him about the advantages of the
various apartments and why you decided to buy one rather than any of the
others.

1. PISO a estrenar c. Concepción Arenal, 900.000 p. 3 hab., com.,
20 m.2, coc. completa, lav. baño, aseo, exterior, mucho sol, esc. entrada
150.000 ptas. resto 10 años. Informes en Ausias March 51. Tls. 245-64-67
y 246-1300.

2. PISO estupendo zona Las Cortes, 932.000 ptas. 3 hab., com., coc.,
armarios baño calef. a gas c. tel., terraza, grande, asc. Entrada a convenir,
resto pagará 5.000 pesetas más resto hipoteca. Consúltenos en Ausias
March 51. Tels. 245-64-67 y 246-1300.

3. PISO Sepúlveda—Urgel, 4 hab., com., living, baño com., terraza, muy soleado 1.100.000 entrada p. 500.000 resto 6 años. Tel 254-75-43 mañanas A.P.I.

At the advanced level, such classified ads can be used as a basis for a practical writing project. Students can learn a great deal from the advertisements for positions vacant.

W 49 ADMINISTRATIVA—Buena remuneración, precisa empresa de Barcelona para su Departamento de Contabilidad, señorita joven, buena presencia, imprescindible catalán hablado, estudios de bachillerato o comercio, experiencia en trabajos administrativos. Absoluta reserva. Entrevista, tel. 254-90-32.

From a number of such listings, the students may make a list of the kinds of qualities and qualifications which seem to be sought (*buena presencia, estudios de bachillerato o comercio, experiencia en trabajos administrativos* and so on). They may then list in Spanish the qualifications they feel they possess, select an advertisement, and write an application for the position advertised.

THE IDEA FRAME

Dehydrated sentences and cloze tests control the structures the students will use. Some experienced teachers feel that progress toward expressive writing is more rapid if content rather than structure is controlled.[3] The student, relieved of the complete responsibility for the development of the content, can concentrate his energies on vigorous writing and can experiment with various possibilities for expressing an idea. (In this sense, the advertisements of W48 and W49 can be considered idea frames.)

1. The idea frame may be related to current reading. For instance, the reading passage R49 may be taken as a basis for writing activities. Here we have a short account of an apparent increase in the number of adolescents who run away from home. The following idea frames can be developed from the passage:

W 50 (I) A questionnaire is developed in such a way that, when it is answered consecutively, it produces a coherent paragraph:

1. ¿A qué problema social suelen referirse los periódicos españoles?
2. ¿Qué hacían los adolescentes que huían de casa, en el pasado?
3. ¿Por qué huyen de casa los adolescentes hoy día?

4. ¿Dónde viven la mayoría de los universitarios alemanes?

5. Según *Triunfo*. ¿cuál es la situación de los adolescentes en Francia?

A set of questions like this provides the student with a developing situation and some essential vocabulary. It should not, however, be the final stage. The student should then be asked to write creatively, thus reusing language material he has just acquired in new ways to express his own ideas.

W 51 (1) ¿Qué piensa Ud. acerca de las causas de ese problema social? En su parecer, ¿qué efecto puede tener sobre los padres la fuga de su hijo? ¿Y sobre el mismo adolescente?

2. Stevick's microtexts can provide useful idea frames (see Chapter 2, p. 51). After a text has been discussed orally, students may be asked to describe a similar situation in which they found themselves, the implications for this particular situation of the arguments in the text, the reasons why they could not agree with the writer of the text, and so on.

3. *The land of make-believe.*

The students as a group invent an imaginary setting as a background for some of their writing activities.

W 52 (E, I, or A) The students *invent a country,* give it a name (*Banagualpa?*), design its map, describe its history, its economy, its living conditions, and its problems with its neighbors. (If the class is working in small groups, each group has its own country and displays its map prominently on its section of the bulletin board.) From time to time, they write about events which affect *la República de Banagualpa.*

—El gobierno de Banagualpa ha declarado su intención de crear una universidad en San Simón, capital de la provincia de Tacuara. Explique usted las razones de esa decisión, describa los planes del Ministerio de Educación e Información banagualpense y las reacciones de los estudiantes de la vieja universidad de la capital de Banagualpa.

—¡Emergencia Nacional! Bajo el pretexto de proteger el régimen democrático de Banagualpa, el gobierno del vecino país de Eldorado acaba de invadir el territorio banagualpense. Se dice que una división del ejército eldoradeño ya se encuentra en las afueras de San Simón. Usted es corresponsal de la Radio Nacional de Banagualpa y debe escribir los boletines de noticias que va a transmitir esa radio durante los tres primeros días de la guerra.

W 53 (E or I) The students *invent a family* and keep a copy of all the data: number of children and their names, ages, and interests, cousins, aunts, and uncles, where they live, what they do for a living and what they enjoy doing in their leisure, their friends, neighbors, and pets, some of their well-remembered joys and misfortunes, and their hopes and plans for the future. They occasionally tackle problems like the following:

—La tía Cordelia, quien vive en un pueblecito de Andalucía, acaba de escribirles a sus parientes madrileños para informarlos de su próximo matrimonio con su amigo de juventud, don Tomás Porrón y Butifarra. Ella tiene 72 años. El tiene solamente 80. Escriba usted la correspondencia resultante de la noticia (cartas de una sobrina, de un ahijado, las respuestas de la tía Cordelia, etc.).

W 54 (E) For the elementary level, a treasure island (*la isla del tesoro*) is a fruitful notion. The students themselves will provide plenty of ideas for bringing it into existence and for projects associated with it. If the class is divided into groups, each group may use the same island but have its own theories on where and how the treasure is hidden.[4]

INTEGRATED LANGUAGE ACTIVITIES WITHIN AN IDEA FRAME
Writing with visual

1. (E or I) *Objects.* Students are shown some object and asked to write a *concise description* which would distinguish it from all other objects, e.g., a pencil, a book, an eraser, or a window. The descriptions are read out in class and other students try to show how the descriptions could apply to other objects. The written description is then further refined to meet these objections.

Variation. (E) An adaptation of *Kim's Game* (*¿De qué se acuerda Ud.?*). Students are shown briefly a tray of jumbled objects. Each student may look at the tray for one minute. Students then list as many objects as they can remember with a short descriptive comment, e.g., *un pañuelo blanco con flores azules.* Students read out their lists with descriptions and discuss the objects they forgot.

2. (E or I) *Persons.* Students write descriptions of no more than two sentences in length of persons in the class, in school, in the news, on television, or pictured in the textbook. No names are given. The descriptions written by one group are circulated to other groups who try to guess who has been described.

3. (E or I) *Pictures.* Students bring to class pictures selected from magazines or newspapers. Photographs of unexpected situations are useful.

These are distributed at random. Students write anecdotes, descriptions, or explanations about the pictures which are then read to the class. Each student may correct his version as he reads it and other students suggest improvements. The student then rewrites his version for grading. Students select by vote the most interesting compositions which will be posted, with the picture, on the bulletin board or reproduced in the class newspaper.

4. (E or I) *Cartoons.* Students working in pairs are given cartoon strips (*tiras cómicas*) without balloons (*globos*) or captions (*leyendas, títulos*). Each student writes captions for his series of sketches (*lenguaje escrito*), developing the story line. They then exchange cartoons and write balloon dialogue for each other's stories (*lenguaje hablado*). Pairs work together in perfecting their cartoons which are later displayed on the bulletin board for the amusement of the rest of the class. (Note: single picture cartoons are more difficult since they require witty comments. These may be used at the advanced level.)

5. (I or A) *Films.* Short silent films and documentary sound films may be used to stimulate written composition.

Writing with speaking and listening

Many activities are listed in C67, under Writing. To these may be added the following:

1. (E or I) The composition is given orally and discussed with other students before being written in its final form. (See *Oral Reports* in Chapter 1.)

2. (E or I) After students have acted out dialogues they have studied, they write, singly or in groups, original dialogues which recombine the material in new situations. They then act their dialogues for the rest of the class.

3. (E or I) Students are given a partial dialogue, that is, with the utterances of one participant but not the other. They make up the other half of the dialogue so that it fits in with the half supplied. (See also *Situation Tapes* in Chapter 1.) They then act out their different versions. (Originality and whimsicality are encouraged.)

4. (E or I) Activities 1, 2, and 3 in the section *Writing with visual,* p. 280, may be performed orally.

5. (E or I) *Charlando.* This is an old party game which makes an amusing writing exercise for groups of eight or less. The eight questions below are typed on a sheet with plenty of space, not only for the written answer but also to allow the paper to be turned back to hide what has been written. Student A answers the first question, turns back the sheet to hide the answer, and passes the sheet to Student B, who does likewise with the second question. The paper is passed on for all eight questions. Each student in the group begins a sheet, so that up to eight sheets can be

circulating at once. When the last questions have been answered, the papers are unfolded and the incongruous results are read to the group.

Preguntas: 1. ¿Quién?
2. ¿Encontró a quién?
3. ¿Dónde?
4. ¿Qué le dijo él?
5. ¿Qué le contestó ella?
6. ¿Qué hicieron los dos?
7. ¿Cuál fue el resultado de eso?
8. ¿Tiene una moraleja ese cuento?

6. (I or A) *Vamos a contar un cuento.* This is also played in groups. Each person is given a sheet of paper on which is written the opening sentence of a story. He reads what is written and adds a sentence of his own. The papers are then circulated around the group, with each student adding a sentence to each story. The last student in each case writes a concluding sentence and gives the story a title. The completed stories are then read aloud to the group.

7. (I or A) *¿Qué piensa Ud. de eso?* Students bring in information on current controversial issues which they present to the class. After class discussion of the data and the problem, students write out their own opinions on the issue, with any supporting information they have been able to find. They then present this viewpoint orally to the class, or to a small group, as a basis for further discussion.

8. (E) Students listen to a story on tape or as told to them by the teacher or an advanced student. They then write the story out in their own words, adding embellishments in keeping with the theme as they wish.

9. (I or A) Students take a story they have been reading, rewrite it in simple Spanish, then tell the story to an elementary class.

10. (I or A) Students interview in Spanish visiting native speakers or Spanish-speaking local residents about their special interests and then write up the interview for the class newspaper or the bulletin board. If the school newspaper can be persuaded to print the interview in Spanish, this will arouse the curiosity of other students about language study. (If no native speakers are available, a fellow Spanish teacher agrees to be interviewed in Spanish on some hobby or special interest.)

11. (E or I) Students are given a skeleton outline with blanks of a lecture, discussion, interview, story, or play they are to hear on tape. (At the elementary level, the outline may be like C57; at the intermediate level it will omit segments of vital information.) After listening, students either complete the outline or use it as a guide in writing up their own account of what they heard.

12. (I or A) Students listen to interviews with, or speeches by, political leaders, national figures, artists, or writers. They make notes on what they

have heard; they complete their notes in group discussion with other listeners; finally, they use the material they have noted in a research project.

13. (I or A) Students complete a written research project on a leading Spanish or Spanish-American personality. After this has been presented to the class and discussed, the students listen to a speech by, or interview with, this personality.

14. (I or A) Students watch a Spanish-language documentary film and use the information in it for a written research project.

15. (E) *Writing with listening at the beginning stage:* Postovsky[5] reports an experiment in which adult students of Russian performed written drills from spoken input, without speaking themselves, for one month of intensive study (six hours per day with additional homework). They heard only native speakers. At that stage, they were superior in morphology and also in pronunication to the regular audiolingual group. This approach is not necessarily transferable to other age groups and other situations, but it has interesting implications.

Writing with reading

Some suggestions have already been given in the section on *Integrating the Language Skills* in Chapter 7. To be able to write well, the student needs to read widely, thus familiarizing himself with the way recognized Spanish-language writers write. He must, through much experience with written texts, develop his ability to assimilate information directly in Spanish and to think in Spanish, so that his writing acquires the rhythms and associations of the Spanish-language writer.

1. (E or I) Students rework the linguistic material of a story by rewriting it from the viewpoint of a different character or from the changed perspective of one of the characters when writing in retrospect. R56 may be rewritten from the point of view of the old man living in the house or R49 as a reminiscence of a runaway person some years later.

2. (I or A) After careful reading of a text, students sum up its main thrust by giving it a title. They then identify the *main topics* and trace *the development of thought* through each paragraph. The processes associated with C52, C53, and C54 may be applied at this point. The students set down the main ideas in a logical sequence in simple active declarative sentences. This skeleton outline is then put away. Another day, the students take the outline and write a text of their own from it. They then compare their text with the original to see what they can learn linguistically from the comparison.

3. (I or A) The appropriate use of *logical connectives* is a problem in writing a foreign language, yet it is essential to the coherent development of ideas. This subject is discussed in Chapter 7, R50 and R51. The procedure in R51 can be applied to full paragraphs and to a reasoned argument of several paragraphs in length.

4. (I or A) An excellent intellectual and linguistic exercise is the *resumen:* the gathering together of the main ideas of the text in succinct summary form. This is a useful art in this busy age. To do this well, the student has to understand the text fully and rethink it in concentrated terms which he expresses in Spanish. Applied to sophisticated texts, this is certainly an advanced-level activity, but it can be practiced with less complicated texts at the intermediate level.

5. (I or A) Writing can be associated with *rapid reading.* Students need to learn to skim through informational material to draw from it the specific facts they require for some definite project. For this, they are given a set of questions beforehand and a specific period of time to find and write down the information from a long article or a chapter of a book.

(E) This approach can be used also with narrative material for *extensive reading,* as soon as students begin to read longer passages for pleasure. It can also serve as a familiarization process before the students study sections of the material in detail.

6. (I or A) Where students are encouraged to read Spanish articles and books of their own choice from an extensive reading library, they should be encouraged to write short *reactions* of a paragraph or two to what they have read. These brief communications should not be stereotyped book reports or summaries of the content, but quite personal, reflecting the concern of the student with some aspect of the reading material, information he gained from it, or imaginative ideas which came to him as he read it. The most interesting of these may, with the writer's permission, be posted on the bulletin board to encourage or discourage other students from choosing the same reading material. (This moves beyond the frame to expressive writing.)

7. (I) Benamou suggests the cloze procedure for introductory courses in *literature* for developing sensitivity to the author's choice of a particular word in preference to other semantic alternatives. He says, "This procedure has to do with both structure and divergence. There is structure when one can bring an incomplete text to a close without effort, that is, when the context itself provides enough clues as to the missing element. What matters is understanding the structural organization of the whole. There is divergence when the author's choice at this point in the message is not the expected end but rather an unexpected element. Here, the divergence between what the reader is expecting and what the author has said provides a measure of the style."[6]

8. (A) Further sensitivity to literary style can be encouraged at the advanced level by means of attempts to write short passages in imitation of the style and approach of particular authors.

9. Further suggestions will be found later in this chapter in *Normal Purposes of Writing,* 3 and 4.

PRACTICE IN STYLES OF WRITING (A)

Arapoff has suggested a format within which students may practice various styles of writing. Taking the content of a simple dialogue, students are encouraged to rewrite it in the form of direct address, narration, paraphrase, summary, factual analysis, assertion, in essay form, as argumentative analysis, with evaluation of the argument, as a critical review which objectively examines the validity of the evidence, as a term paper. This interesting approach should be studied in the original article, "Writing: A Thinking Process."[7]

Shortening Arapoff's sequence somewhat, the teacher would proceed as follows.

1. Students would be given a short dialogue like W55 as *foundational content.*

W55
ENRIQUE	Hola, María.
MARÍA	Hola, Enrique.
ENRIQUE	¿A dónde vas?
MARÍA	Pues, voy a la playa. ¿Quieres venir conmigo?
ENRIQUE	Pero, ¡si va a llover! Fíjate en esas nubes grises.
MARÍA	¡Qué va! No es posible que empiece a llover otra vez. ¡Hace una semana que llueve todos los días!

2. Next students rewrite W55 as *direct address in a narrative framework.*

W56 —Buenos días, María—dice Enrique al encontrarla en la calle.
—Buenos días, Enrique—contesta ella.
—¿A dónde vas? —le pregunta él.
—Pues, voy a la playa. ¿No quieres venir conmigo? —le pregunta ella.
—Pero, ¡si va a llover! —contesta él, señalando el cielo con el dedo. —¡Fíjate en esas nubes grises!
—¡Qué va! —contesta María —No es posible que empiece a llover otra vez. ¡Hace una semana que llueve todos los días!

3. Students then write a paraphrase of W55 in *narrative form.*

W57 Al encontrar a María en la calle, Enrique la saluda y ella lo reconoce de pronto. Al preguntarle él adónde va, ella le contesta que va hacia la playa y lo invita a acompañarla. Enrique le dice que va a llover y le muestra el cielo cubierto de nubes grises. María se resiste a creer que pueda llover, porque ya hace una semana que llueve constantemente.

4. This is followed by a *sumario,* written very concisely in one or two sentences.

W 58 Cuando María invitó a Enrique a acompañarla a la playa, él le dijo que iba a llover, pero ella no quiso creer que pudiera empezar a llover de nuevo después de una semana de lluvia.

5. Next, the main argument of the passage is set out in the form of an *assertion.*

W 59 Enrique y María no estaban de acuerdo sobre el tiempo. El era pesimista y ella optimista.

6. Finally, this analysis leads to a short *essay* on optimists and pessimists.

W 60 Escriba usted una composición corta sobre el asunto siguiente: el optimista frente al pesimista.

7. The further steps proposed by Arapoff—*argumentative analysis, evaluation of the arguments, critical review* of the essay, and *term paper* would require a careful study of styles of writing. The complete project would be a very interesting undertaking for a Spanish major, who must learn at some stage to write various kinds of essays, seminar and term papers, and even critical reviews, for literature courses.

IV. Expressive writing or composition

If we wish students to write Spanish spontaneously, we must give them opportunities to acquire confidence in their ability to write. We must, however, expect shavings on the floor in the process. Learning to write is not a natural development like learning to speak. As Arapoff has observed: "Everyone who is a native speaker is not necessarily a 'native writer.' "[8]

Our students will have varying degrees of interest in writing as a form of self-expression, even in their native language. If they are to submit willingly to the discipline of learning to write well in Spanish, they will need to see some *purpose in the writing activity.* In this way writing is differently motivated from speaking, which is an activity in which most people readily and frequently engage every day of their lives. In speaking, a student without much to contribute can often adroitly involve others and support them enough, with his attention and interest, to free himself of the necessity to participate fully. (This support function is a normal form of communicative involvement which the student of a foreign language should also learn to fulfill acceptably.) Faced with a blank page, however, the unimaginative student does not have this alternative.

Personality plays an important role in writing, as it does in speaking. Some feel inhibited as soon as they take pen in hand, although they might have expressed themselves orally without inhibitions. These students need a clearly defined topic, often an opening sentence, or even a framework, to get them started. Just as some are terse in speech, others are incapable of being expansive in writing—they do not waste words and elaborate the obvious. These students find it hard to write a full paragraph, or a complete composition, on something as irrelevant to their preoccupations as "What I did last weekend" or "A day on a farm." We must not forget that there are also some students who are most reluctant to expose their real thoughts on paper, sometimes because, in their experience, teachers have never really cared what they thought. In speech they can be vague, whereas in writing, this is rarely acceptable, except in poetry. For them also, writing as a class exercise is unappealing.

For these reasons among others, we cannot expect all of our students to achieve a high standard of expressive writing in our foreign-language class. For many, we will be satisfied if they are able to say what they want or need to say with clarity and precision.

There are students, of course, who enjoy writing, and these will want to write from the beginning. Many of them will have already acquired a style of writing in their native language which has been praised and encouraged. Such students often feel frustrated when they find they cannot express themselves in the foreign language at the same level of sophistication as they do in their native language. In their efforts to do so, they often load their writing with poorly disguised translations of their English thought. The enthusiasm of these students must be encouraged, while they are guided to see that writing well in another language means thinking in the forms of that other language. This does not mean just the adoption of its semantic distinctions and syntactic structures, but also its approach to logic and the development of an idea. Even in writing style, there are culturally acquired differences.[9] A student whose native culture encourages allusive and indirect rhetorical development finds it hard to be explicit, just as one who has learned to express his ideas by building logical step on logical step finds it difficult to indulge in what seem to him digressions from the line of thought. Even students who are natural writers need guidance in adapting to the rhetorical style of a new language.

WHAT WRITING MAY BE CALLED "EXPRESSIVE"?

"Expressive" writing does not necessarily mean imaginative or poetic writing. Not all students have the gift of imagination. Writing is expressive if it says what the student wants it to say in the situation. If writing is to be a natural, self-directed activity, the student must have the choice between writing for practical purposes or creating a work of imagination. Even where guidance is offered, that is, where the student is given a structure and facts on which to base his writing, he should always have the privilege of ignoring what is offered if he can write from his own inner inspiration.

What is needed is writing for the *normal purposes of writing,* not just as a self-contained language exercise. In a diversified foreign-language program,[10] students have the opportunity to concentrate on the use of Spanish for specific purposes: the study of literature, the reading of contemporary informational materials, concentrated aural-oral development, translation or simultaneous interpretation, the learning of special skills through Spanish (e.g., Spanish or Spanish-American cooking, music, or art), or the acquiring of certain subject matters taught in Spanish (e.g., Spanish or Spanish-American history or political institutions). Clearly, then, what is "expressive" in such cases depends on the student's own goals.

Except in specialized programs, where students learn to write in the language in order to study in the same classes as native speakers, writing should not be a distinctive activity. It should, rather, be a natural ingredient in ongoing activities. Since one writes better in a language on a subject which one has experienced in that language, students more inclined to the practical should have experiences learning in Spanish about practical things, while imaginative topics will spring naturally out of experiences (whether graphic, aural, or visual) with literature of the imagination.

NORMAL PURPOSES OF WRITING

These will be organized in six categories under two main headings: *Practical* (everyday living, social contact, getting and giving information, study purposes) and *Creative* (entertainment, self-expression).

Practical use

　　1. *Everyday living.*

　　a. *Forms and applications.* Students learn to fill in customs declarations, passport applications, entry permits, identity information, and applications for posts abroad. (The professor who wished to spend his sabbatical doing research at the *Biblioteca Nacional* hardly impressed the administration with his command of Spanish when he wrote down his wife's occupation as *esposa de casa* instead of *sus labores.*) Where there are Spanish-speaking communities nearby, students may go and help monolinguals fill in social security, medical benefit, or welfare claims.

　　b. *Arrangements and records.* Students should know how to write notes and notices setting out arrangements for travel, meetings, concerts, dances, weekend camps, or competitions. They should be able to write up short accounts of activities for Spanish club records or for the class or school newspaper.

c. *Orders and complaints.* Students should know how to order goods and services, and how to protest errors in shipping or billing, shoddy quality of goods, or neglect of services. They should be able to write for hotel rooms, information on study abroad, or subscriptions to newspapers and magazines. They should know the correct formulas for commercial and official correspondence of various kinds.[11] These can all be given a realistic twist by basing them on information in newspapers and tourist pamphlets. Students may write, for instance, to the *Ministerio de Información y Turismo* or the university in the town in which they are interested and request information for friends and relatives, if not for themselves, or for use with a research project.

2. *Social contact.* Students should learn the correct formulas for congratulations and various greetings, and ways of notifying others of family events or changes of circumstances. They should be encouraged to use this knowledge by sending such greetings and announcements to friends and correspondents, or displaying them on the bulletin board.

Students should be encouraged to write to correspondents in Spain and Spanish-speaking areas. Classes should be twinned with classes of a similar level abroad, so that they may exchange projects giving personal, local, and national information, youth trends and customs, ways of spending leisure time, and so on.

3. *Getting and giving information.* Students gather information for projects, collate it, and report it to others in written form. They prepare comments in writing on controversial articles in newspapers and magazines for later presentation as oral reports or for circulation in the class as a basis for discussion. They may take articles reporting the same event from two Spanish-language newspapers (or discussing the same topic from two magazines), and write résumés of the content for discussion in class. They may prepare items of international, national, local, or school news for wall, class, or school newspapers. They may take turns in preparing weekly bulletins of news from Spanish-language newspapers or newscasts for their own class and for distribution to more junior classes. They distribute similarly reviews of Spanish-language films which are being shown at school or in the local area.

4. *Study purposes.* Students who intend to make Spanish a major study need practice in taking notes of lectures (*conferencias*) and of reading material (*lecturas*). They should know how educated native speakers of Spanish develop a line of thought. They need to be able to write good summaries (*resúmenes*), reports (*informes*), essays (*composiciones, ensayos*), and literary analyses (*análisis literarios*).

Creative expression

5. *Entertainment.* Students write skits, one-act plays, or scripts for their own radio and television programs (which may be taped or shown on

closed-circuit television for the entertainment of other classes). They write out program notes for a fashion parade, or captions for a display of students' baby pictures or unidentified photographs of famous people. They write parodies of well-known advertisements or radio and television commercials. They prepare puzzles and mystery stories for other members of the class to solve.

6. *Self-expression.* Students write stories, poems, nonsense rhymes (*trabalenguas*), nursery rhymes, biographical sketches, and autobiographical narratives. They keep personal records of their thoughts and experiences as resources from which to draw material for creative writing. (A good starting point for the inexperienced, or those lacking in confidence, is the writing of a story, poem, or autobiographical incident in the style of an author they have just been reading.)

WRITING AS A CRAFT

Even with motivation to express oneself in written form, coherent, readable material does not necessarily flow from the pen. Nor is such writing merely a matter of composing carefully constructed grammatical sentences. Lucid writing is only possible when the writer has clarified his own thinking on the subject and knows how he wishes to present his viewpoint or develop his argument. The idea may be obscure, even esoteric or hermetic, but the writer knows that this is what he wants to say and the reader tries to penetrate his thought. Muddled thinking, however, leaves the reader confused and frustrated.

Arapoff calls the process basic to writing "purposeful selection and organization of experience."[12] If one of the objectives of the Spanish course is ability to write well and expressively in Spanish, then the teacher must guide the student in developing his skills in analyzing his thoughts, shaping them into central and subordinate ideas, and developing a line of thought which carries the reader to the heart of the matter. The Spanish teacher cannot presume that the students already know these things from some other course.

How can we interest students in the process of reflecting on what they really want to say and organizing it before starting to write? This initial stage becomes more attractive as a group experience. The students in the group pool their ideas, break off to gather more information if necessary, discuss various ways of organizing their ideas into a central line of thought, with major topics and subordinate ideas related to these major topics. They decide on a title to express the central theme, a way of introducing the material so that the reader's attention is caught, and the type of conclusion to which they will direct the development of thought. The actual writing is then done in small groups (or individually, if there are students who prefer to work alone). The draft elaboration of the theme is then discussed by the group; the choice of words is refined, and the syntactic structure is tightened up, with transitional elements supplied where these are still lacking. Finally the rhythm and flow of the writing receive special attention, as the completed text is read aloud. The group texts are then dittoed for presentation to and discussion by the class as a whole.

This type of group elaboration of a composition ensures some proofreading for inaccuracies of spelling and grammar. Valette[13] suggests that the group approach be used also to establish criteria for correcting and assessing the texts prepared by the groups. The students are asked to rank the compositions before them in order of preference. They then "describe which qualities they think characterize a good composition. The class might come up with categories such as: organization, good opening sentence, appropriate use of vocabulary, original imagery, etc." The class then looks over each composition and rates it on a scale decided on by themselves and weighted according to group decision. After the class has perfected its scale in relation to the actual compositions it is considering, this rating scale is adopted by the teacher for grading tests of writing. Valette's procedure has two advantages: the students consider the system fair since they participated in its design and modification, they also understand by what criteria their writing will be graded, and they have guidelines for improving their work in the future.

Some teachers will object that this system cannot ensure that all errors in the text are corrected. This is true. The question arises: for expressive writing should all inaccuracies and errors be corrected in every composition? Most of us have ourselves experienced the discouragement of staring in horror at a veritable forest of red marks and comments on a piece of writing over which we had toiled in the belief that we were achieving something worthwhile. The place for fastidious correction is at the stage of cognition and production exercises. If students are making serious errors persistently, more practice exercises should be provided at the point of difficulty. When students are writing to express their ideas, corrections should focus on incomprehensibility, or inapt word choice, and errors in grammatical form or syntactic structure which mislead the reader. The most serious mistakes must be those which native readers can tolerate the least, rather than those kinds of inaccuracies which native writers themselves commit. Students can be trained to proofread their work for blemishes, as suggested in the previous chapter, but penalizing students for sheer inaccuracy of surface detail at the expressive stage encourages the production of dull, unimaginative, simple sentences, with students taking refuge in the forms they have thoroughly mastered over a long period of study.

With expressive writing, students should learn to check their completed drafts for things other than accents and spelling errors. They should be looking at the way their thought falls naturally into paragraphs and their use of logical connectives and other transitional devices which show the development of thought and cement internal relationships. They should seek ways to eliminate repetitions, tighten the structure through judicious use of complex and compound sentences, and highlight ideas through nuances of word choices and their combinations.

The ever-present danger of anglicisms in structure and lexical choice cannot, of course, be ignored. Students should be sensitized to this problem, which is most likely to arise when they try to express a complex idea in the foreign language. Students should be encouraged to break down a complex idea into a series of simple active affirmative declarative sentences in Spanish which represent the facets of its meaning, and then to rebuild them into a complex or compound sentence which responds to the rules of combination and modification in Spanish as they know them. Francis Bacon said: "Reading maketh a full man, conference a ready man, and writing an exact man."[14] It is when we try to express our meaning that we discover where our ideas are fuzzy or incomplete. Trying to set down the elements of our meaning in simple form pinpoints areas of confusion and uncertainty and forces us to ask ourselves what we are really trying to say. Then, and then only, can we seek the best way to express our ideas in another language.

It cannot be emphasized too strongly that students learn to write well in Spanish by doing all the planning and drafting of their compositions, and discussion of appropriate content, *in Spanish*. The teacher must help the student from the beginning to acquire confidence in writing directly in the foreign language. Where students have done their initial planning and early writing in English and have then translated what they wanted to say into Spanish, the writing is usually stilted and anglicized, lacking the feeling for the language and natural flow and rhythm toward which the student should be aiming. If the flexibility measures recommended earlier in this chapter are adopted, students will have experience, even at the elementary level, in trying to express their own ideas and imaginings in *Spanish*. Where the writing program is associated with oral language activities of the creative type described in Chapter 2, students begin to think in Spanish and to compose Spanish sentences spontaneously without nervousness or inhibition.

Correcting and evaluating expressive writing

A number of systems for grading expressive writing have been proposed, each of which has merits for particular situations or students with specific aims.

The following guidelines have emerged from the experience of many teachers.

1. One learns to write sequential prose by writing sequential prose.

Practice exercises are merely muscle-flexing. What one does correctly in structured practice, one does not necessarily observe when trying to express one's own meaning.

2. It is better to draw a student's attention to a few important faults in his writing at a time and to encourage him to improve these, rather than to confuse him with a multiplicity of detail which he cannot possibly assimilate immediately.

3. The persistent errors of a number of students lead to group discussions and practice. At the intermediate and advanced levels these errors provide a logical framework for a review of grammar based on existential frequency of commission.

4. Students should be encouraged to keep checklists of their own weaknesses, since these, as with errors in spoken language, will vary from individual to individual.

5. Time should be taken in class for students to check their work before submitting it for grading. Editing is a normal part of native-language writing and should be equally normal for foreign-language writing. Research has shown that students "can reduce their grammatical and mechanical errors—including spelling and capitalization—more than half by learning how to correct errors before submitting their papers."[15]

6. Similarly, class time should be given to the perusing and immediate correction of a script in which the errors have been marked, so that the student may ask questions and receive explanations as he needs them.

7. An active correction process is more effective than the passive reading by the student of corrections written in by the instructor.

8. Several active correction processes have been proposed:

a. Errors are merely underlined. Students, alone or in groups, decide in what way their writing was inadequate and make changes.

b. Errors are underlined and marked with a symbol which acts as a guide to the kind of error made (e.g., T = tense, A = agreement, V = lexical choice, etc.).

c. Errors are underlined and given numbers which refer to sections of a brief review of grammar rules to which all students have access.

d. Errors are underlined, with no comment or symbols, but no grade is assigned until the student resubmits a corrected script.

e. Errors are not indicated specifically, but a check mark is placed in the margin opposite the line where the error occurs. The student must identify the actual error himself.

f. Knapp[16] adopts a positive, rather than a negative, approach to grading expressive writing. He establishes a Composition Check-List of items to which students should pay attention in writing compositions. While correcting, he assigns red pluses for all items successfully handled. Students try, from composition to composition, to increase the number of pluses on their individual checklists. Lack of pluses arouses student concern so that they seek help in overcoming specific weaknesses. (Careless mistakes are merely underlined.)

9. Writing in more felicitous expressions can be time-wasting for the teacher unless he makes few such suggestions, discusses these with the students, and encourages them to use the suggested expressions in later writing.

Scoring systems

The subjective nature of grades assigned to written expression has long been criticized. Where one teacher is involved and the students know what that teacher expects, the unreliability of the scoring and ranking is reduced. In allotting a grade, an experienced teacher is considering the interplay of a number of factors. If the number of scripts is not too great, and the teacher is not too tired or harassed, his grading will normally be reasonably consistent.

Inexperienced teachers would, however, do well to consider what qualities they are looking for and to assign grades according to some weighted system until they acquire more confidence. Where more than one corrector is involved with the ranking of one group or of parallel groups, agreement should be reached on the weighting they are assigning to different factors.

The following weighted checklist is proposed for discussion:

W 61 *Weighted assessment scheme for expressive writing in a foreign language.*

1. Organization of content (focus, coherence, clarity, originality)

                                                                20 per cent

2. Structure
   - a. sentence structure (appropriateness and variety)
   - b. morphology (accurate use of paradigms, adjective agreements, forms of pronouns, etc.)
   - c. use of verbs (forms, tenses, moods, sequence of tenses, agreements, etc.)   40 per cent
3. Variety and appropriateness of lexical choices   20 per cent
4. Idiomatic flavor (feeling for the language, fluency)   20 per cent

Commentary

1. At the advanced level, there will also be consideration of content in addition to organization of content. Further variation of this checklist will be developed where students have reached the stage of writing in Spanish essays on literary, cultural, or other informational subjects.

2. Students should be aware of the criteria adopted for the assessment of their writing.

Research in native-language writing[17] has shown that for assessment of achievement, two compositions on different subjects written on two separate occasions produce a more reliable evaluation than one composition. It has been found that the performance of good writers varies more than that of poor writers. The fairest procedure is to assess the student according to the grade of the more successful of the two compositions. Apart from the common factor of day-to-day variability in inspiration and energy, the finding seems intuitively transferable to the assessment of foreign-language writing, in that a particular student may find one composition topic unduly cramping from the point of view of content or vocabulary area.

Translation

Translation is both a skill and an art, of considerable practical and esthetic value in the modern world, as it has been down the ages. It provides access for millions to the scientific and technical knowledge, the great thoughts, the artistic achievements, and the societal needs and values of the speakers of many tongues.

In foreign-language teaching, it has been at different periods either an accepted or a controversial element, depending on prevailing objectives and teaching preferences. It was a keystone of the learning and testing process in the grammar-translation approach. Direct-method theorists de-emphasized it as a learning device, excluding it from early instruction as much as possible while admitting it as an art at advanced stages. Audio-lingual textbooks usually printed English translations of the early Spanish dialogues and included translation drills for practice. Translation of continuous passages from the native language into the foreign language was, however, considered an advanced exercise in this approach also.

Unfortunately, much of the discussion of the place of translation in foreign-language learning has been at cross-purposes, since the kind of translation and its function in the learning process have not been specified. The following aspects of translation need to be differentiated in such discussion.

1. Translation may be from the foreign language into the native language or from the native language to the foreign language.
2. Translation may be *oral* or *written.*
3. Translation may be used as a *learning* or a *testing* device or it may be practiced for its intrinsic value as a *practical skill* or a *discriminating art.*
4. Translation may be *simultaneous,* as in oral interpretation, which draws on the interpreter's internalized knowledge of both languages, or

carefully *edited* and re-edited, after consultation of dictionaries and grammars, as in literary or technical translation.

5. *Oral translation* from the foreign language to the native language may be a classroom technique by which the teacher rapidly clarifies the meaning of an unfamiliar word or phrase in listening or reading exercises. It may be the way the student is required to demonstrate his aural or reading comprehension. It may also, at the advanced level, be a sophisticated activity like oral interpretation. (Since most professional oral interpreters translate only from the foreign language into their native, or dominant, language, this would also be the direction of any classroom practice of this demanding process.) Oral translation from the native to the foreign language may be used for practice or testing of the application of grammatical rules.

6. *Written translation* into the native language may be a device to test comprehension of factual detail. On the other hand, written translation into Spanish may be used to test application of the rules of grammar, as in the translation of sample sentences, or of passages of English constructed along the lines of W29 and W63. Either type of translation may be an advanced activity to test ability to transfer meaning comprehensively and elegantly from one language code to the other.

In view of these many ways in which the term "translation" is used, it is difficult to take a position for or against its use in the foreign-language class. Rather, one should consider the possible contributions to language learning of each of these activities at various levels in relation to the objectives of the course.

The main objection to translation as a teaching device has been that it interposes an intermediate process between the concept and the way it is expressed in the foreign language, thus hindering the development of the ability to think directly in the new language. It may be argued that even when students are taught by direct methods, they often mentally interpose this intermediate translation process themselves in the early stages. Such mental translation usually disappears as a superfluous step when students become familiar with the language through continual exposure to it. Teachers will need to decide for themselves which position they will take in this controversy, whether to eschew all translation or use it judiciously for certain purposes. Here we will discuss such judicious use and also opportunities to engage in translation as an activity in its own right at the advanced level.

TRANSLATION AS A TEACHING/LEARNING DEVICE
Translation from the foreign to the native language

This process is useful for clarifying the meaning of certain abstract concepts, some function words and logical connectives, and some idiomatic expressions which context alone does not illuminate. Such translation, if used too frequently, can become a crutch, reducing the amount of effort given to inferencing[18]—a process which is of considerable importance in autonomous language use. Some teachers like to make quick oral checks of comprehension of reading and listening materials by asking for native-language equivalents of certain segments of the messages. In moderation, and in association with other checks of comprehension conducted in the foreign language itself, this procedure can pinpoint and eliminate some areas of vagueness for the student.

In the early stages, some judicious translation of common expressions can familiarize students with different levels of language. Such expressions will normally be presented through situations in which they would be used. Even then, however, it is not always perfectly obvious to the student that different relationships are expressed by the choice, for instance, of *Buenos días, Francisco. ¿Cómo está usted?* rather than, *Hola, Paco, ¿Qué hubo?*

Translation from the native to the foreign language

1. *Translation of isolated sentences.* This process as a practice exercise has been brought into disrepute by its excesses. Sentences of improbable or infrequent occurrence, constructed so that they positively bristle with problems, have made language learning an ordeal for many students, without doing more than convincing them of their inadequacies. Such sentences may still be found in many contemporary textbooks.

The process can be useful, however, when a set of short sentences which focus on a particular grammatical feature is used as a stimulus for eliciting formulations in Spanish, as in the following examples.

W 62 For practicing the form and order of pronoun objects before the verb.

Diga en español:
1. I give him the book.
2. I give her the book.
3. He gives her the book.
4. He gives me the book.
5. She gives it to me.
6. He gives it to her . . .

Commentary

W62 is a familiarization exercise. Conducted orally, it may be a chaining activity, with students proposing short sentences for each other to translate. It may appropriately be accompanied by action. See also G51.

2. *Ejercicio de imitación.* This is a specially constructed exercise which is useful for identifying student problems in grammatical and vocabulary

usage in written Spanish. The instructor extracts from a passage of
Spanish, which has been read and studied, useful features he wishes the
student to be able to use. He then prepares for translation into Spanish
an English text which requires the use of these features. The student trans-
lates the passage without consulting the original on which it is based and
then examines the original to see where he can improve or correct his
translation. Group discussion is useful at this stage.

W 63   *Ejercicio de imitación* based on R38.

Tradúzcase al español:

After a five-day visit to Barcelona, Johnny and Guillermo were about to
take the train for Italy. They were met at the station by Gloria Berenguer,
a pleasant Catalan girl who had been at the university with them in the
United States. She had shown them around the city during their stay, and
now she was there to say good-bye to them.

"Gloria," said Guillermo, "would you and Johnny get on the train and
try to find an empty compartment? I'd better stay here and keep an eye on
the baggage." . . .

TRANSLATION AS A SPECIALIZED STUDY[19]

Once we go beyond the transposition into Spanish of sentences and
sequences of sentences that either parallel what the student has already
encountered or test what he is learning at the time, we approach translation
as a demanding, often frustrating, study in its own right. Genuine translation involves the exploration of the potential of two languages. It not only
involves the student in serious consideration of the expressive possibilities
of the foreign language, but also extends his appreciation of the semantic
extensions and limitations of his own language, and the implications for
meaning of its syntactic options. It is, then, an appropriate undertaking in
an advanced course, or even at the intermediate level when a particular
group of students is especially interested in attaining competence in it. It
may be offered as an advanced option in an individualized or small-group
program, or as a specialized course among diversified options.

Translation must be distinguished from the extracting of information
from a text. Much information can be gleaned without exact translation,
although readers may resort to translation at times to clarify important
details. (See *Reading for Information* in Chapter 6, p. 171.)

Translation and meaning

The teacher will want to sensitize students interested in translation to the
many facets of meaning with which they will have to deal. This provides
an excellent context for familiarizing them with basic concepts of linguistics.

Translation involves careful analysis of the meaning of the source text. Students consider various aspects of the meaning they have extracted and rethink it in terms of the target language so that as little is added and as little is lost as possible. They learn a great deal as they discover that it is not always possible to attain exact equivalance and as they evaluate possible versions to see which most fully captures all the implications of the original. They will find that they need to look beyond single words, segments of sentences, or even complete sentences to whole stretches of discourse as they make their decisions. Much can be thrashed out in group working sessions as they ask themselves some searching questions[20] about the text they wish to translate.

1. What type of writing does the passage represent: descriptive, narrative, conversational, expository, argumentative, polemical, or some other? What are the features of this style in the target language?

2. What is the overall meaning of this passage in its context in a larger discourse? Is it a serious development of ideas or is it satirical? Is it deliberately vague? Is the original inaccurate or fallacious? It is carelessly put together? (Any of these characteristics, and many others, must be faithfully reproduced.)

3. Is the tone of the passage assured, hesitant, dogmatic, humorous, solemn, neutral, or something else?

4. Is the passage boring, repetitive, exciting, laconic, provocative, mysterious . . . ?

5. Is the general structure such that it can be reproduced in the translation, or would an equivalent in the other language require different sentence division or repositioning of segments for emphasis or for other reasons?

6. How can the time relationships in the source text be most clearly expressed in the target languages? (This is not always a question of which tenses to select.)

7. For which lexical items is the semantic content different from seemingly equivalent lexical items in the target language? Should additional lexical items be introduced to carry the meaning which would otherwise be lost, or can this extra meaning be carried by grammatical morphemes, or by implications from syntactic choices?

W 64 He ate in the dark or by the light through the stove door left ajar. There was still no lamp, no candle. The fixer set a small splinter aside to mark the lost day *and crawled onto his mattress.*[21]

Commentary

The very expressive segment we have italicized indicates how quite simple expressions may be very difficult to translate succinctly into another language. He "crawled onto his mattress" in English contains the ideas not only of movement, direction, and weariness, but also the almost animal level of life to which the fixer has been reduced. *El se arrastró hasta su colchón* contains the ideas of movement, direction, and weariness, without the feeling of hopelessness of the original. On the other hand, *arrastrarse* is perhaps closer in meaning to "to crawl" than it is to "to crawl onto," and therefore a different rendering, such as: *el se desmoronó en su colchón* would probably capture more faithfully the intended meaning of the original passage. The fact that even among native speakers of Spanish there is not total agreement as to which translation is superior serves to highlight the difficulty of rendering in one language a thought originally conceived (or expressed) in another.

8. Do superficially equivalent expressions in the original and in the proposed translation have different denotative (referential) meaning or connotative (emotive) meaning? (*Falsos amigos*[22] fall into these categories.)

9. Are there sociolinguistic or emotional levels of language or specialized fields of knowledge implicit in the text which will need careful attention in the translation?

10. Are there culturally related items in the source text which will need to be rethought in relation to the cultural concepts of the speakers of the target language, or should literal translations be used for these to preserve in the translation the foreign flavor of the original?

11. Are there figurative, rhetorical, or specifically literary aspects of the language of the original which require careful transposition?

12. Are there any idiosyncratic features of the author's style observable in this passage? Are there any mechanisms in the target language which would convey the same impression?

Clearly such a task is formidable for a language learner. If students are not to become discouraged, they will need to be given much practice with translation graded in difficulty, with particular passages selected because they allow the student to focus on specific problems. Students will also derive considerable benefit from pooling ideas in group preparation of a final translation, and from discussion of the efficacy of published translations of passages they themselves have attempted to translate.

W 65 Compare this English translation with the original Spanish passage from *Requiem por un Campesino Español* by Ramón J. Sender.[23] Do you think the translator has captured the level of language and tone of the original and reproduced the full meaning?

A. Mosén Millán se decía: es pronto. Además, los campesinos no han acabado las faenas de la trilla. Pero la familia del difunto no podía faltar.

Seguían sonando las campanas que en los funerales eran lentas, espaciadas y graves. Mosén Millán alargaba las piernas. Las puntas de sus zapatos asomaban debajo del alba y encima de la estera de esparto. El alba estaba deshilándose por el remate. Los zapatos tenían el cuero rajado por el lugar donde se doblaban al andar, y el cura pensó: tendré que enviarlos a componer. El zapatero era nuevo en la aldea. El anterior no iba a misa, pero trabajaba para el cura con el mayor esmero, y le cobraba menos. Aquel zapatero y Paco el del Molino habían sido muy amigos.

B. Mosén Millán said to himself: "It's too soon. Besides, the peasants haven't finished their threshing yet." But the dead man's family would have to come. Those slow, ponderous and solemn funeral bells were still tolling. Mosén Millán stretched his legs and the tips of his shoes appeared from below his alb and rested on the rush mat. The alb was ravelling at its hem, his shoes were cracked where they bent in walking. "I'll have to send them to be repaired," thought the priest. The cobbler was newly arrived in the village. The former one had not attended Mass, but he had worked for the priest with the greatest care and had charged him less. That cobbler and Paco had been fast friends.

W 66 Discuss the decisions made by the translator of this passage from *Un millón de Muertos* by José María Gironella. Do you consider them necessary and effective?

A. Una hora después, todos los milicianos que participaron en la gran operación se habían retirado a sus casas y casi todos dormían. Dormía incluso el catedrático Morales, a quien de repente entraba una gran fatiga. Dormía también Cosme Vila, el cual había abierto la puerta de la alcoba descalzo y de puntillas para no despertar al pequeño. Su mujer le preguntó, en la oscuridad: "¿Qué hora es?" Cosme Vila contestó, desnudándose: "Las cuatro y media."

A las cinco empezó la gran operación del dolor. Mientras hubo estrellas en el cielo y camiones repletos de milicianos recorrieron la ciudad, ningún familiar de ningún detenido, ni siquiera de los que fueron arrancados de sus hogares aquella misma noche, se atrevió a salir. Había corrido la voz de lo que iba a suceder; pero tener miedo no era excusa válida para enfrentarse con las patrullas. Así que, a lo largo de la noche, el alma murió a cada chirriar de neumático y los ojos se clavaron en las rendijas de la persianas.

B. An hour later, all the militiamen who had taken part in the big roundup had gone home and most of them were asleep. Professor Morales was sleeping, too, suddenly overtaken by immense weariness. Shortly after opening the bedroom door on tiptoe in his bare feet so as not to awaken the child, Cosme Vila too had sunk into sleep. His wife had spoken out of the darkness, asking, "What time is it?" and Cosme Vila had replied as he was undressing, "Four-thirty."

The exodus of the bereft began at five. As long as there were still stars in the sky and trucks filled with militiamen roaming the streets of the city, no relative of any detained man, not even of those dragged from their homes that very night, would dare to go out. News of what had been about to happen had spread rapidly, but to be afraid was no valid excuse for confronting the patrols. Accordingly, throughout the night, the soul fainted at every slither of tires and the eyes remained riveted on the slats of the venetian blinds.[24]

Translation into English

As with other aspects of the foreign-language course, translation can begin with *useful things which are near at hand.*

1. Students translate Spanish *labels, slogans,* and *advertisements,* trying to produce English versions which ring true to the commercial style to which they are accustomed. This activity can lead to interesting discussions of differences of approach to the consumer.

2. Students translate *instructions* for the use of products for local merchants (car salesmen or hair stylists, for instance) or for relatives, or *cooking recipes* for themselves or friends. Where necessary, they use specialized dictionaries to help them.

3. Students translate interesting sections of *letters from correspondents* to publish in the school newspaper or share with others in the geography or social studies class.

4. Students translate *historical documents,* such as the *Carta de las Naciones Unidas,* for use in their history class; selections from important *political speeches* or *communiqués* (taken from newspapers or news magazines) for a political science or international relations class; *scientific articles* for the science class; or words of *songs* for the school choir.

5. Some students become interested in attempting the translation of passages in all kinds of styles and moods; others try to develop real proficiency in scientific or technical translation in specialized fields.

6. Some students, deeply interested in language and in literature, might work together (or individually) to produce an English *poem* which is a translation of a Spanish poem. (A translation of a poem in poetic form is a new creation.) This would be submitted for publication in the school magazine.

Techniques for translation into English. Early attempts at this type of exercise often result in gibberish (Spanglish).

W 67 Tradúzcase al inglés:

Un mundo asombrado y temeroso es el que se enfrenta hoy al falso dilema de orden indiscriminado, dictatorial, o terrorismo anárquico. El largo período de terror en Latinoamérica, los secuestros de embajadores, las frecuentes desviaciones de naves aéreas y los hechos de los guerrilleros urbanos, sacuden al hombre y lo hacen pedir el retorno al orden, al respeto, a las normas tradicionales de convivencia nacional o internacional.
(From *Siempre,* México, D.F., adapted.)

Student's translation:
A shady, frightful world confronts itself in the false dilemma of discriminatory order, dictatorial, or terroristic anarchy. The large period of terror in Latin America, the sequestrations of ambassadors, the frequent deviations of airships and the facts of the urban guerrillas, shake the man and make it ask for the return to the order, the respect, the traditional norms of national or international living together.

Commentary

1. Many a student has felt frustrated when this type of translation was rejected. He knew what most of the passage was about and could have answered a comprehension test fairly adequately. This student does not understand what a translation should be like.

2. Many of the weaknesses of this type of response can be corrected by asking students to read their translations aloud. As they read, they become conscious of the odd quality of their English and often correct it as they proceed. Group discussion helps to refine the final version.

3. Group discussion before individual writing of the translation is also helpful in impressing on the student that the passage had a sensible, sequential meaning. Part of the translation may be written on the chalkboard or the overhead projector as the group works it over. The students then complete the translation individually, comparing their versions with each other to decide on the best possible translation.

4. Before considering their translation final, students should ask themselves the following six questions:

a. Have I respected contrasts between Spanish and English structure?
b. Have I fallen for any *"falsos amigos"*?

c. Have I used my common sense with time relations?

d. Have I used all the clues in the passage to help me translate unfamiliar words?

e. Have I used the appropriate style and level of language?

f. Is my final translation English or Spanglish?

Translation into Spanish

We can place translation from the native language into the foreign language in perspective, as a student activity, by asking ourselves the question which has become one of the central preoccupations of this book: To what normal uses can such an activity be put? For translation into the native language, we were able to find many uses. For translation into the target language, the only one which springs immediately to mind is the translating of school brochures, local area information booklets, or articles from school magazines or newspapers for inclusion in a twinned schools exchange project, or for sending to a Spanish-speaking correspondent who does not know English. Otherwise, it is difficult to think of possible occasions when a student would be called on to perform this task. In writing letters or preparing reports, students should be encouraged to write directly in Spanish, not to translate scripts they have composed in English.

We should consider the production of an acceptable translation into Spanish as a means, not an end—a means for developing sensitivity to the meanings expressed in a stretch of discourse in one's own language and to the different linguistic mechanisms used by the two languages to convey these meanings. Students learn to translate ideas, not words. This type of exercise is, therefore, an analytic activity. Through a comparative examination of the syntactic and semantic systems of English and Spanish and the cultural contexts in which they operate, the student attempts to expand his own potential for expression in the Spanish language.

Techniques for translation into Spanish. 1. If students are to gain the benefits of a comparative study of two language systems, teachers must avoid the types of passages one finds in some textbooks which distort English into near-Spanish to make the translation process "easier" for the student, e.g., "He says that he calls himself Juan Martínez. The only bad thing that he has is that he is accustomed to eating even when he has not hunger."

2. Since this is an intellectual exercise—an active, conscious process of attacking linguistic problems—it is a suitable project for group discussion and preparation before the individual prepares his own draft.

3. Students will begin by analyzing certain basic stylistic factors which will affect the whole translation, e.g., It the passage informal and conversational in tone so that I should use non-literary, or at any rate non-formal

expressions and vocabulary items, as well as short sentences, rather than long sentences with several embedded clauses?

4. Students will learn to use monolingual and bilingual dictionaries and grammars efficiently to verify the appropriateness of their proposed translations.

5. Students will learn to check their own work for basic inaccuracies in writing (incorrect choice of auxiliaries, mistakes in spelling and accents). This mechanical task should be the student's own responsibility. (Students may keep checklists of the types of mistakes to which they are prone.) Students may help each other by double-checking each other's work.

6. Group correction and discussion of the translations proposed by the students in relation to the model translation presented by the teacher is more effective than returning individually corrected scripts, since it focuses the student's attention on one thing at a time and gives him several opinions to consider.

7. Translation into Spanish should be a *study of translation techniques.* Several variants may be tried.

a. Students may compare their translations with a professional translation of the same passage, discussing the merits and insufficiencies of the two versions.

b. Students may be given a translation of the passage which was made by a student in another class. They then discuss proposed corrections and improvements to this translation before attempting their own version.

c. Students may discuss the qualities of the translations of the same passage by two professional translators.

d. Students in one group may translate a Spanish passage into English, then pass their translation to another group to translate into Spanish. Subsequent discussion of the original Spanish passage, the English translation, and the re-translation will illuminate many of the problems of conveying every aspect of meaning in a translation and the variety of ways in which a sentence may be interpreted.

EXPLORING THE DICTIONARY

We profess that one of our aims in teaching foreign language is to open up to our students the world of language itself. Part of this world is the wonder of words—their multiplicity, their variety, their elasticity, their chameleon-like quality of changing and merging in different environments. We know that different languages view reality from different perspectives and that many of these cultural differences are reflected in words and in their nuances of meaning. Yet frequently we keep our foreign-language learners impoverished in this area, depriving them of the opportunity to explore another world of words.

For this, the dictionary can be an invaluable friend. Instead of steering our students away from it, we should teach them to use it effectively. We should provide interesting opportunities for them to familiarize themselves with various kinds of dictionaries as aids in their pursuit of personal fluency in speech and writing.

Of course, the dictionary can mislead the neophyte. Until the student has learned how to consult a dictionary, there will be the inevitable crop of *El tocadiscos está fuera de orden* and *Espero que tengas un buen tiempo allá.* We must provide the kinds of experiences that will make these aberrations a passing phase.

Quite early, and certainly by the intermediate level, our student should have learned that there are two kinds of dictionaries available to him: the monolingual (the kind to which he is accustomed in his native language) and the bilingual (which he will certainly find in the attic or in the local bookshop if he does not find it in the classroom). Each of these, then, should be accessible to him and he should learn to use them purposefully.

1. *The monolingual dictionary.* For the Spanish student, this may mean the *Pequeño Larousse Ilustrado* (and, at advanced levels, a work such as the *Diccionario de Uso del Español*).

a. It will be easy to interest the student in the *Pequeño Larousse Ilustrado* by introducing him to the second half (*Parte Artes, Letras, Ciencias*) and encouraging him to seek quick answers there to many questions which arise in history, geography, art, music, social studies, classical mythology, and literature.

This initial interest can be quickened by a few competitive general knowledge quizzes which draw him into the second hal fof the *Pequeño Larousse,* showing him that it is not difficult to extract information there, even though it is in Spanish. (The clues to finding the answers in W68-69 will not appear in the students' quizzes.)

W 68 (I or A)

1. The famous Spanish painter, Picasso, has a painting called *Guernica* which is supposed to have been inspired by the atrocities committed in the Spanish Civil War. What exactly is Guernica? (The answer is found under the entry *Guernica.*)

2. When did the Spanish Civil War take place and what were some of its political consequences? (The answer is found under the entry *España.*)

3. We hear a great deal about the different regions of Spain such as *Cataluña, Andalucía, Valencia,* etc. Locate those regions on the map of Spain (located near the entry *España*), list them and look up information on each one of them.

4. What was the so-called *Armada Invencible?* What do you know about the Spanish king who organized it? (Answers under the entries *Armada Invincible* and *Felipe II.*)

Note: It may seem that some of these questions provide information which could be broken down to form further questions, but this questionnaire is not intended as a test. Since its purpose is to arouse interest in searching for information in the *Pequeño Larousse* the questions should provide interesting reading in themselves. For intermediate and advanced students the questions may very well be written in Spanish, so long as the general appearance of the quiz is not so forbidding as to be self-defeating.

b. Next, the student can be encouraged in spare moments to browse through the first half of the book looking at the *illustraciones*.

W 69 (E or I) 1. In order to describe an object, such as a car, one has to know the names of its parts. What is the Spanish for: (a) bumper, (b) headlight, (c) windshield, (d) hood? (Answers from the plate: *Carrocería*.)

2. Students may know that Spanish regional dresses include a variety of styles of headgear. Have them look up *sombrero* and then look up other cross-referenced items (e.g., *tocado, boina, gorro, gorra*). What do these types of headdress look like?

3. You may think you know the meaning of *el pensamiento* because you know *yo pienso*. What other meaning does it have? (Answer from the illustration in the text.)

Very soon, groups of students, or individuals, should be enthusiastic enough to make up their own questions to try out on each other.

c. Next we introduce the student to the *bold-face entries* in the main text.

W 70 (E or I) 1. A *casa* is a house and a *casilla* is a little house.

What is the Spanish for a little flower, a small square, a small street, a small bottle?

d. Finally we move to the *small type*.

W 71 (I) 1. *¡Hombre!* is often heard in familiar speech. What does this exclamation mean?

2. Spanish borrows English words, just as the English language has borrowed words'like *marina, mulatto, savvy,* and *tornado*. Sometimes these English borrowings are used in ways rather different from their native usage.

What is the meaning of (a) *un smoking,* (b) *el auto-stop,* (c) *un lunch,* (d) *un crismas* (*christmas*), (e) *un dogo?*

e. From this point on, it should be possible to incorporate the consultation of the *Pequeño Larousse* into as many activities as possible and to direct students to it to find out many things for themselves.

f. Word formation is a fascinating study, already discussed in R4-5 and R68-71. Advanced students should pursue this area further for its intrinsic interest.

W72 (A) From a source such as the *Diccionario de Uso del Español,* comment on the relationships between the pairs of words below. From the dictionary, write down a sentence showing the use of each:

a. *pelea*   pelear
   plan   planear
   lágrima   lagrimear ...

b. *ridículo*   ridiculizar
   carbón   carbonizar ...

c. *duda*   dudoso
   horror   horroroso ...

d. *rojo*   rojizo
   enfermo   enfermizo ...

2. *The bilingual (or Spanish-English, English-Spanish) dictionary.* It is this dictionary which every student has tucked away in his desk, usually in a very abbreviated paperback edition, and to which he refers to produce the howlers with which every teacher is familiar.

a. We should help our students by recommending a dependable, reasonably priced bilingual dictionary which will be used consistently during their studies, so that they will know how to use it when they are on their own.

b. A larger, more comprehensive bilingual dictionary will be available for reference in the classroom and in the library, alongside the monolingual Spanish dictionaries discussed.

c. Students will be given practice exercises in dictionary search so that they become familiar with the various features—pronunciation guides, abbreviations for parts of speech (e.g., v = *verbo,* verb; va = *verbo activo o transitivo,* active or transitive verb), levels of language and usage (e.g., colloquial, familiar, slang, archaic, or obsolete), dialectal variations (CAm = Central American, SAm = South American), relationships with other words (i.e., the rubric under which to find derivatives) grammatical indicators (e.g., with an adverb of interest: *pedirle algo a alguien*), and sample sentences demonstrating general use and inclusion in specifically idiomatic expressions.

d. Finally, and most importantly, students will be trained to check meaning in both parts of the dictionary. The lady who, wishing to compliment a helpful salesgirl, looked in her pocket dictionary and said, *Usted es muy enferma, señorita,* could have been saved much embarrassment had she checked the various Spanish entries for *patient* in the Spanish-English section before taking the plunge. Exercises like W73 and W74 are easy to construct and interesting to work out with the help of the dictionary.

W73 (I or A) Find out from a bilingual dictionary how to express in Spanish the expressions italicized in the following sentences:

1. This is *a famous picture* by Picasso.
2. He loves *to take pictures.*
3. I love *the pictures of the Spanish countryside* in this book.
4. You're just *the picture of your mother.*
5. She's as *pretty as a picture.*
6. *The pictures of the presidents* are on the stamps.
7. My little sister likes me to "read" to her from *her picture book.*
8. *I can picture him* standing on the beach on the Costa Brava.

W74 (I or A)

1. If you saw the following signs in Barcelona, what would they mean to you: (a) *Se alquilan pisos desde 3.000* and (b) *Mantenga limpia España?*

2. What does this road sign mean: *Peatón: en carretera, circula por tu izquierda?*

3. Suppose you hear a Spaniard say of a certain person: *Es muy dueño de sí mismo.* What would you say he meant by that?

4. What is the difference between *echarse a las espaldas* and *echarse sobre las espaldas?*

EXPLORING THE GRAMMAR

Students at the advanced level who wish to write well must learn to find answers to their own questions about written Spanish. At this stage they should be given practice in formulating the questions they want answered in such a way that they can find the information they need in a Spanish grammar book like Martin Alonso's *Gramática del español contemporáneo,* or Manuel Seco's *Gramática esencial del español,* or Samuel Gili y Gaya's *Curso superior de sintaxis española.* For this, they need to know the basic grammatical terms in Spanish so that they can make efficient use of the indexes to these grammars.

If a student wishes to know whether he should write—"¿El profesor? Lo vi en el jardín hace diez minutos," or—"¿El profesor? Le vi en el jardín hace diez minutos," he will need to know that this is a question of *leísmo* vs. *loísmo,* and that he will find an answer for it under the main entry *Pronombres,* item *leísmo, laísmo y loísmo.*

Learning terms of this type is unexciting, but it can be made more appealing by giving the student interesting problems to solve through personal search in the grammar book. When he feels at home with it, he will enjoy finding his own answers instead of asking other people.

Questions like the following may be proposed. (The indications given here as to how this information might be obtained from Martin Alonso's *Gramática del español contemporáneo* would not be given to the students.)

W75 (A)

1. Cuando *hubimos terminado* la tarea, empezamos a charlar.

Is the tense found in literary or spoken Spanish, or both?

(Answer: The name of the tense is found by looking at the tense tables for the various conjugations where one finds *pretérito anterior. Pretérito actual y anterior de indicativo* is then found in the index (*Índice analítico de materias*) under the heading *Tiempos,* which indicates the section where the matter is discussed.

2. In writing a letter, a student wants to say that he found Madrid full of cars. Should he write (a) or (b)?

a. Madrid estaba lleno de coches.

b. Madrid estaba llena de coches.

(Answer: The student looks for *Género* in the *Índice analítico de materias.* There he finds several subheadings and finally selects *Género según la significación* where he reads:

Femeninos:

[...] 3.º los nombres de ciudades y poblados terminados en *a:* la inmortal Roma [...] Hoy la tendencia es al masculino: *medio Londres y todo París lo sabe. Madrid modernísimo y Buenos Aires muy extenso de circuito.*)

3. When does one use:

grande   *or* gran
cualquiera   *or* cualquier
primero   *or* primer
bueno   *or* buen?

(Answer: The students look for the main entry *Adjetivo,* item *Apócope adjectiva* in the *Índice analítico.*)

4. Can proper names be pluralized in Spanish as they can in English? (e.g., the Waltons, the Williamsons.) If so, when and how? Is there any difference in meaning between *los Leal* and *los Leales?*

Answer: the student looks for the main entry *Sustantivo,* item *Accidentes nominales . . . Número.*)

Students can be asked to propose their own problems, which will be worked into a *search questionnaire.*

Suggested assignments and projects

Communicating (chapters 1–3)

1. Write a situational dialogue suitable for the second month of instruction. Write a critique of the first draft of your dialogue, then rewrite it if necessary. From your final dialogue write a spiral series and a situation tape. (You may find that what you have written needs considerable adaptation for the situation tape. You should try the script for the tape out on several people to see if it is workable.) If you have the facilities available, record your tape in the form in which it would be used by students.

2. Choose a grammatical feature. Write a grammar-demonstration dialogue to display the various facets of this feature. Construct a unit showing how you would exploit this feature in guided oral practice, in student-directed practice, and then in some natural language activity. (Consult also chapter 4.)

3. Design a module for small-group activity which explores some facet of the everyday culture of Spain or some other Spanish-speaking country. Include natural communicative activities and some culminating display for sharing the material with the whole class.

4. Take a unit or lesson from a direct method textbook and examine the types of activities proposed. Design a learning packet for individualized

instruction or a unit for small-group work using this material. (Remember that individualized instruction does not mean independent study. This distinction is important if communication skills are to be developed.)

5. Design in detail for fourth-year high school, fourth semester of college, or advanced level college an aural-oral communication course based entirely on natural uses of language. Your course should supply ample opportunity for developing facility in listening to all kinds of Spanish and for expressing oneself in different situations and styles of language. (Think of ways of stimulating genuinely self-directed activity by the students. Do not make the course dependent on expensive equipment and aids which you could not realistically expect to be available in the average foreign-language department.)

6. Take two textbooks designed specifically for conversation courses. Analyze and comment on the types of communicative activity they promote, using the following heads as an outline.

Situations. For what situations is practice provided? Are these adequate? useful? culturally illuminating? Could the material be adapted easily to other situations?

Normal uses of language. How do the types of activities proposed relate to the normal communicative categories of chapter 2? What other categories can you establish from this examination?

Strategies of communication. What techniques for expressing personal meaning within a limited knowledge of the language do these texts encourage? What other strategies do learners of a foreign language need to practice? How could these be incorporated into these texts?

7. Design two listening comprehension tests—one multiple-choice and the other based on natural language activities. Discuss for each of the tests the problems involved in assessment of the degree of listening skill and in administration in a practical teaching situation.

8. Design in detail a course for developing facility in listening along with facility in reading. State the level at which the course would be offered and give your reasons for offering it at that level. (See also chapters 6 and 7.)

Oral practice for the learning of grammar (chapter 4)

9. Take six Type A exercises from current textbooks and show how each could be developed as a Type B exercise.

10. Take a unit for grammatical practice from a current textbook, classify the types of exercises proposed, and design further exercises of the types described in chapter 4 which are not already included but which you would consider suitable for practicing this area of grammar.

11. Draft a series of oral exercises for teaching the use of the interrogative pronouns in Spanish. Draw freely from the various types described in chapter 4, passing from teacher demonstration to student-directed application to autonomous student production.

12. Examine critically the oral exercises for the learning of grammar on a set of tapes accompanying a current textbook. What are their best features and their weaknesses? Propose types of exercises which would, in your opinion, make them more interesting and more useful for developing ability to use the language in interaction.

Teaching the sound system (chapter 5)

13. Make a tape of your own reading of the evaluation passage S44. Choose the four most striking weaknesses in your production (see S43) and work out articulatory descriptions, empirical recommendations, and remedial exercises which would help students to correct these same faults.

14. Work out some multiple-choice items to test aural discrimination of [b:ƀ]; [d:đ]; [g:ǥ]; [s:h]; /s:θ/; /r:r̄/ when they occur in context in normal word groups.

15. Make some tapes of your students conversing in Spanish. From an analysis of these tapes, list in descending order of frequency the ten features of Spanish pronunciation and intonation for which you consider they need the most remedial practice. Compare your list with those of other students or teachers and discuss the differences.

Reading (chapters 6 and 7)

16. Take a survey of interests in reading material in the class you are teaching (or in which you are practice teaching). Find suitable materials in Spanish to meet these interests at different stages of reading development. List these (with complete bibliographic information) and explain the reasons for your selection.

17. a. Take a reading passage or story your students have found difficult to read and another they enjoyed but did not consider particularly difficult.

b. Compare the two texts according to level of difficulty of vocabulary, structural complexity, interest of content, familiarity or unfamiliarity of content, any other criteria you consider relevant.

c. Ask your students to write down why they found one passage difficult and the other accessible.

d. Compare (b) and (c) and give what seems to you the most reasonable explanation of the students' reactions to the two texts.

18. Undertake a survey of Spanish-language newspapers and magazines (from Spain, Hispano-America, and Spanish-speaking population centers of the United States). Examine various aspects of their content and language and rate them appropriate for Stages 4, 5, or 6.

19. The physical aspects of a reading text are important factors in readability. Examine a number of books for reading development in Spanish from the point of view of:
    a. varieties of type (italics, boldface, etc.) and length of line;
    b. layout (spacing, headings and subheadings, breaks in the text);
    c. convenience of supplementary helps (glosses, notes, etc.);
    d. usefulness and attractiveness of illustrative material;
    e. general appearance of the body of the text;
    f. attractiveness and durability of the cover;
    g. any other physical features which have attracted your attention.

20. Find two textbooks which include the same reading selection. Compare the way the material has been presented and exploited in each (adaptation, if any, of the original text, layout, glosses and supplementary helps, types of questions and exercises, interest and usefulness of these for a particular stage of reading development, integration of reading with other skills).

21. Examine some Spanish-language children's books and comic books from the point of view of vocabulary level, grammatical complexity, and content. Class them as possibilities for supplementary reading at specific stages of reading development.

Writing (chapters 8 and 9)

22. On separate occasions within the same week, give your students three tests of one grammatical feature (e.g., form and position of pronoun objects): a multiple-choice test, a cloze test, and a set of stimulus sentences to translate into Spanish. Make graphs of the number of errors made by the students on each test. Repeat the tests in a different order for another

feature and examine these results as well. Give an analysis of what this informal experiment has revealed about the relative difficulty and discriminatory power of the three tests, and the most persistent problems for the students who are learning these features.

23. Examine a textbook for elementary language instruction. What part does writing play in this book? Are the writing activities integrated with the other skills? Are they imaginative and interesting for students of the age to which the book is directed? Are they purposeful? What suggestions can you make to improve their effectiveness?

24. Examine a manual for advanced Spanish composition. Do the types of activities provided leave scope for personal initiative? Are they directed toward normal purposes of writing? What aspects of writing have been ignored? What suggestions would you make for a revised edition of the manual?

25. Examine a book (A) written for instruction in the writing of the native language (English or Spanish). Compare it with a book (B) intended to improve foreign-language writing. What ideas can be gleaned from the study of A for the improvement of B, or vice versa?

Appendix

System of symbols used in this book to represent Spanish sounds*

Phones	Phonemes	As in Spanish (orthographic)
[á]	/á/†	m<u>a</u>dre, tom<u>a</u>
[b]	/b/	am<u>b</u>os, in<u>v</u>ierno
[b̶]	/b/	ha<u>b</u>er, la<u>v</u>ar
[ĉ]	/ĉ/	<u>ch</u>ico
[θ]	/θ/ (Castilian)	bra<u>z</u>o; co<u>c</u>er
[d]	/d/	<u>d</u>on<u>d</u>e
[d̶]	/d/	a<u>d</u>iós
[é]	/é/	tom<u>é</u>, sab<u>e</u>
[f]	/f/	<u>f</u>echa
[g]	/g/	<u>g</u>anga, <u>g</u>uitarra
[g̶]	/g/	ro<u>g</u>ar, lle<u>g</u>ué
[í]	/í/	d<u>i</u>me, cas<u>i</u>
[i̯]	/i/	b<u>i</u>en; ba<u>i</u>le, ha<u>y</u>
[k]	/k/	<u>c</u>asa, a<u>qu</u>ella

* The source of this system is John B. Dalbor's *Spanish Pronunciation: Theory and Practice*.

† Note that the stress on vowel phonemes is indicated as optional, that is, /á/ stands for /a/ or alternatively /á/. Examples are given in orthographic representation for both cases. Thus, *toma* /tóma/ exemplifies the unstressed variant, while *madre* /mádre/ exemplifies the stressed variant.

317

Phones	*Phonemes*	*As in Spanish (orthographic)*
[l]	/l/	lado
[ḷ]	/ḷ/ (Castilian)	llamar
[m]	/m/	tomar
[n]	/n/	bueno
[ŋ]	/n/	tengo, cinco
[ñ]	/ñ/	año
(ʹ)[o]	(ʹ)/o/	cosa, caso
[p]	/p/	padre
[r]	/r/	hora
[r̄]	/r̄/	torre, risa
[s]	/s/	ser, queso
	(Latin American)	brazo, cocer
[z]	/s/	desde, mismo
[h]	/s/ (Latin American)	hasta, manos, perdiz
[t]	/t/	tomar
(ʹ)[u]	(ʹ)/u/	duro, sultán
[u̯]	/u/	bueno, causa
[w]	/w/	hueso
[x]	/x/	ajo, gente
[y]	/y/	mayo
	(Latin American)	llamar

Additional symbols (used in transcribing English items)

æ	nap
a	far
aɪ	nice
eɪ	name
ə	elevate, an apple, umbrella
ɫ	fell, gaul
ʃ	sure, ashes
ʔ	an iceman (the glottal stop occurs between the words)

Notes

Abbreviations used in notes and bibliography

ADFL	*Bulletin of the Association of Departments of Foreign Languages* (MLA, New York)
AFLT	*American Foreign Language Teacher* (Detroit, Michigan)
FLA	*Foreign Language Annals* (American Council on the Teaching of Foreign Languages)
IJAL	*International Journal of American Linguistics*
IRAL	*International Review of Applied Linguistics*
MLJ	*Modern Language Journal* (National Federation of Modern Language Teachers' Associations)
NEC	Reports of the Working Committees of the Northeast Conference on the Teaching of Foreign Languages
LL	*Language Learning* (University of Michigan, Ann Arbor)
TQ	*TESOL Quarterly* (Teachers of English to Speakers of Other Languages)

1 Communicating

1. The terms "skill-getting" and "skill-using" have been borrowed from Don H. Parker, "When Should I Individualize Instruction?" in Virgil M. Howes, ed.,

Individualization of Instruction: A Teaching Strategy (New York: Macmillan, 1970), p. 176.

2. The rationale for interaction activities of this type is set out in "Talking Off the Tops of Their Heads," in Wilga M. Rivers, *Speaking in Many Tongues* (Rowley, Mass.: Newbury House, 1972a), pp. 20–35.

1. STRUCTURED INTERACTION

1. How this can be done is discussed fully in W. M. Rivers, "From Linguistic Competence to Communicative Competence," in *TQ* 7 (1973), pp. 25–34.

2. Valdelomar, Abraham, "El Vuelo de los Cóndores," in Doris King Arjona and Carlos Vásquez Arjona, eds., *Quince Cuentos de las Españas* (New York: Charles Scribner's Sons, 1971), p. 74.

3. All comments in parentheses in the description of the five styles are based on M. Joos, *The Five Clocks* (New York: Harcourt, Brace and World, 1961). For a more detailed analysis of the conversational register from the point of view of Transactional Engineering Analysis, see L. A. Jakobovits and B. Gordon, *The Context of Foreign Language Teaching* (Rowley, Mass.: Newbury House, 1974), Chapter 3.

4. Víctor Ruiz Iriarte, *El Carrusell,* Marion P. Holt, ed. (New York: Appleton-Century-Crofts, 1970), pp. 20–21.

5. John R. Searle, *Speech Acts: An Essay in the Philosophy of Language* (Cambridge, Eng.: Cambridge University Press, 1969), p. 16.

6. Ibid.

7. "Semantics plays a central role in syntax," according to George Lakoff in "On Generative Semantics," in D. D. Steinberg and L. A. Jakobovits, eds., *Semantics* (Cambridge, Eng.: Cambridge University Press, 1971), p. 232, note *a*.

8. Discussed more fully in Wilga M. Rivers, *Teaching Foreign-Language Skills* (Chicago: The University of Chicago Press, 1968), pp. 78–80.

9. C. Gattegno, *Teaching Foreign Languages in Schools: The Silent Way* (Reading, Eng.: Educational Explorers Ltd., 1963). 2d ed. 1972 (New York: Educational Solutions). The Silent Way is described in more detail in two articles in *ADFL* 5 (1973–74): C. Dominice, "The Silent Way: A Student looks at Teaching" (pp. 23–24), and C. Perrault, "The Silent Way: An Experienced User Speaks" (pp. 25–26).

10. Gattegno (1963), p. 39.

11. Ibid., p. 21.

12. Ibid., p. 40.

13. Ibid., p. 24.

14. The Gouin series is described in detail, with class procedure, in R. Titone, *Teaching Foreign Languages: An Historical Sketch* (Washington, D.C.: Georgetown University Press, 1968), pp. 33–37. A similar approach to the beginning stages was taken by M. D. Berlitz, the founder of the Berlitz schools.

15. This quotation is from François Gouin, *The Art of Teaching and Studying Languages,* trans. H. Swan and V. Bétis, (London: George Philip and Son; New York: Charles Scribner's Sons, 1892), p. 131. This has a contemporary ring. The Berkeley linguist Wallace Chafe considers the verb to be central in seman-

tics. In *Meaning and the Structure of Language* (Chicago: The University of Chicago Press, 1970) he suggests as "a general principle that semantic influence radiates from a verb" (p. 190) and in his work he considers the verb central and the noun peripheral (p. 96).

16. Gouin (1892), p. 162.

17. Ibid., p. 171. To bring the original Spanish example as printed into conformity with contemporary usage, *hácia* in line 1 has been changed to *hacia* and *de* in line 2 to *a*.

18. The use of the *Ud.* or *tú* form in this case will depend on the age of the students and the approach the teacher has decided to take to this aspect of the language. Many teachers use *Uds.* to older students and expect this form in return, while encouraging students to use *tú* to each other. In this way students have regular practice in switching from one to the other.

19. See J. J. Asher, "The Learning Strategy of the Total Physical Response: A Review," *MLJ* 50 (1966), 79–84. Asher claims that the association of action and sound results in longer retention, at least for listening comprehension.

20. Developed by the Institute of Modern Languages in Washington, D.C., and described in John Schumann, "Communication Techniques," *TQ* 6 (1972), 143–46.

21. E. B. de Sauzé's approach is described in E. B. de Sauzé and V. Condon, *The Cleveland Plan for the Teaching of Modern Languages with Special Reference to Spanish* (Philadelphia: The John C. Winston Company, 1931). Ralph Hester, ed., in *Teaching a Living Language* (New York: Harper and Row, 1970), p. x, claims that the verbal-active method, a "rationalist direct method," derives from de Sauzé. Yvone Lenard dedicated her verbal-active textbook, *Parole et Pensée* (New York: Harper and Row, 1965) to Emile B. de Sauzé, a "maître de l'enseignement."

22. Y. Lenard, "Methods and Materials, Techniques and the Teacher" in Hester, ed. (1970), p. 37.

23. Karl C. Diller, "Linguistic Theories of Language Acquisition," in Hester, ed. (1970), pp. 16–17, 18; and also K. C. Diller, *Generative Grammar, Structural Linguistics, and Language Teaching* (Rowley, Mass.: Newbury House, 1971), pp. 25, 27.

24. Lenard in Hester, ed. (1970), p. 36.

25. Ibid., p. 50.

26. Ibid., p. 55.

27. From Y. Lenard, *Parole et Pensée: Introduction au français d'aujourd'hui.* 2e éd. (New York: Harper and Row, 1971), p. 341. (Adapted by the authors)

28. L. G. Kelly in *25 Centuries of Language Teaching* (Rowley, Mass.: Newbury House, 1969) traces the use of the dialogue in foreign-language teaching back to the *colloquium* of the Middle Ages (p. 120).

29. Terrence L. Hansen and Ernest J. Wilkins, *Español a lo Vivo: Level II,* 2d ed. (Lexington, Mass.: Xerox College Publishing, 1972), pp. 1–2. The teaching of a foreign culture in the language class is discussed in detail in Rivers (1968), Chap. 11, "Cultural Understanding," and the psychological factors which should be considered are analyzed in Rivers (1964), Chap. 12.

Many useful techniques for teaching a foreign culture are described in H. N. Seelye, *Teaching Culture: Strategies for Foreign Language Educators* (Skokie, Ill.: National Textbook Co., 1974), and Northeast Conference Reports 1960, 1972, and 1976.

30. There seems to be a misconception among some foreign-language teachers that only learning grammar rules and working deductively and analytically can be called "cognitive." Actually, from the point of view of cognitive psychology, any process which requires students to think, to extract meaning from any symbolic behavior (action, strange utterance, pictorial representation), to work out generalizations from examples or instances (induction), is a cognitive operation. See "The Foreign-Language Teacher and Cognitive Psychology," in Rivers (1972a), pp. 81–83.

31. Earl W. Stevick of the Foreign Service Institute, Washington, D.C., originated the "microwave cycle" which he described in "UHF and Microwaves in Transmitting Language Skills," in E. W. Najam and Carleton T. Hodge, eds., *Language Learning: The Individual and the Process, IJAL* 32, 1, Part 2 (1966), Publication 40 of the Indiana University Research Center in Anthropology, Folklore, and Linguistics, pp. 84–94. In *Adapting and Writing Language Lessons* (Washington, D.C.: Foreign Service Institute, 1971), pp. 310–15, Stevick explains that he developed this device from the question-answer technique of Thomas F. Cummings in *How to Learn a Foreign Language* (New York: privately published, 1916), and that *he now prefers the term Cummings device*. The device has been used with good results in Peace Corps and Foreign Service Institute materials in a variety of languages. Chapter 6 and Appendices P, Q, and R of Stevick (1971) give detailed examples of the device in languages as diverse as English, French, Lao, Bini, Kikuyu, and Ponapean.

32. Stevick (1971), p. 311.

33. Ibid., pp. 312–13.

34. Stevick (1966), p. 92.

35. Stevick (1971), p. 314.

36. Ibid., p. 37.

37. Lenard in Hester (1970), p. 50, says, "There should be [an oral composition] for every lesson, to be followed the next day by a written one. The oral composition becomes, in fact, the most important exercise of the verbal-active method in building the elements of which fluency is composed: the ability to speak at length, aloud, clearly and confidently, in front of other people, and to use the words and structures that you know freely and correctly in order to say what you mean."

38. Ibid. (Translated by the authors)

39. Ibid., p. 56.

40. Francis A. Cartier reports that a team of programmers under his direction at the Defense Language Institute English Language Branch has developed a series of situational conversations on tape along these lines for individual learning and practice. These tapes seek to elicit certain structures. It was found that students experienced a definite feeling of rapport with the speakers and would work through the tapes several times to try to improve their efforts.

2. AUTONOMOUS INTERACTION

    1. Rivers (1968), p. 201.

    2. Emma M. Birkmaier, "The Meaning of Creativity in Foreign Language Teaching," *MLJ* 55 (1971), p. 350.

    3. Abraham H. Maslow, *Motivation and Personality*. 2d ed. (New York: Harper and Row, 1970), Chapter 4: "A Theory of Human Motivation" sets out this hierarchy. Its importance in communication in the foreign-language classroom is discussed in Earl W. Stevick, "Before Linguistics and Beneath Method" in Kurt Jankowsky, ed., *Language and International Studies,* Georgetown University Round Table on Languages and Linguistics 1973 (Washington, D.C.: Georgetown University Press, 1973), pp. 99–106.

    4. C. B. Paulston and H. R. Selekman, "Interaction Activities in the Foreign Language Classroom or How to Grow a Tulip-Rose." *FLA* 8 (1975). Selekman experimented with these games in a Hebrew school in Pittsburgh.

    5. Paulston and Selekman (1975) tell of the shock and disappointment experienced by one of Selekman's students when he discovered that the ostensibly monolingual person to whom he thought he was speaking spoke perfect English.

    6. Described fully in Paulston and Selekman (1975).

    7. Alexander Lipson, "Some New Strategies for Teaching Oral Skills," in Robert C. Lugton, ed., *Toward a Cognitive Approach to Second Language Acquisition* (Philadelphia: Center for Curriculum Development, 1971), pp. 231–44.

    8. Paulston and Selekman (1975).

    9. Lipson (1971), p. 240.

    10. Stevick (1971), pp. 365–90.

    11. Passage transcribed word for word from a tape of authentic conversation made in Panama, R.P., by a colleague of one of the authors.

    12. Stevick (1973), p. 100.

    13. Ibid.

3. LISTENING

    1. P. T. Rankin, "Listening Ability: Its Importance, Measurement, and Development," *Chicago Schools Journal* 12, pp. 177–79, quoted in D. Spearritt, *Listening Comprehension—A Factorial Analysis* (Melbourne: Australian Council for Educational Research, 1962), p. 2.

    2. Spearritt (1962), pp. 92–93. Spearritt adds: "There is some evidence that performance on listening comprehension tests is related to performance on inductive reasoning, verbal comprehension and certain types of memory tests."

    3. R. E. Troike, "Receptive Competence, Productive Competence, and Performance," in J. E. Alatis, ed., *Linguistics and the Teaching of Standard English to Speakers of Other Languages or Dialects*. Report of the Twentieth Annual Round Table Meeting on Linguistics and Language Studies (Washington, D.C.: Georgetown University Press Monograph No. 22, 1970), pp. 63–73.

    4. See T. Bever, "The Cognitive Basis for Linguistic Structures," in J. R. Hayes, ed., *Cognition and the Development of Language* (New York: John Wiley and Sons, 1970), and "Linguistic and Psychological Factors in Speech Perception

and Their Implications for Teaching Materials," in Rivers (1972a), pp. 94–107.

5. These two levels, the recognition and selection levels, are discussed fully in relation to listening comprehension in Rivers (1968), pp. 142–43.

6. N. Chomsky in *Aspects of the Theory of Syntax* (Cambridge, Mass.: The MIT Press, 1965), p. 9, says that "a generative grammar is not a model for a speaker or a hearer. It attempts to characterize in the most neutral possible terms the knowledge of the language that provides the basis for actual use of language by a speaker-hearer."

7. For some perceptual strategies, see Bever in Hayes, ed. (1970), pp. 287–312.

8. Colin Cherry, *On Human Communication* (New York: John Wiley and Sons, 1957), p. 277.

9. Ibid.

10. Excerpt from a conversation with Spanish graduate students at the University of Illinois at Urbana-Champaign, recorded in 1974 by one of the co-authors (M. M. A.), who takes this opportunity to thank Ms. Montserrat Dejuan and Messrs. Rafael Castillo and Manuel Puerta for their kind cooperation.

11. For a detailed discussion of hearing as a stochastic process, that is, based on expectations, see Charles F. Hockett, "Grammar for the Hearer," in R. Jakobson, ed., *On the Structure of Language and Its Mathematical Aspects* (Providence, R.I.: American Mathematical Society, 1961), pp. 220–36.

12. See Jerald R. Green, *A Gesture Inventory for the Teaching of Spanish* (Philadelphia: Chilton Books, 1968).

13. For a discussion of adverbs of interest in Spanish, see R. P. Stockwell, J. D. Bowen, and J. W. Martin, *The Grammatical Structures of English and Spanish* (Chicago: The University of Chicago Press, 1965). *Beneficiary, recipient* (of an object or a service), and related concepts are treated in M. A. K. Halliday, "Language Structure and Language Function," in John Lyons, ed., *New Horizons in Linguistics* (Harmondsworth, Middlesex: Penguin Books, 1970), pp. 140–65.

14. The following books provide information on Cataluña: Sergio Vilar, *Cataluña en España, aproximación desde Cataluña al espíritu y los problemas de las regiones españolas* (Barcelona: Aymá, S. A., Editora, 1968); Julián Marías, *Consideración de Cataluña* (Barcelona: Aymá, S. A. Editora, 1966); George Orwell, *Homage to Catalonia* (London: Secker and Warburg, 1938).

15. For colloquial language and conversational styles, consult Martin Alonso, *Gramática del Español Contemporáneo* (Madrid: Ediciones Guadarrama, 1968), Chapter 13: "Laboratorio de la palabra hablada," pp. 401 ff.

16. Short-wave broadcast from Ecuador, recorded in Spring, 1974. It has not been possible to identify the station.

17. Short-wave broadcast from Radio Nacional de España, recorded in Spring, 1974. Most geographical names can be located in *Pequeño Larousse Ilustrado*. Proper names are often pronounced according to the usual Spanish sound-symbol correspondences, but the teacher should listen to the news broadcasts first and prepare the students for any unexpected pronunciations.

18. Short-wave broadcast of Radio Nacional de España in Spring, 1974.

19. A detailed description of these stages is given in Rivers (1972a), pp. 97–

104. See also U. Neisser, *Cognitive Psychology* (New York: Appleton-Century-Crofts, 1967), Chapter 7: Speech Perception.

20. Asher (1966), pp. 79–80.

21. Ibid., pp. 80–82.

22. G. A. Miller's term in "The Magical Number Seven, Plus or Minus Two: Some Limits on Our Capacity for Processing Information," *Psychological Review* 63 (1956), pp. 81–96. Reprinted in G. A. Miller, *The Psychology of Communication. Seven Essays.* (New York: Basic Books, 1967). See also Leopoldo Wigdorsky, "Research in Applied Linguistics and its Impact upon Foreign Language Teaching Materials," in G. E. Perren and J. L. M. Trim, eds., *Applications of Linguistics: Selected Papers of the Second International Congress of Applied Linguistics,* (Cambridge, Eng.: Cambridge University Press, 1971), pp. 463–69.

23. The pros and cons of the backward buildup technique are discussed in detail in Rivers (1968), pp. 171–72.

24. Other structural features which students should learn to recognize rapidly are listed in Rivers (1972a), p. 103.

25. Processes involved in fluent reading are compared with processes of listening in Rivers (1972a), pp. 105–6.

26. Edited excerpt from a recorded conversation (see note 10 of this chapter).

27. The information in this paragraph and the quotation are from "Research in Listening Comprehension," by Andrew Wilkinson, *Educational Research* 12 (1970), pp. 140–41.

28. Excerpt from a recorded conversation (see note 10 of this chapter).

29. Bever in Hayes, ed. (1970), p. 291.

30. This is basic to the controversy between the transformational-generative grammarians who support the standard theory and the generative semanticists. Chomsky has stated that "there must be, represented in the mind, a fixed system of generative principles that characterize and associate deep and surface structures in some definite way—a grammar, in other words, that is used in some fashion as discourse is produced or interpreted" (*Language and Mind,* 1st ed., 1968, p. 16). According to G. Lakoff, "the theory of generative semantics claims that the linguistic elements used in grammar have an independent natural basis in the human conceptual system. . . . Generative semantics takes grammar as being based on the independently given natural logical categories, . . . and on natural logical classes. . . ." (from "The Arbitrary Basis of Transformational Grammar" in *Language* 48, pp. 77–78).

31. These are basic to Charles Fillmore's Case Grammar. Fillmore adds other functions such as instrument and experiencer.

32. Bever in Hayes, ed. (1970), pp. 286–99. The strategies are described as follows: Strategy A p. 290, Strategy B p. 294, Strategy C p. 296, Strategy D p. 298.

33. In transformational-generative grammar each clause is considered a sentence and assigned the symbol S.

34. I. M. Schlesinger, *Sentence Structure and the Reading Process* (The Hague: Mouton, 1968), pp. 122–41.

35. Excerpt from an unidentified short-wave program recorded in Spring, 1974.

36. Based on a pamphlet entitled *"Gastronomía,"* published by Spain's *Ministerio de Información y Turismo.*

37. This chart is a completely revised and expanded version of the one in Rivers (1968), pp. 151–54.

38. Short-term retention, as used in this chart, is not synonymous with short-term memory. Echoic memory is useful for only a few seconds, during which the listener still has recourse to the raw data. Active verbal memory (immediate memory or short-term memory) can hold from five to nine cognitive chunks (e.g., short phrases or groups of digits) created by the listener. This material is then recoded for storage in long-term memory. The expression "short-term retention," as used in this chart, is a pragmatic one, referring to the short interval that elapses before what the student has heard is put to some active use. The student is not expected to hold the material in his memory for use at a later stage, as he is for the long-term retention of Stage D.

39. *¡Vamos a Ver!* and *Tal Como Es* (Saint Paul, Minn.: EMC Corporation) are of this type. Based on BBC language programs, these materials maintain the students' attention for a variety of reasons: suspense, ordinary situations which provide much practice in practical language use, and interest in what native speakers have to say about their everyday lives. More material along these lines would be useful.

40. A similar technique is described by S. Belasco in "C'est la Guerre? or Can Cognition and Verbal Behavior Co-exist in Second-Language Learning?" in R. C. Lugton, ed. (1971), pp. 223–25. In Belasco's approach, the student is provided from the beginning with a text with visual hints to deviations from standard style of language. Here, at the advanced level, we suggest a purely listening and writing task.

41. Teachers seeking further information on literary techniques of this type should consult E. Correa Calderón, and Fernando Lázaro, *Cómo se comenta un texto literario* (Salamanca: Ediciones Anaya, S. A., 1966) and Rafael Lapesa Melgar, *Introducción a los estudios literarios* (Salamanca: Ediciones Anaya, S. A., 1968).

4. ORAL PRACTICE FOR THE LEARNING OF GRAMMAR

1. Adapted from E. C. Hills and J. D. M. Ford, *First Spanish Course* (Boston: D.C. Heath and Co., 1917), pp. 26–28.

2. Ibid., p. 23.

3. The use of substitution tables has been traced back to Erasmus in the sixteenth century. See L. Kelly, *25 Centuries of Language Teaching* (Rowley, Mass.: Newbury House, 1969), p. 101. Harold Palmer gives examples of substitution tables and advocates their use in *The Scientific Study and Teaching of Languages* (London: Harrap, 1917).

4. An interesting analysis of drills into mechanical, meaningful, and communication categories is made in C. B. Paulston, "The Sequencing of Structural Pattern Drills," *TQ* 5 (1971), pp. 197–208. The subject is also discussed in W. M. Rivers, "Talking off the Tops of Their Heads" in Rivers (1972a), pp. 20–35.

5. The concept of Type A and Type B exercises is developed more fully in W. M. Rivers, "From Linguistic Competence to Communicative Competence," *TQ* 7 (1973), pp. 25–34.

5. TEACHING THE SOUND SYSTEM

1. It is presumed that most trainee teachers and practicing teachers have at some time studied the Spanish sound system. This very sketchy introduction to terminology is included for the benefit of the occasional student to whom it is new. It is customary to use square brackets [ʰ] for phonetic or allophonic representations and slashes /b/ for phonemic representations. The system of symbols used in this chapter is set out in the Appendix.

2. For further information on this subject, see S. A. Schane, *Generative Phonology* (Englewood Cliffs, N.J.: Prentice-Hall, 1973) and S. Saporta and H. Contreras, *A Phonological Grammar of Spanish* (Seattle: University of Washington Press, 1962).

3. Tomás Navarro Tomás, *Studies in Spanish Phonology* (Coral Gables, Fla.: University of Miami Press, 1968), p. 36.

4. Ibid., pp. 37–38.

5. P. Delattre, *Comparing the Phonetic Features of English, French, German and Spanish* (London: Harrap, 1965), p. 55.

6. Ibid., p. 56.

7. Ibid., p. 55.

8. Sometimes a student will succeed in making the correct sound in a somewhat different way, but most students will need the teacher's help and will profit from precise instructions.

9. For a thorough discussion of the production of /r/ and /r̄/ and their variants, see T. Navarro Tomás, *Manual de Pronunciación española,* 16th ed. Publicaciones de la *Revista de filología española,* Núm. III (Madrid: Raycar, S.A., 1971), pp. 115–24. See also J. Rodríguez-Castellano, *Ejercicios de pronunciación española* (New York: Charles Scribner's Sons, 1965), pp. 19–20, and R. L. Hadlich, J. S. Molton, and M. Montes, *A Drillbook of Spanish Pronunciation* (New York: Harper and Row, 1968), p. 147.

10. C. H. Prator, Jr., *Manual of American English Pronunciation,* rev. ed. (New York: Holt, Rinehart and Winston, 1957), p. 83.

11. L. E. Armstrong, *The Phonetics of French* (London: Bell, 1959), p. 110. First published 1932.

12. R. P. Stockwell and J. D. Bowen, *The Sounds of English and Spanish* (Chicago: The University of Chicago Press, 1965), p. 49.

13. W. E. Bull, *Spanish for Teachers: Applied Linguistics* (New York: The Ronald Press, 1965), p. 64. Note that the production of /r/ *simple* is very similar to that of the British English fricative /r/ described by Armstrong in S1.

14. The phonemic notations /r̄/ and /rr/ are both found in various sources to symbolize the *vibrante multiple.* For consistency within this text /r̄/ will be the preferred symbol except when quoting from a source using /rr/.

15. Bull (1965), p. 65.

16. R. L. Politzer and C. H. Staubach, *Teaching Spanish: A Linguistic Orientation,* rev. ed. (New York: Blaisdell, 1965), p. 78.

17. Rodriguez-Castellano (1965), p. 21.

18. Stockwell and Bowen (1965), p. 57.

19. For a thorough discussion of these types of problems, together with numerous examples which can be incorporated into drills, see Stockwell and Bowen (1965), pp. 43–65.

20. For information on *sinéresis* and *sinalefa,* see Hadlich, et al. (1968), pp. 81–83 and 200–201.

21. The two rhymes quoted here are popular jingles for which the authors have been unable to locate a written source. Both rhymes were taught to one of the authors, one by his teacher in a FLES class, the other by a former student from Puerto Rico.

22. V. R. Iriarte, *Amador, el Optimista,* adapted in Barbara Kaminar de Mujica and Eyra Marcano, eds., *Lecturas para Pensar y Discutir* (New York: Harcourt Brace Jovanovich, 1972), p. 60, with several small additions by the authors to cover certain pronunciation problems.

II The Written Word
6 READING I: PURPOSES AND PROCEDURES

1. More research is needed to determine which basic grammatical relations in Spanish are essential to enable a person to read Spanish with comprehension.

2. J. McGlathery describes such a course in "A New Program of Substitute and Supplementary German Language Courses," in W. M. Rivers, L. H. Allen, et al., eds., *Changing Patterns in Foreign Language Programs* (Rowley, Mass.: Newbury House, 1972), pp. 248–53.

3. Luis Leal and Joseph H. Silverman, *Siglo Veinte* (New York: Holt, Rinehart and Winston, 1968), pp. 82–83.

4. Some students are able to reach this stage more rapidly through the experience of living for a time in a Spanish-speaking community—unfortunately many are not.

5. A. Díaz-Cañabete, "La muerte de una tertulia" in *La España Moderna,* Thomas R. Hart and Carlos Rojas, eds. (Englewood Cliffs, N. J., Prentice-Hall, 1966), pp. 77–79.

6. M. A. Buchanan, *A Graded Spanish Word Book* (Toronto: University of Toronto Press, 1927), p. 7.

7. H. A. Keniston, *A Standard List of Spanish Words and Idioms* (Lexington, Ky.: D. C. Heath, 1949), p. iv.

8. Ibid., p. vi.

9. Madrid: Consejo Superior de Investigaciones, Instituto "San José de Calasanz."

10. A. Juilland and E. Chang-Rodriguez, *Frequency Dictionary of Spanish Words* (The Hague: Mouton, 1964), p. v.

11. M. Cervantes de Saavedra, "La Gitanilla" from *Novelas Ejemplares,* in *De Todo un Poco,* Book I, C. Castillo and C. F. Sparkman, eds. (New York: D.C. Heath, 1936).

12. N. Brooks, *Language and Language Learning: Theory and Practice,* 2d ed. (New York: Harcourt, Brace & World, 1964), pp. 120–25.

13. This concept is explained more fully in the article "Linguistic and Psychological Factors in Speech Perception with their Implications for Teaching Materials," in Rivers (1972a), pp. 94–107.

14. *A-LM Spanish Level One,* 2d ed., Modern Language Staff (New York: Harcourt, Brace & World, 1969), p. 69.

15. Klaus A. Mueller, Luis Vargas, Roberto B. Franco, and Davis Woodward, *Spanish for Secondary Schools, First Level,* Part Two (Boston: D. C. Heath and Co., 1963), p. 36.

16. *A-LM Spanish Level One,* 2d ed., p. 83 (with *ordena a eliminar* corrected to *ordena eliminar*).

17. Mueller, Vargas, Franco, and Woodward (1963), p. 38.

18. *A-LM Spanish Level One,* 2d. ed., p. 194.

19. P. Pimsleur, *Sol y Sombra: Lecturas de Hoy* (New York: Harcourt Brace Jovanovich, 1972), pp. 15–17. This book includes selections of varying levels of difficulty; it is for this reason that the reader will find excerpts from it illustrating more than one level of reading development. The article quoted here appears in Primer Nivel which contains only the first 500 of the 1,000 most familiar words established by Pimsleur as the basis for his book.

20. As in the reading method described in Rivers (1968), pp. 22–24.

21. J. K. Leslie, *Cuentos y Risas, A First Reader in Spanish* (New York: Oxford University Press, 1952), pp. 3–4 (with *calle del Cangallo* corrected to *calle Cangallo*).

22. *Spanish: Reading for Meaning,* Modern Language Staff of Harcourt, Brace & World (New York: Harcourt, Brace & World, 1966), pp. 12–13.

7. READING II: FROM DEPENDENCE TO INDEPENDENCE

1. The matter of systems and subsystems of language has been discussed in "Contrastive Linguistics in Textbook and Classroom," in Rivers (1972a), pp. 36–44.

2. The question of verbal aspect is further complicated by the fact that it is sometimes implicit in the meaning of the verb, and sometimes expressed by grammatical means. The interested reader will find more information on this important topic of Spanish grammar in S. Gili y Gaya, *Curso superior de sintaxis española* (Barcelona: Publicaciones y Ediciones SPES, S.A., séptima edición, 1960), Ch. XI, *Teoría general de los tiempos,* as well as in C. H. Stevenson, *The Spanish Language Today* (London: Hutchinson University Library, 1970), Ch. 11, *The tense-aspect,* and in R. L. Hadlich, *A Transformational Grammar of Spanish* (Englewood Cliffs, N.J.: Prentice-Hall, 1971), Ch. 5. In R42 we focus on the aspectual contrast between the *pretérito perfecto absoluto* and the *pretérito imperfecto* (respectively called *pretérito* and *imperfecto* for short). These contrasting manners of expressing past events and circumstances are discussed in M. M. Ramsey, *A Textbook of Modern Spanish,* rev. by R. K. Spaulding (New York: Holt, Rinehart and Winston, 1956), Ch. XVII, pp. 315–28.

3. "La Luna Roja," by Roberto Arlt, in *Imaginación y Fantasía: Cuentos de*

las Américas, rev. ed., edited by Donald A. Yates and John B. Dalbor (New York: Holt, Rinehart and Winston, 1968), p. 100.

4. "El Sombrero de Tres Picos," by Pedro A. de Alarcón in Ramsey (1956), p. 327.

5. The distinction being made here is between (1) How (manner)? questions like: *¿Cómo abrió la puerta? Abrió la puerta con la llave* (directly quoted from the text), and (2) How (explanation)? questions like: *¿Cómo podía ella saber que su vecina no estaba en casa? Porque todas las ventanas estaban cerradas y generalmente la vecina las dejaba abiertas* (drawn from several parts of the text).

6. From "La Grulla," in William F. Giese and Manuel Salas, *Spanish Grammar and Reader* (New York: The Dryden Press, 1942), p. 189.

7. G. A. C. Scherer, "Programming Second Language Reading," in G. Mathieu, ed., *Advances in the Teaching of Modern Languages,* Vol. 2 (London: Pergamon, 1966), p. 113.

8. Ibid., pp. 114–15.

9. Ibid., p. 120.

10. Pimsleur (1972), pp. 78–79 (two marginal glosses omitted). R48 and R49 are from the Segundo Nivel. In addition to having a larger vocabulary base than R36, they reflect a gradually increasing number and variety of verb forms and tenses.

11. Ibid., pp. 119–20.

12. From *Obras Completas de Don Francisco de Quevedo Villegas,* Vol. 2, Luis Astrana Marín, ed. (Madrid: M. Aguilar, 1932), p. 73.

13. From *Obras Completas,* 8th ed. (Madrid: Aguilar, S.A. de Ediciones, 1954), pp. 454, 455, 464.

14. From *Canción* (Madrid: Aguilar, 1961), p. 126. Original publication date 1936 (Madrid: Editorial Signo).

15. From Azorín (José Martínez Ruiz), "Castilla—Las Nubes," in *Obras Completas,* Vol. 2 (Madrid: M. Aguilar, 1947), pp. 704–5.

16. From Anna María Matute, "La Conciencia," in *Historias de la Artámila* (Barcelona: Ediciones Destino, 1961), p. 119.

17. Scherer (1966), p. 123.

18. In P. G. Evans, *An Elementary Spanish Reader* (New York: Charles Scribner's Sons, 1960), pp. 167–68.

19. Stuart Hoffman, quoted in *Glamour,* August, 1972, p. 39.

20. In Gloria Durán and Manuel Durán *Vivir Hoy* (New York: Harcourt, Brace Jovanovich, 1973), p. 170 (glosses omitted).

21. William G. Moulton, *A Linguistic Guide to Language Learning* (New York: Modern Language Association, 1966), p. 18.

22. For further discussion along these lines, see "Linguistic and Psychological Factors in Speech Perception . . ." in Rivers (1972a), pp. 94–107.

8. WRITING AND WRITTEN EXERCISES: THE NUTS AND BOLTS

1. L. S. Vygotsky, *Thought and Language,* trans. E. Hanfmann and G. Vakar (Cambridge, Mass.: The MIT Press, 1962), p. 97.

2. Differences between spoken and written language have been discussed in

Chapter 1 (C2-6). The subjct should be studied in depth in syntax classes for future teachers.

3. The table in W3 is based on the example provided by M. Aupècle in "La langue française écrite en milieu étranger à l'école primaire," in *Le Français dans le monde,* No. 99 (1973), p. 26. Even more elaborate combination tables from R. Moody and N. Arapoff are reproduced in C. B. Paulston, "Teaching Writing in the ESOL Classroom: Techniques of Controlled Composition," *TQ* 6 (1972), pp. 43–44, where they are called "correlative substitution exercises."

4. There are many exceptions to nearly all the categories one might set up in this area. Some are more dependable than others, e.g., *-ismo* m.: *el comunismo, el fascismo,* etc. Some often-taught generalizations are better avoided, such as the notion that nouns ending in *a* are feminine. Students who learn such "rules of thumb" continue, even at the advanced stage, to say "**La problema es que . . . , *Estaba en la sofá. . . .*" (* is a linguistic convention to indicate sentences which would not be acceptable to a native speaker.)

5. Deduction and induction are discussed at the beginning of Chapter 4.

6. According to Piaget's theory of cognitive development, it is not until somewhere between twelve and fifteen years that the average child reaches the stage of "formal operations," where he is able to use verbal, symbolic forms of reasoning freely. See J. S. Bruner, R. R. Olver, et al., *Studies in Cognitive Growth* (New York: John Wiley & Sons, 1966).

7. It is difficult to randomize deliberately the positions of the correct answers in a pattern of A's, B's, and C's. One way of ensuring that one is not subconsciously arranging them in some way is to allot numbers to the letters and then arrange the correct choices according to a set of telephone numbers selected at random from the telephone book. E.g., A = 1; B = 2; C = 3; D = 4; E = 5; F = 6; the phone numbers are 352-1808; 463-7496; 359-1990; the pattern of correct answers for twelve questions will be C E B A D F C D F C E A. The first part of this randomization has been applied to W14.

8. The whimsicality of the extrapolation in this title is admitted. It was by means of comparison with the same inscription in demotic and classical Greek that Champollion was able to decipher the hieroglyphics on the Rosetta Stone.

9. There have been included here some of the most frequent forms of *deber* that the students will encounter. The full complexities of the subject should be studied by the teacher in an advanced grammar book. Special attention should be given to the use of *deber de* + infinitive to indicate obligation or necessity. On this matter, see Samuel Gili y Gaya's *Curso superior de sintaxis española* (Barcelona: Publicaciones y Ediciones SPES, S.A., séptima edición, 1960), paragraph 96, and M. M. Ramsey and R. K. Spaulding's *A Textbook of Modern Spanish* (New York: Henry Holt and Co., 1956), chapter 26. The examples in this section have been culled from a newspaper (*El Nacional* of Mexico City), from private memos, and from recorded conversations. Notice that the form *ha debido* in W 30 No. 12 can mean either "must have" (inference or supposition) or "has had to" (necessity or obligation). In such cases, only the context can make clear which meaning is intended by the speaker.

10. For a definition of *aspect,* see references in Chapter 7, Note 2.

11. Some modern textbooks prefer to use the term *mode* for the indicative,

subjunctive, and imperative, because the older term *mood* has misleading connotations.

    12. R. Braddock, R. Lloyd-Jones, and L. Schoer, *Research in Written Composition* (Champaign, Ill.: N.C.T.E., 1963), p. 83.

    13. This was the finding also for native English writers in the Buxton Study, reported in Braddock et al. (1963), pp. 58–70.

9.   WRITING AND WRITTEN EXERCISES II: FLEXIBILITY AND EXPRESSION

    1. From Julio Camba's *"El turista yanqui,"* in *La Rana Viajera* (Boston: D. C. Heath, 1928), pp. 138–40.

    2. *La Vanguardia Española,* September 15, 1972.

    3. M. Bracy, "Controlled Writing vs. Free Composition," *TQ* 5 (1971), p. 244.

    4. For further suggestions along these lines, see K. Sandburg's "writing laboratories," quoted in Paulston (1972), pp. 57–58.

    5. V. Postovsky, "Effects of Delay in Oral Practice at the Beginning of Second Language Learning," dissertation written at the University of California, Berkeley, in 1970, and reported by S. Ervin-Tripp, "Structure and Process in Language Acquisition," in J. E. Alatis, ed., *Bilingualism and Language Contact: Anthropological, Linguistic, Psychological, and Sociological Aspects,* Monograph No. 23 (Washington, D.C.: Georgetown University Press, 1970), p. 340.

    6. M. Benamou, *Pour une nouvelle pédagogie du texte littéraire* (Paris: Hachette/Larousse, 1971), pp. 12–13. [Excerpt translated by the authors.] Other useful references for the teaching of literature are: T. E. Bird, ed., *Foreign Languages: Reading, Literature, and Requirements* (1967 *NEC*) and *MLJ* 56 (1972), of which the theme is "The Teaching of Foreign Literatures," W. Lohnes, special ed., and Harold K. Moon, *Spanish Literature: A Critical Approach* (Lexington, Mass.: Xerox College Publishing, 1972).

    7. N. Arapoff, "Writing: a Thinking Process," *TQ* 1 (1967), pp. 33–39. Reprinted in H. B. Allen and R. N. Campbell, eds. *Teaching English as a Second Language: A Book of Readings,* 2d ed. (New York: McGraw-Hill, 1972), pp. 199–207.

    8. N. Arapoff, "Discover and Transform: A Method of Teaching Writing to Foreign Students," in *TQ* 3 (1969), p. 298.

    9. This subject is discussed in an interesting article by R. B. Kaplan, "Cultural Thought Patterns in Inter-Cultural Education," *LL* 16 (1966), pp. 1–20, reprinted in K. Croft, ed., *Readings on English as a Second Language* (Cambridge, Mass.: Winthrop, 1972).

    10. A number of possibilities for diversification are described in W. M. Rivers, L. H. Allen, et al., eds., *Changing Patterns in Foreign Language Programs* (Rowley, Mass.: Newbury House, 1972).

    11. Formulas for beginning and ending all kinds of letters as well as for greetings, invitations, and announcements, are set out in Laurel H. Turk and Agnes M. Brady, *Spanish Letter Writing* (Boston: D. C. Heath and Co., 1942) and in José Carlos Garcia Martín, *Correspondencia Comercial* (México, D.F.: Harper and Row Latinoamerica, Harla, S.A., 1973).

    12. Arapoff (1967) in Allen and Campbell, eds. (1972), p. 200.

13. R. M. Valette in "Developing and Evaluating Communication Skills in the Classroom," *TQ* 7 (1973), pp. 417–18.

14. Francis Bacon, *Of Studies* (1598).

15. R. L. Lyman, "A Co-operative Experiment in Junior High School Composition" (1931), quoted in Braddock, et al. (1963), p. 35.

16. D. Knapp, "A Focused, Efficient Method to Relate Composition Correction to Teaching Aims," in Allen and Campbell, eds. (1972), pp. 213–21.

17. See "The Writer Variable" in Braddock, et al. (1963), pp. 6–7, where the research of G. L. Kincaid and C. C. Anderson is reported.

18. For more information on inferencing, see Aaron S. Carton, "Inferencing: A Process in Using and Learning Laguage," in P. Pimsleur and T. Quinn, eds. *The Psychology of Second Language Learning* (Cambridge, Eng.: Cambridge University Press, 1971), pp. 45–58.

19. Teachers interested in translation should be familiar with books like E. A. Nida, *Toward a Science of Translating* (Leiden: E. J. Brill, 1964) and J. C. Catford, *A Linguistic Theory of Translation* (London: Oxford University Press, 1965). See also W. M. Rivers, "Contrastive Linguistics in Textbook and Classroom" in Rivers (1972a), pp. 36–44.

20. Note that, since these questions apply to both types of translation, the expression "source text" refers to a text in either Spanish or English, and the "target language" is the one into which the passage is being translated.

21. From B. Malamud, *The Fixer* (New York: Farrar, Straus and Giroux, 1966), p. 215.

22. *Falsos amigos* are discussed in *Reading for Information* in Chapter 6.

23. Both A and B are from the bilingual edition *Requiem por un Campesino Español—Requiem for a Spanish Peasant* (New York: Las Americas Publishing Co., 1960), pp. 6–7. The English translation is by Elinor Randall.

24. Passage A is from José María Gironella's *Un Millón de Muertos* (Barcelona: Editorial Planeta, 1961), and Passage B is from the English translation of the same book, entitled *One Million Dead,* by Joan MacLean (New York: Doubleday and Co., 1963), first and second paragraphs of Chapter One.

General bibliography

Alatis, J. E., ed. 1969. *Linguistics and the Teaching of Standard English to Speakers of Other Languages or Dialects.* Georgetown University Round Table on Languages and Linguistics. Washington, D.C.: Georgetown University Press.

———, ed. 1970. *Bilingualism and Language Contact: Anthropological, Linguistic, Psychological, and Sociological Aspects.* Georgetown University Round Table on Languages and Linguistics. Washington, D.C.: Georgetown University Press.

Allen, E. D., and Valette, R. M. 1972. *Modern Language Classroom Techniques: A Handbook.* New York: Harcourt Brace Jovanovich.

Allen, H. B., and Campbell, R. N., eds. 1972. *Teaching English as a Second Language: A Book of Readings.* 2d ed. New York: McGraw-Hill.

Alonso, M. 1968. *Gramática del español contemporáneo.* Madrid: Ediciones Guadarrama.

Alter, M. P. 1970. *A Modern Case for German.* Philadelphia: American Association of Teachers of German.

Altman, H. B., ed. 1972. *Individualizing the Foreign Language Classroom: Perspectives for Teaching.* Rowley, Mass.: Newbury House.

Altman, H. G., and Politzer, R. L., eds. 1971. *Individualizing Foreign Language Instruction.* Rowley, Mass.: Newbury House.

Arapoff, N. 1967. "Writing: A Thinking Process." *TQ* 1:33–39.

———. 1969. "Discover and Transform: A Method of Teaching Writing to Foreign Students." *TQ* 3:297–304.

Asher, J. H. 1966. "The Learning Strategy of the Total Physical Response: A Review." *MLJ* 50:70–84.

Bartley, D. E., and Politzer, R. L. 1969. *Practice-Centered Teacher Training: Spanish.* Philadelphia: Center for Curriculum Development.

Beinhauer, W. 1963. *El español coloquial.* Madrid: Editorial Gredos.

Belasco, S. 1970. "C'est la Guerre? or Can Cognition and Verbal Behavior Co-exist in Second-Language Learning?" *MLJ* 54:395–412. Reprinted in Lugton, R. C., ed. (1970), pp. 191–230.

Birkmaier, E. M., ed. 1968. *Foreign Language Education: An Overview.* Britannica Review of Foreign Language Education, Vol. 1. Chicago: Encyclopaedia Britannica.

――――. 1971. "The Meaning of Creativity in Foreign Language Teaching." *MLJ* 55:345–53.

Bowen, J. D., and Stockwell, R. P. 1960. *Patterns of Spanish Pronunciation: A Drillbook.* Chicago: The University of Chicago Press.

Bracy, M. 1971. "Controlled Writing vs: Free Composition." *TQ* 5:239–46.

Braddock, R., Lloyd-Jones, R., and Schoer, L. 1963. *Research in Written Composition.* Champaign, Ill.: National Council of Teachers of English.

Brooks, N. 1964. *Language and Language Learning: Theory and Practice.* 2d ed. New York: Harcourt, Brace & World.

Buchanan, M. A. 1927. *A Graded Spanish Word Book.* Toronto: University of Toronto Press.

Bull, W. E. 1965. *Spanish for Teachers: Applied Linguistics.* New York: The Ronald Press.

Calderón, Correa, E., and Lázaro, F. 1966. *Cómo se comenta un texto literario.* Salamanca: Ediciones Anaya, S. A.

Catford, J. C. 1965. *A Linguistic Theory of Translation.* London: Oxford University Press.

Chastain, K. 1971. *The Development of Modern Language Skills: Theory to Practice.* Philadelphia: Center for Curriculum Development.

Croft, K., ed. 1972. *Readings on English as a Second Language.* Cambridge, Mass.: Winthrop.

Dalbor, J. B., 1969. *Spanish Pronunciation: Theory and Practice.* New York: Holt, Rinehart and Winston.

Delattre, P. 1965. *Comparing the Phonetic Features of English, French, German and Spanish.* London: Harrap.

Diller, K. C. 1971. *Generative Grammar, Structural Linguistics, and Language Teaching.* Rowley, Mass.: Newbury House.

Dodge, J. W., ed. 1971. *The Case for Foreign Language Study.* New York: Northeast Conference and MLA/ACTFL.

Finocchiaro, M., and Bonomo, M. 1973. *The Foreign Language Learner: A Guide for Teachers.* New York: Regents Publishing Co.

Frey, H. J. 1974. *Teaching Spanish: A Critical Bibliographic Survey.* Rowley, Mass.: Newbury House.

Fries, C. C. 1945. *Teaching and Learning English as a Foreign Language.* Ann Arbor, Mich.: University of Michigan Press.

García Martin, J. C. 1973. *Correspondencia comercial.* Mexico, D.F.: Harper and Row Latinoamerica, Harla, S. A.

Gattegno, C. 1963. *Teaching Foreign Languages in Schools: The Silent Way.* Reading, Eng.: Educational Explorers. (2d ed. 1972. New York: Educational Solutions.)

George, H. V. 1972. *Common Errors in Language Learning: Insights from English.* Rowley, Mass.: Newbury House.

Gili y Gaya, S. 1960. *Curso superior de sintaxis española.* Barcelona: Publicaciones y Ediciones SPES, S. A., séptima edición.

Gouin, F. 1892. *The Art of Teaching and Studying Languages.* Trans. H. Swan and V. Bétis. London: George Philip and Son; New York: Charles Scribner's Sons.

Green, J. R. 1968. *A Gesture Inventory for the Teaching of Spanish.* Philadelphia: Chilton Books.

Grittner, F. 1969. *Teaching Foreign Languages.* New York: Harper and Row.

――――, ed. 1974. *Student Motivation and the Foreign Language Teacher.* Skokie, Ill.: National Textbook Company.

――――, and LaLeike, F. H. 1973. *Individualized Foreign Language Instruction.* Skokie, Ill.: National Textbook Company.

Harris, D. P. 1969. *Testing English as a Second Language.* New York: McGraw-Hill.

Hester, R., ed. 1970. *Teaching a Living Language.* New York: Harper and Row.

Howes, V. M., ed. 1970. *Individualization of Instruction: A Teaching Strategy.* New York: Macmillan.

Hulp, L. B., 1974. *Let's Play Games in Spanish,* Vols. 1 and 2. (Skokie, Ill.: National Textbook Co.)

Jakobovits, L. A. 1970. *Foreign Language Learning. A Psycholinguistic Analysis of the Issues.* Rowley, Mass.: Newbury House.

――――, and Gordon, B. 1974. *The Context of Foreign Language Teaching.* Rowley, Mass.: Newbury House.

Jankowsky, K., ed. 1973. *Language and International Studies.* Georgetown University Round Table on Languages and Linguistics. Washington, D.C.: Georgetown University Press.

Jarvis, G. A., ed. 1974. *Responding to New Realities.* ACTFL Review of Foreign Language Education, Vol. 5. Skokie, Ill.: National Textbook Company.

――――., ed. 1975. *The Challenge of Communication.* ACTFL Review of Foreign Language Education, Vol. 6. Skokie, Ill.: National Textbook Company.

Jespersen, O. 1904. *How to Teach a Foreign Language.* London: George Allen and Unwin Ltd. Reissued, 1961.

Juilland, A. and Chang-Rodriguez, E. 1964. *Frequency Dictionary of Spanish Words.* The Hague: Mouton and Co.

Kaplan, R. B. 1966. "Cultural Thought Patterns in Inter-Cultural Education." *LL* 16:1–20.

Kelly, L. G. 1969. *25 Centuries of Language Teaching.* Rowley, Mass.: Newbury House.

Keniston, H. 1941. *A Standard List of Spanish Words and Idioms.* Lexington: D. C. Heath and Co.

Knapp, D. 1972. "A Focused, Efficient Method to Relate Composition Correction to Teaching Aims." In Allen, H. B., and Campbell, R. N., eds., (1972), pp. 213–21.

Lambert, W. E., and Tucker, R. 1972. *The Bilingual Education of Children*. Rowley, Mass.: Newbury House.

Lange, D. L., ed. 1970. *Individualization of Instruction*. Britannica Review of Foreign Language Education, Vol. 2. Chicago: Encyclopaedia Britannica.

————, ed. 1971. *Pluralism in Foreign Language Education*. Britannica Review of Foreign Language Education, Vol. 3. Chicago: Encyclopaedia Britannica.

————, and James, C. J., eds. 1972. *Foreign Language Education: A Reappraisal*. ACTFL Review of Foreign Language Education, Vol. 4. Skokie, Ill.: National Textbook Company.

Lenard, Y. 1970. "Methods and Materials, Techniques and the Teacher." In Hester, R., ed. (1971), pp. 33–64.

Logan, G. E. 1973. *Individualized Foreign Language Learning: An Organic Process*. Rowley, Mass.: Newbury House.

Lohnes, W., spec. ed. 1972. *The Teaching of Foreign Literatures* (Theme). *MLJ* 56, No. 5.

Love, F. W., and Honig, L. J. 1973. *Options and Perspectives: A Sourcebook of Innovative Foreign Language Programs in Action, K-12*. New York: Modern Language Association.

Lugton, R. C., ed. 1971. *Toward a Cognitive Approach to Second Language Acquisition*. Philadelphia: Center for Curriculum Development.

Melgar, R. L. 1968. *Introducción a los estudios literarios*. Salamanca: Ediciones Anaya, S. A.

Moskowitz, G., 1970. *The Foreign Language Teacher Interacts*. rev. ed. Minneapolis: Association for Productive Teaching.

Moulton, W. G. 1966. *A Linguistic Guide to Language Learning*. New York: Modern Language Association.

Navarro Tomás, T. 1968. *Studies in Spanish Phonology*. Coral Gables, Fla.: University of Miami Press.

Nida, E. A. 1964. *Toward a Science of Translating*. Leiden: E. J. Brill.

Northeast Conference (1959): F. D. Eddy, ed. *The Language Learner*. Containing: Modern Foreign Language Learning: Assumptions and Implications; A Six-Year Sequence; Elementary and Junior High School Curricula; Definition of Language Competences Through Testing.

Northeast Conference (1960): G. R. Bishop, ed. *Culture in Language Learning*. Containing: An Anthropological Concept of Culture; Language as Culture; Teaching of Western European Cultures; Teaching of Classical Cultures; Teaching of Slavic Cultures.

Northeast Conference (1961): S. L. Flaxman, ed. *Modern Language Teaching in School and College*. Containing: The Training of Teachers for Secondary Schools; The Preparation of College and University Teachers; The Transition to the Classroom; Coordination between Classroom and Laboratory.

Northeast Conference (1962): W. F. Bottiglia, ed. *Current Issues in Language Teaching*. Containing: Linguistics and Language Teaching: Programmed Learning; A Survey of FLES Practices; Televised Teaching.

Northeast Conference (1963): W. F. Bottiglia, ed. *Language Learning: The Intermediate Phase.* Containing: The Continuum: Listening and Speaking; Reading for Meaning; Writing as Expression.

Northeast Conference (1964): G. F. Jones, ed. *Foreign Language Teaching: Ideals and Practices.* Containing: Foreign Languages in the Elementary School; Foreign Languages in the Secondary School; Foreign Languages in Colleges and Universities.

Northeast Conference (1965): G. R. Bishop, ed. *Foreign Language Teaching: Challenges to the Profession.* Containing: The Case for Latin; Study Abroad; The Challenge of Bilingualism; From School to College.

Northeast Conference (1966): R. G. Mead, Jr., ed. *Language Teaching: Broader Contexts.* Containing: Research and Language Learning: Content and Crossroads: Wider Uses for Foreign Languages; The Coordination of Foreign-Language Teaching.

Northeast Conference (1967): T. E. Bird, ed. *Foreign Languages: Reading, Literature, and Requirements.* Containing: The Teaching of Reading; The Times and Places for Literature; Trends in FL Requirements and Placement.

Northeast Conference (1968): T. E. Bird, ed. *Foreign Language Learning: Research and Development.* Containing: Innovative FL Programs; The Classroom Revisited; Liberated Expression.

Northeast Conference (1969): M. F. Edgerton, Jr., ed. *Sight and Sound: The Sensible and Sensitive Use of Audio-Visual Aids.* Containing: Non-Projected Visuals; Sound Recordings; Slides and Filmstrips; The Overhead Projector; Motion Pictures; Television; Let Us Build Bridges.

Northeast Conference (1970): J. Tursi, ed. *Foreign Languages and the "New" Student.* Containing: A Relevant Curriculum: An Instrument for Polling Student Opinion; Motivation in FL Learning; FL's for All Children?

Northeast Conference (1971): J. W. Dodge, ed. *Leadership for Continuing Development.* Containing: Professional Responsibilities; Inservice Involvement in the Process of Change; Innovative Trends in FL Teaching; Literature for Advanced FL Students.

Northeast Conference (1972): J. W. Dodge, ed. *Other Words, Other Worlds: Language-in-Culture.* Containing: On Teaching Another Language as Part of Another Culture; Sociocultural Aspects of FL Study; Ancient Greek and Roman Culture; France; Quebec: French Canada; An Approach to Courses in German Culture; Italy and the Italians; Japan: Spirit and Essence; The Soviet Union; Spain; Spanish America: A Study in Diversity.

Northeast Conference (1973): J. W. Dodge, ed. *Sensitivity in the Foreign Language Classroom.* Containing: Interaction in the FL Class; Teaching Spanish to the Native Spanish Speaker; Individualization of Instruction.

Northeast Conference (1974): W. C. Born, ed. *Toward Student-Centered Foreign-Language Programs.* Containing: The Teacher in the Student-Centered FL Program; Implementing Student-Centered FL Programs; FL's and the Community.

Northeast Conference (1975): W. C. Born, ed. *Goals Clarification: Curriculum, Teaching, Evaluation.*

Northeast Conference (1976): W. C. Born, ed. *Language and Culture: Heritage and Horizons.*

Oller, J., Jr., and Richards, J. 1973. *Focus on the Learner.* Rowley, Mass.: Newbury House.

Palmer, H. 1917. *The Scientific Study and Teaching of Languages.* London: Harrap.

Paulston, C. B. 1971. "The Sequencing of Structural Pattern Drills." *TQ* 5:197–208.

———. 1972. "Teaching Writing in the ESOL Classroom: Techniques of Controlled Composition." *TQ* 6:33–59.

———, and Selekman, H. R. "Interaction Activities in the Foreign Language Classroom or How to Grow a Tulip-Rose." *FLA* 8.

Perren, G. E., and Trim, J. L. M., eds. 1971. *Application of Linguistics: Selected Papers of the Second International Congress of Applied Linguistics.* Cambridge, Eng.: Cambridge University Press.

Pillet, R. A. 1974. *Foreign-Language Study: Perspective and Prospect.* Chicago: The University of Chicago Press.

Politzer, R. L. and Staubach, C. H. 1965. *Teaching Spanish: A Linguistic Orientation.* Rev. ed. New York: Blaisdell.

Prator, C. H. 1957. *Manual of American English Pronunciation.* Rev. ed. New York: Holt, Rinehart and Winston.

Recuentro de vocabulario español. 1952. Río Piedras: University of Puerto Rico.

Reichmann, E., ed. *The Teaching of German: Problems and Methods.* Philadelphia: National Carl Schurz Association.

Rivers, W. M. 1964. *The Psychologist and the Foreign-Language Teacher.* Chicago: The University of Chicago Press.

———. 1968. *Teaching Foreign-Language Skills.* Chicago: The University of Chicago Press.

———. 1972a. *Speaking in Many Tongues.* Rowley, Mass.: Newbury House.

———, Allen, L. H., et al., eds. 1972b. *Changing Patterns in Foreign Language Programs.* Rowley, Mass.: Newbury House.

———. 1973a. "From Linguistic Competence to Communicative Competence." *TQ* 7:25–34.

———. 1973b. "Testing and Student Learning." In O'Brien, M. C., ed., *Testing in Second Language Teaching: New Dimensions.* Dublin: ATESOL, and Dublin University Press, pp. 27–36.

———. 1973c. "The Non-Major: Tailoring the Course to Fit the Person—not the Image." In Jankowsky, K., ed. (1973), pp. 85–97. Also *ADFL Bulletin* 5, 2:12–18.

———. 1975a. "Students, Teachers and the Future." *FLA* 8: 22–32.

———. 1975b. "The Natural and the Normal in Language Learning." *LL* 21, No. 2.

Sauzé, E. B. de and Condon, V. 1931. *The Cleveland Plan for the Teaching of Modern Languages with Special Reference to Spanish.* Philadelphia: The John C. Winston Co.

Scherer, G. A. C. 1966. "Programming Second Language Reading." In Mathieu, G., ed. *Advances in the Teaching of Modern Languages*. Vol. 2. London: Pergamon, pp. 108–29.

Schumann, J. H. 1972. "Communication Techniques." *TQ* 6: 143–46.

Seco, M. 1972. *Gramática esencial del español*. Madrid: Aguilar S. A. de Ediciones.

Seelye, H. N. 1974. *Teaching Culture: Strategies for Foreign Language Educators*. Skokie, Ill.: National Textbook Company.

Spolsky, B., ed. 1972. *The Language Education of Minority Children*. Rowley, Mass.: Newbury House.

Stack, E. M. 1966. *The Language Laboratory and Modern Language Teaching*. Rev. ed. New York: Oxford University Press.

Steiner, F. 1975. *Performing with Objectives*. Rowley, Mass.: Newbury House.

Stevick, E. W. 1966. "UHF and Microwaves in Transmitting Language Skills." In Najam, E. W. and Hodge, C. T., eds., *Language Learning: The Individual and the Process*. *IJAL* 32, 1, Part 2. Publication 40 of the Indiana University Research Center in Anthropology, Folklore, and Linguistics.

———. 1971. *Adapting and Writing Language Lessons*. Washington, D.C.: Foreign Service Institute.

———. 1973. "Before Linguistics and Beneath Method." In Jankowsky, K., ed. (1973), pp. 99–106.

Stockwell, R. P., and Bowen, J. D. 1965. *The Sounds of English and Spanish*. Contrastive Structure Series. Charles A. Ferguson, Gen. ed. Chicago: The University of Chicago Press.

———, Bowen, J. D., and Martin, J. W. 1965. *The Grammatical Structures of English and Spanish*. Contrastive Structure Series. Charles A. Ferguson, Gen. ed. Chicago: The University of Chicago Press.

Sweet, H. 1899. *The Practical Study of Languages*. London: Dent. Reprinted 1964. London: Oxford University Press.

Titone, R. 1968. *Teaching Foreign Languages: An Historical Sketch*. Washington, D.C.: Georgetown University Press.

Troike, R. C., and Modiano, N. 1975. *The Proceedings of the First Inter-American Conference on Bilingual Education*. Arlington, Va.: Center for Applied Linguistics.

Turk, L. H., and Brody, A. M. 1942. *Spanish Letter Writing*. Boston: D. C. Heath and Co.

Valette, R. M. 1967. *Modern Language Testing: A Handbook*. New York: Harcourt, Brace & World.

———, and Disick, R. S. 1972. *Modern Language Performance Objectives and Individualization: A Handbook*. New York: Harcourt Brace Jovanovich.

———. 1973. "Developing and Evaluating Communication Skills in the Classroom." *TQ* 7:407–24.

West, M. 1941. *Learning to Read a Foreign Language and Other Essays on Language-Teaching*. London: Longmans.

Wilkins, D. A. 1972. *Linguistics in Language Teaching*. Cambridge, Mass.: The MIT Press.

Supplemental bibliography

SOME INTRODUCTORY READINGS IN LINGUISTICS AND PSYCHOLOGY OF LANGUAGE LEARNING

Aid, F. M., *Semantic Structures in Spanish: A Proposal for Instructional Materials*. Washington, D.C.: Georgetown University Press.

Alarcos Worach, E. 1970. *Estudios de gramática functional del español*. Madrid: Editorial Gredos.

Allan, J. P. B., and Corder, S. P., eds. 1973. *Readings for Applied Linguistics*. Vol. 1. London: Oxford University Press.

Alonso Pedraz, M. 1955. *Ciencia del lenguage y arte del estilo*. 4 ed. rev. Madrid: Aguilar.

Bolinger, D. 1975. *Aspects of Language*. 2d ed. New York: Harcourt Brace Jovanovich.

Bruner, J. S., Olver, R. R., et al. 1966. *Studies in Cognitive Growth*. New York: John Wiley and Sons.

Carroll, J. B. and Freedle, R. O., eds. 1972. *Language Comprehension and the Acquisition of Knowledge*. Washington, D.C.: V. H. Winston and Sons.

Chafe, W. 1970. *Meaning and the Structure of Language*. Chicago: The University of Chicago Press.

Cherry, C., 1957. *On Human Communication*. New York: John Wiley and Sons.

Chomsky, N. 1957. *Syntactic Structures*. The Hague: Mouton.

————. 1965. *Aspects of the Theory of Syntax*. Cambridge, Mass.: The MIT Press.

————. 1972. *Language and Mind*. Enlarged ed. New York: Harcourt Brace Jovanovich. Original ed. 1968.

341

————. 1972. *Studies on Semantics in Generative Grammar.* The Hague: Mouton.

Corder, S. P. 1973. *Introducing Applied Linguistics.* Harmondsworth, Middlesex, Eng.: Penguin Books.

Criado de Val, M. 1969. *El verbo español.* Madrid: Sociedad Anónima Española de Traductores y Historias.

Elgin, S. H. 1973. *What Is Linguistics?* Englewood Cliffs, N.J.: Prentice-Hall.

Ervin-Tripp, S. M. 1973. *Language Acquisition and Communicative Choice.* Selected and introduced by A. S. Dil. Stanford: Stanford University Press.

Ferguson, C. A., and Slobin, D. I., eds. 1973. *Studies of Child Language Development.* New York: Holt, Rinehart and Winston.

Fernandez-Rampirez, S. 1951. *Gramática española: los sonidos, el nombre y el pronombre.* Madrid: Manueles de la Revista de Occidente.

Fishman, J. A. 1971. *Sociolinguistics: A Brief Introduction.* Rowley, Mass.: Newbury House.

Fodor, J. A., Bever, T. G., and Garrett, M. F. 1974. *The Psychology of Language: An Introduction to Psycholinguistics and Generative Grammar.* New York: McGraw-Hill.

Gardner, R. C., and Lambert, W. E. 1972. *Attitudes and Motivation in Second-Language Learning.* Rowley, Mass.: Newbury House.

Giglioli, P. P. 1972. *Language and Social Context.* Harmondsworth, Middlesex: Penguin Books.

Halliday, M. A. K. 1973. *Explorations in the Functions of Language.* London: Edward Arnold.

Hayes, J. R., ed. 1970. *Cognition and the Development of Language.* New York: John Wiley and Sons.

Hockett, C. 1961. "Grammar for the Hearer." In Jakobson, R., ed. *On the Structure of Language and its Mathematical Aspects.* Providence, R.I.: American Mathematical Society, pp. 220–36.

Huey, E. B. 1968. *The Psychology and Pedagogy of Reading.* Cambridge, Mass.: The MIT Press. Original publication: Macmillan, 1908.

Joos, M. 1961. *The Five Clocks.* New York: Harcourt, Brace & World.

Lakoff, G. 1971. "On Generative Semantics." In Steinberg, D. D., and Jakobovits, L. A., eds., *Semantics.* Cambridge, Eng.: Cambridge University Press, pp. 232–96.

————. 1972. "The Arbitrary Basis of Transformational Grammar." *Language* 48:77–78.

Lakoff, R. 1972. "Language in Context." *Language* 48:907–27.

Lambert, W. E. 1972. *Language, Psychology and Culture.* Selected and introduced by A. S. Dil. Stanford: Stanford University Press.

Langacker, R. W. 1967. *Language and its Structure: Some Fundamental Linguistic Concepts.* New York: Harcourt, Brace & World.

Lewis, E. G. 1974. *Linguistics and Second Language Pedagogy: A Theoretical Study.* The Hague: Mouton.

Lyons, J. 1968. *Introduction to Theoretical Linguistics.* Cambridge, Eng.: Cambridge University Press.

————., ed. 1970. *New Horizons in Linguistics*. Harmondsworth, Middlesex: Penguin Books.

Maslow, A. H. 1970. *Motivation and Personality*. 2d ed. New York: Harper and Row.

Miller, G. A. 1967. *The Psychology of Communication: Seven Essays*. New York: Basic Books. Published 1969 as *Psychology and Communication*. London: Pelican.

————, ed. 1973. *Communication, Language, and Meaning: Psychological Perspectives*. New York: Basic Books.

Neisser, U. 1967. *Cognitive Psychology*. New York: Appleton-Century-Crofts.

Nilsen, D. L. F. and A. P. 1975. *Semantic Theory: A Linguistic Perspective*. Rowley, Mass.: Newbury House.

Pimsleur, P., and Quinn, T., eds. 1971. *The Psychology of Second Language Learning*. Cambridge, Eng.: Cambridge University Press.

Politzer, R. L. 1972. *Linguistics and Applied Linguistics: Aims and Methods*. Philadelphia: Center for Curriculum Development.

Real Academia Española. 1973. *Esbozo de una nueva gramática de la lengua española*. Madrid: Espasa-Calpe, S.A.

Schane, S. A. 1973. *Generative Phonology*. Englewood Cliffs, N.J.: Prentice-Hall.

Schlesinger, I. M. 1968. *Sentence Structure and the Reading Process*. The Hague: Mouton.

Schumann, J. H., and Stenson, N., eds. 1974. *New Frontiers in Second Language Learning*. Rowley, Mass.: Newbury House.

Searle, J. R. 1969. *Speech Acts: An Essay in the Philosophy of Language*. Cambridge, Eng.: Cambridge University Press.

Slobin, D. I. 1971. *Psycholinguistics*. Glenview, Ill.: Scott, Foresman.

Smith, F. 1971. *Understanding Reading*. New York: Holt, Rinehart & Winston.

Spearritt, D. 1962. *Listening Comprehension: A Factorial Analysis*. Melbourne: Australian Council for Educational Research.

Vygotsky, L. S. 1962. *Thought and Language*. Trans. E. Hanfmann and G. Vakar. Cambridge, Mass.: The MIT Press.

Index

218–19, 233, 235, 249. *See also* Listening, with comprehension questions

Radio, 39, 53, 57, 63, 102, 103, 105; newscasts, 42, 67–69, 88, 100, 103, 104, 233
Rapid speech. *See* Spoken Spanish
Rationalist direct method. *See* Direct method
Reading, 22; aloud, 100, 161, 163, 190–91, 234–35; direct, 178, 197, 198, 207, 213, 233, 283; of expository material, 221, 224; extensive, 203, 206, 209, 222, 233, 284; of informal material, 177; for information, 171–77, 211, 224, 235, 288, 298; intensive, 203–6, 207–8, 209–10, 211–15; for literary analysis, 178, 212, 266, 289; objectives of, 171, 179, 190, 198; pre-reading, 190; of recombinations, 190, 194–96, 197; speed of, 206, 234–35; with speaking, 40–41, 58, 177, 191–92, 210, 233; stages of development in, 178, 189–90, 314, 315, *stage one, 190–94, stage two, 194–97, stage three, 197–202, stage four, 203–9, stage five, 209–15, stage six, 215;* student's interests in, 171, 178–79, 206, 209–10, 314–15; teaching of, 177, 216–17, 235, 297, 314; with writing, 191, 194–95, 209, 211, 219, 228–29, 232, 272, 278, 283–84. *See also Consultorio sentimental;* Listening, with reading; Microtexts; Testing; Vocabulary
Recall, 32, 78, 80, 82, 95, 230–31, 232. *See also* Memory
Reception, 4. *See also* Listening
Recombination. *See* Dialogues; Reading
Records. *See* Tapes and records
Redundancy, 7–8, 11, 31, 55, 60, 62–63, 68, 80–81
Register. *See* Style of language
Rejoinders, 23, 31, 33, 38, 256
Repetition, 31–32, 114–15, 160
Repetition exercises. *See* Drills
Replacement exercises. *See* Exercises
Research projects, 50, 51, 52, 177, 233–34, 243–44, 282–84, 289
Restatements. *See* Drills, conversions
Résumé (*resumen* or *sumario*), 224, 232, 233, 284, 286, 289
Retention. *See* Memory
Role-playing, 27, 33, 45, 52–53, 98, 100, 101, 105, 198, 233, 270, 281. *See also* Dramatization
Rosetta procedure. *See* Exercises
Rule-governed behavior. See Rules
Rules, 109–10, 125–26, 239, 249; deductive explanation of, 33, 106, 247, 248; inductive discovery of, 18, 21, 23, 32, 106, 205, 262–63; internalization of, 14; rule-governed behavior, 14, 15, 21, 54

SAAD'S (simple, active, affirmative, declarative sentences), 8, 80, 82, 97, 98, 99, 101, 283, 292
Sainetes. See Dialogues, recreational
Semantics, 15, 65, 79, 86, 137, 205–6, 229, 231, 261, 262, 298, 299, 318 n.7, 318 n.15; generative, 84, 323 n.30. *See also* Lexical choice; Meaning; Vocabulary
Semantic-syntactic decoding. *See* Listening models of processes
Sentence modification. *See* Drills; Exercises, written
Short stories, 64, 206, 209, 215, 233
Silent Way (Gattegno), 17–18, 73
SI line. *See* Simultaneous interpretation
Simultaneous interpretation, 56, 139, 288, 295; SI line (Stevick), 56
Sinalefa, 7–8, 9, 157, 160, 165, 194, 326 n.20
Sinéresis, 157, 160, 165, 326 n.20
Situations: with dialogues, 27, 29, 36–38, 312; for natural language use, 45–48, 52–53, 56, 128, 139, 313, 324 n.39; in structured learning, 15, 19, 20, 107, 117, 118, 119–20, 125, 134–35, 194, 210, 256, 270, 272, 313. *See also* Conversation; Dialogues; Interview technique; Role playing; Tapes, *Situation*
Situation tapes. *See* Tapes and records
Skill-getting and skill-using, 4–5, 238. *See also* Intensive practice; Communication
Skits. *See* Dialogues, recreational
Slides. *See* Visual aids
Social relations, 46
Songs, 52, 53, 58, 73, 95, 99, 104, 234, 302
Sound-production exercises. *See* Exercises, for production of sounds
Sound-symbol correspondence, 87–88, 163, 190, 191, 192–93, 236, 322 n.17. *See also* Spelling
Sound system. *See* Phonological system
Spanglish, 246, 269, 303
Spanish language: characteristics of, 7; contemporary usage, 7–14, 24–25, 57, 123–24, 136, 142–43, 177–78; differences between spoken and written Spanish, 7–9, 102, 238, 281; effects of position of stress in, 9–11; regional differences in, 52, 58, 102, 142–43; written, 210, 238, 239, 241. *See also Ataque suave;* Intonation; Phonological system; *Sinalefa; Sinéresis;* Spoken Spanish; Stress
Spanish-speaking areas outside Spain: materials related to, 42, 52, 64, 102, 104, 198–99, 206, 215, 233, 312, 315
Speaking, 14–15, 21–22, 44–57, 287; through immediate communication 6; middle position for, 6–7; progressive development of, 6; with writing, 41, 48, 238–39, 281–83. *See also* Communication; Discussion; Listening,

with speaking; Normal purposes of language; Reading, with speaking
Speech acts (Searle), 15
Spelling, 70, 87–88, 163, 173, 191, 192–93, 239, 241, 243, 291. *See also* Sound-symbol correspondence
Spoken Spanish, 7–14, 55–56, 60–63; consultative, 12; formal, 11–12, 68, 161; informal, 9, 11–12, 13, 67, 76, 98, 177–78, 193, 238; rapid, 8–9, 13, 101. *See also* Spanish language; Stress; Style of language; *Tu* and *usted*
Stimulus sentences. *See* Translation, drills
Stress, 9–11, 18, 119, 143, 155–56, 159, 160, 163, 164, 244. *See also* Spanish language
Student interest. *See* Reading; Teacher-student relations
Style of language, 11–12, 14, 15, 31, 58, 64, 102, 161, 179, 297, 300, 304, 313; and Joos's five styles, 11. *See also* Spanish language, written; Spoken Spanish
Stylistics, 284–86, 300–302, 304–5
Subjunctive. *See* Tenses and moods
Substitution exercises. *See* Drills
Substitution or variation tables, 118–19, 240–41, 324 n.3
Suffixes. *See* Vocabulary, prefixes and suffixes
Summary. *See* Résumé
Syllables in Spanish, 143, 164, 194, 324 n.22. *See also Ataque suave; Sinalefa; Sinéresis*
Syntactic system, 15–16, 60, 64–66, 238, 247–49, 253, 267, 315; signals or cues of, 75–76, 84–85, 201–2, 262

Tags, 8, 63, 121–22, 125
Tapes and records: exercises on, 114–16, 161, 314; for pronunciation practice, 161, 163–66, 314; *Situation,* 42–43, 91–92, 100, 312, 320 n.40; uses for, 7, 17, 57, 58, 64, 69, 73, 95, 98, 99, 102, 103, 104, 105, 233, 242, 243, 282, 289. *See also* Language laboratory
Teacher proficiency, 57, 265–66
Teachers, non-native, 54, 57
Teacher-student relations, 19, 44, 45, 50–51, 54–55, 57, 110, 171, 174, 252, 262, 286–87, 291, 295. *See also* Personality of student
Telephone, 45, 48–49, 101, 104, 128, 134–35
Television, 46–47, 53, 90, 103, 234
Tenses and moods, 121, 127, 134, 138, 177–78, 203–4, 208, 252–53; Conditional, 127, 252–54, 270; future, 25, 26, 28, 29, 76, 97, 99, 120–21, 138, 201, 247–48; imperative, 72–73, 113; infinitive, 133; past, 138, 203–5, 241, 256–57, 258–59, 260, 264–65, 310; participles, 127, 226, 241; present, 25, 76–77, 99, 110, 120, 252–54; subjunctive, 127, 133, 205, 252–54, 266. *See also* Aspect
Tests; cloze, 98, 261, 276, 278, 284, 315; con-

struction of, 250–61; correction of, 250, 257, 258; in drills, 122; of grammar, 250–53, 256–61, 276, 315; of interaction, 56; of listening comprehension, 59, 77–78, 89–95, 313, 321 n.3.2; multiple choice, 77, 89, 89–95, 96–97, 98, 100, 220–22, 228–29, 250–56, 313, 315, 329 n.7; of oral drills, 115, 118; of pronunciation, 163–66; of reading comprehension, 78–79, 217–25, 261; of spelling, 191; true-false, 77, 89, 96, 100, 222–23; of vocabulary, 224, 254–55
Textbooks, 22, 107–11, 170, 192, 313, 314, 315, 316; dialogues in, 14, 26, 29; exercises in, 137, 139, 229, 261, 274–75, 297; pronunciation in, 154; readings in, 207, 209, 213–14
Tongue-twisters, 154, 161
Total immersion, 6
Total physical response, 20, 72. *See also* Actions in language learning
Transfer, 141, 144–47, 157–59, 269
Transformational-generative grammar, 122–23, 126–27, 141–42, 322 n.6, 323 n.30, 323 n.33; deep and surface structure, 126, 192
Transformations. *See* Drills, conversion
Translation, 22, 32, 136, 178–79, 209, 287, 295–305, 331 n.19; drills, 136–39, 297; as a learning device, 107–12, 205, 259–60, 296–98, 309, 315; English into Spanish, 296, 297–98, 304–5; Spanish into English, 296–97, 302–4. *See also* Grammar-translation approach; Normal purposes of language
Travel abroad, 57, 102, 104, 215
True-false questions. *See* Testing
Tu and *usted,* 12, 14, 24–25, 83–84, 110, 319 n.18
Twinned schools, 64, 289, 304

Uncertainties of a message. *See* Listening, models of processes

Verb, importance of, 19, 21, 318–19 n.15
Verbal-active approach, 21–22, 41, 97, 319 n.21. *See also* Direct method, rationalist
Visual aids: flannel board, 27, 96; flashcards, 27, 32, 87–88, 96, 119, 194; objects, 42, 96, 280–81; overhead projector, 51, 88, 194, 235, 242, 303; pictures, 17, 27, 32, 40–41, 42, 46, 78, 96, 99, 117, 119, 120, 134, 158, 191, 192, 197, 198, 216, 240; puppets, 27, 37. *See also* Bulletin board; Cartoons and comic books; Films; Television
Vocabulary, 60, 68, 112, 115, 137, 203, 254, 305, 307–9, 315; for aural recognition, 86–88, 98, 99; building and maintaining of, 225–32; cognates in, 172–73, 175–76, 186–87, 197, 198, 199, 200, 203, 207, 209, 213, 216; compound words in, 172; *falsos amigos*

in, 174, 186, 303; function words in, 171, 174, 176, 179, 187, 296; learning of, 16–17, 18, 31, 32, 38, 132–33, 216; logical connectives in, 84, 210–11, 283, 292, 296; prefixes and suffixes in, 172, 226–27, 308; for reading, 171, 174–75, 197, 198, 200, 203, 207, 208, 209, 215, 221; specialized, 19, 47, 68, 69, 86–88, 99, 179. *See also* Exercises, for vocabulary; Frequency lists; Lexical choice; Testing; Word formation

Voicing. *See* Pronunciation

Wall newspapers. *See* Bulletin board

Word counts. *See* Frequency lists

Word formation, 172, 226–27, 307–8

Writing, 7, 19, 22, 236, 315; abstract quality of, 236–37, 239; advanced, 285–86, 287, 290–92; cultural differences in, 287; development of thought in, 283, 287, 290; expressive, 239, 250, 268, 269, 271, 284, 286–95, 316; within a framework, 269–71, 276–77, 287, *dehydrated sentences for, 276, 278;* within idea frame, 278–84; in the language, 239, 246–67; literary usage for, 7 (*see also* Spanish language, written); models of, 238; production, 239, 247, 268–86; with visual, 279–80; writing down, 237, 239–46, *copying, 240–41, reproduction, 241–43. See also* Communication, in writing; Composition, correction of; Emotional factors; Exercises, written; Listening, Reading, Speaking, with writing; Normal purposes of language

Written script in teaching, 33